D1290950

Collecting and Investing Strategies for United States Gold Coins

By: Jeff Ambio

Collecting and Investing Strategies
for United States Gold Coins
By: Jeff Ambio

Copyright © 2008
ZYRUS PRESS INC.

Published by:
ZYRUS PRESS INC.
PO Box 17810, Irvine, CA 92623
Tel: (888) 622-7823 / Fax: (800) 215-9694
www.zyruspress.com
ISBN# 978-1-933990-10-1 (paperback)

Coin images reproduced within this work with permission from
Bowers and Merena and Rare Coin Wholesalers.

Dedication

This book is dedicated to my best friend—my beautiful and loving wife Misty Renee. Without her patience and support my career as a numismatic professional would hardly be possible.

Acknowledgments

Several individuals and firms contributed to the publication of this book. First and foremost I would like to thank my publisher, Bart Crane, and the entire staff at Zyrus Press. Without Bart's willingness to take on this project and work around my sometimes hectic schedule, this book would never have reached completion.

Special thanks also goes to Elaine Dinges and Bowers and Merena Auctions, as well as Steve Contursi and the team at Rare Coin Wholesalers, for providing the images of the beautiful coins pictured in this book. Their continued support for all of my numismatic endeavors is greatly appreciated.

Finally, I would like to recognize Steve Deeds. As president of Bowers and Merena Auctions and, more importantly, a close personal friend, Steve has always made himself available to provide guidance and assistance on all aspects of numismatics. Especially appreciated are the many hours that he spent providing valuable insights into the rare coin market for projects related to the completion of my M.B.A. As a mentor, Steve has provided me with many of the skills and values necessary to be a successful and upstanding member of the professional numismatic community.

About the Author

Jeff Ambio holds a degree in History from Cornell University and a Masters of Business Administration from Pepperdine University. Upon his graduation from Cornell in 1998, Ambio chose to turn a life-long love of coins into a full-time career, which has since blossomed into a successful and rewarding numismatic profession. Today, few can lay claim to so prolific a career in so short a period of time. Ambio's numismatic resume reads like a directory of the most prestigious auction companies in America, and his writings provide collectors with volumes of much needed coin collecting knowledge and information.

Ambio's first position in the numismatic business was as Cataloger and Catalog Production Manager of U.S. coins with Heritage Auction Galleries in Dallas, Texas. During his tenure with Heritage, Jeff handled thousands of rare and exotic coins, produced dozens of auction catalogs, and designed many of the marketing pieces published by the firm.

In 2004, Ambio moved to California, taking positions at Superior Galleries of Beverly Hills, and later at Bowers & Merena Auctions of Irvine. At Bowers & Merena, Ambio held the title of Director of Numismatics. Jeff also served as Vice President of Numismatics at Rare Coin Wholesalers of Dana Point, California.

In addition to extensive numismatic cataloging and marketing experience, Jeff is a widely read numismatic author. His writings and articles are credited with ground-breaking work in the field and have appeared in numerous numismatic journals, including *Rare Coin Investment Trends*, *The Gobrecht Journal*, *Numismatic News*, and *Coin World*.

Early in his career, Ambio's achievements as a numismatist were honored with a scholarship to attend the American Numismatic Association (ANA) Summer Seminar. In 2007, Jeff came full circle, returning this time to the ANA Summer Seminar as an instructor and originator of the course "Attributing United States Coins." In addition to several regional and local organizations, Jeff is a member and supporter of the ANA and the NLG.

In 2007, Ambio returned to his lakeside home in Texas, where he now works as a technical and marketing consultant for rare coin auction houses, dealerships and brokerage firms across America. Jeff is the loving husband of Misty Renee, and the proud father of one son, Tristan Drew. In his spare time, he enjoys freshwater fishing and studying European military history.

Table of Contents

Table of Contents Cont.

Preface

I count myself as one of the few people in this great nation of ours blessed with the opportunity to turn a life-long passion for coin collecting into a full-time career as a professional numismatist. I have played a leading role in the production of many of the largest, most important rare coin auctions that have been presented to the public since the late 1990s. More recently, I was given the honor of researching and marketing the inventory of a leading numismatic wholesaler—an inventory that includes some of the rarest coins available in today's market, many with simply extraordinary, virtually unbelievable technical quality and eye appeal. Countless hours spent "walking the aisles" at local, regional and national conventions provided the opportunity to peruse the inventories of many other influential dealers and "compare notes" with my fellow numismatic professionals. And as the author of several widely distributed articles, market analyses and numismatic brochures, I have gained keen insight into the dynamics of rarity, desirability and other market forces as they guide the performance of all types of United States coins.

Through it all, I have realized one important truth—the knowledge and insight needed to successfully collect and/or invest in rare United States coins is not readily accessible to the average enthusiast. Third-party certification, by guaranteeing authenticity and providing a widely accepted grade level at which an individual coin is likely to trade, has certainly removed some of the risk formerly associated with buying and selling in the rare coin market. The Internet has also made information such as certified population reports, catalog descriptions and auction prices realized much more accessible than it was, say, 20 years ago. Nevertheless, it remains an undeniable truth that the expertise required to interpret and apply this data can only be obtained through years of immersion in the market. Many of the keys to building a successful collecting and investing strategy, therefore, are themselves locked in the heads of experienced numismatic professionals.

You need only remember such famous individuals as Louis E. Eliasberg, Sr., John Jay Pittman and Harry W. Bass, Jr. to realize that collectors and investors can also acquire the knowledge necessary to assemble a world-class collection or lucrative portfolio. You must understand, however, that these numismatists had several critical advantages over the majority of today's rare coin enthusiasts. They assembled the majority of their collection at a time when the market was less competitive due to the presence of fewer collectors and investors. They had the financial means and freedom to travel the country, if not the world, in search of the finest coins available. And they had close personal relationships with the leading dealers and auctioneers of their day to guarantee that they were always "in the loop" as coins became available for sale or market conditions changed. In fact, many of today's numismatic professionals would give their "grading eye" for half of the resources that someone like John Jay Pittman had at his disposal.

What about the average collector or investor in the 21st century? What if you have only a few hundred or a few thousand dollars to devote to yearly rare coin purchases? Or what if you are an investor with a genuine interest in numismatic rarities and several million dollars to spend, but are perhaps wary of diving headfirst into a new, unfamiliar market that has a language and culture all its own? And what if family responsibilities, work schedules or other lifestyle considerations make it well-nigh impossible to attend auctions and conventions on a regular basis in order to keep abreast of changing market conditions? Is the successful pursuit of numismatics beyond your reach?

Absolutely not. There are numismatic professionals who are ready and willing to share their knowledge, act as the eyes and ears of their clients on the convention circuit and provide one-on-one assistance in building collections and investment portfolios.

As God has blessed me with the experience and contacts required to count myself as a respected professional in today's numismatic community, I feel it is my duty to share what I have learned to the benefit of others. It is my sincere hope that this book—which is devoted to the regular-issue gold series of 1795-1933—provides you with a valuable glimpse into an important area of the numismatic market and provides meaningful assistance in your search for a successful strategy through which to pursue these most regal of United States coins.

Jeff Ambio
Texas, July 2007

Introduction

The Appeal of United States Gold Coins

Gold. The long-term ownership or even short-term possession of this precious metal has served as a universal indicator of wealth, power and prestige for centuries. What has been true for kings, governments and titans of industry throughout the ages is also true for numismatists in the 21st century. The collector or investor who can count rare United States gold coins among his or her holdings is almost always an individual who has met with considerable success in life's endeavors. In addition, dealers who either dabble or specialize in gold coins have in their inventory an excellent calling card for success as a numismatic professional.

That even the short-term possession of rare gold coins is an important status symbol becomes more obvious when you consider the typical sale conducted by one of today's leading auction houses. The financial success of a sale often depends on the number of gold coins consigned and the performance of these pieces on auction day. This makes perfect sense given the fact that consignments of gold coins constitute the majority of value embodied within an auction. What you might not realize is that the success of a sale in terms of its current and future marketing value for the auction house is also closely linked to the quality of its gold offerings. Pre-sale advertisements, highlight listings, catalog covers and post-sale news releases often devote generous amounts of space to gold coins. And rest assured that, if at all possible, the auctioneer will schedule gold coin lots to sell on a Friday and/or Saturday evening to guarantee maximum exposure among dealers, collectors, investors and, yes, future consignors. Clearly, much of the appeal of gold coins is the societal or industry status that accrues to those who own and handle them.

Gold coins are also popular because they possess greater intrinsic value than coins struck in virtually any other metallic content. Even non-numismatists automatically assume that a gold coin is a valuable coin, and with good reason. The most undesirable survivor of a common issue in the Gold Dollar series still has significant value due to its bullion content. In essence, the value of the precious metal within the coin establishes a baseline below which it cannot realistically trade. Many collectors and investors, particularly those new to the market, are drawn to gold coins because the intrinsic value of these pieces provides a sense of security when making purchases. "Even if numismatic demand for my gold coin suddenly evaporates, it will still retain at least some value due to its precious metal content," or so I have heard several collectors and investors remark.

Sheer beauty also explains why many gold coins enjoy such a strong following in today's numismatic market. The U.S. gold coin family includes many series whose designs are numbered among the most beautiful ever produced in our nation's Mint. The Indian Quarter Eagle and Half Eagle of 1908-1929, with their unique incuse design, and Augustus Saint-Gaudens' inspired designs for the Eagle and Double Eagle series of 1907-1933 are classic examples of United States gold coins whose beauty enjoys universal recognition in numismatic circles. Other designs are desirable because they offer significant clues about the values and artistic tastes of our forebears. There are few other pieces of art more indelibly linked to the era of George Washington, John Adams and Thomas Jefferson than the Capped Bust Right gold coins struck during the late 1790s and early 1800s. Finally, even a relatively banal design such as that employed for the various Liberty gold series during the 19th and early 20th centuries can be extremely beautiful when represented by a high-grade, nearly blemish-free example.

Another solid foundation upon which the long-standing popularity of gold coins rests is rarity. Many issues in the U.S. gold series are rare in an absolute sense, and all are rare (or conditionally challenging) in the highest Mint State grades. The difficulty that you will encounter when searching for an attractive, problem-free example of many U.S. gold issues adds considerably to the "thrill of the hunt," itself a motivating factor for many collectors and investors who decide to enter the numismatic market.

Throughout the pages of this book, you will encounter additional factors that help to explain the strong and seemingly ever-growing demand that rare United States gold coins enjoy in the numismatic market. It is probably true, nevertheless, that you will not be able to provide a comprehensive list of all the varied reasons that have attracted you to the U.S. gold coin series. In fact, there is probably only one thought running through your head at the time of purchase: "I did it. I achieved another milestone in the pursuit of the finest numismatic collection or investment portfolio that my money can buy."

Only at moments of greater reflection are you likely to recall all of the conscious and subconscious impulses that combined to create an unavoidable, uncontrollable desire to add that key-date Liberty Half Eagle or beautiful Saint-Gaudens Double Eagle to your set. It is also probable that during the Saturday morning trips to the bank's safe deposit box, or the Sunday afternoons at home sharing the joys of collecting with children and grandchildren, the longing to leaf through the pages of the latest auction catalog or book an airline ticket to the next convention will start stirring in your soul. Pretty soon, you will reach for a copy of your favorite numismatic reference and start dreaming of the next coin to add to your collection or investment portfolio. And if you reach for this book, you have already decided that your next numismatic purchase will be a gold coin.

The Parameters of this Study

This book focuses on the United States regular-issue gold series struck from 1795 through 1933. These are the most popular and widely recognized gold coins in all of U.S. numismatics. The Commemorative gold coins struck from 1903-1926 have been excluded because the factors that determine their absolute and high-grade rarity are different from those that rule the fate of issues struck for use in circulation or, in the case of proof gold, yearly sale to a select group of advanced numismatists. The same can be said for modern gold Commemoratives struck beginning in 1984, a discussion of which you will also not find in the following pages.

Territorial gold coins, while subject to the same demands and rigors of commerce experienced by branch mint issues struck during the same era, are also not included in this book. The market for these rarities is distinct from that of the regular-issue United States gold series, with its own dynamics and a relatively small number of dedicated buyers. Such is also the case for most patterns and related issues struck in gold. A notable exception, however, is the Four-Dollar Gold Stella. While all Stellas are technically patterns (Congress never authorized regular-issue production of this denomination), most numismatists consider the inclusion of an example a requirement for the completion of a type set of regular-issue U.S. gold coins.

Finally, and perhaps surprisingly, I have decided not to include an analysis of the United States Mint's American Eagle gold bullion series. These coins can certainly be fun to collect, and the completion of a set of Mint State and/or proof examples is within reach for many buyers. These pieces are technically not coins, however, but rather bullion in coin form. With the exception of a few issues with slightly lower mintages or the Mint State examples struck from unpolished proof dies, these pieces really belong in the precious metals market. Investors, therefore, should probably view bullion coins as just that: bullion.

How to Use this Book

By reading Chapter 1, you will gain an understanding of the various strategies available for building a meaningful collection or investment portfolio of United States gold coins. Throughout the remainder of this book, I provide a detailed analysis of each major type in the classic U.S. gold series of 1795-1933 within the framework of these collecting and investing strategies. In each case, however, it is up to you to decide on the strategy that you want to follow for that particular type. Remember, you can choose to follow one strategy for all types in the entire U.S. gold series or select different strategies for different types. Both paths will lead to the formation of a desirable and rewarding collection.

Once you have chosen the path that you will follow in your pursuit of U.S. gold coins, the appropriate subsections in each chapter of this book identify the specific issues and grades that I believe are best suited to the attainment of your goals. Finally, I have also provided physical characteristics for individual types and issues, pricing data and, where relevant, words of caution to better equip you as you endeavor to build the finest collection or investment portfolio of United States gold coinage.

Methodology and a Disclaimer on Investing in Rare Coins

This book is based on my observation of countless gold coins as well as my evaluation of auction listings and published certified population reports. The number of coins graded and encapsulated by PCGS and NGC can also be a powerful tool in determining *relative rarity*. While PCGS and NGC publish this information, it has severe limitations when it comes to determining *absolute rarity*.

In the quest for an ever-higher grade, or *upgrade*, a coin may be removed from its holder and resubmitted to a grading service. When the same coin is submitted more than once, it skews the figures reported by PCGS and NGC. The leading third-party certification services seek to track and adjust for resubmissions by encouraging dealers, collectors and investors to return the inserts. In theory, this merely requires submitters to retain the insert from the holder in which the coin was removed, or broken out of, and to send them to the grading service. In practice, however, many individuals simply toss these small, yet significant pieces of paper into the trash. Others store their old inserts and return them to the services at pre-determined intervals of time, for example, once every six months. During the intervening time period, the person's inserts will still be listed as distinct coins in the PCGS and/or NGC population reports.

I have also used select numismatic reference books including *A Guide Book of United States Coins* by R. S. Yeoman, Walter Breen's *Complete Encyclopedia of U.S. and Colonial Coins* and *Encyclopedia of U.S. Gold Coins* by Jeff Garrett and Ron Guth during preparation of this study, but only to verify facts such as mintage figures, weight standards, etc. Unless otherwise stated, historical trends are based on prices realized or average prices realized as reported by leading rare coin auction houses, as well as my knowledge of select private treaty sales.

Bear in mind that I am offering my opinion about how and what to collect. Like any collectible or investment, there is no crystal ball listing future values for a collection or a particular coin. Gather enough numismatic experts in a room today and they will likely each hold different opinions about the *current* merits, attributes and even the actual value of a particular coin. In the end, the market dictates. With that said, most prices I list in this catalog are factual in nature, though I do make every effort to point out coins that I think are undervalued or that have greater potential to appreciate in value. I also make suggestions regarding how much you can expect to pay for certain coins. Remeber, however, that the prices of common-date or generic gold coins fluctuate daily with the spot price of gold bullion. It goes without saying that ultimately the choice of what to buy and how much to pay is yours. Armed with the right information, you will make better choices. Reading this book is certainly the most important step you will make in that direction.

CHAPTER ONE

Popular Collecting and Investing Strategies

There are several ways to build a meaningful collection or investment portfolio of United States gold coins. Collectors that specialize in these pieces can pursue more than one strategy, sometimes simultaneously but more often sequentially as their passion for numismatics evolves, their interests shift or their collecting/investing budget changes. The strategies outlined here form the framework within which I have evaluated each type in the regular-issue U.S. gold series.

Short Type Set

A definite consideration for the new collector or investor, this is one of the easiest ways to assemble a meaningful set of United States gold coins. A short type set includes one example each of a select group of U.S. gold series that have at least one factor in common. Examples are numerous and include:

Popular 20th Century Types, a four-piece set that includes:

Indian Quarter Eagle
Indian Half Eagle
Indian Eagle
Saint-Gaudens Double Eagle

Liberty Gold Coinage, a four-piece set that includes:

Liberty Quarter Eagle
Liberty Half Eagle
Liberty Eagle
Liberty Double Eagle

Liberty Double Eagle Types, a three-piece set that includes:

Type I Liberty Double Eagle
Type II Liberty Double Eagle
Type III Liberty Double Eagle

This method of collecting offers tremendous flexibility in that you define the parameters of the set. Regardless of what short set you choose to assemble, I advise selecting the most common business strike issues of each type in the highest grade that your numismatic budget will support.

Complete Type Set

Assembling a complete type set is perhaps the most popular way to begin a pursuit of United States gold coins. In this form, type collecting involves acquiring a single representative of each major design in the U.S. gold series. You should seek an example of the most common business strike issue of each type in the highest grade that you can afford.

Type collecting can allow you to become familiar with the various gold series produced in the United States Mint, as well as their peculiarities in terms of strike, absolute rarity and grade distribution among surviving examples. In time, you might even develop an affinity for one particular type of gold coin and graduate to more specialized forms of set building.

A complete type set of United States gold coins includes 34 examples, one each of the following types:

Gold Dollar, Type I
Gold Dollar, Type II
Gold Dollar, Type III
Capped Bust Right Quarter Eagle, No Stars Obverse
Capped Bust Right Quarter Eagle, Stars Obverse
Capped Bust Left Quarter Eagle
Capped Head Left Quarter Eagle, Large Diameter
Capped Head Left Quarter Eagle, Reduced Diameter
Classic Quarter Eagle
Liberty Quarter Eagle
Indian Quarter Eagle
Three-Dollar Gold
Four-Dollar Gold Stella
Capped Bust Right Half Eagle, Small Eagle Reverse
Capped Bust Right Half Eagle, Large Eagle Reverse
Capped Bust Left Half Eagle
Capped Head Left Half Eagle, Large Diameter
Capped Head Left Half Eagle, Reduced Diameter
Classic Half Eagle
Liberty Half Eagle, No Motto
Liberty Half Eagle, Motto
Indian Half Eagle
Capped Bust Right Eagle, Small Eagle Reverse
Capped Bust Right Eagle, Large Eagle Reverse
Liberty Eagle, No Motto
Liberty Eagle, Motto
Indian Eagle, No Motto
Indian Eagle, Motto
Liberty Double Eagle, Type I
Liberty Double Eagle, Type II
Liberty Double Eagle, Type III
Saint-Gaudens Double Eagle, High Relief
Saint-Gaudens Double Eagle, No Motto
Saint-Gaudens Double Eagle, Motto

Advanced Type Sets

There are several possible ways to customize a gold type set so that the final product is better suited to your collecting or investing goals.

Rarer Issues: Instead of opting for the most common date in the series, you might want to select a rarer issue to represent the type. I have even encountered a few collectors that are assembling gold type sets using key-date issues—a challenging task, to be sure, but one that offers many rewards as long as you have deep pockets and considerable patience.

Major Subtypes: Several series in the U.S. gold family include significant subtypes, or major design changes, that are not represented in basic type sets due to rarity and/or cost. The 1838 and 1839/8 Liberty Eagles, for example, feature a noticeably different obverse portrait than the other issues in the No Motto series. Another example is the No Motto Indian Eagle of 1907. The Wire Rim, Rolled Edge and No Periods coins represent different designs along the evolution from Augustus Saint-Gaudens' original vision for this coin to the version that Mint officials believed would serve best for mass production. The inclusion of these major subtypes can add considerably to the parameters and, hence, desirability of a type set.

Issuing Mint: The first branch mints opened their doors in 1838 at a time when there were only two gold series in production: the Classic Quarter Eagle and Half Eagle. From that year forward, virtually all U.S. gold denominations were struck not only in the main coinage facility in Philadelphia, Pennsylvania, but also in one or more of the six branch mints that operated at various times during United States history. (I have excluded the West Point Mint from this study because it opened 51 years after the end of the classic U.S. gold series in 1933.) A popular alternative to assembling a basic type set is to add one example from each mint in which a particular series was produced. The result will be a much larger collection that includes 89 coins, as follows:

Gold Dollar, Type I: (5) Coins

Philadelphia Mint
Charlotte Mint
Dahlonega Mint
New Orleans Mint
San Francisco Mint

Gold Dollar, Type II: (5) Coins

Philadelphia Mint
Charlotte Mint
Dahlonega Mint
New Orleans Mint
San Francisco Mint

Gold Dollar, Type III: (4) Coins

Philadelphia Mint
Charlotte Mint
Dahlonega Mint
San Francisco Mint

Capped Bust Right Quarter Eagle, No Stars Obverse: (1) Coin

All struck in the Philadelphia Mint

Capped Bust Right Quarter Eagle, Stars Obverse: (1) Coin

All struck in the Philadelphia Mint

Capped Bust Left Quarter Eagle: (1) Coin
All struck in the Philadelphia Mint

Capped Head Left Quarter Eagle, Large Diameter: (1) Coin
All struck in the Philadelphia Mint

Capped Head Left Quarter Eagle, Reduced Diameter: (1) Coin
All struck in the Philadelphia Mint

Classic Quarter Eagle: (4) Coins
Philadelphia Mint
Charlotte Mint
Dahlonega Mint
New Orleans Mint

Liberty Quarter Eagle: (5) Coins
Philadelphia Mint
Charlotte Mint
Dahlonega Mint
New Orleans Mint
San Francisco Mint

Indian Quarter Eagle: (2) Coins
Philadelphia Mint
Denver Mint

Three-Dollar Gold: (4) Coins
Philadelphia Mint
Dahlonega Mint
New Orleans Mint
San Francisco Mint

Four-Dollar Gold Stella: (1) Coin
All struck in the Philadelphia Mint

Capped Bust Right Half Eagle, Small Eagle: (1) Coin
All struck in the Philadelphia Mint

Capped Bust Right Half Eagle, Large Eagle: (1) Coin
All struck in the Philadelphia Mint

Capped Bust Left Half Eagle: (1) Coin
All struck in the Philadelphia Mint

Capped Head Left Half Eagle, Large Diameter: (1) Coin
All struck in the Philadelphia Mint

Capped Head Left Half Eagle, Reduced Diameter: (1) Coin
All struck in the Philadelphia Mint

Classic Half Eagle: (3) Coins
Philadelphia Mint

Charlotte Mint
Dahlonega Mint

Liberty Half Eagle, No Motto: (5) Coins
Philadelphia Mint
Charlotte Mint
Dahlonega Mint
New Orleans Mint
San Francisco Mint

Liberty Half Eagle, Motto: (5) Coins
Philadelphia Mint
Carson City Mint
Denver Mint
New Orleans Mint
San Francisco Mint

Indian Half Eagle: (4) Coins
Philadelphia Mint
Denver Mint
New Orleans Mint
San Francisco Mint

Capped Bust Right Eagle, Small Eagle: (1) Coin
All struck in Philadelphia Mint

Capped Bust Right Eagle, Large Eagle: (1) Coin
All struck in Philadelphia Mint

Liberty Eagle, No Motto: (3) Coins
Philadelphia Mint
New Orleans Mint
San Francisco Mint

Liberty Eagle, Motto: (5) Coins
Philadelphia Mint
Carson City Mint
Denver Mint
New Orleans Mint
San Francisco Mint

Indian Eagle, No Motto: (2) Coins
Philadelphia Mint
Denver Mint

Indian Eagle, Motto: (3) Coins
Philadelphia Mint
Denver Mint
San Francisco Mint

Liberty Double Eagle, Type I: (3) Coins
Philadelphia Mint

> *New Orleans Mint*
> *San Francisco Mint*

Liberty Double Eagle, Type II: (3) Coins
> *Philadelphia Mint*
> *Carson City Mint*
> *San Francisco Mint*

Liberty Double Eagle, Type III (5) Coins
> *Philadelphia Mint*
> *Carson City Mint*
> *Denver Mint*
> *New Orleans Mint*
> *San Francisco Mint*

Saint-Gaudens Double Eagle, High Relief: (1) Coin
> *All struck in Philadelphia Mint*

Saint-Gaudens Double Eagle, No Motto: (2) Coins
> *Philadelphia Mint*
> *Denver Mint*

Saint-Gaudens Double Eagle, Motto: (3) Coins
> *Philadelphia Mint*
> *Denver Mint*
> *San Francisco Mint*

Proof Type Set

One of the more challenging forms of type collecting is to assemble a set of each design in the U.S. gold coin family in proof format. For many collectors, however, proof type collecting as defined in the preceding sentence is not a realistic goal. Many early gold types are unknown in proof, while all pre-1859 gold coins that are universally accepted as proofs are exceedingly rare. A more inviting goal, therefore, is to build a proof type set comprised solely of those gold series that were either in production in 1859, or were first struck in a later year. Even then you will have your work cut out for you, as all proof issues in the regular-issue United States gold series are rare. While individual examples of such later types as the Liberty Half Eagle with Motto and Indian Quarter Eagle do appear in the market fairly often, they always command significant premiums that are commensurate with their rarity. If you have considerable financial resources and above-average patience, however, the completion of a 15-coin proof type set of U.S. gold is an obtainable goal. This set must include one example of each of the following types:

> *Gold Dollar, Type III*
> *Liberty Quarter Eagle*
> *Indian Quarter Eagle*
> *Three-Dollar Gold*
> *Four-Dollar Gold Stella*
> *Liberty Half Eagle, No Motto*
> *Liberty Half Eagle, Motto*
> *Indian Half Eagle*

Liberty Eagle, No Motto
Liberty Eagle, Motto
Indian Eagle, Motto
Liberty Double Eagle, Type I
Liberty Double Eagle, Type II
Liberty Double Eagle, Type III
Saint-Gaudens Double Eagle, Motto

Assembling a Complete Set

This will likely be the final level of collecting that you reach after experimenting with one or more forms of type collecting. Before beginning to assemble a complete set of a specific U.S. gold coin, you should make sure that you have become so enamored with that series that there is no longer a desire to acquire examples of any other type. Your goal now will be to assemble a specialized collection that is as complete as possible for your chosen series. This form of collecting could take one of several forms:

Complete Year Set: A prevalent form of series collecting in the U.S. gold market involves assembling a complete year set of a chosen type. The Mint in which a specific example was struck is irrelevant, but I advise selecting the most common issue of the date.

Date and Mint Set: One of the most prevalent forms of series collecting in the U.S. gold market is to assemble a complete date and mint set of a specific type. Examples include a complete set of Three-Dollar gold pieces, a complete set of No Motto Liberty Eagles and a complete set of all types of Liberty Double Eagles.

Die Variety Set: Despite the tremendous accomplishment achieved by Harry W. Bass, Jr. (the only numismatist to assemble a nearly complete collection of early U.S. gold coins by die variety), this method of collecting remains in its infancy as far as regular-issue U.S. gold coins are concerned. The issues delivered in the Philadelphia Mint from 1795 through early 1834 contain many of the most dramatic and easily distinguishable die varieties in the U.S. gold series. Unfortunately, examples of even "common" die marriages are expensive coins. As a result, and assuming a grade of AU-55 for each coin, it will cost at least $550,000 to acquire a complete set of the seven-known die varieties in the 1795-1797 Capped Bust Right, Small Eagle Ten-Dollar series. Die marriages in the later U.S. gold series are mostly minor and not all that noteworthy, although there are some interesting varieties in the Charlotte, Dahlonega, New Orleans and Carson City gold series that are gaining steadily in popularity.

Proof Set: A more challenging way to assemble a complete year set of many series in the U.S. gold family is to acquire one example of each proof delivery. As with proof type collecting, the year 1859 is a realistic cutoff point for this strategy. Even California industrialist Ed Trompeter did not go back beyond 1858 when assembling his legendary collection of proof gold. The task is already formidable enough when confined to the 1858/59-1915 era.

A Complete Set by Issuing Mint: Yet another variant of series collecting is to focus on all coins struck within a particular Mint, sometimes regardless of denomination and/or type. A few examples include: a complete set of Charlotte Mint Gold Dollars, Quarter Eagles and Half Eagles; a complete set of New Orleans Mint Half Eagles; and a complete set of Liberty Double Eagle struck in the Carson City Mint. The Charlotte, Dahlonega and Carson City Mints are the most popular coinage facilities for this kind of series collecting, followed by the New Orleans Mint in the second tier. On the other hand, the Denver and San Francisco Mints have hardly any adherents among series collectors, while the Philadelphia Mint is usually not considered a candidate for this type of collecting. (An unstated prerequisite for many series collectors assembling sets by issuing mint seems to be the presence of a mintmark!) The San Francisco Mint, in particular, offers considerable opportunities. Many early S-mint gold coins are similar in rarity to Charlotte, Dahlonega and Carson City Mint issues, yet they often sell for considerably less. What's more, the gold coins struck in the San Francisco Mint during the 1850s, 1860s and 1870s possess considerable historic appeal due to their association with the California Gold Rush and the taming of the frontier.

Investing Tips

In today's market of high, seemingly ever-increasing prices for rare coins, the line that used to divide collectors and investors is becoming more blurred. This is perhaps nowhere more evident than in the market for U.S. gold.

Collectors no longer freely dole out a few hundred dollars for a gold coin without first conducting research into the issue's past price performance. Indeed, I am meeting more and more collectors who are more accurately described as collector-investors. This newer breed of numismatist is often defined as a person whose primary interest in coins is their history, beauty and/or rarity but who also desires to protect his or her financial investment in collecting as much as possible. Pure investors, on the other hand, usually focus on the future growth potential of the coins that they buy and sometimes believe that other numismatic considerations such as historical appeal are of only secondary importance.

With both types of numismatists in mind, the investing sections of this book will highlight a few issues that have the best potential for future price appreciation given the right market conditions and general economic circumstances.

CHAPTER TWO

Considerations for Buying Rare U.S. Gold Coins

As the value of rare United States coins has steadily increased, so too has the number of sellers in the market. Most dealers are honest, reputable experts who thoroughly enjoy buying, selling and studying coins. Many of them even got their start in the industry as collectors, and almost all possess tremendous knowledge of rare coins and the market in which they trade. What's more, reputable dealers are usually very willing to share their expertise and offer sound advice that can prove invaluable when building a meaningful collection or investment portfolio. The benefits of a relationship with a recognized industry expert are numerous, and you should get to know as many reputable dealers as possible and enlist their aid in the attainment of your collecting and/or investing goals. This advice is particularly sound if you are planning on specializing in a certain type of U.S. gold coin. Many dealers also specialize in particular types of coins, their buying and selling activities providing them with comprehensive, up-to-date information that may not be available in print.

There are many possible ways to find a reputable United States coin dealer. Chartered by Congress in 1891, the American Numismatic Association (ANA) is the leading hobby organization in U.S. numismatics. The association's website, www.money.org, maintains a searchable database of member dealers. Another excellent source is the Professional Numismatists Guild (PNG), an organization of rare coin and paper money experts whose members are held to high standards of integrity and professionalism. Members of the PNG can be found at the organization's website, www.pngdealers.com. Both the ANA and the PNG are non-profit organizations.

One of the most underutilized methods of finding a reputable numismatic dealer is simply to ask other collectors and investors for recommendations. Word-of-mouth can be a powerful tool. Honest, knowledgeable dealers will enjoy a good reputation among veteran buyers, while less-trustworthy individuals or companies are often treated accordingly in the collector and investor communities. A prerequisite for carrying out this kind of research might be to join a local, regional or national numismatic association. Not only can membership in an organization such as the ANA put you in touch with other collectors and investors, but it could provide access to research tools, current events and other useful technical and market information

Many of the coins that trade in today's numismatic market pass through auctions instead of being bought and sold outright by dealers. Auction houses are also excellent places to buy rare gold coins. The catalogs that these firms produce not only strive to provide detailed descriptions of a coin's physical attributes, but they often contain a wealth of historical and analytical information. The best sources for finding reputable auction houses are the ANA, PNG and by word-of-mouth.

Auctioneers offer another powerful, yet underutilized tool for the gold specialist: the lot viewing sessions that take place in the weeks or days leading up to an auction. Through these venues, you can view large numbers of gold coins in all price ranges. And the more coins that you view, the more familiar you will become with third-party grading standards and issue-specific characteristics such as strike, luster and color. If schedules and budgets permit, I strongly suggest spending some time at auction lot viewing. Registration is required to participate, but it is usually free and there is almost never an obligation to bid.

After finding a reputable dealer and/or auctioneer, what else should you consider before buying your first gold coin? Whether you are a veteran collector or a beginner, it is a good idea to acquire only those pieces that have been graded and encapsulated by Professional Coin Grading Service (PCGS) and Numismatic Guaranty Corporation (NGC). Founded in 1986 and 1987, respectively, these two firms revolutionized the numismatic industry. Coins submitted to these services are evaluated by teams of professional numismatic graders and authenticators. Pieces that are determined to be genuine, unaltered and problem-free for their respective level of preservation are assigned a numeric grade on a 1-70 scale. The coins are then sonically sealed in tamper-evident plastic holders with a paper insert that lists the date, denomination, grade, variety (if applicable) and a unique barcode for identification purposes. Once certified by PCGS or NGC, a coin carries a grade that can help to determine the level at which it will trade in the market. PCGS and NGC-certified coins enjoy universal acceptance, and they also have a high level of liquidity due to the strong reputations that these firms enjoy. In short, PCGS and NGC are the standards for the rare coin industry of the 21st century. They provide a measure of confidence for both novice and veteran collectors when trading in a dynamic market.

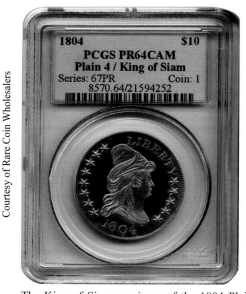 

Courtesy of Rare Coin Wholesalers

The King of Siam specimen of the 1804 Plain 4 Eagle in a PCGS holder and an 1808 Quarter Eagle certified by NGC. I strongly recommend acquiring only those pieces that have been graded and encapsulated by these two services due to the reputations that PCGS and NGC enjoy in most numismatic circles.

You should consider one additional point as far as certified coins are concerned. Grading is subjective, particularly since eye appeal can be an important component of a coin's value. A characteristic that I consider attractive might be construed as a negative in your eyes, or vice versa. For example, I might prefer prooflike coins with a degree of reflectivity to their surfaces. You, however, could be assembling a set with coins that possess uniform mint frost on both sides. It is always a good idea to evaluate coins— even certified pieces—firsthand before buying. In-person inspection will allow you to get comfortable with a coin's assigned grade and determine whether or not the piece will make an attractive addition to your set.

CHAPTER THREE

Type I Gold Dollars

Courtesy of Rare Coin Wholesalers

SPECIFICATIONS

Year(s) Issued: *1849-1854*
Issuing Mint(s): *Philadelphia, Charlotte, Dahlonega, New Orleans, San Francisco*
Authorizing Act: *March 3, 1849*
Designer: *James Barton Longacre*
Weight: *1.672 grams*
Composition: *90% gold, 10% copper*
Diameter: *13 millimeters*
Edge: *Reeded*

History

The first Gold Dollars struck in the United States were issued in 1831 by the private minting firm of Christopher Bechtler. The coins produced by Bechtler and his family were intended to meet the acute need for circulating coinage created by the discovery of gold in Lower Appalachia during the late 1820s. The first Gold Dollars struck in the United States Mint, however, were not produced until 1849. Once again, the driving factors were brought about by a regional gold rush.

James Marshall discovered gold in California's American River on January 24, 1848. Beginning that year, but particularly in 1849 when thousands of "Forty-Niners" began flooding into California from the Eastern states, immense quantities of newly mined California gold entered the world market. While certainly a boon for many sectors of the U.S. economy, and a blessing to those individuals who got rich out West, the California

Gold Rush upset the delicate balance between gold and silver in the avenues of commerce.

What happened as far as the United States' circulating coinage is concerned can be summarized as follows. As more and more of the yellow precious metal emerged from the earth in California, the value of silver reckoned in gold rose sharply. It did not take long for the nation's silver coins to be worth more as bullion than as a circulating medium of exchange. Once this happened, bullion dealers and speculators began hoarding silver coins. These pieces were eventually melted, sometimes after being sold overseas for a profit, but more typically after they were returned to the Mint to provide bullion for lighter-weight silver coins as authorized by the Act of February 21, 1853. The first coins to disappear from circulation in the Eastern United States were the large Silver Dollars, which probably only enjoyed limited domestic circulation during the 1840s anyhow. To replace the Silver Dollar and create an outlet for California gold, Congress authorized production of a Gold Dollar on March 3, 1849.

James Marshall, the man who discovered gold in California's American River on January 24, 1848 and triggered the largest gold rush in United States history. (Public Domain Image)

To design the new coin the United States Mint turned to Chief Engraver James Barton Longacre, who had obtained his position after Christian Gobrecht's death in 1844. Longacre's initial design for the Gold Dollar features a left-facing portrait of Liberty as the central design element on the obverse. Liberty is wearing a coronet inscribed LIBERTY, and 13 stars encircle the border. On the reverse, a wreath surrounds the denomination 1 DOLLAR and the date. The legend UNITED STATES OF AMERICA is around the border and the mintmark, if one is present, is positioned below the wreath.

Coinage of the Type I Gold Dollar commenced in 1849 and continued into 1854. During that time period, the Philadelphia, Charlotte, Dahlonega, New Orleans and San Francisco Mints struck a total of 12,565,273 examples. At 13 millimeters in diameter, this is the smallest regular-issue U.S. gold coin. Ironically, its size would eventually prove to be the downfall of the Type I Gold Dollar. After numerous complaints reached the Mint that the diminutive coin was difficult to handle and easily confused with some of the smaller silver coins then in circulation, the federal government had little choice but to terminate the Type I Gold Dollar and replace it with the larger Type II design. This occurred in August of 1854, at which time the Mint also ordered banks to return Type I examples to the Treasury Department for melting and recoinage. By 1861, at least 8 million of the 12+ million examples coined had suffered this fate, leaving a net mintage of approximately 4 million coins for the type.

Short Type Set

This design is not one of the more popular among collectors assembling short type sets of U.S. gold coins. You should not be deterred by this fact, however, since the Type I

Gold Dollar is closely related to several other gold series and, as such, readily lends itself to inclusion in one or more short type sets. These include:

Gold Dollar Types, a three-piece set including:

> ***Type I Gold Dollar***
> *Type II Gold Dollar*
> *Type III Gold Dollar*

Gold Coin Types Designed by James Barton Longacre, a seven-piece set including:

> ***Type I Gold Dollar***
> *Type II Gold Dollar*
> *Type III Gold Dollar*
> *Three-Dollar Gold*
> *Type I Double Eagle*
> *Type II Double Eagle*
> *Type III Double Eagle*

Small-Denomination Gold Coins of the 19th Century, a four-piece set that includes:

> ***Type I Gold Dollar***
> *Type II Gold Dollar*
> *Type III Gold Dollar*
> *Three-Dollar Gold*

Complete Type Set

With more than 9 million coins produced, the 1851, 1852 and 1853 comprise the majority of Type I Gold Dollars struck. Along with the 1854 Type I, these three issues are the most plentiful Gold Dollars of this design, and they are strong candidates for inclusion in a type set. You should have little difficulty locating a circulated or Mint State survivor of one of these issues in today's market, at least through the MS-64 grade level. As a Gem (MS-65 or finer), however, this type can be quite elusive in numismatic circles.

Circulated Examples: The 1851, 1852, 1853 and 1854 Type I are plentiful in the various About Uncirculated grades, and the price differential between EF-40 and AU-58 is less than $150. Given these facts, it makes most sense to opt for a coin in AU-58, at which grade level you will probably have to pay somewhere in the range of $200-$300.

Mint State Examples: The Mint State type collector should consider acquiring a Type I Gold Dollar that grades at least MS-64. Near-Gems appear quite regularly in the market, and numerous buying opportunities will provide the opportunity to select a coin that is premium quality for the grade and possessed of above-average eye appeal. The asking price for an 1851, 1852, 1853 or 1854 Type I in MS-64 will be in the range of $1,500-$2,000.

More patience is required if you are assembling a type set of Gem-quality coins. MS-65s, however, do appear at auction and large conventions several times each year. The 1853 has the largest certified population in this grade for the type, and a PCGS MS-65 sold for $4,888 at auction in May of 2007.

There are some truly breathtaking survivors of the P-mint issues in this series, although Superb Gems usually appear in the market with much less frequency than those of their Type III counterparts. I had the privilege of cataloging an 1852 graded MS-69 by PCGS in the fall of 2005 that sold for $50,600 at auction. There is also a more current auction record (January 2006) of $92,000 for a common-date Type I Gold Dollar in MS-69.

General Characteristics: The best-looking Type I Gold Dollars possess rich orange-gold color and full, satin or frosty luster. A few rose-gold and reddish-gold coins also exist, and these are also extremely attractive in higher Mint State grades. The P-mint issues are almost always sharply struck.

Words of Caution:Whether you are buying a circulated or Mint State Type I Gold Dollar, use a 10x loupe to examine the surfaces. This is normally not advised, as under such magnification even the highest-grade coins are apt to reveal at least a couple of trivial blemishes. The Type I Gold Dollar, however, is a very small coin whose surfaces are difficult to appreciate with the naked eye. A loupe will help reveal abrasions that, while small in an absolute sense, are large relative to the size of a Gold Dollar. And a small abrasion on a small coin is just as detrimental as a large abrasion on a large coin.

Significant abrasions are seldom encountered on Gold Dollars in higher Mint State grades because the numeric designations assigned by PCGS and NGC take surface preservation into account. Circulated coins, however, will show a greater number of abrasions due to time spent in commercial channels. Since the common Type I Gold Dollars are relatively plentiful in the various AU grades, I suggest waiting until a relatively smooth example comes along.

STRATEGIES FOR INCLUDING THE TYPE I GOLD DOLLAR IN A COMPLETE TYPE SET

Most Desirable Issue(s): *1851, 1852, 1853, 1854 Type I*

Most Desirable Grade(s), Circulated Coins: *AU-58*

Estimated Cost: *$200-$300*

Key to Collecting: *Coins free of sizeable abrasions with relatively smooth surfaces*

Most Desirable Grade(s), Mint State Coins: *MS-64 or finer*

Estimated Cost: *$1,500 and up*

Key to Collecting: *Rich orange-gold, reddish-gold or rose-gold color; full satin or frosty luster; a sharp strike*

Advanced Type Set

Rarer Issues: There are two issues in the Type I Gold Dollar series that are particularly attractive for advanced type purposes. The first is the 1850. With just 481,953 pieces produced, the original mintage of this delivery is 24% that of the 1852, 15% that of the 1851 and just 12% that of the 1853. Yet the 1850 does not command much of a premium through MS-64. An NGC-certified example in that grade traded for $1,840 during an early 2007 auction, which is actually in the range of $1,500-$2,000 for the 1851, 1852 and 1853 in the same grade.

Gem 1850 Gold Dollars appear in the market with much less frequency than those of the 1851-1853 Philadelphia Mint issues. This is understandable given the relative population figures of these deliveries. As of March 2007, PCGS and NGC combined have graded 257 1853 Gold Dollars in MS-65. The corresponding total for the 1850 is only 24 coins, which suggests that the latter issue is approximately 10 times rarer in this grade. Prices do not reflect this fact, however, as evidenced by an 1850 in NGC MS-65 that sold for $4,888 in early 2006. This is the same price realized by an 1853 graded MS-65 at PCGS that crossed the auction block in May of 2007. Clearly, the 1850 is an underrated Gold Dollar in today's market.

Another Type I Gold Dollar that is attractive for better-date type purposes is the 1849 No L. As the first Gold Dollar struck in the United States Mint, this is a historic issue. It is also a one-year type, as all other issues in the Type I Gold Dollar series display the designer's initial L on the truncation of the bust. A scarce coin with only 1,000 examples believed to have been struck, Mint State survivors are actually more plentiful than the original mintage might suggest. (Many pieces were preserved as the first coins of their kind.) Nevertheless, the 1849 No L is rarer than the 1851, 1852 and 1853 by a factor of 5-15 times depending on the specific issue and level of preservation being compared. At $2,000-$3,500, MS-64s are particularly inexpensive relative to similarly graded examples of the more common P-mint issues. Gems are pricier, but not to a degree that is commensurate with their relative rarity. A PCGS MS-65 sold for $5,750 through auction in April of 2007, although I believe that they should be trading for hundreds of dollars more.

STRATEGIES FOR INCLUDING THE TYPE I GOLD DOLLAR IN A TYPE SET OF RARER ISSUES

Most Desirable Issue(s): *1849 No L, 1850*

Most Desirable Grade(s), Circulated Coins: *AU-58*

Estimated Cost:

    1849 No L: *$400-$500*

    1850: *$200-$300*

Key to Collecting: *Coins free of sizeable abrasions with relatively smooth surfaces*

Most Desirable Grade(s), Mint State Coins: *MS-64 or finer*

Estimated Cost:

    1849 No L: *$2,000 and up*

    1850: *$1,750 and up*

Key to Collecting: *Yellow-gold or orange-gold color; no individually conspicuous abrasions; full satin or frosty luster; a sharp strike*

Major Subtypes: Three coins are required for the completion of a set of Type I Gold Dollars that illustrates the major design changes in this series. The most significant subtypes are concentrated in the first year of issue. Most coins of this type display a Closed Wreath on the reverse, but the Philadelphia Mint used an Open Wreath design to deliver many of the 688,567 pieces struck during 1849. The Open Wreath design also comprises the entire mintage of the 1849-D and 1849-O, as well as an extremely small percentage of the mintage for the 1849-C. I recommend the 1849 with the designer's initial L to represent the Open Wreath design. Five examples certified MS-64 by PCGS or NGC sold at auction from January-May, 2007. In each case the coins realized between $2,041 and $2,760.

As previously stated, the first 1,000 Gold Dollars struck in the Philadelphia Mint lack the designer's initial L on the truncation of the bust. The 1849 No L, therefore, is also an important subtype in this series.

Unlike their later-date counterparts, 1849-dated Gold Dollars typically possess softer color in yellow-gold or orange-gold shades. Reddish-gold or rose-gold survivors are in the minority. Most examples of the 1849 Open Wreath and 1849 No L issues are well struck, and satiny luster is dominant among Mint State survivors.

The third and final subtype in the Type I Gold Dollar series is the Closed Wreath reverse. The common-date 1851, 1852, 1853 and 1854 Type I are all strong candidates to represent this design.

STRATEGIES FOR INCLUDING THE TYPE I GOLD DOLLAR IN A TYPE SET OF MAJOR SUBTYPES

Required Number of Coins: *Three*

Major Subtype #1: *No L*

Most Desirable Issue(s): *1849 No L*

Major Subtype #2: *Open Wreath*

Most Desirable Issue(s): *1849 with L*

Major Subtype #3: *Closed Wreath*

Most Desirable Issue(s): *1851, 1852, 1853, 1854 Type I*

Issuing Mint: You will have to acquire five coins to represent all of the Mints that struck Type I Gold Dollars. The Philadelphia Mint requirement has already been sufficiently addressed; the 1851, 1852, 1853 and 1854 Type I are the best type candidates due to their relative availability in the market.

Moving on to the branch mints, we come to the Charlotte facility. All C-mint Type I Gold Dollars are scarce-to-rare coins, and the 1849-C Open Wreath is virtually unobtainable with only four examples positively confirmed. The most realistic type candidate among C-mint Gold Dollars is the 1851-C, which appears at auction with relative frequency in both circulated and Mint State grades. This issue is also one of the most consistently well-struck Type I Gold Dollars from the Charlotte Mint. In fact, enough sharply detailed coins have survived that I strongly advise holding out for one of those pieces. Coins that grade AU-50 or finer with a minimum number of abrasions are most desirable. In AU-50, this issue will set you back at least $1,750, while AU-58s are priced in the neighborhood of $2,500. Expect to pay at least $10,000 for an 1851-C Gold Dollar that grades MS-64. Most examples that I have examined possess yellow-gold or green-gold color and, in higher grades, satin-to-frosty surfaces.

The Dahlonega Mint requirement is going to be a bit more challenging to satisfy than that for the Charlotte Mint. Indeed, D-mint Type I Gold Dollars are universally rare coins, and most are poorly struck, noticeably abraded and worn to one degree or another. The first-year 1849-D, however, was saved in limited quantities as the premier Gold Dollar struck in the Dahlonega Mint. In fact, AU and Mint State coins are actually offered quite frequently in large auctions and on the bourse floor of major conventions. An AU-50 or higher-graded example with a well-balanced strike, yellow-gold or green-gold surfaces and no singularly conspicuous blemishes is particularly attractive for type purposes. This issue will start at $2,000 in AU-50, while a PCGS AU-58 brought $3,220 at auction in early 2007. In MS-64, you will have to spend between $15,000 and $20,000 to acquire an 1849-D Gold Dollar in a PCGS or NGC holder.

Courtesy of Rare Coin Wholesalers

The 1849-D appears to have been saved in limited quantities as the first Gold Dollar struck in the Dahlonega Mint. AU and Mint State examples are usually offered frequently enough to satisfy the buyer that exercises a little bit of patience.

Compared to its North Carolina and Georgia counterparts, the New Orleans Mint will be a snap to represent in a mintmarked Type I Gold Dollar set. The highest mintages in this O-mint series belong to the 1851-O and 1853-O, and these two issues are the most realistic candidates for low-grade circulated type purposes. If you are looking for an AU representative, however, the 1849-O is a better choice. As the first New Orleans Mint gold coin of its denomination, many '49-O Gold Dollars were plucked from circulation after a very short time. A PCGS AU-58 commanded $517 from the winning bidder when it appeared at auction in April of 2007.

In Mint State, the 1849-O must once again yield to the 1851-O and 1853-O in terms of market availability. Regardless of the exact issue and/or grade level you choose to pursue, locating a relatively smooth-looking example will not be an easy task. In fact, I believe that high-grade, attractive New Orleans Mint gold coins are among the more underrated pieces in numismatics. If you also subscribe to this theory, I suggest waiting until a premium-quality example becomes available. Your chances of catching the eye of another collector when the time comes to sell will be greatly improved if you exercise a bit of patience now. Many of the most attractive 1851-O and 1853-O Gold Dollars are concentrated at the MS-64 grade level. Of particular importance in this regard is that near-Gems will usually possess relatively few wispy abrasions. An 1851-O in PCGS MS-64 sold for $4,888 at auction in early 2007.

Courtesy of Bowers and Merena

In Mint State, the 1853-O appears to be one of the more attractive New Orleans Mint Gold Dollars for type purposes. Locating a relatively smooth-looking example at any grade, however, will probably not be an easy task. Even the coin pictured here possesses a sizeable scrape in the right-obverse field—the kind of individually distracting feature that the buyer might want to avoid.

The San Francisco Mint struck its first Gold Dollars in 1854—the final year of the Type I design and the first of the Type II motif. All 1854-S Gold Dollars display the Type I design, and an example of this issue is absolutely required for completion of a gold type set by issuing mint. This is one of the rarest Type I Gold Dollars, and the '54-S is particularly underrated when compared to the C- and D-mint issues in this series. Due to the rarity of examples in today's market, you should downplay the importance of numeric grade when pursuing this issue. A problem-free coin certified by PCGS or NGC with relatively smooth-looking surfaces represents a significant find. You will be particularly pleased with your acquisition if you avoid coins with large distractions in prime focal areas. (By prime focal areas on a Type I Gold Dollar I mean Liberty's face and neck on the obverse and the date and mintmark areas on the reverse.) This is no mean feat, but an 1854-S Gold Dollar that fits this profile is well positioned to increase in value as this issue gains in stature among gold collectors. In AU-55, the 1854-S is a $1,500-$2,000 coin, while an NGC MS-62 commanded $3,220 at auction in early 2006.

STRATEGIES FOR INCLUDING THE TYPE I GOLD DOLLAR IN A TYPE SET BY ISSUING MINT

Required Number of Coins: *Five*

Issuing Mint #1: *Philadelphia, Pennsylvania*

Most Desirable Issue(s): *1851, 1852, 1853, 1854*

Key to Collecting: *Rich orange-gold, reddish-gold or rose-gold color; full satin or frosty luster; a sharp strike; free of sizeable abrasions*

Issuing Mint #2: *Charlotte, North Carolina*

Most Desirable Issue(s): *1851-C*

Key to Collecting: *AU-50 or higher grade; relatively smooth surfaces; yellow-gold or green-gold color; relatively bold strike*

Issuing Mint #3: *Dahlonega, Georgia*

Most Desirable Issue(s): *1849-D*

Key to Collecting: *AU-50 or higher grade; relatively smooth surfaces; yellow-gold or green-gold color; relatively bold strike*

Issuing Mint #4: *New Orleans, Louisiana*

Most Desirable Issue(s): *1849-O (AU only), 1851-O, 1853-O*

Key to Collecting: *Relatively bold strike; relatively smooth surfaces*

Issuing Mint #5: *San Francisco, California*

Most Desirable Issue(s): *1854-S (only option)*

Key to Collecting: *Any grade; problem-free surfaces that are free of sizeable and/or individually conspicuous abrasions*

Proof Type Set

With only a single proof Type I Gold Dollar listed at the major certification services as of May 2007—an 1850 in PCGS Proof-60—including a specimen striking of this design in a type set is not a realistic goal for most numismatists.

Assembling a Complete Set

Year Set: A complete year set of Type I Gold Dollars includes only six coins, and the attainment of this goal is well within reach of many collectors. The Philadelphia Mint issues are the most common and, hence, also the most attractive candidates for this strategy. A circulated year set is easy to complete, fun to assemble and relatively affordable at an estimated total cost of only $1,200-$1,800 in AU-58. Nevertheless, you should consider focusing on coins that grade MS-64 or finer. Uncirculated P-mint Gold Dollars of this type appear in the market on a regular basis, and they are attractive coins when possessed of a sharp strike, vibrant luster and original color. A Mint State set also has the potential to outperform a circulated one when the time comes to sell. In MS-64, you can acquire one example each of the 1849 Open Wreath, 1850, 1851, 1852, 1853, and 1854 Type I for approximately $10,000.

Date and Mint Set: Due to the rarity and high value of the Charlotte and Dahlonega Mint issues, assembling a complete date and mint set of Type I Gold Dollars will be beyond the reach of many collectors. With ample resources, however, you can normally complete this 25-piece set within two or three years. (This discussion does not include the virtually uncollectible 1849-C Open Wreath.) Grades of MS-64 or finer are most attractive for the Philadelphia Mint issues. The Charlotte and Dahlonega Mint deliveries, as well as the 1854-S, will require some compromising, however, and any coin that grades at least AU-50 deserves serious consideration. I suggest adopting a more focused view as far as the New Orleans Mint issues are concerned, for example, coins that grade at least AU-55, if not AU-58. Following the strategy outlined here, a complete date and mint set of Type I Gold Dollars excluding the 1849-C Open Wreath will require at least $45,000.

If you choose to assemble a date and mint set of Type I Gold Dollars, I advise selecting coins with as sharp a strike as possible and relatively smooth surfaces for their respective issue and grade. Remember, however, that the C- and D-mint issues typically come softly impressed with noticeably abraded surfaces. The same can be said for the 1854-S and many of the O-mint deliveries, at least as far as surface preservation is concerned. The completion of an AU-Mint State set of Type I Gold Dollars is a significant feat that will establish the numismatist as a veteran of the market.

Die Variety Set: Type I Gold Dollars are seldom collected by die marriage, with the exception of the Charlotte and Dahlonega Mint issues whose varieties have garnered some attention among Southern gold specialists. Much research still needs to be done on this series, particularly as far as the P-mint issues are concerned. Unless you are assembling a set of C-, D-, or O-mint coins, and then only after consulting with a recognized expert, I caution against paying a premium for a Type I Gold Dollar advertised as a rare die variety.

Proof Set: It is impossible to assemble a complete set of proof Type I Gold Dollars because many P-mint issues are either unknown in this format or are currently unobtainable for private ownership.

A Complete Set by Issuing Mint: The prospects are much brighter as far as assembling a complete set of Type I Gold Dollars by issuing mint is concerned. The Charlotte, Dahlonega and New Orleans Mint issues are all strong candidates for this kind of collecting, and many impressive sets have already been formed. Most mintmarked sets of Type I Gold Dollars are assembled as part of a larger collection, including C-mint Gold Dollars or O-mint gold coins of all denominations. If you concern yourself solely with the Type I Gold Dollar, however, you will have a much easier time completing the task since there are just five or six issues each reported for the Charlotte, Dahlonega and New Orleans Mints. Excluding the 1849-C Open Wreath, any one of these sets is well within reach of the collector with above-average means. Completing this task will provide a strong sense of accomplishment, and it could also serve as an excellent springboard for a larger collection of Southern gold.

In order to prepare yourself to tackle this strategy, it is important to evaluate the potential cost associated with assembling a complete set of Type I Gold Dollars by issuing Mint. Focusing exclusively on the Dahlonega Mint issues (of which there are six) and the AU-55 grade level, you should expect to pay at least $25,000 to complete a set.

Investing Tips

You can assemble a potentially lucrative portfolio of Type I Gold Dollars by following any of the recommended collecting strategies outlined above. When financial return outweighs collecting goals, however, you should focus solely on Mint State coins. All Type I Gold Dollars are theoretically obtainable in Mint State, even the ultra-rare 1849-C Open Wreath. With the market's emphasis on technical quality and numeric grade, and the accessibility of third-party certification reports to help in assessing relative rarity, I suggest that you purchase examples at or above the level at which the respective issue becomes conditionally rare. For the Philadelphia Mint issues in this series, MS-65 is the cutoff point. For those deliveries produced in the Charlotte, Dahlonega and San Francisco facilities, MS-60 is a much more realistic option. The O-mint issues are more difficult to address as a group, although MS-60 will also work well for most of these deliveries.

CHAPTER FOUR

Type II
Gold Dollars

Courtesy of Rare Coin Wholesalers

SPECIFICATIONS

Year(s) Issued: *1854-1856*
Issuing Mint(s): *Philadelphia, Charlotte, Dahlonega, New Orleans, San Francisco*
Authorizing Act: *March 3, 1849*
Designer: *James Barton Longacre*
Weight: *1.672 grams*
Composition: *90% gold, 10% copper*
Diameter: *15 millimeters*
Edge: *Reeded*

History

Due to their extremely small size, Type I Gold Dollars were unpopular with the contemporary public. To increase the denomination's acceptability in commercial channels, the Mint increased the diameter from 13 millimeters to 15 millimeters while making the coins thinner so that they would still conform to the specified weight standard. The Philadelphia Mint struck its first Type II Gold Dollars in 1854. The Charlotte, Dahlonega and New Orleans Mints joined the parent facility in 1855. In 1856, however, only the San Francisco Mint struck Type II Gold Dollars, the other Mints either refraining from producing this denomination or utilizing the newly introduced Type III motif. Struck in just three years and comprised of a mere six issues, the Type II Gold Dollar is one of the shortest-lived series in all of U.S. numismatics.

Although the Mint intended this design to improve the fortunes of the denomination as a circulating medium of exchange, the Type II series was a serious setback for the Gold Dollar. Chief Engraver James Barton Longacre executed this design in too high relief for the coinage presses of the mid-1850s to handle. The result was a plethora of weakly struck coins, their devices shallow in appearance and overly susceptible to wear in the avenues of commerce. It is no wonder that the Mint hurried the improved Type III design into production, the first pieces flowing from the presses in the Philadelphia and Dahlonega Mints in 1856.

The Type II Gold Dollar design is superficially similar to that of the Type I. On the obverse, however, Liberty is wearing a feathered headdress instead of a coronet, and the reverse wreath is more complex with corn, cotton, maple and tobacco leaves. Look for a mintmark on the reverse below the knot of the bow that binds the wreath.

Short Type Set

Like its Type I counterpart, the Type II Gold Dollar is not popular with gold collectors that are assembling short type sets. This is unfortunate because the type is challenging to collect and, thus, not attractive for collectors that are looking to specialize in a certain series. In addition, a high-grade Type II Gold Dollar will add considerably to the importance of a small holding of United States gold coins. There are several short type sets that will have to include an example of the Type II Gold Dollar, as follows:

Gold Dollar Types, a three-piece set including:
> *Type I Gold Dollar*
> ***Type II Gold Dollar***
> *Type III Gold Dollar*

Gold Coin Types Designed by James Barton Longacre, a seven-piece set including:
> *Type I Gold Dollar*
> ***Type II Gold Dollar***
> *Type III Gold Dollar*
> *Three-Dollar Gold*
> *Type I Double Eagle*
> *Type II Double Eagle*
> *Type III Double Eagle*

Small-Denomination Gold Coins of the 19th century, a four-piece set that includes:
> *Type I Gold Dollar*
> ***Type II Gold Dollar***
> *Type III Gold Dollar*
> *Three-Dollar Gold*

Complete Type Set

The total mintage for the Type II Gold Dollar is a mere 1,633,426 pieces. The Philadelphia Mint struck approximately 94% of this total during 1854 and 1855. Indeed, these two P-mint deliveries constitute the majority of Type II Gold Dollars in today's market, and they are the only realistic type candidates in this brief series.

Circulated Examples: The circulated type collector will experience little difficulty locating an 1854 Type II or 1855 Gold Dollar either at auction or on the bourse floor of even a regional numismatic trade show. The frequency with which AU-55 and AU-58 survivors trade is one reason why you might want to focus on one of these two grade levels. There are other reasons, however, one of which has to do with the poor striking quality that most survivors possess. Below the Choice AU level, this often inadequately produced type can appear excessively soft in detail as wear intermingles with striking incompleteness to obliterate key elements of the design. The rim of the Type II Gold Dollar also proved inadequate to protect the coin from the rigors of commercial use, and many examples acquired large abrasions, if not outright damage. The longer the coins remained in circulation, the greater the probability that they would become impaired. Finally, Type II Gold Dollars appear to have been favorites of coin jewelry manufacturers, and many survivors show evidence of polishing, solder and rim damage from having been mounted. It is sound advice to insist on acquiring only problem-free coins certified by PCGS or NGC to avoid the risk of acquiring a former jewelry piece.

In addition to the aforementioned features, you should demand that your Type II Gold Dollar possesses above-average detail for the assigned grade and relatively few abrasions. I believe that examples with even a single large distraction are undesirable, even if their surfaces are otherwise quite smooth.

In AU-55, an example of one of these issues will cost $500-$650. The price in AU-58 will increase to $975.

Mint State Examples: Much has been written about the rarity of the Type II Gold Dollar in Mint State. This is not always true, and the 1854 Type II and 1855 are actually a bit overrated in the lower Mint State grades. Even a casual perusal of major auction catalogs is sufficient to illustrate that Uncirculated survivors of these issues trade fairly often through the MS-62 grade level. Considering that such pieces are apt to be heavily abraded and/or deficient in luster, to say nothing of possessing the characteristic striking softness for the type, you should avoid the 1854 Type II and 1855 in MS-60, MS-61 or MS-62. Examples in those grades are usually unattractive and are not the kind of coin that you would want to try selling in the future.

Beginning in MS-63, the type issues in this series are conditionally scarce, and any coin that grades finer than MS-64 is quite rare from a market availability standpoint. Even through MS-66, however, the 1854 Type II and 1855 are usually offered for sale several times yearly. This is a benefit to the buyer, as there will be more opportunities to select an above-average example for inclusion in a type set.

An 1854 Type II or 1855 Gold Dollar in MS-63 will cost $9,000-$12,000, while an 1855 in NGC MS-64 crossed the auction block at $13,800 in early 2007. The price for the type jumps considerably in MS-65, at which level you should expect to pay at least $30,000 for a PCGS or NGC-certified Gem. I am aware of two 1855s in PCGS MS-66 that sold through auction in 2007. The first example traded for $51,750 while the second piece commanded $43,125 from the winning bidder.

General Characteristics: The typical 1854 Type II and 1855 Gold Dollar offered in today's market are softly struck over the highpoints of Liberty's portrait on the obverse and (most distractingly) at the letters LL in DOLLAR and one or more of the digits in the date in the center of the reverse. Despite what is sometimes written in auction catalogs and other references, however, it is not impossible to locate a sharply struck Type II Gold Dollar. I have handled quite a few survivors of the P-mint issues that are boldly struck, and the occasional sharply struck example does turn up. When such a coin is also in a higher Mint State grade with full luster and original orange-gold or rose-gold color, the beauty of the Type II Gold Dollar is readily evident. Uncirculated examples typically display thick, billowy, satin-textured luster.

In circulated grades, the 1854 Type II and 1855 usually display lighter color in either yellow-gold or pale rose-gold shades. Choice AU pieces almost always come with at least faint remnants of original mint luster in the more protected areas of the design.

Courtesy of Bowers and Merena

An 1854 Type II Gold Dollar with an average strike. Notice the softness of detail on the haircurls over Liberty's brow on the obverse and at the digit 8 in the date on the reverse.

Words of Caution: In addition to incompleteness of strike, the typically encountered 1854 Type II or 1855 Gold Dollar exhibits clashmarks in the fields around the central design elements. There are as-struck features caused when dies come together without an intervening planchet. Since they were imparted during the minting process and are quite common for the type, clashmarks will not result in a lower grade from PCGS or NGC. Clashmarks can be distracting, however, particularly if they are bold enough to interfere with your ability to appreciate key design elements. You should avoid purchasing a Type II Gold Dollar if the clashmarks it possesses significantly reduce the overall eye appeal. Examples of the 1854 Type II and 1855 issues that are completely free of clashmarks are rare, but they do exist and are obtainable as long as you are not in a hurry to complete your type set.

STRATEGIES FOR INCLUDING THE TYPE II GOLD DOLLAR IN A COMPLETE TYPE SET

Recommended Issue(s): *1854 Type II, 1855*

Most Desirable Grade(s), Circulated Coins: *AU-55, AU-58*

Estimated Cost: *$500-$975*

Key to Collecting: *Yellow-gold or rose-gold color; remnants of original luster; above-average detail for the grade; no sizeable or individually conspicuous abrasions*

Most Desirable Grade(s), Mint State Coins: *MS-63 or finer*

Estimated Cost: *$9,000 and up*

Key to Collecting: *Billowy satin luster; rich orange-gold or rose-gold color; at least a bold strike, but preferably sharp definition and most importantly in the center of the reverse; freedom from excessive clashmarks*

Advanced Type Set

Rarer Issues: Of the six issues in the Type II Gold Dollar series, only two readily present themselves as potential candidates for inclusion in an advanced type set of rarer issues. The first is the 1855-O, which I believe to be among the more underrated coins in the entire U.S. Gold Dollar series. Survivors from an original mintage of 55,000 pieces are scarce in all circulated grades and decidedly rare in Mint State. The second is the equally elusive 1856-S, which was produced to the extent of just 24,600 coins.

Courtesy of Bowers and Merena

The 1855-O and 1856-S are both underrated rarities in the Type II Gold Dollar series that might serve well in an advanced type set. Both issues tend to carry numerous detracting abrasions, so one should look for a coin with relatively smooth-looking surfaces for the assigned grade.

Due to the rarity of the '55-O and '56-S in Mint State, I recommend acquiring examples that grade AU-55 or AU-58. Even low-grade Mint State examples represent a fleeting buying opportunity when they appear in the market, and they are usually the province of specialized collectors. In AU-55, the '55-O will sell for $2,250-$7,000. The '56-S is a $3,500-$4,000 coin in AU-55 and a $5,000-$7,000 piece in near-Mint.

The typical 1855-O Gold Dollar possesses yellow-gold color, while the 1856-S usually tends more toward an orange-gold hue. (A small number of 1855-O Gold Dollars exhibit green-gold tinting, but these coins are not encountered all that often.) Both issues tend to carry numerous detracting abrasions, so look for a coin with relatively smooth surfaces for the assigned grade. Examples that still retain some mint luster are usually satiny in texture. The quality of strike varies, but it will typically be above average for a mintmarked Gold Dollar from the mid-1850s, particularly one of the Type II design.

STRATEGIES FOR INCLUDING THE TYPE II GOLD DOLLAR IN A TYPE SET OF RARER ISSUES

Most Desirable Issue(s): *1855-O, 1856-S*

Most Desirable Grade(s): *AU-55 or AU-58*

Estimated Cost: *$2,250-$7,000*

Key to Collecting: *Yellow-gold or orange-gold color, relatively abrasion free for the assigned grade*

Major Subtypes: There are no major design changes in the Type II Gold Dollar series, and a single example will suffice for the numismatist assembling an advanced type set with this focus.

Issuing Mint: This five-piece set is among the most challenging to assemble in all of U.S. numismatics. Even despite the aforementioned striking problems and potential difficultly of locating an example with above-average eye appeal, the 1854 Type II or 1855 will pose no problem in the assembly of this set. Once again, I suggest acquiring a coin that grades AU-55, AU-58 or finer than MS-62.

The branch mints are another matter entirely, as each mintmarked issue in the Type II Gold Dollar series is unique for its issuing coinage facility. The 1855-C is elusive in all grades and is currently unknown in any grade above MS-62. The 1855-D is even rarer, the original mintage a scant 1,811 pieces. On the other hand, there are a few exceptional '55-D Gold Dollars that grade MS-63 and MS-64. The typically offered survivor of both issues grades no finer than EF, however, and even an AU-50 example would make a noteworthy addition to a numismatic holding. The '55-C will cost at least $9,000 in AU-50, while a '55-D in the same grade is worth at least $20,000. Strike is definitely going to be a problem with both of these issues, and a coin with above-average detail, no singularly distracting abrasions and pretty yellow-gold or rose-gold color represents a significant find in today's market.

The 1855-O and 1856-S, previously discussed above as probable candidates for inclusion in a type set of rarer issues, are both also required for the completion of an advanced type set based on issuing mint.

Courtesy of Bowers and Merena

Rare in an absolute sense and difficult to locate with strong eye appeal, the 1855-C and 1855-D Gold Dollars are likely to serve as significant roadblocks to the completion of a type set by issuing mint.

STRATEGIES FOR INCLUDING THE TYPE II GOLD DOLLAR IN A TYPE SET BY ISSUING MINT

Required Number of Coins: *Five*

Issuing Mint #1: *Philadelphia, Pennsylvania*

Most Popular Issue(s): *1854 Type II, 1855 (only options)*

Key to Collecting: *AU-55, AU-58 or finer than MS-62 in grade; bold-to-sharp strike; no singularly distracting abrasions*

Issuing Mint #2: *Charlotte, North Carolina*

Most Popular Issue(s): *1855-C (only option)*

Key to Collecting: *AU-50 or higher grade; relatively smooth surfaces; yellow-gold or pale rose-gold color; relatively bold strike; no singularly distracting abrasions*

Issuing Mint #3: *Dahlonega, Georgia*

Most Popular Issue(s): *1855-D (only option)*

Key to Collecting: *AU-50 or higher grade; relatively smooth surfaces; yellow-gold or pale rose-gold color; relatively bold strike; no singularly distracting abrasions*

Issuing Mint #4: *New Orleans, Louisiana*

Most Popular Issue(s): *1855-O (only option)*

Key to Collecting: *AU-55 or finer grade; yellow-gold color; relatively abrasion free for the assigned grade*

Issuing Mint #5: *San Francisco, California*

Most Popular Issue(s): *1856-S (only option)*

Key to Collecting: *AU-55 or finer grade; orange-gold color; relatively abrasion free for the assigned grade*

Proof Type Set

It is possible to include the Type II Gold Dollar in a proof type set of United States gold coinage, but you should only consider this task if you have particularly deep pockets and a lot patience. Both the 1854 Type II and 1855 are exceedingly rare in proof format. You are more likely to encounter a proof 1855 in today's market, but there are still only 12 examples listed at PCGS and NGC (May/2007), and this number probably includes at least a few resubmissions. One of the finest is the specimen once owned by John Jay Pittman. The coin currently grades Proof-66 Deep Cameo at PCGS and it sold for an impressive $316,250 at auction in early 2007.

Assembling a Complete Set

Year Set: On the other hand, a complete year set of Type II Gold Dollars is probably within reach for many collectors. You need only acquire three examples to complete this set. The Philadelphia Mint issues in this series will satisfy the requirements for 1854 and 1855, while the rarer 1856-S must suffice for that year. The same grades and surface characteristics outlined above for the type collector will also appeal to the collector assembling a year set of this type.

Date and Mint Set: As far as the Type II Gold Dollar is concerned, this set is essentially the same as an advanced type set by issuing mint. The only difference is that the numismatist will have to acquire an example of both the 1854 Type II and 1855. This is a challenging, yet obtainable goal, particularly if you are willing to acquire circulated examples for some or all of the branch mint issues.

Die Variety Set: I am unaware of any major work on die varieties for the 1854 Type II, 1855 or 1856-S Gold Dollars. On the other hand, two die marriages have been confirmed for the 1855-D—an interesting fact for such a low-mintage coin, and an expensive proposition if you choose to assemble a complete set of Type II Gold Dollars by die variety. As demand for Type II Gold Dollars among die variety collectors is very limited, and since that demand will probably not increase substantially in the foreseeable future, I do not recommend this strategy for this series. If you are particularly enamored with the Type II Gold Dollar, then assembling a date and mint set is a more appropriate strategy.

Proof Set: This deceptively easy set requires only two coins to complete. The extreme rarity of both the 1854 Type II and 1855 in proof format, however, has prevented most collectors from attempting this feat. On the other hand, the late John Jay Pittman did own a proof 1854 Type II and 1855 Gold Dollar at the same time. If you are looking to follow in his footsteps, I suggest setting aside at least $700,000 to acquire a pair of Gem-quality examples.

A Complete Set by Issuing Mint: There are only four mintmarked issues in the Type II Gold Dollar series, one each from the Charlotte, Dahlonega, New Orleans and San Francisco Mints. While many collectors specialize in Southern gold, and many would be wise to take a serious look at the early S-mint issues of all denominations, branch mint Type II Gold Dollars are typically acquired only as part of larger collections. If you plan to focus on the various gold denominations struck in the Charlotte and Dahlonega Mints, you will find that the 1855-C and 1855-D Gold Dollars are costly, key-date issues that will probably number among your later acquisitions.

Investing Tips

The Type II Gold Dollar series possesses several potentially lucrative opportunities for the numismatic investor. There is a very strong collector base underlying the market for Type II Gold Dollars. To date, type collectors have been fairly successful at keeping the price for attractive examples of the 1854 Type II and 1855 issues high. Additionally, Southern gold specialists are numerous enough to guarantee that any problem-free 1855-C, 1855-D or (to a lesser extent) 1855-O will command a strong premium when it appears in the market. Even the 1856-S—a product of a coinage facility with relatively few adherents—will continue to gain steadily in price as more collectors begin to appreciate the issue's true rarity in AU and Mint State grades.

In order to take full advantage of the investment potential of Type II Gold Dollars, I suggest concentrating on Mint State examples or, in the case of the mintmarked issues, coins that grade at least AU-55. Regardless of exactly which grade level(s) and issue(s) you choose to pursue, patience will serve you in good stead. Sharply struck examples of the 1854 Type II and 1855 are particularly desirable, as are bolder-than-average representatives of the 1855-C, 1855-D, 1855-O and 1856-S. Such coins do exist, but they do not trade with any degree of frequency. I also believe that you should avoid coins with excessive clashmarks (some evidence of die clashing, however, is usually acceptable) and/or individually detracting abrasions, particularly if they are in prime focal areas.

In the specific case of the 1854 Type II and 1855, coins that grade MS-66 or finer and possess full, satiny luster and rich orange-gold or rose-gold color are highly desirable for numismatic investment purposes. These coins are very rare from a condition standpoint—PCGS and NGC report just 53 examples that grade MS-66 or finer in the entire Type II Gold Dollar series (May/2007)—and they are extremely beautiful coins to behold. An 1855 in PCGS MS-66 crossed the auction block at $64,200 in early 2004, while a simply breathtaking example of the same issue in PCGS MS-67 sold for $86,250 one year later.

CHAPTER FIVE

Type III
Gold Dollars

Courtesy of Rare Coin Wholesalers

SPECIFICATIONS

Year(s) Issued: *1856-1889*
Issuing Mint(s): *Philadelphia, Charlotte, Dahlonega, San Francisco*
Authorizing Act: *March 3, 1849*
Designer: *James Barton Longacre*
Weight: *1.672 grams*
Composition: *90% gold, 10% copper*
Diameter: *15 millimeters*
Edge: *Reeded*

History

The definitive design for the United States' circulating Gold Dollar made its debut in 1856 with deliveries from the Philadelphia and Dahlonega Mints. The Type III motif was executed by Chief Engraver Longacre, and it was a much more durable product than the artist's Type II design. The two types are actually very similar in appearance, but the latter was prepared in lower relief for improved striking quality and durability in the avenues of commerce. Liberty's portrait is also noticeably larger on Type III examples.

For much of the era during which it was struck, the Type III Gold Dollar did not see widespread circulation. The denomination certainly served a useful purpose when it was authorized in 1849, but its fortunes eroded significantly with the onset of the Civil War in 1861. Gold was hoarded in the Eastern states beginning early in the conflict, and mintage figures at the Philadelphia Mint dropped accordingly. The Confederate takeover of the Charlotte and Dahlonega facilities in 1861 ensured that no more Gold Dollars would ever be produced in the South after that year. (The New Orleans Mint actually struck its final coins of this denomination in 1855 while the Type II design was still current.) The San Francisco Mint never produced the Type III Gold Dollar in significant quantity, and a delivery of 3,000 pieces in 1870 was the facilities' final contribution to this series.

With the exception of the 1873 and 1874 deliveries, yearly Gold Dollar mintages in the Philadelphia Mint never again approached pre-Civil War levels. Despite limited production runs, however, many of the post-1875 issues are fairly plentiful in Mint State due to widespread hoarding at the time of issue. Unlike earlier U.S. gold coins, late-date Gold Dollars were kept stateside instead of being exported. Many examples, therefore, survived for future generations of numismatists.

By 1889, the federal government finally conceded that the production of limited quantities of Gold Dollars that were not needed in circulation was futile. Congress abolished this denomination the following year with the act of September 25, 1890.

The Philadelphia Mint struck proof Type III Gold Dollars every year from 1856-1889. Many of these issues have extremely limited mintages, and those for the 1856, 1857 and 1858 have been lost to history because they were never recorded by Mint employees.

Short Type Set

The potential for including a Type III Gold Dollar in a short type set of U.S. gold coinage is underappreciated in today's market. In addition to its Type I and Type II counterparts, the Type III Gold Dollar shares characteristics with several other gold types that might serve as a useful foundation upon which to build a small, yet meaningful collection. A few of the more obvious possibilities are:

Gold Dollar Types, a three-piece set including:

Type I Gold Dollar
Type II Gold Dollar
Type III Gold Dollar

Gold Coin Types Designed by James Barton Longacre, a seven-piece set including:

Type I Gold Dollar
Type II Gold Dollar
Type III Gold Dollar
Three-Dollar Gold
Type I Double Eagle
Type II Double Eagle
Type III Double Eagle

Small-Denomination Gold Coins of the 19th Century, a four-piece set that includes:

Type I Gold Dollar
Type II Gold Dollar
Type III Gold Dollar
Three-Dollar Gold

Complete Type Set

As the longest-running type in the Gold Dollar series, it should come as no surprise to read that the Type III offers more candidates for inclusion in a circulated or Mint State type set than its predecessors.

Circulated Examples: Some of the most attractive issues in this series for circulated type purposes are the higher-mintage Philadelphia Mint deliveries. These include the 1856 Slant 5 (of particular desirability due to its first-year status), 1862 and 1874. Worn survivors of dates such as these are plentiful in numismatic circles—so plentiful, in fact, that I would almost caution against acquiring a circulated example for a type set. A few 1874s in AU-58 sold for about $180-$250 at auction in late 2006/early 2007 while MS-62s realized only $300-$400 during the same general time period. Since the price difference between these two grades is not all that great, I believe that there is considerable benefit to stretching a bit to buy a Mint State coin.

If you prefer to acquire a circulated Type III Gold Dollar to match the rest of the coins in your gold type set, or if you would rather put the extra money toward another numismatic acquisition, AU-58 is the most desirable grade. There are plenty of opportunities to acquire a coin with virtually intact luster, sharp striking detail and relatively few abrasions.

Courtesy of Bowers and Merena

Plentiful in an absolute sense due to relatively high mintages, the 1862 and 1874 are two issues that the circulated type collector might want to consider when looking for a Type III Gold Dollar.

Mint State Examples: Contrary to the aforementioned strategies for the Type I and Type II Gold Dollars, I advise focusing on one of the lower-mintage Type III Gold Dollars when assembling a Mint State type set. Many late-date Type III Gold Dollars were widely saved at the time of issue and are more plentiful in high grades than their limited original mintages might suggest. Gem and Superb Gem examples of issues such as the 1880 (just 1,600 business strikes produced), 1881 (original mintage: only 7,620 pieces) and 1882 (a mere 5,000 coins struck for use in circulation) appear in the market on a fairly regular basis. What's more, these issues almost always come sharply struck with vibrant, satin or semi-prooflike luster and beautiful color. An example that grades at least MS-65 will make a lovely addition to a type set, and a limited original mintage is likely to keep demand strong in the coming decades. Select Gem-quality examples of these three issues that sold through auction in 2006/2007 include:

> **1880**: *A coin certified MS-65 by PCGS traded for $3,738 in August of 2006.*
> **1880**: *A PCGS MS-66 sold for $2,990 in early 2007.*
> **1881**: *An NGC MS-65 brought $2,530 when it appeared at auction during the spring of 2006.*
> **1881**: *Conversely, the sum of only $2,990 was required to secure an NGC MS-66 during an early 2007 auction.*
> **1882**: *The winning bidder paid $2,645 for a PCGS MS-65 that crossed the auction block in March of 2007.*

If you are looking for an even higher-quality example, $4,250-$5,000 will be sufficient to secure an 1880, 1881 or 1882 Gold Dollar in MS-67.

General Characteristics: Just to reiterate, you should have no difficulty acquiring a sharply struck and attractive Type III Gold Dollar for inclusion in a type set. The P-mint issues come in a wide variety of colors and luster types, and you can certainly hold out for a coin that best suits your taste.

Words of Caution: With so many attractive examples from which to choose, pursuing this type should be a fun and relaxing pastime. Do not allow yourself to be pressured into buying one of the more common P-mint issues. If you are not completely satisfied with the coin, let it go and wait for a more appealing example to come along. Likewise, if you find a desirable Type III Gold Dollar and an equally attractive representative of one of the earlier Gold Dollar types but cannot afford to purchase both pieces simultaneously, it is better to buy the other piece first. It is much easier to find attractive Type III Gold Dollars in auctions and dealers' inventories.

STRATEGIES FOR INCLUDING THE TYPE III GOLD DOLLAR IN A COMPLETE TYPE SET

Most Desirable Issue(s)

Circulated Grades: *1856 Slant 5, 1857, 1858, 1859, 1861, 1862, 1873 Open 3, 1874*

Mint State Grades: *1880-1889*

Most Desirable Grade(s), Circulated Coins: *AU-58*

Estimated Cost: *$180-$250*

Key to Collecting: *Virtually intact mint luster; sharply struck devices; no individually detracting abrasions*

Most Desirable Grade(s), Mint State Coins: *MS-65 or finer*

Estimated Cost: *$2,500 and up*

Key to Collecting: *Full mint luster; original color; sharp striking detail*

Advanced Type Set

Rarer Issues: There are many issues in the Philadelphia Mint Type III Gold Dollar series that are attractive for advanced type purposes. Most of the low-mintage deliveries struck during the 1863-1872 era have smaller extant populations than those produced after 1875. This indicates that exportation and melting of Gold Dollars was more common during and immediately after the Civil War than it was beginning in the mid-1870s. Issues such as the 1867 and 1869 are encountered with less frequency in today's market than, say, the 1881 and 1882. On the positive side, most surviving Gold Dollars from the 1863-1872 era are Mint State, virtually all are well struck and many display gorgeous prooflike surfaces. While it will certainly cost you more in the short run, adding a rarer Type III Gold Dollar is a great way to increase the desirability of your type set when the time comes to sell. Technical quality, eye appeal and cost should be of concern, so I suggest obtaining an example that grades at least MS-62 as a suitable compromise. The cost for these issues will vary, but you should anticipate spending at least $1,500.

STRATEGIES FOR INCLUDING THE TYPE III GOLD DOLLAR IN A TYPE SET OF RARER ISSUES

Most Desirable Issue(s): *Philadelphia Mint issues dated 1863-1872*

Most Desirable Grade(s): *MS-62 or finer*

Estimated Cost: *$1,500 and up*

Key to Collecting: *Sharp striking detail; richly original color; full mint bloom, which is frequently semi- or fully prooflike*

Major Subtypes: There are no significant subtypes in the Type III Gold Dollar series, the design remaining unchanged during its 34-year lifespan.

Issuing Mint: You will need to acquire four coins to complete a set of Type III Gold Dollars using this strategy. The P-mint requirement has already been addressed, the low-mintage issues struck after 1875 being most attractive for Mint State type purposes.

There is not much choice where the Charlotte Mint is concerned as only two Type III Gold Dollar issues were produced in this Southern coinage facility. In my experience, there are more examples of the 1857-C than the 1859-C available in numismatic circles. This should come as no surprise given a higher mintage for the 1857-C. Indeed, I wholeheartedly recommend this issue for C-mint type purposes. Not only do examples appear in the market with relative frequency, but you should have an easier time locating a fairly well-struck coin. Nevertheless, you will probably have to accept some degree of striking incompleteness when purchasing an 1857-C Gold Dollar. While the Type III design was a decided improvement over its Type II predecessor, the Southern coinage facilities continued to experience considerable difficulty producing this denomination until the onset of the Civil War. Also be mindful of the fact that dull, usually orange-gold surfaces characterize most surviving the 1857-C Gold Dollars. To mitigate these detractions somewhat and have a decent chance of securing a coin with better-than-average eye appeal, I suggest concentrating on pieces that grade at least AU-50 and possess a decent strike. Freedom from an excessive number of distracting abrasions is also a significant asset. There are not all that many 1857-C Gold Dollars that fit these criteria. The realistic collector should be patient when pursuing this issue and, even then, be willing to compromise a bit in one or two areas where they feel comfortable yielding some ground. Plan on setting aside at least $3,000 before entering the market for an 1857-C that grades AU-50.

Courtesy of Bowers and Merena

The 1857-C seems like the issue of choice for the collector that is looking for a representative of Type III Gold Dollar production in the Charlotte Mint. Not only are survivors more plentiful than those of the 1859-C delivery, but one should have a better chance of locating a fairly well-struck 1857-C.

Courtesy of Bowers and Merena

The 1859-D turns up now and then in the finer circulated and Mint State grades, and the average survivor of this 4,952-piece delivery is fairly well struck by the standards of the issuing Mint. A coin that grades at least AU-50 is usually preferable, particularly if it is also free of singularly detracting abrasions with rose-gold or, better yet, orange-gold color.

There are more issues in the D-mint Type III Gold Dollar series, and the advanced type collector should have an easier time than that experienced pursuing the Charlotte

Mint issues. Nevertheless, the 1860-D and 1861-D are not realistic candidates for type purposes. Both issues are key-date rarities with peculiar striking characteristics that only the dedicated Southern gold specialist will appreciate. On the other hand, the 1859-D turns up now and then in the finer circulated and Mint State grades, and the average survivor of this 4,952-piece delivery is fairly well struck by Dahlonega Mint standards. A coin that grades at least AU-50 is preferable, particularly if it is also free of singularly detracting abrasions with rose-gold or, better yet, orange-gold color. The '59-D will cost at least $2,800 in that grade.

The San Francisco Mint contributed five issues to the Type III Gold Dollar series, and all are scarce-to-rare coins that do not trade all that often in the U.S. rare coin market of the early 21st century. There are a few more survivors of the 1860-S than the 1857-S, 1858-S, 1859-S and 1870-S, but Mint State examples of all issues are seldom encountered. In order to acquire a coin with technical quality that matches that of the C and D-mint examples that you purchase, I advise purchasing an 1860-S that grades at least AU-50. At that level of preservation, the 1860-S is worth a minimum of $675. Most examples that I have encountered are sharply struck with surfaces that range from light yellow-gold color to a warmer orange-gold cast.

STRATEGIES FOR INCLUDING THE TYPE III GOLD DOLLAR IN A TYPE SET BY ISSUING MINT

Required Number of Coins: *Four*

Issuing Mint #1: *Philadelphia, Pennsylvania*

Most Desirable Issue(s): *1880-1889*

Key to Collecting: *MS-65 or finer in grade; full mint luster; original color; sharp striking detail*

Issuing Mint #2: *Charlotte, North Carolina*

Most Desirable Issue(s): *1857-C*

Key to Collecting: *AU-50 or higher grade; better-than-average strike; relatively smooth-looking surfaces*

Issuing Mint #3: *Dahlonega, Georgia*

Most Desirable Issue(s): *1859-D*

Key to Collecting: *AU-50 or higher grade; bold strike; no singularly distracting abrasions; pale rose-gold or orange-gold color*

Issuing Mint #4: *San Francisco, California*

Most Desirable Issue(s): *1860-S*

Key to Collecting: *AU-50 or finer grade; sharp strike; no singularly distracting abrasions*

Proof Type Set

This is the only Gold Dollar design that most numismatists can hope to represent in a type set of proof gold. The most plentiful proof Gold Dollars in today's market are survivors of those issues produced from 1884-1889. Any of these dates should be a potential target for the type collector. Coins that grade Proof-64 are particularly desirable due to their combination of strong technical quality and relatively affordable cost. Examples have sold in the range of $4,000-$6,000 during auctions conducted in 2006 and early 2007. The price nearly doubles in Proof-65, and below the Proof-64 level even the small Gold Dollar will usually show at least a few distracting hairlines or tiny contact marks.

Many late-date proofs of this type display bold field-to-device contrast. This is an attractive, highly desirable finish, and the proof type collector should look for a coin that includes a Cameo designation as part of the grade. (Deep/Ultra Cameo specimens are rarer and more difficult to obtain, although an 1887 in NGC Proof-64 UCAM did sell for $5,578 during a late 2006 auction.) Another positive characteristic to emphasize is rich orange-gold color.

STRATEGIES FOR INCLUDING THE TYPE III GOLD DOLLAR IN A PROOF TYPE SET

Most Desirable Issue(s): *1884-1889*

Most Desirable Grade(s): *Proof-64 Cameo*

Key to Collecting: *Bold field-to-device contrast; rich orange-gold color; full striking definition*

Assembling a Complete Set

Year Set: Judging by collections and portfolios offered at auction over the past decade, most numismatists have never even contemplated assembling a year set of Type III Gold Dollars. I find this surprising, since the completion of such a set is not a particularly formidable task, even in predominantly Mint State grades. The Philadelphia Mint issues are relatively obtainable through at least MS-64. In fact, many of the later-date issues in this series are hardly ever encountered in worn condition. Nevertheless, several issues might require you to accept an AU example, and these include the 1863 and 1875. The 1875, however, should be the only substantial hurdle on the path to completion of this year set. Only 400 business strike Gold Dollars were struck in 1875, and survivors are exceedingly rare and seldom encountered at even the largest numismatic events. Even so, patience will be rewarded as AU and Mint State examples are offered on occasion. Such pieces typically appear in auctions, where they receive considerable attention from catalogers. An example certified MS-63 by NGC realized $9,775 during a sale conducted in the early spring of 2007.

Given the rarity and consequent cost of this issue, you might be tempted to compromise with an impaired 1875 Gold Dollar that has been graded by Numismatic Conservation Service (NCS, a part of NGC) or American Numismatic Association Certification Service (ANACS, originally founded by the ANA but no longer affiliated with that association). I do not believe that this is a wise strategy, although NCS and ANACS certainly render valuable service to the numismatic community by authenticating and encapsulating impaired coins that are not eligible for certification at PCGS or NGC. The relative ease with which you can acquire problem-free examples of most other P-mint issues in this series will leave a cleaned or damaged 1875 sticking out like a sore thumb in a complete set. This, in turn, can harm the presentation of the set as whole when the time comes to sell.

Date and Mint Set: Fifteen issues are all that differentiate a date and mint set of Type III Gold Dollars from a year set, and this total includes both date logotypes of the 1856 and 1873. Most of those issues are scarce-to-rare in all grades and at least three are potential stoppers the likes of the 1875. In order to be realistic about your chances of completing a well-matched date and mint set of Type III Gold Dollars, you should try to acquire coins that grade AU. This grade level holds the only real chances of success for issues such as the 1856-D, 1857-C, 1857-D, 1860-D and 1861-D, and probably also the 1863 and 1875. Even in AU-50, however, expect to invest considerable time and at least $85,000 into acquiring a representative of each issue in this series. Few collectors have attempted this feat, and even fewer have succeeded, so make sure that you have the resources to sustain a long, uphill battle before beginning a date and mint set of this type.

Die Variety Set: To date, this type has garnered little attention from die variety specialists, and with good reason. Most issues have limited mintages that required only a single set of dies to produce. The only significant die variety in the Type III Gold Dollar series is the 1862 Doubled Die Obverse, examples of which have yet to command a significant premium in numismatic circles.

Proof Set: It is possible to assemble a complete set of proof Type III Gold Dollars, as the Philadelphia Mint struck examples in this format every year from 1856 through 1889. Only affluent collectors, however, should consider embarking on this task. Many issues have extant populations of fewer than 20 coins, and some would be hard pressed to muster even 10 survivors. Even if you do possess the necessary funds ($100,000+ for just the following three issues in Proof-65/66), securing an example of the 1856, 1874 and 1877 is going to take a considerable amount of time. There are some coins that are simply so rare that an example will appear in the market only once every few years.

A Complete Set by Issuing Mint: The Charlotte and Dahlonega issues in this series have long been popular with collectors that specialize in Southern gold. Try to assemble the set in AU and Mint State grades, but recognize that the 1856-D, 1860-D and 1861-D are going to be particularly challenging and costly at any level of preservation. In fact, you must have at least $50,000 to spend in order to acquire examples of just these three issues in AU-55.

An overlooked but potentially rewarding set is a complete collection of Type III Gold Dollars struck in the San Francisco Mint. There are only five S-mint issues in this series and, while all are scarce-to-rare, examples are undervalued at today's prices. This set has an added benefit: once assembled, you need acquire only the 1854-S Type I and 1856-S Type II to have a complete collection of San Francisco Mint Gold Dollars. Coins that grade at least AU-50 and possess relatively smooth-looking surfaces would form a lovely set. The task might be more difficult than you initially expect, but it is achievable given adequate time and resources. As far as the latter are concerned, one example each of the 1857-S, 1858-S, 1859-S, 1860-S and 1870-S in AU-50 will require at least $6,000.

Investing Tips

There are several widely recognized key-date issues in the Type III Gold Dollar series that have long been highly regarded in numismatic circles. Coins such as the 1861-D and 1875 (the latter in both business strike and proof formats) are always accompanied by considerable fanfare and strong selling prices when an example appears in the market. While these issues could serve as a potentially profitable addition to an investment portfolio, you might want to take a more unorthodox view toward the Type III Gold Dollar. There are many underrated deliveries in this series whose true rarity has yet to be fully appreciated in the numismatic market. Mint State examples of the 1857-S, 1858-S, 1859-S and 1860-S are anything but common, but they rarely number among the more eagerly anticipated highlights in numismatic auctions. I can say the same for proofs such as the 1856, 1874 and 1877. All of these coins exist in very limited numbers, and demand for attractive examples can only increase in the coming decades.

Courtesy of Bowers and Merena

Focusing on rare, key-date issues such as the 1861-D and 1875 represents one possible way for the numismatic investor to target the Type III Gold Dollar series.

CHAPTER SIX

Capped Bust Right, No Stars Obverse Quarter Eagle

Courtesy of Rare Coin Wholesalers

SPECIFICATIONS

Year(s) Issued: *1796 only*
Issuing Mint(s): *Philadelphia only*
Authorizing Act: *April 2, 1792*
Designer: *Robert Scot*
Weight: *4.37 grams*
Composition: *91.67% gold, 8.33% silver and copper*
Diameter: *20 millimeters (approximate)*
Edge: *Reeded*

History

The Quarter Eagle is the last of the three original gold denominations (Quarter Eagle, Half Eagle and Eagle) that the United States Mint placed into circulation during the 1790s. Unlike later deliveries in Robert Scot's Capped Bust Right series, the first 963 pieces struck do not display stars around the obverse border. Significant as a one-year type, the 1796 No Stars Quarter Eagle is also popular as the only early U.S. gold coin without stars as part of the obverse design.

All 1796 No Stars Quarter Eagles are believed to have been struck on September 22 and December 8 of that year. Estimates on the number of coins that have survived vary, but I believe that fewer than 150 examples are known in all grades.

The First United States Mint in Philadelphia. This small complex of buildings served as the nation's only coinage facility through 1833. The first Quarter Eagles were struck within its walls in 1796. (Historical Society of Philadelphia)

Short Type Set

I can think of only two short type sets of U.S. gold coins that will require a representative of this issue. This is not a popular way to collect the Capped Bust Right, No Stars Quarter Eagle. Most collectors that I have met would rather acquire an example as part of a specialized early gold collection or a larger type set. Either of these proposed short sets, however, could serve as a stepping stone on the path to a more expansive holding.

Quarter Eagle Types, an eight-piece set including:
*** Capped Bust Right, No Stars Obverse***
Capped Bust Right, Stars Obverse
Capped Bust Left
Capped Head Left, Large Diameter
Capped Head Left, Reduced Diameter
Classic
Liberty
Indian

Capped Bust Right Gold Coinage, a six-piece set including:
*** Capped Bust Right Quarter Eagle, No Stars Obverse***
Capped Bust Right Quarter Eagle, Stars Obverse
Capped Bust Right Half Eagle, Small Eagle Reverse
Capped Bust Right Half Eagle, Large Eagle Reverse
Capped Bust Right Eagle, Small Eagle Reverse
Capped Bust Right Eagle, Large Eagle Reverse

Complete Type Set

This type is one of the most challenging and costly to acquire in the entire family of United States gold coinage. As previously stated, the Capped Bust Right, No Stars Obverse Quarter Eagle is a one-year type. With a paltry original mintage of 963 pieces, this 18th century issue is understandably rare. In fact, I believe that fewer than 150 coins have survived in all grades. With so few coins extant and strong competition from type collectors and gold specialists, it is not wise to be overly concerned with grade when it comes to the 1796 No Stars Quarter Eagle. Any example certified by PCGS or NGC represents an important potential addition to a collection or investment portfolio. Nevertheless, you might want to focus on circulated or Mint State coins depending on your numismatic budget and/or personal preferences.

Circulated Examples: The majority of 1796 No Stars Quarter Eagles that have survived display at least some degree or wear, and most are concentrated in the EF-40 through AU-58 grade range. As of March 2007, PCGS had also seen five coins in the various VF grades. An example at any of these levels of preservation will fit comfortably into a type set of United States gold, even if most of the other coins in the set are Mint State. An example graded AU-55 by PCGS brought $92,000 when it was offered through a September 2006 auction.

Courtesy of Bowers and Merena

The majority of 1796 No Stars Quarter Eagles that have survived display at least some degree of wear, and most are concentrated in the EF-40 through AU-58 grade range. An example at any of these levels of preservation could fit comfortably into a type set of United States gold, even if most of the other coins in the set are Mint State. The EF coin pictured here retains overall bold definition, and the surfaces are not excessively abraded for an early U.S. gold coin that saw about 20 points of circulation.

Mint State Examples: Uncirculated 1796 No Stars Quarter Eagles are in the minority among surviving examples, and they always garner considerable attention when presented to potential buyers. Coins certified by PCGS and NGC grade predominantly MS-60 through MS-62. Each service does report a single coin in MS-65, the PCGS-certified example realizing an impressive $1.38 million when it crossed the auction block in June of 2005. Lower-grade examples include an NGC MS-61 that sold for $253,000 in early 2007. The inclusion of a Mint State 1796 No Stars Quarter Eagle is one of the most instantly recognizable signs of an important holding in today's rare coin market.

General Characteristics: Most survivors of this one-year type are softly struck to one degree or another. This characteristic is well known among numismatic professionals, as well as many collectors and investors. As such, you should not experience much difficulty selling a 1796 No Stars Quarter Eagle due to incompleteness of strike. However, a few high-grade examples are well struck with relatively bold definition over the central highpoints and nicely detailed denticles around the borders. Holding out for one of these pieces will definitely pay dividends when the time comes to sell.

The majority of 1796 No Stars Quarter Eagles that have survived possess color toward the deeper end of the spectrum, predominantly green-gold, khaki-gold or a blend of both shades. Those that retain some degree of original luster are either satiny or prooflike. With the possible exception of the two or three highest-graded examples, scattered abrasions will be present on one or both sides. Nevertheless, try to avoid coins with large distractions, particularly if they are in one of the prime focal areas. Several pieces also display adjustments marks, which are a normal part of the production process for many silver and gold coins struck in the early U.S. Mint. These features, which appear as narrow depressions in a coin's surface, were created when Mint employees filed an overweight planchet prior to striking in order to make it conform to the specified weight standard. If excessive, however, adjustment marks can reduce a coin's eye appeal even though they will not reduce the numeric grade assigned by PCGS or NGC. You might have difficultly discerning adjustment marks from post-striking damage. If this is the case, be sure to solicit the expert opinion of a numismatic professional before making a purchase.

Words of Caution: Quite a few of the 1796 No Stars Quarter Eagles that I have seen possess significant problems associated with polishing, repairs and other mishandling. The rarity of this issue, as well as the infrequency with which examples are offered for sale, might tempt you to accept an impaired coin. If you are worried at all about the resale potential of your numismatic holdings, however, I urge you to pass over such pieces, even if they are certified as genuine by services such as NCS or ANACS. I have handled several impaired 1796 No Stars Quarter Eagles and can honestly say that most are unattractive coins. And when the time comes to sell, rest assured that potential buyers will always focus first and foremost on the impairments. This happens time and again with even the rarest United States coins. It is best, therefore, to stretch for a problem-free example or select a coin in a lower grade than most other pieces in your type set.

On the other hand, it is not a good idea to hesitate if you are in the market for a problem-free 1796 No Stars Quarter Eagle and an example in your price range becomes available. Coins certified by PCGS and NGC are always in demand and, once snatched up for inclusion in a collection or investment portfolio, it may be several years before they re-enter the market. Be mindful of fleeting buying opportunities when they present themselves.

STRATEGIES FOR INCLUDING THE CAPPED BUST RIGHT, NO STARS OBVERSE QUARTER EAGLE IN A COMPLETE TYPE SET

Most Desirable Issue(s): *1796 No Stars Obverse (only option)*

Most Desirable Grade(s), Circulated Coins: *Any grade*

Estimated Cost: *In AU-55, $95,000 and up*

Key to Collecting: *PCGS or NGC certification; green-gold or khaki-gold color; no sizeable or individually conspicuous abrasions; a coin that is free of an excessive number of adjustment marks*

Most Desirable Grade(s), Mint State Coins: *MS-60 or finer*

Estimated Cost: *$200,000 and up*

Key to Collecting: *PCGS or NGC certification; green-gold or khaki-gold color; no sizeable or individually conspicuous abrasions; a coin that is free of an excessive number of adjustment marks*

Advanced Type Set

Since this early gold type is represented by just one issue, there are no special options available for the advanced type collector.

Proof Type Set

The United States Mint did not strike any proof Quarter Eagles in 1796 of either the No Stars Obverse or Stars Obverse types.

Assembling a Complete Set

Die Variety Set: Other than acquiring an example for inclusion in a type set, the only other way to collect the 1796 No Stars Obverse Quarter Eagle is by die variety. There are two die marriages known, but even so I would not recommend this strategy. For starters, the 1796 No Stars is rare and costly as a type. Buying two examples, therefore, will increase your financial burden significantly. Second, only one die marriage is realistically obtainable. The other has a surviving population of fewer than 10 coins. Finally, Quarter Eagles are the least popular early gold denomination to collect by variety. The majority of issues were struck from just a single die pair and, where it does exist, variation within an individual year is usually minor. There is, therefore, little demand for even the rarest die varieties in the early Quarter Eagle series.

Investing Tips

A high-profile rarity that enjoys strong demand from type collectors and advanced gold specialists, the 1796 No Stars Quarter Eagle has performed very well over the past several decades. The following graph illustrates the recent price appreciation for this issue in AU-50, a highly desirable level of preservation for the type.

You will be best served to consider only PCGS and NGC-certified examples for inclusion in a numismatic investment portfolio. In addition, look for a coin with above-average striking detail and relatively smooth surfaces. The exact grade that you choose is less important as both circulated and Mint State survivors are in extremely limited supply.

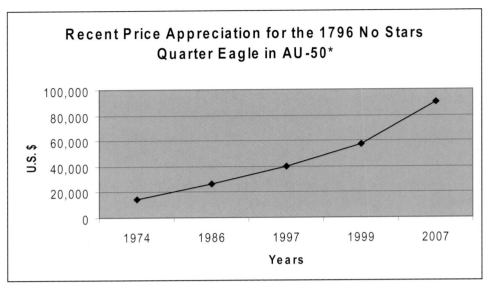

*Most values represent prices realized for PCGS and NGC-certified examples as reported by leading rare coin auction firms. 2007 value is the author's estimate of the current retail price for the issue in AU-50.

CHAPTER SEVEN

Capped Bust Right, Stars Obverse Quarter Eagles

Courtesy of Rare Coin Wholesalers

SPECIFICATIONS

Year(s) Issued: *1796-1807*
Issuing Mint(s): *Philadelphia only*
Authorizing Act: *April 2, 1792*
Designer: *Robert Scot*
Weight: *4.37 grams*
Composition: *91.67% gold, 8.33% silver and copper*
Diameter: *20 millimeters (approximate)*
Edge: *Reeded*

History

The final batch of Quarter Eagles struck in the Philadelphia Mint during 1796 introduced the Stars Obverse variant of the Capped Bust Right design. This design is also the work of Robert Scot, first chief engraver of the United States Mint, and the addition of obverse stars is the most significant differentiating feature between the two types. Both major variants of the Capped Bust Right Quarter Eagle display a right-facing bust of Liberty as the central obverse device. Liberty is wearing a soft cap, the word LIBERTY is above and the date is below. The reverse is a rendition of the Great Seal of the United States with the legend UNITED STATES OF AMERICA around the border.

During the years that the Philadelphia Mint produced Capped Bust Right, Stars Obverse Quarter Eagles, the most popular denomination among gold bullion depositors was the Half Eagle. Since silver and gold coins were struck at the request of bullion depositors during the early decades of U.S. Mint operations, and few Two-and-a-Halves were ordered during the late 1700s and early 1800s, all issues in this series were produced in extremely limited numbers. As many examples were later melted due to rising bullion prices on the world market, this series now ranks as one of the rarest in all of U.S. numismatics.

Short Type Set

As with its No Stars predecessor, the Stars Obverse Quarter Eagle is not immediately recognizable as a coin that would make a fitting addition to a short type set. Nevertheless, I am aware of two sets in which an example of this type will have a prominent position. Both sets would serve very well as a closed collection, or they could be completed on your way to assembling a larger holding of U.S. gold coinage.

Quarter Eagle Types, an eight-piece set including:
> *Capped Bust Right, No Stars Obverse*
> **Capped Bust Right, Stars Obverse**
> *Capped Bust Left*
> *Capped Head Left, Large Diameter*
> *Capped Head Left, Reduced Diameter*
> *Classic*
> *Liberty*
> *Indian*

Capped Bust Right Gold Coinage, a six-piece set including:
> *Capped Bust Right Quarter Eagle, No Stars Obverse*
> **Capped Bust Right Quarter Eagle, Stars Obverse**
> *Capped Bust Right Half Eagle, Small Eagle Reverse*
> *Capped Bust Right Half Eagle, Large Eagle Reverse*
> *Capped Bust Right Eagle, Small Eagle Reverse*
> *Capped Bust Right Eagle, Large Eagle Reverse*

Complete Type Set

Many type collectors concentrate on first-year issues. These deliveries are historically significant, and they will number among the more plentiful issues of their respective type as long as the contemporary public set aside a significant number of examples. In the specific case of the Capped Bust Right, Stars Obverse Quarter Eagle, however, the opposite end of the series actually offers better prospects for acquiring a relatively affordable type candidate.

Circulated Examples: Sixty-to-seventy percent of the circulated Quarter Eagles of this type that I have handled over the past decade have been dated 1807. This is the final issue of the Capped Bust Right type, and it is the most plentiful in today's market. The majority of worn survivors grade Extremely Fine or About Uncirculated, and any individual grade in this range would serve well for type purposes. This is a scarce and expensive type, and you should not be ashamed to include a problem-free EF or AU 1807 Quarter Eagle in an otherwise Mint State set. Examples in EF-40 cost at least $8,750, while an individual example in AU-58 required $21,850 from the winning bidder when it appeared at auction in August of 2006.

Courtesy of Rare Coin Wholesalers

The 1807 is the most frequently encountered Capped Bust Right, Stars Obverse Quarter Eagle in today's market. As a result, this final-year issue is often selected for inclusion in gold type sets.

Mint State Examples: The final-year 1807 is also an attractive Mint State type candidate. Such pieces are considerably rarer than their circulated counterparts, but they are offered with greater frequency than Mint State survivors of other issues in this series.

Based on the relative availability of coins as listed in the PCGS and NGC population reports, I suggest acquiring an example that grades MS-61 or MS-62. A PCGS-certified coin in MS-62 brought $46,000 at auction in mid-2007, while an NGC MS-61 commanded $32,200 during the fall of 2006. A few Choice 1807 Quarter Eagles are also known, and there is even a single MS-65 listed at PCGS (May/2007).

General Characteristics: Whether circulated or Mint State, the typically encountered 1807 Quarter Eagle displays yellow-gold or orange-gold color. I have seen fewer reddish-gold and green-gold examples, although pieces with these colors are still attractive coins. Striking quality is generally good, but a few survivors are a bit softly impressed over the highpoints in and around the centers. Enough boldly struck coins are known, however, that you should avoid an 1807 Quarter Eagle with below-average detail.

While scuffy surfaces are the norm for early gold coins in EF, AU and lower Mint State grades, it is best to pass over an 1807 Quarter Eagle with large and/or singularly conspicuous abrasions. A satiny texture characterizes the luster quality of most high-grade survivors, although a few pieces possess noticeable semi-reflective tendencies in the fields.

Words of Caution: As a gold coin produced in the early United States Mint, the 1807 sometimes comes with adjustment marks on one or both sides. These features are a normal part of the minting process, and they are perfectly acceptable to the professional graders at PCGS and NGC.

If you find adjustment marks distracting, however, enough 1807 Quarter Eagles exist without these features that you should hold out until one of those coins is made available for purchase. On the other hand, I have met some collectors that believe adjustment marks are an interesting result of the rustic conditions that prevailed in the early U.S. Mint. Even if you are in that category, I must still advise that an excessive number of adjustment marks can interfere with major design elements on one or both sides of a coin.

STRATEGIES FOR INCLUDING THE CAPPED BUST RIGHT, STARS OBVERSE QUARTER EAGLE IN A COMPLETE TYPE SET

Most Desirable Issue(s): *1807*

Most Desirable Grade(s), Circulated Coins: *EF-40 through AU-58*

Estimated Cost: *$8,750-$25,000*

Key to Collecting: *Free of large and/or singularly distracting abrasions; few, if any adjustment marks*

Most Desirable Grade(s), Mint State Coins: *MS-60 or finer*

Estimated Cost: *$30,000 and up*

Key to Collecting: *Free of large and/or singularly distracting abrasions; few, if any adjustment marks; yellow-gold or orange-gold color; overall bold striking detail*

Advanced Type Set

Rarer Issues: This series includes several rarer issues that sell for little more than type prices. Examples are the 1802/'1', 1804 14-Star Reverse, 1805 and 1806/4, Stars 8x5. All of these issues have smaller surviving populations in circulated grades than the 1807, but they do not command much of a premium in EF or AU. The 1806/4, Stars 8x5 is particularly desirable because it is an overdate with an impressively low mintage of 1,136 pieces. An EF-40 will cost at least $9,500, while sale prices for AU-58s have reached as high as $25,000-$30,000.

Courtesy of Rare Coin Wholesalers

Incompleteness of strike is often a problem for the Capped Bust Right, Stars Obverse Quarter Eagle, as evidenced by the obverse of this beautiful 1802/'1' graded MS-65 by NGC. Notice that there is essentially no definition over the central highpoints.

In Mint State, the 1802/'1' and 1804 14-Star Reverse are also desirable issues. Both are appreciably rarer than the 1807 in all Mint State grades, but auction prices realized have been similar through MS-62. In fact, an 1802/'1' in NGC MS-62 brought $32,200 at auction in 2005 and an 1804 14-Star Reverse in PCGS MS-61 sold for the same amount just a few months earlier.

On the negative side, the 1802/'1', 1804 14-Star Reverse, 1805 and 1806/4, Stars 8x5 will typically display a softer strike than the 1807. This is the price that you will have to pay to acquire a scarcer example of this type. Still, try to go down fighting by searching for a coin with at least emerging detail over the central highpoints and in most areas at the rims. Color varies widely for these issues, so you should on insist on acquiring a coin that best suits your taste in this area. Those pieces that retain original luster are predominantly satiny or semi-prooflike in sheen.

STRATEGIES FOR INCLUDING THE CAPPED BUST RIGHT, STARS OBVERSE QUARTER EAGLE IN A TYPE SET OF RARER ISSUES

Most Desirable Issue(s): *1802/'1', 1804 14-Star Reverse, 1805 (circulated grades only), 1806/4, Stars 8x5 (circulated grades only)*

Most Desirable Grade(s): *EF-40 or finer*

Estimated Cost: *$9,500 and up*

Key to Collecting: *Above-average striking detail in the centers and at the rims; no sizeable or individually mentionable abrasions*

Major Subtypes: You can have a lot of fun assembling an advanced type set of Capped Bust Right, Stars Obverse Quarter Eagles by major subtype. Several design changes are known, and they are most readily distinguishable by the number and arrangement of stars on both the obverse and the reverse. In fact, this is the most visually dynamic early Quarter Eagle series as far as subtypes are concerned. Given the scarcity of the type as a whole, however, as well as the rarity of some of the issues required to represent certain varieties, I can only endorse this strategy among well-funded collectors. If you are in this category, then be advised that a complete set of major subtypes in the Capped Bust Right, Star Obverse Quarter Eagle series must include six coins.

STRATEGIES FOR INCLUDING THE CAPPED BUST RIGHT, STARS OBVERSE QUARTER EAGLE IN A TYPE SET OF MAJOR SUBTYPES

Required Number of Coins: *Six*

Major Subtype #1: *16-Star Obverse, 16-Star Reverse, Tall-Neck Eagle*

Most Desirable Issue(s): *1796 Stars Obverse (only option)*

Major Subtype #2: *13-Star Obverse, Stars 7x6, 16-Star Reverse, Tall-Neck Eagle*

Most Desirable Issue(s): *1797 (only option)*

Major Subtype #3: *13-Star Obverse, Stars 6x7, 13-Star Reverse, Short-Neck Eagle*

Most Desirable Issue(s): *1798 Wide Date, 5 Berries*

Major Subtype #4: *13-Star Obverse, Stars 8x5, 13-Star Reverse, Short-Neck Eagle*

Most Desirable Issue(s): *1802/'1', 1806/4, Stars 8x5*

Major Subtype #5: *13-Star Obverse, Stars 8x5, 14-Star Reverse, Short-Neck Eagle*

Most Desirable Issue(s): *1804, 14-Star Reverse (only option)*

Major Subtype #6: *13-Stars Obverse, Stars 7x6, 13-Star Reverse, Short-Neck Eagle*

Most Desirable Issue(s): *1805, 1807*

Issuing Mint: Since all Capped Bust Right, Stars Obverse Quarter Eagles were struck in the Philadelphia Mint, you need acquire only a single example of this design to complete a gold type set by issuing mint.

Proof Type Set

The United States Mint did not strike proof Quarter Eagles of this type.

Assembling a Complete Set

Year Set: In order to complete a year set of this early gold type, you will need to acquire eight coins. The 1796 Stars Obverse, 1797, 1798, 1802/'1', 1805 and 1807 must be purchased. For the remaining two dates in this series, the more obtainable 1804 14-Star Reverse and 1806/4, Stars 8x5 are desirable. Consider assembling the set in VF-AU grades. Even then, however, you will experience considerable difficultly locating an example of the 1796 Stars Obverse (original mintage: just 432 coins) and 1797 (only 427 pieces struck). And if you are fortunate enough to find problem-free representatives of these key-date issues, be prepared to pay handsomely for the honor of adding the coins to your set. The 1796 Stars is actually about three times rarer than its identically dated No Stars counterpart, and a PCGS AU-58 commanded $161,000 when it appeared at auction in August of 2006. A 1797 in the same grade will also carry a price tag of at least $100,000.

Date and Mint Set: A challenging task, assembling a complete set of Capped Bust Right, Stars Obverse Quarter Eagles per the listings in the 2008 edition of *A Guide Book of United States Coins* by R.S. Yeoman will require 10 acquisitions. In addition to the 1796 Stars and the 1797, you must now contend with the elusive 1806/5, Stars 7x6 and the exceedingly rare 1804 13-Star Reverse. The 1804 13-Star Reverse has a certified population of only five coins at PCGS and NGC (March/2007), so you might not be able to give serious thought to this strategy. For the stout of heart, consider throwing out the grade requirements and prepare for a long, costly search. On the other hand, it is wise to concentrate on coins certified by one of the two major grading services rather than compromising with an impaired example. Making this decision now will reduce potential difficulties when the time comes to sell.

Die Variety Set: Compared to most other early U.S. gold series, the Capped Bust Right, Stars Obverse Quarter Eagle will seem quite tempting to the die variety specialist. After all, there are only 13 die marriages known for the entire type. On the other hand, at least one of these varieties (1804 13-Star Reverse) is exceedingly rare, and many others are only slightly less challenging to collect. To the best of my knowledge, the late Harry W. Bass, Jr. is the only collector to have embarked on the task of assembling a complete set of

Capped Bust Right, Stars Obverse Quarter Eagles by die variety. The fact that he succeeded (Bass actually assembled the most complete set of early U.S. die varieties of all time) means that the possibility does exists for another collector to follow in his footsteps.

Proof Set: As previously stated, the United States Mint did not strike Capped Bust Right, Stars Obverse Quarter Eagles in proof format.

A Complete Set by Issuing Mint: All Quarter Eagles of this type were struck in the Philadelphia Mint, so a complete set by issuing mint would correspond to a complete date and mint set.

Investing Tips

Although there are numerous possible collecting strategies for this rare early gold type, I believe that the investor should acquire only a single example. This type is too rare (and individual examples are too costly) to invite a large number of specialized collectors, and demand is correspondingly low for some of the more elusive issues and varieties. A notable exception is the rare 1796 Stars Obverse, which enjoys a fairly strong following among advanced type collectors due to its first-year status.

As a rule, however, you should acquire only a single example of this type in the highest grade that you can afford. The final-year 1807 is the most desirable Capped Bust Right, Stars Obverse Quarter Eagle for numismatic investing purposes. Acquire a coin in Mint State, and make sure that it has been certified by PCGS or NGC. The most attractive examples that I have handled possess vibrant luster, relatively distraction-free surfaces for the assigned grade, a bold strike and a lack of significant adjustment marks. Such examples already enjoy strong demand, as evidenced by the performance of MS-62s at auction since the turn of the 21st century.

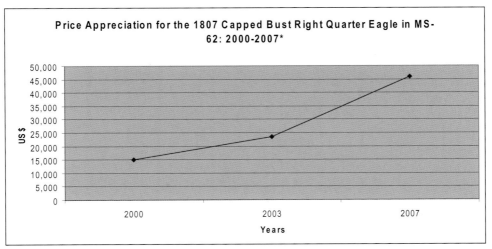

*Values represent prices realized for PCGS and NGC-certified examples as reported by a leading rare coin auction firm.

The investor could do very well with an attractive, high-grade 1807 Quarter Eagle in the coming decades, particularly if the number of gold type collectors.

CHAPTER EIGHT

Capped Bust Left Quarter Eagle

Courtesy of Rare Coin Wholesalers

SPECIFICATIONS

Year(s) Issued: *1808 only*
Issuing Mint(s): *Philadelphia only*
Authorizing Act: *April 2, 1792*
Designer: *John Reich*
Weight: *4.37 grams*
Composition: *91.67% gold, 8.33% silver and copper*
Diameter: *20 millimeters (approximate)*
Edge: *Reeded*

History

Born Johann Matthaus Reich in Germany, John Reich fled his native land for the United States to escape the ravages of the Napoleonic Wars. Although he initially worked as an indentured servant, the United States Mint soon recognized Reich's talent and hired him as assistant engraver. He served in that capacity from 1807 through 1817.

John Reich's most famous, popular and widely collected contribution to the U.S. coinage family is the Capped Bust Half Dollar that made its debut in 1807. The artists' Half Eagle first appeared at around the same time. Over the next eight years, Reich also adapted the basic Capped Bust motif for use in the Dime, Quarter and Quarter Eagle series.

The Capped Bust Left Quarter Eagle was struck in only one year–1808–from a single die marriage that Reich engraved himself. His "signature" is present on the obverse as a notch on the outermost point of star 13. A mere 2,710 pieces were produced. The Mint would not strike any more Quarter Eagles until 1821, when it introduced the Capped Head Left design.

Some numismatic researchers believe that early die breakage explains why there is only a single Quarter Eagle delivery from the 1808-1820 era. While this almost certainly has something to do with why so few examples were struck in 1808, the author believes that the absence of another Quarter Eagle delivery until 1821 is due to the continued unpopularity of the denomination with gold bullion depositors. Limited mintages for the Capped Head Left series of 1821-1834 lend support to this theory.

Short Type Set

Two short sets present themselves as possibilities for the gold collector that wants to highlight this important one-year type. The second option is more attractive because it includes just two coins, although I suggest expanding into a larger type set after achieving that goal.

Quarter Eagle Types, an eight-piece set including:

Capped Bust Right, No Stars Obverse
Capped Bust Right, Stars Obverse
Capped Bust Left
Capped Head Left, Large Diameter
Capped Head Left, Reduced Diameter
Classic
Liberty
Indian

Capped Bust Left Gold Coinage, a two-piece set including:

Capped Bust Left Quarter Eagle
Capped Bust Left Half Eagle

Complete Type Set

As a one-year type with a limited original mintage, the 1808 is an understandably challenging coin to acquire in any grade. Few coins have survived (most numismatists accept a figure of 125-150 pieces), and examples rarely remain on the open market for long. As with the 1796 No Stars Quarter Eagle, you should seriously consider any PCGS or NGC-certified 1808 Quarter Eagle that is offered either for outright purchase or through auction. Even in worn condition, a problem-free survivor of this issue will serve as a highlight in any numismatic holding.

Circulated Examples: Circulated 1808 Quarter Eagles outnumber Mint State survivors by about two-to-one. The typically encountered circulated example grades EF or AU, although a handful of Fine and VF pieces have also survived. A PCGS VF-35 that appeared at auction in 2006 sold for $54,625, while a coin graded AU-50 at the same service crossed the auction block for $80,000 earlier that year.

Mint State Examples: While not quite as rare as the 1796 No Stars at this level of preservation, the 1808 Quarter Eagle is still extremely challenging to locate in Mint State. Most Uncirculated survivors grade MS-60 through MS-62. There are, however, a couple of Choice and Gem pieces extant. One of the finest examples known is an NGC MS-63 that realized $287,500 at auction in early 2007. An NGC MS-61 that traded almost exactly one year earlier commanded $143,750 from the winning bidder.

General Characteristics: Color for this issue is usually orange-gold, green-gold or khaki-gold. Softness of detail around the peripheries is characteristic of virtually all known examples, and a lack of denticles in most areas is a result of the manner in which Reich engraved the dies. On the other hand, the central design elements are usually boldly, if not sharply defined. In fact, there seems to be very little variation between survivors as far as striking quality is concerned. You should not, therefore, be overly concerned with this characteristic when evaluating an example for potential purchase. High-grade survivors typically display satiny surfaces, coins in the MS-60 through MS-62 range usually a bit subdued in sheen.

Unless you are planning to acquire one of the few Choice or Gem-quality coins extant, expect some degree of scuffiness when selecting an 1808 Quarter Eagle for inclusion in your collection. Many examples also display moderate-size abrasions, and a few possess short pin scratches and/or tiny nicks. The leading third-party certification services recognize that a smooth-looking 1808 Quarter Eagle is virtually impossible to obtain through the MS-62 level of preservation and will usually encapsulate examples with a few wispy grazes and/or nicks. These features are not overly worrisome as far as this particular type is concerned, but I would not accept a coin with large abrasions in a prime focal area. Even then, however, do not be too picky or else you could eliminate most potential candidates in your price range.

Adjustment marks are not as prevalent for this issue as they are for the earlier Quarter Eagle types. When present, they are usually minor and concentrated in one or two areas at the rims.

Words of Caution: This issue has a peculiar "look" that is the result of the manner in which the Mint executed the design. Peripheral striking weakness is the norm, and this attribute helps to explain why many survivors exhibit a relatively large number of wispy abrasions and moderate-size distractions for a gold coin of this size. (The rim proved inadequate to protect the coins in circulation.) Viewing old auction catalogs is a good idea, as is visiting a couple of lot viewing sessions for current sales. Both will allow you to become familiar with the characteristics of this issue before you consider making a purchase.

One final word of caution as far as the 1808 Quarter Eagle is concerned. Do not consider acquiring an impaired example that is either not certified at all or graded by a third-party service other than PCGS or NGC. You will be tempted to ignore my advice in light of the hefty premiums that relatively problem-free examples command. Having handled several impaired survivors of this delivery, however, I am confident that you will not be happy adding an impaired 1808 Quarter Eagle to your collection. This is one of several early U.S. Mint issues that, when offered with impairments, is likely to possess numerous severe problems. (The 1794 Flowing Hair Silver Dollar is another example.) Polishing, whizzing, rim damage and repairs are among the more frequently seen impairments, and each can severely inhibit eye appeal on their own, let alone when they are encountered side-by-side on a single example. What's more, even a severely mishandled 1808 Quarter Eagle will almost certainly require a substantial financial investment. (A former jewelry piece with EF Details as certified by ANACS still brought $25,565 at auction in early 2007.) Before you even consider writing out a five or six-figure check, insist on acquiring a relatively problem-free example with above-average eye appeal. In addition to being more attractive to view, a PCGS or NGC-certified coin will also better protect your financial investment.

Courtesy of Rare Coin Wholesalers

The 1808 Quarter Eagle is one of several early U.S. Mint issues that, when offered with impairments, is likely to possess numerous severe problems. Notice the area of extensive tooling in the obverse field before Liberty's portrait on the example pictured here. In addition, both sides of this coin have been harshly cleaned. Despite the hefty premiums that relatively problem-free survivors command, it is probably not a good idea to acquire an impaired 1808 Quarter Eagle that is either not certified at all or graded by a third-party service other than PCGS or NGC.

STRATEGIES FOR INCLUDING THE CAPPED BUST LEFT QUARTER EAGLE IN A COMPLETE TYPE SET

Most Desirable Issue(s): *1808 (only option)*

Most Desirable Grade(s), Circulated Coins: *Any grade*

Estimated Cost: *In VF-35 or finer, $50,000 and up*

Key to Collecting: *PCGS or NGC certification; orange-gold, green-gold or khaki-gold color; relatively abrasion free by the standards of the issue as well as the assigned grade*

Most Desirable Grade(s), Mint State Coins: *MS-60 or finer*

Estimated Cost: *$140,000 and up*

Key to Collecting: *PCGS or NGC certification; orange-gold, green-gold or khaki-gold color; relatively abrasion-free by the standards of the issue as well as the assigned grade; bold-to-sharp striking detail over the central design elements*

Advanced Type Set

Since this early gold type is represented by just one issue, there are no special options available for the advanced type collector.

Proof Type Set

The United States Mint did not strike proof Quarter Eagles of this type.

Assembling a Complete Set

This gold type is represented by a single issue and a single die marriage. A complete set, therefore, will require only a single example.

Investing Tips

This issue is a famous numismatic rarity, and examples are always eagerly greeted by numismatic professionals, collectors and investors when they appear in the market. With a limited population of surviving examples, the 1808 Quarter Eagle is poised for dramatic price appreciation should numismatics continue to grow in popularity. Historic performance, while not a guarantee of future growth, supports this theory. Take for example coins graded MS-60 and MS-61, which have increased in value since the early 1990s:

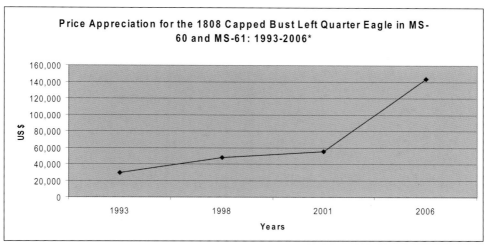

Price Appreciation for the 1808 Capped Bust Left Quarter Eagle in MS-60 and MS-61: 1993-2006*

*Prices represent individual or average prices realized for examples certified by PCGS and NGC as reported by a leading numismatic auctioneer.

A high-grade 1808 Quarter Eagle certified by PCGS or NGC will definitely serve as a centerpiece in a numismatic investment portfolio.

CHAPTER NINE

Large Diameter Capped Head Left Quarter Eagles

Courtesy of Bowers and Merena

SPECIFICATIONS

Year(s) Issued: *1821-1827*
Issuing Mint(s): *Philadelphia only*
Authorizing Act: *April 2, 1792*
Designer: *Robert Scot, after John Reich*
Weight: *4.37 grams*
Composition: *91.67% gold, 8.33% silver and copper*
Diameter: *20 millimeters (approximate)*
Edge: *Reeded*

History

After a 12-year hiatus, the United States Mint resumed Quarter Eagle production in 1821. Assistant Mint Engraver John Reich, creator of the Capped Bust Left motif used for this denomination in 1808, left federal employment in 1817. The task of designing the new Quarter Eagle, therefore, fell to aging Chief Engraver Robert Scot (died 1823). While there are definite differences between the artists' work, Scot relied very heavily on the Quarter Eagle design of his predecessor. The new Two-and-a-Half also features a left-facing portrait of Liberty in the center of the obverse. Liberty is once again wearing a soft cap inscribed LIBERTY, and the date is still positioned along the lower border. On the other hand, Scot's portrait is focused solely on Liberty's head as opposed to the entire bust, and his arrangement of 13 stars encircles much of the periphery instead of being split seven left, six right.

The reverses of both designs are even more similar, a spread-wing eagle clutching an olive branch in its right talon and three arrows in its left. The Latin motto E PLURIBUS UNUM is inscribed on a scroll above the eagle's head, and the legend UNITED STATES OF AMERICA is around the periphery. Scot's eagle displays more uniform wing feathers, however, and he also seems to have gone to greater lengths than Reich to ensure that the denticles on both sides show distinctly after striking.

To distinguish it from the preceding type, the Quarter Eagle introduced in 1821 is known as the Capped Head Left design. Those examples struck through 1827 possess a larger, less-uniform diameter than their counterparts produced from 1829-1834.

There are only five issues in the Large Diameter Capped Head Left Quarter Eagle series, and all were produced in extremely limited numbers. Apparently, contemporary bullion depositors continued to overlook this denomination in favor of the Half Eagle. This theory also helps to explain why the Mint did not strike any Quarter Eagles in 1822 and 1823. Many examples of this type were melted during the 1830s as rising gold prices forced their bullion value to outstrip their monetary value.

Short Type Set

I am aware of two short type sets that would feature this early Quarter Eagle design in a prominent manner. Both are challenging to assemble due to the rarity of many or all of the types that they include.

Quarter Eagle Types, an eight-piece set including:

Capped Bust Right, No Stars Obverse
Capped Bust Right, Stars Obverse
Capped Bust Left
Capped Head Left, Large Diameter
Capped Head Left, Reduced Diameter
Classic
Liberty
Indian

Capped Head Left Gold Coinage, a four-piece set including:

Capped Head Left Quarter Eagle, Large Diameter
Capped Head Left Quarter Eagle, Reduced Diameter
Capped Head Left Half Eagle, Large Diameter
Capped Head Left Half Eagle, Reduced Diameter

Complete Type Set

Due to a combination of limited original mintages and widespread melting, all issues in this short-lived series are significant numismatic rarities. Very few examples appear even in large auctions or at major conventions. As such, I urge decisiveness when you are presented with an opportunity to add an example of this type to your set.

Circulated Examples: For every single example of the 1821, 1824/1 and 1827 that I have encountered, I have also handled approximately two survivors of the 1825 issue. Indeed, the 1825 is the most appropriate type candidate in this series, although describing the 1825 as "common" would be doing the issue a great injustice. Attractive, problem-free examples appear at auction only once every year to year-and-a-half, and they always elicit strong bids.

With the exception of a handful of Fine and Very Fine examples, most circulated 1825 Quarter Eagles that have survived grade Extremely Fine or About Uncirculated. Due to the extreme rarity of the type as well as the issue, even a lower-grade survivor would make a significant addition to a gold type set. A coin that grades EF-40 will require you to pay at least $8,500, while an NGC AU-58 that appeared at auction in early 2007 sold for $18,400.

Mint State Examples: The 1825 is also attractive for Mint State type purposes. Examples are fairly evenly distributed from MS-60 through MS-64, and any grade in this range will serve with distinction in a type set. A PCGS MS-61 traded hands for $29,900 in an April, 2007 auction. There are also two exceptional pieces listed at the major certification services (May/2007): an NGC MS-66 and a PCGS MS-67.

General Characteristics: In addition to its availability relative to the other issues in this series, the 1825 is an important type candidate because most survivors have been carefully produced. A sharp strike is the norm for this issue, and high-grade survivors usually possess vibrant luster with either a satiny or prooflike sheen. Many of the coins that I have observed possess either yellow-gold or orange-gold color. A few green-gold and khaki-gold pieces are also known, as well as an even smaller number with reddish-gold highlights. Large, detracting abrasions are seldom encountered, although circulated and lower-end Mint State pieces will have their fair share of wispy handling marks.

Words of Caution: The best advice that I can offer to the collector that is in the market for an attractive Quarter Eagle of this type is to insist on acquiring a PCGS or NGC-certified example with bold-to-sharp striking detail and no individually mentionable distractions.

> ### STRATEGIES FOR INCLUDING THE LARGE DIAMETER CAPPED HEAD LEFT QUARTER EAGLE IN A COMPLETE TYPE SET
>
> **Most Desirable Issue(s)**: *1825*
>
> **Most Desirable Grade(s), Circulated Coins**: *EF-40 through AU-58*
>
> **Estimated Cost**: *$8,500-$20,000*
>
> **Key to Collecting**: *Relatively sharp definition for the assigned grade; yellow-gold or orange-gold color; remnants of original luster (if appropriate for the assigned grade); no large or individually distracting circulation marks*
>
> **Most Desirable Grade(s), Mint State Coins**: *MS-60 or finer*
>
> **Estimated Cost**: *$28,000 and up*
>
> **Key to Collecting**: *Sharp striking detail; yellow-gold or orange-gold color; vibrant, satiny or prooflike luster*

Advanced Type Set

Rarer Issues: The 1821 and 1827 are strong candidates for inclusion in an advanced type set of better-date coins. These are the bookends of the Large Diameter Capped Head

Left Quarter Eagle series, and they hold immediate appeal for type collectors assembling sets of first or final-year issues. Both are quite a bit rarer than the already elusive 1825, and they are more difficult to locate with a sharp strike.

If you are assembling a type set in circulated grades, focus on the 1821 instead of the 1827. The 1821 has a few more worn survivors than Mint State examples. Coins in the EF-40 through AU-58 grade range will sell for $9,000-$25,000.

If your penchant is for Mint State coins, then the 1827 is the issue of choice. A PCGS MS-64 brought $58,650 in 2004, while an identically graded example traded for $80,500 in early 2005.

As with the 1825, most high-grade 1821 and 1827 Quarter Eagles are satiny or prooflike in sheen. Color varies from yellow-gold on the lighter side to khaki-gold on the deeper end of the spectrum.

Of all issues in this series, the 1821 is the most likely to display sizeable abrasions. A few pieces with an excessively soft strike are also known. Caution is advised when pursuing this issue—try to be as selective as possible while keeping in mind that there are very few examples from which to choose irrespective of striking quality and eye appeal.

STRATEGIES FOR INCLUDING THE LARGE DIAMETER CAPPED HEAD LEFT QUARTER EAGLE IN A TYPE SET OF RARER ISSUES

Most Desirable Issue(s): *1821, 1827*

Most Desirable Grade(s):

    1821: *EF-40 through AU-58*

    1827: *MS-60 or finer*

Estimated Cost:

    1821: *$9,000-$25,000*

    1827: *$25,000 and up*

Key to Collecting: *Above-average striking detail; pleasing luster quality in the higher AU and Mint State grades; relatively distraction-free surfaces, particularly for the 1821*

Major Subtypes: There are no significant design changes in the Large Diameter portion of the Capped Head Left Quarter Eagle series.

Issuing Mint: All Capped Head Left Quarter Eagles were struck in the Philadelphia Mint. If you are assembling a gold type set using this strategy, therefore, you need acquire only a single example of this design.

Proof Type Set

This is the earliest Quarter Eagle series for which proofs are known. I believe, however, that most proof type collectors will forgo the honor of including a Large Diameter Capped Head Left Quarter Eagle in their set. The first-year 1821 is the only issue in this series that is obtainable for private ownership, but it is a major numismatic rarity with only six examples reported at PCGS and NGC (May/2007). A few of those "coins" probably represent resubmissions.

With such a limited number of pieces available, it is understandable that the proof 1821 Quarter Eagle always commands a significant premium when an example is offered in the market. A PCGS Proof-64 Cameo specimen sold for $241,500 during a January 2007 auction.

Assembling a Complete Set

Year Set: Five coins are required for completion of a year set of this early Quarter Eagle type, one example each dated 1821, 1824/1, 1825, 1826/'5' and 1827. This is a challenging task, to say the least, and not only because the key-date 1826/'5' has a combined population at PCGS and NGC of only 20 coins (March/2007). All issues in this series are elusive, and they are not offered for sale with any degree of frequency. Once secured in a collection or investment portfolio, Quarter Eagles of this type often remain off the market for many years. When attractive, problem-free examples do become available, they always command strong prices.

On the other hand, this is a short series, and the collector who is not constrained by financial limitations can put together a nice year set using coins that grade AU-55 for at least $77,500. The majority of the set can be assembled after a couple of years of diligent searching. Only the 1826/'5' will require a longer period of time. You should relax your grading criteria, however, and instead concentrate on acquiring the highest quality that you can locate and/or afford for each issue. Insisting on coins certified by PCGS or NGC is sound advice. And, if at all possible, avoid pieces with excessive striking incompleteness or singularly distracting abrasions.

Date and Mint Set: Since all Large Diameter Capped Head Left Quarter Eagles were struck in the Philadelphia Mint, and there are no major subtypes in the series, assembling a date and mint set of this type has the same requirements for a year set.

Die Variety Set: This is not an exciting series to collect by die variety, provided that one has the financial resources to even consider such an undertaking. The 1821, 1824/1, 1826/'5' and 1827 each have just one die marriage known. With three die pairs confirmed, therefore, the 1825 is the only reason why a complete die variety set of Large Diameter Capped Head Left Quarter Eagles would differ in scope from a year set. I suggest moving on to another series after you complete a year set of Large Diameter Capped Head Left Quarter Eagles. Two die marriages of the 1825 are exceedingly rare and have the smallest surviving populations of all Quarter Eagles of this type.

Proof Set: It is impossible to assemble a complete set of proof Quarter Eagles of this type. Neither PCGS nor NGC has certified a single example of the 1824/1, 1825, 1826/'5' or 1827 in this format (July/2007).

A Complete Set by Issuing Mint: All Quarter Eagles of this type were struck in the Philadelphia Mint, so a complete set by issuing mint corresponds to a complete date and mint set.

Investing Tips

The extreme rarity of all issues in this series and steady demand from gold type collectors means that the Large Diameter Capped Head Left Quarter Eagle is an attractive coin for investment purposes. Acquiring a single example to represent the type is a sound strategy, and a coin that grades at least MS-63 is in a sufficiently high grade to possess strong technical merit and pleasing eye appeal. High-grade survivors of this type are few and far between, and the emphasis on technical quality in today's market will become even more pronounced in the coming decades.

This type has performed very well in the finer Mint State grades in recent years, as evidenced by a brief comparison between two examples in MS-64. An NGC-certified 1824/1 realized $26,400 during a 2001 auction. Four years later, a PCGS-certified 1827 sold for $80,500 at auction. The price increase is even more significant when you consider that the 1827 has a slightly higher PCGS and NGC population in MS-64 than the 1824/1 (May/2007).

CHAPTER TEN

Reduced Diameter Capped Head Left Quarter Eagles

Courtesy of Rare Coin Wholesalers

SPECIFICATIONS

Year(s) Issued: *1829-1834*
Issuing Mint(s): *Philadelphia only*
Authorizing Act: *April 2, 1792*
Designer: *William Kneass, after Robert Scot*
Weight: *4.37 grams*
Composition: *91.67% gold, 8.33% silver and copper*
Diameter: *18.5 millimeters*
Edge: *Reeded*

History

The coming of new technology to the United States Mint in the late 1820s occasioned a series of mostly minor modifications to the Capped Head Left Quarter Eagle. William Kneass, chief engraver from 1824-1840, carried out this work, which is perhaps most readily discerned as a more refined appearance to Liberty's portrait on the obverse and the reverse eagle. A closer examination of the new type will also reveal that the stars and letters are smaller, and that the border is comprised of tiny beads instead of denticles. The careful reader will notice, however, that the title of this chapter is *Reduced Diameter* Capped Head Left Quarter Eagles. Indeed, the most significant difference between the Quarter Eagles struck from 1821-1827 and 1829-1834 is their size.

The introduction of the close collar to the minting process during the late 1820s meant that coins could now be struck with a smaller, more uniform diameter. It also made possible the employment of a pronounced raised rim during the die preparation process, which in turn allowed for higher relief to the devices and greater protection for the coins while in circulation.

Most Reduced Diameter Capped Head Left Quarter Eagles never got to test the protective qualities of the new raised rim, however, as the type saw only limited commercial use. The continued unpopularity of the denomination among the contemporary public might be seen as the primary reason for the limited distribution of Quarter Eagles from 1829-1834. Indeed, bullion depositors placed few orders for coins of this type, and most yearly mintages are concentrated in the range of only 4,000-4,540 pieces. In fact, the only issue with an appreciably different mintage is the first-year 1829, which was produced in even fewer numbers.

Nevertheless, the real explanation for why so few Quarter Eagles of this type reached circulation is actually a steady increase in the price of gold on the world market through the early-to-mid 1830s. By the time most Reduced Diameter pieces were struck, they were already worth more as bullion than as coinage of the realm. The majority of coins passed almost immediately into the hands of speculators, after which they were melted. A few fortunate pieces were held as part of bank reserves, and these institutions deserve much of the credit for the examples that have survived to the present day.

Short Type Set

The collector looking to include the Reduced Diameter Capped Head Left Quarter Eagle in a short type set must consider the following options. The absolute rarity of all pre-1834 U.S. types means that both of these sets will be extremely challenging to assemble.

Quarter Eagle Types, an eight-piece set including:

Capped Bust Right, No Stars Obverse
Capped Bust Right, Stars Obverse
Capped Bust Left
Capped Head Left, Large Diameter
Capped Head Left, Reduced Diameter
Classic
Liberty
Indian

Capped Head Left Gold Coinage, a four-piece set including:

Capped Head Left Quarter Eagle, Large Diameter
Capped Head Left Quarter Eagle, Reduced Diameter
Capped Head Left Half Eagle Large Diameter
Capped Head Left Half Eagle, Reduced Diameter

Complete Type Set

As with its Large Diameter counterpart, the Reduced Diameter Capped Head Left Quarter Eagle is rare in all grades. None of the six issues in this series can even remotely be described as "common," and the final-year 1834 is appreciably rarer than the already elusive 1829-1833 deliveries. Selecting an appropriate type candidate at any level of preservation, therefore, requires patience and considerable financial resources.

Circulated Examples: In terms of market availability and price, there is little difference between the 1829, 1830, 1831, 1832 and 1833 Quarter Eagles. Any of these issues, therefore, will serve well in a type set of U.S. gold. Extremely Fine and About Uncirculated examples constitute the majority of worn survivors, so it makes sense to settle on a numeric grade in the 40-58 range. An 1832 in PCGS AU-55 brought $10,350 at auction in early 2007.

Mint State Examples: Concentrating once again on the 1829-1833 deliveries, you can consider any problem-free Mint State example for inclusion in a type set. Even a lower-grade coin in MS-60 or MS-61 will serve as an important highlight in a numismatic holding. A PCGS-certified 1830 in MS-61 traded for $18,400 in early 2007, while an 1830 graded MS-64 at the same service commanded $46,000 the same month.

There are three particularly impressive survivors of this type reported at the major certification services (May/2007), one example each dated 1829, 1831 and 1833. All of these coins grade MS-67, and the 1829 sold for the kingly sum of $316,250 when it appeared at auction in 2006.

General Characteristics: Most examples of this type are very attractive, with warm orange-gold color and bright, usually prooflike luster. Less exemplary is the striking quality, as many pieces possess some degree of softness to the detail over the central highpoints. This is particularly true of these coins struck beginning in 1832, when Mint employees raised the relief of the obverse design. Boldly and sharply struck pieces do exist, however, but the overall rarity of the type means that it is not prudent to pass up an otherwise acceptable example that is a bit softly impressed.

Courtesy of Bowers and Merena

This beautiful 1831 displays the orange-gold color and bright, prooflike surfaces for which the Reduced Diameter Capped Head Quarter Eagle is known. Notice also that this piece is a bit softly struck on the reverse over the feathers along the left shield border—a problem that is usually more pronounced for the 1832-1834 issues. Nevertheless, the strike that this particular example displays is sufficiently sharp that the buyer should probably not pass over this coin in hopes of finding a bolder-looking representative.

Words of Caution: I have encountered several examples of this type that are extensively impaired due to harsh cleaning, damage and/or other problems. Avoid these coins, particularly since they will still command a significant premium. Getting the most for your money is among the best advice that I can offer when it comes to making purchases in any segment of the numismatic market.

STRATEGIES FOR INCLUDING THE REDUCED DIAMETER CAPPED HEAD LEFT QUARTER EAGLE IN A COMPLETE TYPE SET

Most Desirable Issue(s): *1829, 1830, 1831, 1832, 1833*

Most Desirable Grade(s), Circulated Coins: *EF-40 through AU-58*

Estimated Cost: *$7,500-$17,500*

Key to Collecting: *Relatively bold definition for the assigned grade; orange-gold color; remnants of original luster (if appropriate for the assigned grade); no large or individually distracting circulation marks*

Most Desirable Grade(s), Mint State Coins: *MS-60 or finer*

Estimated Cost: *$18,000 and up*

Key to Collecting: *Overall bold striking detail; orange-gold color; vibrant mint luster*

Advanced Type Set

Rarer Issues: The final-year 1834 is the only issue of this type that is significantly rarer than the others—a curious fact since the 1829 was produced in fewer numbers (3,403 pieces vs. 4,000 coins). I believe that most 1834 Capped Head Left Quarter Eagles never left the Mint, and that the federal government destroyed the majority of the mintage after passage of the Act of June 28, 1834. The melted coins provided bullion for the new lightweight gold coinage. As of March 2007, PCGS and NGC combined have certified only 17 survivors of this issue, a combined population that is very low even by the standards of the type. Since all Capped Head Left Quarter Eagles struck from 1829-1834 are extremely rare coins, and the 1834 is usually encountered worn, you should focus on one of the other issues in this series for inclusion in a type set. There are more opportunities to acquire an example dated 1829-1833, and you will have a much better chance of securing a Mint State coin.

Major Subtypes: There are no major design changes in this short-lived series, but the Mint did raise the relief on the obverse in 1832. There is little practical difference between those coins struck from 1829-1831 and those delivered 1832-1834, so there is not much reason to acquire an example from each time period. You should definitely take this advice to heart if you are on a more limited collecting budget. It is more prudent to husband your resources and acquire a single representative of the type in as high a grade as possible.

Issuing Mint: Since the Philadelphia Mint produced all coins of this type, an advanced gold type set by issuing mint requires only a single Reduced Diameter Capped Head Left Quarter Eagle.

Proof Type Set

It is possible, however unlikely, to represent the Reduced Diameter Capped Head Left Quarter Eagle in a proof type set. Only seven coins have been certified by PCGS and NGC (March/2007), and even this miniscule total is almost certainly inflated by resubmissions. All of the coins listed at the certification services are dated either 1831 or 1833, and they are so costly as to be out of reach for all but the most affluent collectors. In early 2006, an 1831 in NGC Proof-64 Cameo crossed the auction block for $148,350.

Assembling a Complete Set

Year Set: Produced for only six years, this can be a tempting series if you are planning to assemble a complete year set of one of the early U.S. gold series. Looks can be deceiving, however, since assembling a year set of Reduced Diameter Capped Head Left Quarter Eagles is actually an extremely challenging task. Since 2000, however, most issues have been appearing at auction at least once a year, which means that buying opportunities are not as few and far between as you might initially suspect. On the other hand, you should plan on spending at least two years searching in order to procure a problem-free 1834.

Do not be too obsessed with numeric grade when approaching this series for the purposes of completing a year set. Focus on PCGS or NGC-certified coins that possess respectable technical quality and eye appeal for the assigned grade. A set that ranges in grade from EF-40 through, say, MS-62 is an impressive holding that will earn you considerable respect from numismatic professionals as well as other collectors. Even if you concentrate on coins that grade only EF-40, you must expect to pay at least $60,000 to complete this set.

Date and Mint Set: Since there are no branch mint issues or major subtypes in this series, the strategies are the same whether you are assembling a date and mint set or a year set of Reduced Diameter Capped Head Left Quarter Eagles.

Die Variety Set: I am aware of only a single die marriage for each issue in this early gold series. Thus, there is no way to expand a year set of Reduced Diameter Capped Head Left Quarter Eagles by die variety.

Proof Set: As previously stated, the only two Reduced Diameter Capped Head Quarter Eagles that are obtainable in proof format are the 1831 and 1833.

A Complete Set by Issuing Mint: All Reduced Diameter Capped Head Left Quarter Eagles were struck in the Philadelphia Mint. A complete set of this type by issuing mint, therefore, is equivalent to a year set.

Investing Tips

The overall rarity of this type and the extreme unlikelihood that additional examples will enter the market at a future date means that demand will continue to exceed supply. Both variants of the Capped Head Left Quarter Eagle enjoy their greatest demand in today's market as type coins. I suggest, therefore, acquiring just a single example of the Reduced Diameter design. To have the best chance of securing an attractive, high-quality piece, focus on coins that grade at least MS-63 at PCGS or NGC. You should also consider the potential importance of strike among future buyers by avoiding pieces with excessive softness of detail.

CHAPTER ELEVEN

Classic Quarter Eagles

Courtesy of Bowers and Merena

SPECIFICATIONS

Year(s) Issued: *1834-1839*
Issuing Mint(s): *Philadelphia, Charlotte, Dahlonega, New Orleans*
Authorizing Act: *June 28, 1834 and January 18, 1837*
Designer: *William Kneass*
Weight: *4.18 grams*
Composition:
    1834-1836: *89.92% gold, 10.08% silver and copper*
    1837-1839: *90% gold, 10% silver and copper*
Diameter: *18.2 millimeters*
Edge: *Reeded*

History

The vast quantities of silver that flowed from Latin American mines during the early decades of the 19th century severely impeded the ability of the United States Mint to produce gold coins that would fulfill their intended purpose in the avenues of international commerce. (Most early U.S. gold coins did not circulate domestically, but were instead used as part of bank reserves or as payment for foreign debts.) By 1834, the price of gold reckoned in terms of silver had already reached a level that the bullion value of a Quarter Eagle exceeded $2.50. In order to stop the widespread hoarding and destruction of these coins by speculators and others, Congress lowered the weight of the Quarter Eagle from 4.37 grams to 4.18 grams with the Mint Act of June 28, 1834. That act also reduced the gold content to 89.92% from 91.67%, although the government increased it slightly to 90% in 1837 (Act of January 18). Mint employees felt that a new design would distinguish coins struck to the new weight standard from their old-tenor counterparts.

Chief Engraver William Kneass is the man responsible for the type that numismatists now refer to as the Classic Quarter Eagle. While Liberty is still facing left on the obverse with 13 stars around the border and the date below, her portrait is noticeably different from those of the Capped Bust Left and Capped Head Left designs. The soft cap is also gone, but the word LIBERTY is still inscribed on a ribbon that binds Liberty's hair. The reverse is very similar to that of the Capped Head Left motif, but Kneass dropped the scroll upon which E PLURIBUS UNUM had been inscribed. Apparently, the chief engraver felt that omission of the Latin motto would be sufficient to distinguish the reverse of the new lightweight Quarter Eagle from its most immediate predecessor. This is the only regular-issue gold coin of this denomination that features the mintmark on the obverse. The exact location of this feature is in the field between Liberty's portrait and the date.

The Charlotte Mint is one of the three earliest branch mints in U.S. coinage history. The facility commenced operations in 1838 and struck its first Quarter Eagles and Half Eagles during that year. Those coins displayed the Classic design attributed to Chief Engraver William Kneass. (Public domain image)

Production of Classic Quarter Eagles in 1834 is greater than that of all previous yearly deliveries for this denomination combined. The Philadelphia Mint remained very busy with the striking of the new Quarter Eagle through 1836, most of the bullion coming from melted old-tenor gold coins. From 1837 through the series' end in 1839, however, yearly deliveries from the Philadelphia Mint dropped down to the low-to-mid, five-figure range.

In addition to record-breaking mintage figures, the Classic series is significant because it includes the first branch mint Quarter Eagles. The newly opened Charlotte Mint struck 7,880 pieces in 1838, as well as an additional 18,140 coins the following year. Although also commencing coinage operations in 1838, the Dahlonega and New Orleans Mints did not strike their first Quarter Eagles until 1839.

This type is also the earliest Quarter Eagle for which proofs have been positively confirmed for virtually all dates in the series.

Short Type Set

Besides a collection of all regular-issue Quarter Eagle types, an example of this design must be included in a two-piece set of Classic gold coinage.

Quarter Eagle Types, an eight-piece set including:

Capped Bust Right, No Stars Obverse
Capped Bust Right, Stars Obverse
Capped Bust Left
Capped Head Left, Large Diameter
Capped Head Left, Reduced Diameter
Classic
Liberty
Indian

Classic Gold Coinage, a two-piece set including:

Classic Quarter Eagle
Classic Half Eagle

Complete Type Set

Beginning with this series, the rarity structure of Quarter Eagles changes dramatically. The Classic type is much more plentiful in an absolute sense than any of the preceding Quarter Eagle designs. In a general sense, therefore, the type collector should have a much easier time obtaining a desirable example for inclusion in their set.

Circulated Examples: The two most frequently encountered Classic Quarter Eagles in today's market are the 1834 and the 1836 Script 8. The contemporary public saved many 1834 Classic Quarter Eagles as the first of their kind, while the 1836 (both date logotypes combined) boasts the highest mintage in the series. Most of the 547,986 Quarter Eagles struck in 1836 were probably examples of the Script 8 variety, although the Block 8 is only a bit scarcer in today's market. Worn 1834 and 1836 Quarter Eagles are readily obtainable in today's market, and most are concentrated in the VF-AU grade range. With a decent number of coins from which to choose, you can afford to be selective when the time comes to buy.

Due to the relative availability of worn examples in numismatic circles, coins that grade AU-55 or AU-58 are most appropriate for circulated type purposes. Indeed, much of the demand for the Classic Quarter Eagle as a type coin is concentrated at the Choice AU and Mint State levels. If you are concerned about the resale potential of your coins, follow the market's lead as far as this series is concerned. In AU-55 and AU-58, insist on purchasing an example with overall sharp definition and considerable portions of the original mint luster still intact. An 1834 in PCGS AU-55 sold through auction in early 2007 for $1,610, while an 1836 Script 8 graded AU-58 at the same service commanded $2,645 during a March 2007 sale.

Mint State Examples: The 1834 and 1836 Script 8 are also strong candidates for inclusion in a Mint State type set. The majority of Mint State survivors grade no finer than MS-63, however, and even at the lower levels of Mint State this type is somewhat scarce from a market availability standpoint. The more attractive examples grade at least MS-62 with well-struck devices and vibrant mint luster. Expect to pay between $4,500 and $6,500 for an example in MS-62, while an MS-63 will cost $7,000-$9,500.

General Characteristics: Striking quality varies widely for this type, and most examples display at least some degree of softness to the central highpoint definition. Nevertheless, enough boldly and sharply struck coins have survived from the P-mint deliveries that you should hold out for one of those examples.

Carefully preserved, high-grade 1834 and 1836 Classic Quarter Eagles often possess vibrant mint luster that ranges from richly frosted to fully prooflike. The original finish can be a bit subdued in the AU and lower Mint State grades, so be mindful of this fact when searching for a suitable example.

Words of Caution: This was a workhorse type, examples seeing extensive use in the avenues of commerce. Many circulated survivors, even those that are technically problem free, are marred by numerous detracting abrasions. This is even true of coins in AU-55 and AU-58, the grades that hold the most appeal for circulated type purposes. Do not purchase coins with overly scuffy surfaces, or those that possess individually conspicuous abrasions. Enough examples of the 1834 and 1836 issues have survived that you can afford to hold out for a better-looking representative.

STRATEGIES FOR INCLUDING THE CLASSIC QUARTER EAGLE IN A COMPLETE TYPE SET

Most Desirable Issue(s): *1834, 1836 Script 8*

Most Desirable Grade(s), Circulated Coins: *AU-55, AU-58*

Estimated Cost: *$1,500-$3,000*

Key to Collecting: *Relatively bold definition; ample remnants of original luster; surfaces that are free of an excessive number of abrasions and individually conspicuous detractions*

Most Desirable Grade(s), Mint State Coins: *MS-62 or finer*

Estimated Cost: *$4,500 and up*

Key to Collecting: *Vibrant frosty or prooflike luster; yellow-gold, orange-gold or green-gold color; bold-to-sharp striking detail*

Advanced Type Set

Rarer Issues: A common misperception among gold collectors is that all of the Philadelphia Mint issues in this series are relatively easy to obtain. This is most certainly not the case, as the 1835, 1837 and 1838 are scarce and underrated in today's market. (The final P-mint delivery in this series, the 1839, is actually very rare.) The 1837 and 1838 are best suited for advanced type purposes. You should consider only coins that grade AU-55 and AU-58 for circulated type purposes. If your goal is to assemble a Mint State type set, however, look for an example that grades at least MS-62. An 1837 in NCG AU-55 brought $2,415 at auction in 2006, while an 1838 certified MS-62 at the same grading service traded for $9,200 in early 2007.

Courtesy of Bowers and Merena

Scarcer than generally realized, the 1838 Classic Quarter Eagle seems particularly attractive for inclusion in an advanced type set of rarer issues.

Attractive 1837 and 1838 Quarter Eagles are characterized by bold-to-sharp striking detail, vibrant frosty or prooflike luster, good color and a relative lack of distracting abrasions. Most examples that I have seen possess either green-gold or orange-gold surfaces, although the occasional yellow-gold piece does turn up in the market.

STRATEGIES FOR INCLUDING THE CLASSIC QUARTER EAGLE IN A TYPE SET OF RARER ISSUES

Most Desirable Issue(s): *1837, 1838*

Most Desirable Grade(s):

   Circulated Examples: *AU-55, AU-58*

   Mint State Examples: *MS-62 or finer*

Estimated Cost:

   Circulated Examples: *$2,500-$4,000*

   Mint State Examples: *$5,250 and up*

Key to Collecting: *Bold-to-sharp striking detail; richly original color, usually in green-gold or orange-gold shades; relatively few distracting abrasions for the assigned grade*

Major Subtypes: Mint employees tinkered with the design of Liberty's portrait almost every year that the Classic Quarter Eagle was in production. There are five distinct subtypes, and they differ either in the size of the portrait or the configuration of the first curl on top of Liberty's head. These varieties have been gaining in prominence since the early 21st century, a trend that is due at least in part to the sale of the Harry W. Bass, Jr. Collection from 1999-2001. Catalogers at several auction houses have also started reporting varieties for issues that were struck using more than one portrait style.

Obtaining an example of the each of the five major varieties in this series will not pose too much of a problem, particularly if you are willing to accept some AU coins in your set. As these design changes are just beginning to gain wider recognition among gold collectors, I would not pay a substantial premium for a Classic Quarter Eagle advertised as a rare variety. To date, the various portrait styles have been selling for prices that are fairly commensurate with the rarity of their respective issue.

STRATEGIES FOR INCLUDING THE CLASSIC QUARTER EAGLE IN A TYPE SET OF MAJOR SUBTYPES

Required Number of Coins: *Five*

Major Subtype #1: *Small Head*

Most Desirable Issue(s): *1834 Small Head (only option)*

Major Subtype #2: *Large Head*

Most Desirable Issue(s): *1834 Large Head (only option)*

Major Subtype #3: *Head of 1835*

Most Desirable Issue(s): *1835, 1836 Head of 1835*

Major Subtype #4: *Head of 1837*

Most Desirable Issue(s): *1837*

Issuing Mint: You will need to purchase four coins to complete a type set of Classic Quarter Eagles by issuing mint. The Philadelphia Mint requirement is the easiest to fulfill, and you can do so with either an 1834 or an 1836 Script 8. You can decide between circulated and Mint State examples based on personal preferences and/or the size of your collecting budget.

Courtesy of Bowers and Merena

There are two Charlotte Mint deliveries in this series, and the final-year 1839-C usually appears more frequently in the market. Coins that grade at least AU-50 can offer suitably bold definition and the chance that some mint luster might still be present, but some numismatists might want to drop down to the EF-40 or EF-45 levels if their financial resources require such a move.

There are two Charlotte Mint deliveries in this series, and the final-year 1839-C appears more frequently in the market. In addition to other type collectors, you will face competition from Southern gold specialists when pursuing this issue. Coins that grade at least AU-50 offer suitably bold definition and the chance that some mint luster might still be present. You can, however, drop down to the EF-40 or EF-45 levels if financial resources require such a move. Mint State survivors are very difficult to come by since there are few known and most are concentrated in tightly held collections.

An 1839-C certified EF-45 by PCGS sold at auction in October 2006 for $4,025. In AU-55, an example traded hands for $6,325 during May of 2007, while an AU-58 commanded $13,800 earlier that year. Both of these About Uncirculated coins were certified by NGC. Finally, I know of an 1839-C Quarter Eagle in NGC MS-62 that realized $40,250 at auction in late 2006.

Striking quality varies for the 1839-C, but patience can yield an overall boldly struck example. Be prepared to accept scattered abrasions, particularly in the circulated and lower Mint State grades. On the other hand, be firm about avoiding coins with large, singularly detracting marks. The typically encountered survivor displays orange-gold color, although lighter and deeper variations do exist.

The 1839-D is the first Dahlonega Mint Quarter Eagle, and it is the only D-mint issue of the Classic type. Survivors typically display either orange-gold or khaki-gold color.

The numismatist should find it much easier to locate an 1839-O Quarter Eagle than an 1839-C or 1839-D. Extremely Fine-40 is once again a potential lower cutoff point for the type collector, although the buyer with deeper pockets might want to stretch for a piece that grades at least AU-50. At the latter grade level, the 1839-O will usually command at least $2,500.

The final two mints active in the production of this type contributed only a single delivery each. Fortunately, a few examples of the 1839-D were set aside as the first Dahlonega Mint Quarter Eagles in U.S. coinage history. This is still a rare issue in an absolute sense, however, but problem-free survivors are offered with enough frequency that you should have little difficulty acquiring one provided that you have the requisite funds. The most attractive 1839-D Quarter Eagles that I have seen are free of individually conspicuous abrasions and possess sharp striking detail. In order to remain consistent with the 1839-C, a coin that grades at least EF-40 is most appropriate, and the 1839-D will probably start at $3,750 at that level. Orange-gold and khaki-gold colors predominate among survivors of this D-mint delivery.

The contemporary public also saved the New Orleans Mint's initial contribution to the Quarter Eagle series in significant numbers. Indeed, it will be much easier to locate an 1839-O Quarter Eagle than an 1839-C or 1839-D. Extremely Fine-40 is once again a potential lower cutoff point for type purposes, although I advise stretching for a piece that grades at least AU-50 if your pockets are deep enough. In AU-50, the 1839-O is worth about $2,500. Most examples display yellow-gold, orange-gold or green-gold color, and the overall definition is usually suitably bold for a product of this coinage facility.

STRATEGIES FOR INCLUDING THE CLASSIC QUARTER EAGLE IN A TYPE SET BY ISSUING MINT

Required Number of Coins: *Four*

Issuing Mint #1: *Philadelphia, Pennsylvania*

Most Desirable Issue(s): *1834, 1836 Script 8*

Key to Collecting: *AU-55 or higher grade; bold-to-sharp striking detail; good luster quality for the assigned grade; no individually bothersome abrasions*

Issuing Mint #2: *Charlotte, North Carolina*

Most Desirable Issue(s): *1839-C*

Key to Collecting: *EF-40 or higher grade; overall bold definition for the assigned grade; no individually bothersome abrasions; orange-gold color*

Issuing Mint #3: *Dahlonega, Georgia*

Most Desirable Issue(s): *1839-D (only option)*

Key to Collecting: *EF-40 or higher grade; overall bold definition for the assigned grade; no individually bothersome abrasions; orange-gold or khaki-gold color*

Issuing Mint #4: *New Orleans, Louisiana*

Most Desirable Issue(s): *1839-O (only option)*

Key to Collecting: *AU-50 or higher grade; overall bold definition for the assigned grade; no individually bothersome abrasions; yellow-gold, orange-gold or green-gold color*

Proof Type Set

Proofs of this type are exceedingly rare, but they exist in slightly greater numbers than those of the Capped Head Left design. Most survivors are dated either 1834 or 1836, but the combined PCGS and NGC population of these two "common" issues is only 23 pieces

(May/2007). The total number of coins available to private numismatists is much lower, which leads me to believe that many "examples" listed at the major certification services are actually resubmissions. The infrequency with which examples trade, as well as the steep prices that they command, prevents most proof gold type collectors from obtaining a representative of this series. A breathtakingly beautiful 1836 in NGC Proof-66 Ultra Cameo did appear at auction in early 2007, where it sold for $253,000.

Assembling a Complete Set

Year Set: With only six issues required, assembling a complete year set of Classic Quarter Eagles might not seem like a particularly daunting task. It is not, although 1839 might present some difficulty. For 1834, 1835, 1836 and 1837 you have no choice but to acquire an example of the year's Philadelphia Mint issue. For 1838, I believe that the P-mint issue is a more realistic candidate than the 1838-C. On the other hand, the 1839-O is easier to obtain than the higher-mintage 1839. The '39-O has survived in greater numbers, and it is offered with greater frequency than the '39-P. Still, this mintmarked issue will probably be the most expensive addition to your set.

I suggest assembling a year set of Classic Quarter Eagles using coins that grade AU-BU. You might, however, want to acquire the 1839-O in EF if your budget dictates such a move. A complete six-piece year set of Classic Quarter Eagles in AU-50 will set you back at least $10,500.

Date and Mint Set: A complete date and mint set of Classic Quarter Eagles is nearly double the size (11 coins) of a year set if you include both date logotypes of the 1836. The cost for the mintmarked issues might force you to accept coins that grade EF-40 or higher. With this in mind, I suggest avoiding Mint State examples altogether and assembling the set in EF-AU. The coins will be much better matched in terms of physical appearance and eye appeal than if the 1839-C and 1839-D grade EF-40 while a couple of the P-mint coins are Mint State.

Die Variety Set: Considerable research has been done on die varieties in this series, but few collectors have taken notice of the results. Since there does not seem to be considerable competition for the scarcer varieties at this time, significant opportunities exist if you choose to collect the Classic Quarter Eagle by die marriage.

Proof Set: With the exception of a single specimen impounded in the Harry W. Bass, Jr. Core Collection, the 1838 is unknown in proof format. The remaining five Philadelphia Mint issues in the Classic Quarter Eagle series are potentially obtainable in proof format, but examples are so rare that they are beyond reach for most numismatists. Bear in mind also that the proof 1837 Quarter Eagle is currently unique in private hands. The deck will definitely be stacked against you if you try to assemble even a partial set of proof Classic Quarter Eagles.

A Complete Set by Issuing Mint: The mintmarked issues in this series enjoy the largest following among collectors assembling sets of gold coins by issuing mint. Since there are only two C-mint deliveries and one issue each from Dahlonega and New Orleans, it is best to pursue branch mint Classic Quarter Eagles as part of a more expansive holding. Indeed, most specialized collections that include these issues are formed for the purpose of highlighting one or more gold denominations struck in the Charlotte, Dahlonega and/or New Orleans Mints.

Investing Tips

With the exception of Southern gold specialists, most collectors who are in the market for a Classic Quarter Eagle are assembling some sort of gold type set. You should, therefore, stake your bets on an increase in type collector demand by acquiring a single representative of this series in the highest grade that your investing budget will allow. Philadelphia Mint coins that grade MS-64 are best for this purpose. The certified population of the entire series drops off markedly above MS-63, and there are only a handful of survivors that grade MS-65 or finer. What's more, most of the near-Gems that I have handled are very attractive coins. P-mint examples typically display bold-to-sharp striking detail, warm yellow-gold or orange-gold color and vibrant mint luster. Surfaces are either frosty or prooflike in sheen, and they will possess relatively few abrasions if the coin grades MS-64.

CHAPTER TWELVE

Liberty Quarter Eagles

Courtesy of Rare Coin Wholesalers

SPECIFICATIONS

Year(s) Issued: *1840-1907*
Issuing Mint(s): *Philadelphia, Charlotte, Dahlonega, New Orleans, San Francisco*
Authorizing Act: *January 18, 1837*
Designer: *Christian Gobrecht*
Weight: *4.18 grams*
Composition: *90% gold, 10% copper*
Diameter: *18 millimeters*
Edge: *Reeded*

History

The United States Mint introduced a new type of Quarter Eagle in 1840, and Christian Gobrecht is credited with producing the design. Officially appointed Chief Engraver of the United States Mint in the same year, Gobrecht had actually been executing the tasks for this position since 1835, when his predecessor William Kneass suffered a stroke.

This is one of the longest-running types in U.S. coinage history, and the basic design remained unchanged through the series' end in 1907. A portrait of Liberty faces left on the obverse, a coronet inscribed LIBERTY on her head. Thirteen stars encircle the border, and the date is at the lower rim. On the reverse, an eagle with outstretched wings clutches a branch in its right talon and three arrows in its right. There is a shield superimposed over the eagle's breast. The legend UNITED STATES OF AMERICA is above, and the denomination 2½ D. is below. Look for a mintmark on the reverse below the eagle.

A workhorse design, the Liberty Quarter Eagle helped bring the United States through the California Gold Rush, the era of westward expansion, the Civil War, the taming of the frontier and the birth of the American Century. At one time or another, examples were produced in five different mints. The Philadelphia Mint is responsible for all proofs, and these special coins are known for virtually all years in the series.

Short Type Set

Unlike its predecessors in the Quarter Eagle series, the Liberty Two-and-a-Half is a coin that has long been popular for inclusion in short type sets of United States gold. This is due to several reasons, included among which are the relative ease with which problem-free examples can be obtained and the desirability of the larger Liberty gold types (particularly the Double Eagle).

Quarter Eagle Types, an eight-piece set including:

Capped Bust Right, No Stars Obverse
Capped Bust Right, Stars Obverse
Capped Bust Left
Capped Head Left, Large Diameter
Capped Head Left, Reduced Diameter
Classic
Liberty
Indian

Liberty Gold Coinage, a four or eight-piece set depending on how many types the collector wants to represent for the larger denominations. The four-piece set includes:

Liberty Quarter Eagle
Liberty Half Eagle
Liberty Eagle
Liberty Double Eagle

Popular U.S. Gold Types, an eight or ten-piece set including:

Liberty Quarter Eagle
Indian Quarter Eagle
Liberty Half Eagle, Motto
Indian Half Eagle
Liberty Eagle, Motto
Indian Eagle (No Motto and/or Motto)
Liberty Double Eagle (usually a Type III example)
Saint-Gaudens Double Eagle (No Motto and/or Motto)

Complete Type Set

Along with the 1908-1929 Indian, the Liberty Quarter Eagle is the most frequently encountered gold coin of this denomination in the numismatic market. There are thousands of potential type candidates from which to choose, both in circulated and Mint State grades.

Circulated Examples: There are numerous Philadelphia Mint issues in this series that are highly desirable for circulated type purposes. A few of these are the 1861 New Reverse (a.k.a. Type II), 1873 Open 3 and the 1902-1907 issues. The later-date issues in this series are actually so plentiful in Mint State that I do not recommend buying an AU example over a Mint State one. In AU-58, for example, the 1907 is worth approximately $200. The same issue in MS-60 costs only $25-$50 more.

Nevertheless, you might have a very good reason for purchasing a circulated Liberty Quarter Eagle. If this is the case, look for an AU-58 that retains most of the striking detail and original luster. The 1861 New Reverse is particularly attractive as a near-Mint type candidate. It was struck during the far off 19th century, and it has the added desirability of having been produced during the first year of the Civil War. A PCGS AU-58 sold for $253 at auction on May 19, 2007.

Mint State Examples: Concentrate on the post-1895 issues in the Liberty Quarter Eagle series when looking for a Mint State type candidate. These issues did not circulate to an appreciable extent, and many Mint State coins have survived. There are also a significant number of MS-67s extant from the 1902-1907 deliveries.

Through the MS-65 grade level, I like the 1896 as a type coin. It has a low mintage of 19,070 business strikes, yet examples sell for nearly the same price as many of the later-date issues. An 1896 in PCGS MS-65 commanded $2,530 during a March 2007 sale.

If you are interested in acquiring a Liberty Quarter Eagle that grades MS-66 or MS-67, focus on the 1902-1907 issues. MS-66s are worth between $2,000 and $2,750, while MS-67s will set you back at least $3,750.

General Characteristics: With so many coins surviving from several different time periods in U.S. Mint history, it should come as no surprise to read that striking quality and color vary widely throughout this series. As far as strike is concerned, insist on obtaining a coin with razor-sharp detail over all elements of the design. Striking incompleteness is sometimes noted for this type, particularly over the eagle's left (facing) leg feathers.

When it comes to color, you are on your own as far as the Liberty Quarter Eagle is concerned. The best type issues in this series come in a wide variety of colors. Just select an example that you believe is attractive.

There is no reason why you should have to accept a Liberty Quarter Eagle with large, individually conspicuous abrasions. Even in lower grades, do not be afraid to wait until you find an example that is relatively distraction free. In addition to overall smooth surfaces, insist on acquiring a coin with vibrant mint luster and no detracting alloy spots.

Words of Caution: Make sure that the Liberty Quarter Eagle you add to your type set meets with 100% satisfaction. In fact, there are so many attractive examples in the market that you should also consider making this one of the final coins to add to a gold type set. Concentrate time, effort and financial resources on types that are more challenging to collect.

STRATEGIES FOR INCLUDING THE LIBERTY QUARTER EAGLE IN A COMPLETE TYPE SET

Most Desirable Issue(s): *Numerous, including 1861 New Reverse, 1873 Open 3, 1896, 1902-1907*

Most Desirable Grade(s), Circulated Coins: *AU-58*

Estimated Cost: *$200-$300*

Key to Collecting: *Bold definition; ample remaining luster; attractive color; no individually mentionable abrasions*

Most Desirable Grade(s), Mint State Coins: *MS-65 or finer*

Estimated Cost: *$2,000 and up*

Key to Collecting: *Razor-sharp strike; full, vibrant luster; attractive color; smooth surfaces within the context of the assigned grade*

Advanced Type Set

Rarer Issues: There are numerous Liberty Quarter Eagles in the second and third rarity tiers that would fit comfortably into an advanced type set of better-date issues. Strong candidates include early P-mint coins such as the 1843, 1845 and 1850. These issues are among the more common Quarter Eagles from their era, but they are much scarcer than the common dates from the later portion of the series. Coins that grade AU-55 or AU-58 and possess vivid color and at least partial mint luster are usually very attractive. You can acquire such an example for somewhere between $350 and $2,000, depending on the specific issue and grade that you select.

Courtesy of Bowers and Merena

There are numerous Liberty Quarter Eagle deliveries in the second and third rarity tiers that could make a fitting addition to an advanced type set of better-date issues. Potential candidates include early P-mint coins such as the 1843, 1845 and 1850.

The 1843, 1845 and 1850 are all quite rare in Mint State. In addition, striking quality is usually not up to the same standards as that seen on many later-date Philadelphia Mint issues. You are going to have to accept some softness to the detail over the eagle's left (facing) leg feathers and the central obverse highpoint. An 1850 in PCGS MS-63 traded for $3,105 at auction in May of 2007, while an NGC MS-64 went for $4,888 one month earlier.

STRATEGIES FOR INCLUDING THE LIBERTY QUARTER EAGLE IN A TYPE SET OF RARER ISSUES

Most Desirable Issue(s): *1843, 1845, 1850*

Most Desirable Grade(s): *AU-55 or finer*

Estimated Cost: *$350 and up*

Key to Collecting: *No individually distracting abrasions; good color; partial or full mint luster*

Major Subtypes: There are no major design changes in the Liberty Quarter Eagle series, although Mint personnel did introduce a new reverse hub beginning in 1859. Acquiring one representative each of the Old Reverse (1852 or 1853, for example) and New Reverse (1861 New Reverse, 1873 Open 3, etc.) hub varieties will expand a basic gold type set. On the other hand, the 1848 CAL. Quarter Eagle is generally not regarded as a distinct design within the Liberty series, but rather the United States' first commemorative coin.

Issuing Mint: Five coinage facilities struck Quarter Eagles of the Liberty type, and a complete type set by issuing mint is within reach for many collectors. Since the Philadelphia Mint has already been covered in significant detail, let's turn our attention to the branch mints.

The most frequently encountered Liberty Quarter Eagle from the Charlotte Mint is the 1847-C. Fortunately, this issue usually possesses a better-than-average strike by Charlotte Mint standards. Look for a relatively abrasion-free example that grades at least AU-50. An example in that grade as certified by PCGS went for $2,760 in early 2006.

A desirable type candidate also exists for the Dahlonega Mint in the form of the 1843-D. One of the more plentiful Liberty Quarter Eagles from this mint, the '43-D usually possesses a bold-to-sharp strike. Once again, you should focus on coins that grade AU-50 or finer to obtain relatively strong technical quality and eye appeal. Expect to pay at least $3,250 to acquire a problem-free 1843-D Quarter Eagle in AU-50.

There are more options as far as the New Orleans Mint is concerned, but strike will pose more of a problem than it does for the Charlotte and Dahlonega Mints. The 1843-O Small Date and 1854-O are relatively available in numismatic circles. As with all mintmarked Quarter Eagles from the 1840s and 1850s, these issues are very rare in Mint State. I recommend selecting a circulated example, preferably a coin that grades AU-50 through AU-58. Both the '43-O Small Date and the '54-O are worth $500-$1,000 in the various AU grades.

Most 1843-O Small Date and 1854-O Quarter Eagles that I have seen are softly struck around the reverse shield, over the eagle's left (facing) leg feathers and at the haircurls over Liberty's brow. Examples with at least emerging definition in these areas are worth the wait, particularly if they also possess a relative lack of distracting abrasions.

Many extant 1843-O Small Date and 1854-O Quarter Eagles are softly struck around the reverse shield, over the eagle's left (facing) leg feathers and at the haircurls over Liberty's brow. The present example, a survivor of the former delivery, possesses above-average definition.

Many New Orleans Mint Liberty Quarter Eagles are softly struck over the central highpoints, as evidenced by this 1846-O in NGC MS-64.

The author has handled more examples of the 1878-S than any other S-mint delivery in the Liberty Quarter Eagle series, and this seems like the best type candidate from this coinage facility.

The final branch mint that struck Liberty Quarter Eagles is that located in San Francisco, California. I have handled more examples of the 1878-S than any other S-mint Quarter Eagle of this type, and it is the best type candidate from this Mint. Most survivors are in higher grades, and I suggest obtaining an example that grades AU-58. Two PCGS-certified coins in that grade each brought $374 during a March 2007 sale.

The typically encountered '78-S Quarter Eagle possesses satiny luster and orange-gold or rose-gold color. Striking quality varies, mostly from generally bold to a bit soft over the central highpoints.

STRATEGIES FOR INCLUDING THE LIBERTY QUARTER EAGLE IN A TYPE SET BY ISSUING MINT

Required Number of Coins: *Five*

Issuing Mint #1: *Philadelphia, Pennsylvania*

Most Desirable Issue(s): *1861 New Reverse, 1873 Open 3, 1896, 1902-1907*

Key to Collecting: *MS-60 or higher grade; sharp striking detail; vibrant luster; attractive color; no individually bothersome abrasions*

Issuing Mint #2: *Charlotte, North Carolina*

Most Desirable Issue(s): *1847-C*

Key to Collecting: *AU-50 or higher grade; overall bold definition; no individually bothersome abrasions*

Issuing Mint #3: *Dahlonega, Georgia*

Most Desirable Issue(s): *1843-D*

Key to Collecting: *AU-50 or higher grade; overall bold definition; no individually bothersome abrasions*

Issuing Mint #4: *New Orleans, Louisiana*

Most Desirable Issue(s): *1843-O Small Date, 1854-O*

Key to Collecting: *AU-50 or higher grade; above-average striking detail; no individually bothersome abrasions*

Issuing Mint #5: *San Francisco, California*

Most Desirable Issue(s): *1878-S*

Key to Collecting: *AU-58 or higher grade; bold striking detail; no individually bothersome abrasions; orange-gold or rose-gold color*

Proof Type Set

This is the earliest Quarter Eagle series that you can realistically consider for inclusion in a proof type set. Although the 20th century issues exist in slightly greater numbers, the coins struck during the 1892-1899 era are more attractive for type purposes. These issues are still relatively obtainable by proof gold standards, and many of the survivors possess awesome field-to-device contrast. In fact, I suggest purchasing a coin with a Deep or Ultra Cameo designation from one of the two leading certification services.

Coins that grade at least Proof-64 are recommended since they will possess a relative or overall lack of wispy hairlines. The dominant color is usually an orange-gold shade, although the fields will appear to "go black" as the coin rotates away from a light. Insist on 100% full striking detail. You should also look for a coin with an "orange peel" texture. This feature is seen quite often on proof U.S. gold coins from the mid-to-late 19th century, and it is best described as a slightly rippled effect in the fields. "Orange peel" texture is highly desirable to proof gold specialists and, if present, will be a valuable asset when the time comes to sell.

Courtesy of Bowers and Merena

Although the 20th century issues exist in slightly greater numbers, the coins struck during the 1892-1899 era might be more attractive for type purposes as far as the proof Liberty Quarter Eagle series is concerned. These issues are still relatively obtainable by proof gold standards, and many of the survivors possess awesome field-to-device contrast.

A few auction appearances from early-to-mid 2007 should give you an idea of how much proof Liberty Quarter Eagles from the 1890s are worth with a Deep/Ultra Cameo finish:

1892: *Certified Proof-64 Ultra Cameo at NGC; realized $18,975.*
1898: *Certified Proof-64 Deep Cameo at PCGS, realized $10,925*
1894: *Certified Proof-65 Ultra Cameo at NGC; realized $17,480.*
1894: *Certified Proof-66 Ultra Cameo at NGC; realized $20,700.*
1895: *Certified Proof-66 Deep Cameo at PCGS; realized $27,600.*
1897: *Certified Proof-66 Deep Cameo at PCGS; realized $23,000.*

STRATEGIES FOR INCLUDING THE LIBERTY QUARTER EAGLE IN A PROOF TYPE SET

Most Desirable Issue(s): *1892-1899*

Most Desirable Grade(s): *Proof-64 Deep/Ultra Cameo or finer*

Key to Collecting: *Bold field-to-device contrast; orange-gold color; full striking detail; a minimum number of wispy hairlines; "orange peel" texture*

Assembling a Complete Set

Year Set: The length of this series means that assembling a complete set using any criteria is going to be a difficult task. Such is definitely the case with a year set, although you can assemble most of the collection if you focus predominantly on the P-mint issues and aim for coins that grade EF, AU or Mint State. For the years 1865, 1866 and 1875, I recommend the San Francisco Mint issues since they are more obtainable than their P-mint counterparts. The 1841-C, although a scarce-to-rare issue in its own right, will have to substitute for the 1841—the proof-only "Little Princess"—and the 1842-O can take the place of the scarcer 1842-P.

On the other hand, the years 1863, 1864, 1881 and 1885 pose significant problems. The 1863 is a proof-only issue with an original mintage of just 30 coins, while the 1864, 1881 and 1885 were produced in limited numbers in both business strike and proof formats. There are no branch mint alternatives for any of these dates. At least $115,000 is required to obtain an 1863 in Proof-64 and AU-55/AU-58 examples of the 1864, 1881 and 1885. Clearly, the challenge of assembling an entire year set of Liberty Quarter Eagles is great, but the results could be very rewarding if you have sufficient financial resources.

Date and Mint Set: The completion of this set is not a realistic option for most collectors, primarily due to the extreme rarity of the 1848 CAL. and 1854-S. Even if you were to accept the absence of these coins from your "complete" set, there are countless other landmines sprinkled throughout this series in the form of rare, key-date issues. You need only look at the Charlotte and Dahlonega Mint issues, as well as the already-familiar 1864, 1875, 1881 and 1885, to prove the veracity of this statement.

Die Variety Set: With the possible exception of Southern gold specialists assembling sets of Charlotte, Dahlonega and/or New Orleans Mint coinage, there is little collector demand for Liberty Quarter Eagle die varieties. Given the challenge that even a year set represents, I suggest delving no deeper than that level if you are interested in specializing in this series.

Proof Set: Another strategy that I do not recommended for the faint hearted or those operating on a strict budget, the proof Liberty Quarter Eagle series is riddled with rare, virtually unobtainable issues. This is particularly true of the pre-1858 deliveries. A few examples from that era include: 1841—the proof-only "Little Princess"—a legendary rarity; 1842 and 1847, each of which are unobtainable for private ownership; 1855, currently unknown in proof format; and 1856, the only known example is impounded in the Harry W. Bass, Jr. Collection.

Beginning in 1858, and particularly in 1859, proof Liberty Quarter Eagles become somewhat more obtainable. As with all proof gold coins, however, even later-date Liberty Quarter Eagles are rare when viewed in the wider context of numismatics.

If you would like to assemble a set of proof Liberty Quarter Eagles, consider a short set approach to make the task more manageable. An eight-piece set from 1900-1907 is a relatively obtainable goal and will definitely serve as a highlight in a numismatic holding. Built around coins that grade Proof-64, this set will set you back at least $56,000.

Another desirable theme set, and one that is more challenging and costly to complete, encompasses the proof Quarter Eagles struck during the Civil War. Using examples with a numeric grade of Proof-63, a set of proof 1861-1865 Quarter Eagles will require in excess of $125,000.

A Complete Set by Issuing Mint: With the exception of key-date coins and conditionally rare examples, the Philadelphia Mint issues in this series do not garner much attention as a group. The same also holds true for the San Francisco Mint issues, but I believe that it would be an enjoyable and rewarding task to assemble a nearly complete set of Liberty Quarter Eagles from that branch mint. The key word here is "nearly" as the 1854-S is a major rarity and beyond reach for most collectors. Excluding this issue, all of the other S-mint Liberty Quarter Eagles are collectible, although you will have to accept predominantly EF and AU coins in order to improve your chances of completing the set.

Charlotte, Dahlonega and New Orleans Mint Liberty Quarter Eagles have long been popular among Southern gold specialists. Many collectors that pursue Liberty Quarter Eagles from one of these three branch mints do so as part of their quest to assemble more comprehensive collections, such as a complete set of C-mint gold coins.

Investing Tips

Under the right circumstances and market conditions, late-date Liberty Quarter Eagles in grades at or above MS-66 and high-quality proofs from the late 1890s and 1900s possess strong potential for price appreciation. These coins include many of the most beautiful survivors of this design, and they are important for high-grade type purposes. A single business strike in MS-66, MS-67 or even MS-68 will make an important addition to a numismatic portfolio, perhaps accompanied by a Cameo or Deep Cameo proof.

Famous rarities are also candidates for strong future performance, and the Liberty Quarter Eagle series has its share of these coins. Consider acquiring an example of the 1841 "Little Princess," a problem-free 1854-S or a proof 1863. Remember, however, that these issues do not trade all that often, and the number of potential buyers is currently very limited. With these facts in mind, I suggest concentrating on the aforementioned type coins for numismatic investment purposes. Common issues in the finer Mint State grades, as well as late-date proofs, enjoy broader demand. In short, there will be more buyers for those coins when the time comes to sell. If you still want to add a key-date Liberty Quarter Eagle to your numismatic portfolio, consider the following prices realized:

> **1841**: *$109,250 paid for a slightly impaired example in PCGS Proof-53 that sold through a March 2007 auction.*
> **1854-S**: *A PCGS EF-45 example traded for $345,000 at an early 2007 sale.*
> **1863**: *The winning bidder paid $149,500 for an NGC Proof-66 Ultra Cameo that crossed the auction block in early 2007*

CHAPTER THIRTEEN

Indian Quarter Eagles

Courtesy of Rare Coin Wholesalers

SPECIFICATIONS

Year(s) Issued: *1908-1929*
Issuing Mint(s): *Philadelphia, Denver*
Authorizing Act: *January 18, 1837*
Designer: *Bela Lyon Pratt*
Weight: *4.18 grams*
Composition: *90% gold, 10% copper*
Diameter: *18 millimeters*
Edge: *Reeded*

History

The Quarter Eagles and Half Eagles introduced in 1908 are a radical departure from all previous designs in U.S. coinage history. Prepared by Bela Lyon Pratt, a protégé of Augustus Saint-Gaudens, the Indian Quarter Eagle features an incuse design with the devices, date and lettering set below the fields. The redesign of this denomination in 1908 was part of President Theodore Roosevelt's campaign to improve the artistic merits of United States coinage, the first fruits of which were harvested the previous year with the introduction of Saint-Gaudens' Eagle and Double Eagle.

This is arguably the most attractive regular-issue Quarter Eagle ever struck in the United States Mint, although it was widely criticized when first introduced. The contemporary public feared that the incuse design would serve as a magnet for dirt and germs, and some questioned the coins' ability to stack. These objections proved groundless, however, and the Indian Quarter Eagle is now universally admired in numismatic circles.

A left-facing portrait of a Native American wearing a feathered headdress is the focal feature on the obverse. Thirteen stars are arranged around the periphery: six left, seven right. The word LIBERTY is at the upper border, while the date is below. On the reverse, a powerful eagle strides left atop a bundle of arrows. The eagle is clutching an olive branch in its right talon. The motto IN GOD WE TRUST is present in the right field, while the Latin motto E PLURIBUS UNUM is situated in the left field. Pratt's inclusion of the motto E PLURIBUS UNUM represents its first appearance on the Quarter Eagle since 1834. The legend UNITED STATES OF AMERICA is inscribed along the upper border, and the denomination expressed as 2½ DOLLARS lines the lower border. The mintmark location is at the reverse rim before the arrowheads.

The Indian Quarter Eagle was struck from 1908-1915 and then again from 1925-1929. There are only fifteen issues in this series, all but three of which were coined in the Philadelphia Mint. Proofs were also prepared, but only through 1915. The onset of the Great Depression about a year after the October 1929 stock market crash signaled the end of the Indian Quarter Eagle series. Indeed, 1929 was the final year in which the United States Mint produced this denomination. The only gold coins struck in quantity from 1930-1933 were Double Eagles for use in international trade—a testament to the fact that the Indian Quarter Eagle was intended primarily for use within the borders of the United States.

Short Type Set

As a member of the quartet of revolutionary coin designs introduced in 1907-1908, the Indian Quarter Eagle has long enjoyed prominent placement in short sets of 20th century and popular gold types. Of course, you would also have to represent this series in a type set of Quarter Eagles.

Quarter Eagle Types, an eight-piece set including:
Capped Bust Right, No Stars Obverse
Capped Bust Right, Stars Obverse
Capped Bust Left
Capped Head Left, Large Diameter
Capped Head Left, Reduced Diameter
Classic
Liberty
Indian

20th Century Gold Coinage, a four or six-piece set including:
Indian Quarter Eagle
Indian Half Eagle
Indian Eagle (No Motto and/or Motto)
Saint-Gaudens Double Eagle (No Motto and/or Motto)

Popular U.S. Gold Types, an eight or ten-piece set including:
Liberty Quarter Eagle
Indian Quarter Eagle
Liberty Half Eagle, Motto
Indian Half Eagle
Liberty Eagle, Motto

Indian Eagle (No Motto and/or Motto)
Liberty Double Eagle (usually a Type III example)
Saint-Gaudens Double Eagle (No Motto and/or Motto)

Complete Type Set

A frequently encountered type in the numismatic market, the Indian Quarter Eagle is a mainstay of dealer inventories and auction offerings. You should not, therefore, anticipate too much difficulty locating an attractive, problem-free example for inclusion in a circulated or Mint State type set.

Circulated Examples: With the exception of the key-date 1911-D, all issues in the Indian Quarter Eagle series are readily obtainable in circulated grades. Those struck during the 1920s are the most frequently encountered, and a near-Mint example would fit nicely in a type set. Expect to pay between $200 and $300 for a coin that grades AU-58 at PCGS or NGC.

Mint State Examples: The 1925-D is the most common Quarter Eagle of this type. Nevertheless, I do not consider this issue a desirable candidate for Mint State type purposes because many examples are poorly struck over the D mintmark and/or the lowermost feathers in the Native American's headdress. The 1926 is a much better alternative, and it is actually not much rarer than the 1925-D.

The 1926 typically comes with a sharp strike, good color and vibrant luster. The most desirable type candidates are those coins that grade MS-64 or finer because their surfaces will be free of excessive bagmarks. In that grade, the 1926 will cost $1,000-$1,500. The price for an MS-65 increases to $3,500-$4,250.

General Characteristics: Many Indian Quarter Eagles are bluntly defined over the lowermost feathers in the Native American's headdress. This attribute, when present, is easiest to spot if you rotate the coin under a light. A definite "ridge" will appear between the poorly defined portions of the headdress and those that are more sharply detailed. Sharply struck examples do exist for most issues, however, and I urge waiting until one of those coins becomes available. As an aside, incompleteness of detail at the top of the eagle's left wing is always seen on examples of the first-year 1908 due to the manner in which the Mint prepared the dies for that issue.

If you are planning to add a Denver Mint Quarter Eagle to your collection, be sure to also evaluate striking quality over the all-important D mintmark. The mintmark is often softly impressed, and it sometimes appears as little more than a shapeless blob. Try to hold out for an example with a sharp mintmark.

Luster quality for the series varies from a vibrant, satiny or frosty sheen to a more subdued, slightly granular texture. You can mitigate this problem by focusing on an issue like the 1926, which almost always comes with rich mint frost. Survivors of that issue also possess attractive color, the typical piece displaying pretty orange-gold or rose-gold overtones.

Circulated and lower-grade Mint State Indian Quarter Eagles often display numerous abrasions. In fact, some of the coins that have spent actual time in commercial channels possess large, detracting marks. Insist on acquiring a coin that is relatively free of excessive abrasions for inclusion in your gold type set.

Courtesy of Bowers and Merena

The 1926 typically comes with a sharp strike, good color and vibrant luster. The most desirable type candidates seem to be those coins that grade MS-64 or finer because their surfaces are generally free of excessive bagmarks. In that grade, the 1926 will probably cost $1,000-$1,500, while the price will almost certainly increase to $3,500-$4,250 for an MS-65.

Words of Caution: This is one of several gold series for which you can exercise patience. There are numerous coins from which to choose, and you need not feel pressured into purchasing an example with soft striking detail, inferior luster or an excessive number of abrasions.

Die buckling is known for several issues in this series, and it often appears as a raised, ridge-like feature just inside the border on one or both sides of the coin. I cannot think of a reason why you should be concerned over an Indian Quarter Eagle struck from buckled dies since this feature will not have an adverse effect on a coin's grade or desirability.

On the other hand, I had a very disturbing conversation with a less-reputable dealer about 10 years ago. While perusing the bourse floor of a regional coin show in search of an Indian Quarter Eagle to add to a circulated type set, I happened upon the table of a dealer who had several possible candidates in stock. After I took a close look at a few AU examples and commented on the excessive number of abrasions that they possessed, the dealer actually made the argument that "most" detracting marks on the surfaces of Indian Quarter Eagles are "in the die." This is absolutely not true, and there is a definite visual difference between as-struck features such as die cracks and strikethroughs and post-striking abrasions, scratches and other distractions. Be wary of this kind of reasoning if you encounter it in your numismatic travels, and always consult a trusted numismatic professional if you are having difficulty differentiating between pre and post-striking features on a coin's surface.

STRATEGIES FOR INCLUDING THE INDIAN QUARTER EAGLE IN A COMPLETE TYPE SET

Most Desirable Issue(s):

Circulated Grades: *All with the exception of the key-date 1911-D and, possibly, the scarcer 1914 and 1914-D*

Mint State Grades: *1926*

Most Desirable Grade(s), Circulated Coins: *AU-58*

Estimated Cost: *$200-$300*

Key to Collecting: *Bold definition; ample remaining luster; attractive color; surfaces that are free of excessive abrasions*

Most Desirable Grade(s), Mint State Coins: *MS-64 or finer*

Estimated Cost: *$1,000 and up*

Key to Collecting: *Sharp striking detail; full, frosty luster; orange-gold or rose-gold color; no individually conspicuous bagmarks*

Advanced Type Set

Rarer Issues: In circulated grades, the scarcer 1914 or 1914-D will serve very well in a better-date type set. Expect to pay only $200-$300 for an example that grades AU-58.

In Mint State, the 1908 is a popular choice for type purposes due to its first-year status. Other possibilities include the 1909, 1910, 1911, 1912, 1913 and 1915, all of which are scarcer than the 1925-1929 issues in higher grades. The most desirable examples possess above-average definition, good luster and color and no sizeable abrasions. Examples of each of these issues that grade MS-64 can be had for $1,500-$2,750.

Courtesy of Bowers and Merena

In circulated grades, the scarcer 1914 or 1914-D Quarter Eagle could make a noteworthy addition to a better-date type set.

STRATEGIES FOR INCLUDING THE INDIAN QUARTER EAGLE IN A TYPE SET OF RARER ISSUES

Most Desirable Issue(s):

    Circulated Grades: *1914, 1914-D*

    Mint State Grades: *Philadelphia Mint issues dated 1908-1915*

Most Desirable Grade(s):

    Circulated: *AU-58*

    Mint State: *MS-64 or finer*

Estimated Cost:

    Circulated Examples: *$200-$300*

    Mint State Examples: *$1,500 and up*

Key to Collecting: *Above-average definition; pleasing luster quality for the assigned grade; attractive color; surfaces that are free of excessive abrasions*

Major Subtypes: There are no design changes in the Indian Quarter Eagle series, the series remaining unchanged from 1908 through 1929.

Issuing Mint: This is an easy collecting strategy to follow for the Indian Quarter Eagle series since you will need to acquire only two coins. To represent the Philadelphia Mint, I wholeheartedly recommend the 1926.

The only Denver Mint issue that is not among the rarer deliveries in this series is the 1925-D, which is actually one of the most frequently encountered Quarter Eagles of this type. Avoid examples with blunt striking detail over the lowermost feathers in the Native American's feathered headdress and an ill-defined mintmark.

Provided that your numismatic budget will support such acquisitions, acquire a 1926 and 1925-D that grade at least MS-64. PCGS and NGC-certified examples in that grade will possess full mint bloom, relatively smooth surfaces and attractive color in orange-gold or rose-gold shades. All other things being equal, near-Gems will also be less expensive than pieces that grade MS-65 or finer. In fact, a two-piece set that includes one example each of the 1925-D and 1926 in MS-64 can be had for as little as $2,400.

STRATEGIES FOR INCLUDING THE INDIAN QUARTER EAGLE IN A TYPE SET BY ISSUING MINT

Required Number of Coins: *Two*

Issuing Mint #1: *Philadelphia, Pennsylvania*

Most Desirable Issue(s): *1926*

Key to Collecting: *MS-64 or higher grade; sharp striking detail; full, frosty luster; orange-gold or rose-gold color*

Issuing Mint #2: *Denver, Colorado*

Most Desirable Issue(s): *1925-D*

Key to Collecting: *MS-64 or higher grade; above-average striking detail; full, frosty luster; orange-gold or rose-gold color*

Proof Type Set

This is a challenging, yet obtainable type in proof. Although all issues in this series are rare, the real problem with the proof Indian Quarter Eagle is the finish applied by the Mint. Most issues were prepared with a matte, or sandblast texture that can appear dark and/or dull to the uninitiated collector. This is certainly the case with the first-year 1908, which displays noticeably deeper color that any other proof delivery of this type. Even the 1911-1915 deliveries, while noticeably lighter in color than the 1908, still possess the other undesirable attribute of the matte finish: overly delicate surfaces. Nicks and other contact marks often show up as "shiny spots" that I personally find to be very distracting. This characteristic can be particularly worrisome if your numismatic budget dictates that you focus on coins that grade lower than Proof-66.

The 1909 and 1910, on the other hand, were not prepared with a matte texture but rather with a Roman Gold finish that is a blend of satin and semi-reflective characteristics. These issues tend to come bright, and their surfaces are usually better at concealing wispy contact marks, which means that you can obtain a Proof-64 without compromising too much on quality. The 1909 and 1910, therefore, are the most desirable proof Indian Quarter Eagles for proof type purposes, even though they cost a bit more than most matte issues in the same grade. A 1909 certified Proof-64 by NGC sold through auction for $19,550 in 2005. Most survivors of both the proof 1909 and 1910 Quarter Eagle display medium yellow-gold color.

Courtesy of Rare Coin Wholesalers

The typically encountered proof 1909 Indian Quarter Eagle is quite bright with medium-gold color and surfaces that are better at concealing wispy contact marks than those of the 1908 and 1911-1915 issues. The Roman Gold finish employed in 1909 and 1910 is a blend of satin and semi-reflective characteristics.

A Word of Caution: Do not be misled by the reported mintage figures for the 1909 and 1910 into thinking that survivors are more plentiful than they are in reality. The contemporary public did not like either the matte or Roman Gold proofing methods, and many proof Indian Quarter Eagles were melted in the Mint when they failed to sell by the end of the year in which they were struck.

STRATEGIES FOR INCLUDING THE INDIAN QUARTER EAGLE IN A PROOF TYPE SET

Most Desirable Issue(s): *1909, 1910*

Most Desirable Grade(s): *Proof-64 or finer*

Key to Collecting: *Full striking detail; bright satin-to-semi-reflective surfaces; warm medium-gold color; a minimum number of wispy contact marks*

Assembling a Complete Set

Year Set: Unlike the Liberty Quarter Eagle, the Indian Quarter Eagle series is highly conducive to specialized collecting. A complete year set comprises only 13 coins, and it is fairly easy to assemble in grades through MS-64. The only year that might cause you to pause is 1914, for both the Philadelphia and Denver Mint issues are scarce, particularly in higher grades. In order to avoid overly scuffy surfaces and/or sizeable abrasions, I suggest assembling this set using coins that grade at least MS-63. If you would like to complete an entire year set of Indian Quarter Eagles in MS-63, plan on spending approximately $15,000.

Date and Mint Set: By adding only two more coins, you can easily convert a year set of Indian Quarter Eagle into a complete date and mint set. Unfortunately, your last two acquisitions are likely to be the series' key dates: the 1911-D and the 1914. You might be tempted to account for the relative rarity of these two issues by assembling the balance of the set in Mint State and securing the 1911-D and 1914 in AU. This is certainly one way to go, and it will make the task of completing a date and mint set of this series easier and more affordable. However, you need to weigh ease of completion against uniformity of technical quality and eye appeal. I believe that it is worth stretching for Mint State examples of all issues in order to assemble a set of uniformly high quality. Even the key-date 1911-D and 1914 are obtainable in Mint State for a price.

 Courtesy of Bowers and Merena

The collector that decides to assemble a complete date and mint set of Indian Two-and-a-Halves in, say, MS-63 should probably plan on spending at least $36,000. More than half of this cost will almost certainly be required just to secure the key-date 1911-D. An example of that issue in a PCGS MS-63 holder sold for $19,550 during a March 2007 auction.

A complete date and mint set of Indian Quarter Eagles in, say, MS-63 will set you back at least $36,000. More than half of this cost will go to the 1911-D, an example of which sold for $19,550 during a March 2007 auction. The coin was mounted in a PCGS MS-63 holder at the time of sale.

Die Variety Set: As a product of the 20th century United States Mint, the Indian Quarter Eagle was produced using dies that are essentially indistinguishable from one another except for the date and presence/absence of a mintmark. This is not, therefore, a popular way to collect this series.

Proof Set: Over the course of a year or year-and-a-half, an example of each of the eight proof deliveries in this series will appear in the market. Despite the relative frequency with which examples are offered, this series has yet to attract a considerable number of adherents among specialized collectors. One reason is certainly cost, as all proof Indian Quarter Eagles are rare coins that command hefty premiums in the market. Another explanation is the aforementioned physical and aesthetic qualities of the matte-textured finish. Many collectors shy away from these coins because their surfaces are dark and easily marred. In the highest grades (Proof-66 or finer), however, these can be extremely attractive coins, particularly when viewed by a collector that understands the intricacies of the matte and Roman Gold proofing styles. In order to assemble a complete set of proof Indian Quarter Eagles using a mix of Proof-65 and Proof-66 coins, plan on spending at least $210,000.

A Complete Set by Issuing Mint: Undoubtedly, the brevity of this series explains why most specialized collectors choose to assemble a date and mint set instead of focusing on either the Philadelphia or Denver Mint issues in isolation.

Investing Tips

As a beautifully designed, relatively obtainable gold series from the 20th century, the Indian Quarter Eagle enjoys strong demand from type collectors and specialists. MS-65 is a highly desirable grade for most issues in this series, at least insofar as it is the level at which certified populations drop off precipitously. As the key issue in this series, the 1911-D garners significant attention in all Mint State grades, as well as in AU.

Proofs of this type are underappreciated in many numismatic circles. The later-date matte issues such as 1911 and 1912 are actually very attractive, what with the myriad sparkling facts that their surfaces reveal under closer examination with a loupe. You should definitely avoid noticeable "shiny spots," however, which is possible to do if you aim higher than Proof-65.

CHAPTER FOURTEEN

Three-Dollar Gold Pieces

Courtesy of Rare Coin Wholesalers

SPECIFICATIONS

Year(s) Issued: *1854-1889*
Issuing Mint(s): *Philadelphia, Dahlonega, New Orleans, San Francisco*
Authorizing Act: *February 21, 1853*
Designer: *James Barton Longacre*
Weight: *5.015 grams*
Composition: *90% gold, 10% copper*
Diameter: *20.5 millimeters*
Edge: *Reeded*

History

This curious denomination was struck from 1854 through 1889. Other than as an additional outlet for California gold, there was not much need for a Three-Dollar coin. Indeed, this denomination saw very little circulation during the 1850s and early 1860s, and even less, if any, after the Civil War. Mintage figures reflect this fact, as most issues were produced to the extent of fewer than 10,000 pieces. In fact, the first-year 1854 is the only delivery with more than 100,000 coins produced, and just nine of the series' 41 business strike issues have five-figure mintages.

Numismatists have posed additional theories to explain why the federal government authorized a gold coin in this denomination. Some of the more popular ones center on the three-cent postage rate of the day. Indeed, a Three-Dollar coin could prove convenient for purchasing stamps in 100-count quantities. Also mentioned on occasion is the Three-Cent

Silver first struck in 1851. Perhaps the Three-Dollar gold was meant as a convenient way for banks and merchants to exchange these small, easily misplaced silver pieces?

Regardless of exactly why it was produced, the Three-Dollar gold piece is one of the least successful denominations in U.S. coinage history. But the judgment of history was far in the future when Congress authorized this denomination with the Act of February 21, 1853. At that time, the Mint's sole concern was developing a workable design for the new coin.

The task of designing the Three-Dollar gold piece fell to Chief Engraver James Barton Longacre. The design that he created would later be adapted for use on the Type III Gold Dollar. A portrait of Liberty faces left on the obverse, atop her head a feathered headdress with the word LIBERTY inscribed across the band. The legend UNITED STATES OF AMERICA is around the border. On the reverse, a wreath of corn, cotton, tobacco and wheat encircles the denomination 3 DOLLARS and the date. The mintmark, if applicable, will be present in the reverse field below the ribbon knot that binds the wreath.

Short Type Set

The Three-Dollar is one of the more overlooked series among collectors assembling short type sets of U.S. gold coinage. This is perhaps understandable given the fact that the Three-Dollar gold series is unique as a denomination. Nevertheless, the type does share some characteristics with the Gold Dollar and, to a lesser extent, the Liberty Double Eagle.

Gold Coin Types Designed by James Barton Longacre, a seven-piece set including:

Type I Gold Dollar
Type II Gold Dollar
Type III Gold Dollar
Three-Dollar Gold
Type I Double Eagle
Type II Double Eagle
Type III Double Eagle

Small-Denomination Gold Coins of the 19th Century, a four-piece set that includes:

Type I Gold Dollar
Type II Gold Dollar
Type III Gold Dollar
Three-Dollar Gold

Complete Type Set

All Three-Dollar gold pieces are expensive coins, and the series is rarer in an absolute sense than many others in the U.S. gold family. (Examples include the various Liberty series, as well as the popular Indian and Saint-Gaudens coinage of the 20th century). On the other hand, the Three-Dollar gold series does not enjoy a level of market demand that is truly commensurate with its rarity. I see this as an opportunity for type collectors since you will experience less competition for an attractive Three-Dollar gold piece than for, say, a Saint-Gaudens Double Eagle.

Circulated Examples: The majority of circulated Three-Dollar gold pieces that trade hands in the numismatic market are survivors of three issues: 1854, 1874 and 1878. Indeed, these deliveries boast the three-highest mintages in the series, and they can be found in AU-55 or AU-58 with relative ease. These grades are even more desirable because the overall definition will be bold despite light highpoint wear and partial mint luster is usually present. Select prices realized for these issues at the Choice AU grade level include:

> **1854***: An example graded AU-55 by PCGS sold for $1,725 during a May 2007 auction.*
>
> **1854***: During the same month, a coin graded AU-58 at NGC traded for $2,185.*
>
> **1874***: A PCGS AU-55 crossed the auction block for $1,495, also during May of 2007.*
>
> **1874***: Once again in May of 2007, an NGC AU-58 brought $1,840 at auction.*
>
> **1878***: A coin certified AU-55 by PCGS commanded $1,610 from the winning bidder during an early 2007 sale.*
>
> **1878***: An NGC AU-58 sold for $1,840 at auction on May 14, 2007.*

Courtesy of Rare Coin Wholesalers

As one of the most plentiful Three-Dollar gold pieces in today's market, the 1878 has long been a favorite among type collectors.

Mint State Examples: No other Three-Dollar gold piece has a greater Mint State population than the 1878, and this is the most popular issue in the series for type purposes. A plethora of bagmarks confines most Mint State survivors to the lower numeric grades. You can minimize these distracting features while not breaking the bank in the process, however, by selecting an example that grades MS-62 or MS-63. An NGC MS-62 brought $4,370 at auction in mid-2007. At around the same time, a PCGS MS-63 traded for $5,319.

There is also a fair number of near-Gem and Gem-quality 1878 Three-Dollar gold pieces available in today's market. An MS-64 will command $6,500-$7,500, while $12,000-$20,000 is required to obtain an example that grades MS-65.

General Characteristics: Expect the average circulated 1854, 1874 and 1878 Three-Dollar gold piece to possess orange-gold or rose-gold color, sometimes intermingled with more deeply set green-gold undertones. Scattered abrasions are almost always present, but plenty of coins exist whose surfaces are free of sizeable and/or individually mentionable distractions.

For the Mint State 1878, color ranges from orange-gold to rose-gold hues, and the luster is almost always frosty in texture. There is no such thing as a fully struck 1878 Three-Dollar gold piece, but many examples are suitably bold in detail despite isolated softness to the highpoints of the obverse headdress and the lower-reverse wreath.

Words of Caution: If your only interest in the Three-Dollar gold piece is as a type coin, then you can usually view a few pieces before committing to a purchase. In a typical year, the 1854, 1874 and 1878 will appear numerous times at auction and on the bourse floor of major numismatic conventions. If you exercise some patience, you can become more familiar with the attributes of these issues without fear of missing out on a fleeting buying opportunity. On the other hand, I see no reason to wait if you are confronted with an attractive coin that fits into your price range.

Many Three-Dollar gold pieces (particularly the lower-mintage issues) possess striations, or die polish lines in the fields. These features are as struck and, unlike hairlines from a cleaning, are raised on the surface of the coin. Striations will not adversely affect the numeric grade of a Three-Dollar gold piece, but you should avoid pieces with these features if you think that they are distracting. If you are uncertain as to whether lines on a coin are striations or evidence of cleaning or another form of mishandling, consult a recognized numismatic expert before making a purchase.

STRATEGIES FOR INCLUDING THE THREE-DOLLAR GOLD PIECE IN A COMPLETE TYPE SET

Most Desirable Issue(s): *1854 (circulated grades only), 1874 (circulated grades only), 1878*

Most Desirable Grade(s), Circulated Coins: *AU-55, AU-58*

Estimated Cost: *$1,500-$2,000*

Key to Collecting: *Partial mint luster; freedom from excessive and/or individually bothersome abrasions*

Most Desirable Grade(s), Mint State Coins: *MS-62 or finer*

Estimated Cost: *$4,500 and up*

Key to Collecting: *Overall bold strike; frosty luster; orange-gold or rose-gold color; no individually conspicuous bagmarks*

Advanced Type Set

Rarer Issues: The most desirable Three-Dollar gold issues for advanced type purposes are the low-mintage deliveries from the 1879-1889 era. These coins were produced at a time when there was very little demand for Three-Dollar gold pieces in commercial channels. Contemporary dealers and collectors recognized these issues' limited mintages as being potentially desirable to future generations of numismatists, and they set aside significant numbers of Mint State examples. As a result, issues such as the 1879, 1887, 1888 and 1889 hold tremendous appeal for advanced type purposes. The original business strike mintages of these deliveries are just 3,000, 6,000, 5,000 and 2,300 pieces, respectively, but examples appear in the market several times yearly. In grades at or above the MS-62 level, survivors are usually free of individually mentionable abrasions, and they will often possess vibrant luster with a frosty or prooflike sheen. Color varies, but it is generally orange-gold or rose-gold in shade. Price will also vary depending on the issue, but expect to pay at least $5,000 for an example that grades MS-62.

STRATEGIES FOR INCLUDING THE THREE-DOLLAR GOLD PIECE IN A TYPE SET OF RARER ISSUES

Most Desirable Issue(s): *1879, 1887-1889*

Most Desirable Grade(s): *MS-62 or finer*

Estimated Cost: *$5,000 and up*

Key to Collecting: *Bold-to-sharp striking detail; vibrant mint luster, sometimes prooflike; orange-gold or rose-gold color; no individually conspicuous bagmarks*

Major Subtypes: While there are several minor variations in the size of the date and/or lettering between various issues, the basic Three-Dollar gold design remained unchanged from 1854 through 1889. As such, I would be satisfied with including just a single representative of this series in a type set.

Issuing Mint: Four coins are required to complete a set of Three-Dollar gold pieces by issuing mint. Much has already been said about potential type candidates from the Philadelphia Mint, although you should select a Choice AU coin over a Mint State one since the mintmarked issues will force you down to the circulated level.

There is just a single Dahlonega Mint issue in this series, and it is a low-mintage rarity with just 1,120 pieces originally struck. Elusive in all grades, the 1854-D enjoys strong demand from Southern gold specialists as well as advanced type collectors. Expect strong competition when searching for a problem-free example, and expect to pay a handsome sum whether you are successful at securing a coin at auction or through a dealer.

The vast majority of surviving 1854-D Threes are worn to one degree or another, so obtaining a circulated coin is the most realistic option for the type collector. This issue tends to come softly struck, and I suggest focusing on one of the EF or AU grades to acquire a coin with at least fairly bold definition. Deep green-gold or khaki-gold color is the norm, as are numerous abrasions and surfaces that display somewhat of a glossy texture. In sum, this is probably the most challenging Three-Dollar gold piece to locate with strong eye appeal, and you must relax your standards somewhat when looking for a suitable example.

An 1854-D Three graded EF-40 by PCGS brought $21,850 when it appeared at auction in 2005. In AU-50, the price for this issue increases to the $30,000-$35,000 range, while an AU-58 is worth at least $50,000.

The other stand-alone issue in this series is the 1854-O, and it will also pose a significant challenge. Circulated grades from EF-AU offer the best options, and examples in AU-55 and AU-58 will retain at least part of the original satin luster. Look for coins with yellow-gold color, no sizeable or individually conspicuous abrasions and an O mintmark that is at least readily discernible (although it might be somewhat weak due to die polishing in the Mint). A PCGS AU-55 brought $13,800 at auction in 2006, which is actually more than a realized price of $11,500 reported for an example graded AU-58 at NGC from a slightly earlier sale.

There are more options as far as the San Francisco Mint is concerned. The unique 1870-S can be dismissed out of hand, which leaves the 1855-S, 1856-S, 1857-S and 1860-S. All of these deliveries are scarce in circulated grades and rare in Mint State, but the

Courtesy of Bowers and Merena

The 1854-O is the only New Orleans Mint issue in the Three-Dollar gold series, and it may also pose a significant challenge for the advanced numismatist. Circulated grades from EF-AU probably offer the best options for the buyer, and examples in AU-55 and AU-58 often retain at least part of the original satin luster. Look for coins with yellow-gold color, no sizeable or individually conspicuous abrasions and an O mintmark that is at least readily discernible.

1856-S appears with the greatest frequency. In order to be realistic about your chances of finding an affordable coin, the circulated grades are a better option than those at the Mint State level. Coins in EF and AU will usually retain a significant amount of striking detail despite light wear, and most even show traces of original luster. Try to avoid pieces with sizeable abrasions from commercial use—a challenging feat since this issue circulated heavily on the West Coast during the California Gold Rush and early frontier eras. In AU-58, the 1856-S will command at least $6,000.

STRATEGIES FOR INCLUDING THE THREE-DOLLAR GOLD PIECE IN A TYPE SET BY ISSUING MINT

Required Number of Coins: *Four*

Issuing Mint #1: *Philadelphia, Pennsylvania*

Most Desirable Issue(s): *1854, 1874, 1878*

Key to Collecting: *AU-55 or higher grade; orange-gold or rose-gold color; luster quality as befits the assigned grade; bold-to-sharp striking detail; no individually conspicuous abrasions*

Issuing Mint #2: *Dahlonega, Georgia*

Most Desirable Issue(s): *1854-D (only option)*

Key to Collecting: *EF-40 through AU-58 in grade; green-gold or khaki-gold color; relatively bold detail for the issue and the assigned grade*

Issuing Mint #3: *New Orleans, Louisiana*

Most Desirable Issue(s): *1854-O (only option)*

Key to Collecting: *EF-40 through AU-58 in grade; yellow-gold color; discernible detail to the O mintmark; no sizeable or individually conspicuous abrasions*

Issuing Mint #4: *San Francisco, California*

Most Desirable Issue(s): *1856-S*

Key to Collecting: *EF-40 through AU-58 in grade; no sizeable or individually conspicuous abrasions*

Proof Type set

The most frequently encountered proofs in this series are the late-date issues from 1886-1888, although the 1884, 1885 and 1889 are not too far behind. Excluding the 1885 (which sells for a premium due to the extremely low-mintage of its business strike counterpart), all of these issue come highly recommended for proof gold type purposes. The most beautiful examples that I have ever seen possess orange-gold or yellow-gold color, overall smooth surfaces and a bold Cameo or Deep/Ultra Cameo finish. The Cameo grades appear in the market most frequently, and coins with a numeric designation of at least Proof-64 do not possess too many wispy hairlines. Some examples exhibit a bit of haziness in the open fields—this is an as-struck feature that is due to microscopic porosity in the planchet. On its own, this feature should not adversely affect the desirability of a proof Three-Dollar gold coin.

The exact price will vary depending on the issue that you choose to pursue. An 1886 in Proof-64 Cameo, for example, will set you back at least $25,000.

Courtesy of Bowers and Merena

The most frequently encountered proofs in this series are the late-date issues from 1886-1888, any of which will probably be attractive to the proof gold type collector. Some of the most beautiful survivors possess orange-gold or yellow-gold color, overall smooth surfaces and a bold Cameo or Deep/Ultra Cameo finish.

STRATEGIES FOR INCLUDING THE THREE-DOLLAR GOLD PIECE IN A PROOF TYPE SET

Most Desirable Issue(s): *1884, 1886-1889*

Most Desirable Grade(s): *Proof-64 Cameo or finer*

Key to Collecting: *Sharp striking detail; bold field-to-device contrast; orange-gold or yellow-gold color; a minimum number of wispy contact marks*

Assembling a Complete Set

Year Set: More than any other issues, the 1875 and 1876 prevent most collectors from assembling a complete year set of Three-Dollar gold pieces. These are proof-only issues, and no branch mint coins were struck in either of those years. Expect to pay more than $170,000 just to acquire one example each of the 1875 and 1876 in Proof-64.

Even excluding these two deliveries, the completion of this set is still a formidable task due to the presence of several scarce-to-rare business strikes. But, with enough patience and at least $7,200, Extremely Fine examples of such issues as the 1865, 1866, 1867 and 1871 are obtainable. If you choose this strategy for the Three-Dollar gold series, exclude the proof-only 1875 and 1876 and then accept a mix of worn and Mint State coins for the remaining years in the series.

Courtesy of Bowers and Merena

One of the most significant obstacles along the road to completing a set of Three-Dollar gold pieces, the 1876 is a proof-only issue with a reported mintage of just 45 pieces. The specimen pictured here has been certified Proof-65 Ultra Cameo by NGC and probably carries a price tag in excess of $100,000.

Date and Mint Set: It is currently impossible to assemble a complete date and mint set of Three-Dollar gold pieces because the unique 1870-S is impounded in the Harry W. Bass, Jr. Collection. A virtually complete set is obtainable, however, although the task will require deep pockets and also a considerable amount of searching. The good news is that you can confine your date and mint set to the business strikes and, thus, avoid grappling with the rare, proof-only 1873 Open 3, 1875 and 1876. Once again, I advise selecting a mix of circulated and Mint State examples.

Die Variety Set: While at least one serious study has been undertaken on the die varieties in this series, there is currently little collector interest in this facet of the Three-Dollar gold piece. Since assembling even a year set of this denomination is a difficult task, I do not recommend trying to complete a Three-Dollar gold set by die variety. Even if you are successful at identify a rare die marriage, current and anticipated levels suggest that the market will not pay a premium for such a coin at anytime in the foreseeable future.

Proof Set: Proofs are known from each year in the Three-Dollar gold series, although several have unknown or disputed mintages. The rarity of issues such as the 1855, 1856, 1857, 1858, 1873 Open 3, 1873 Closed 3 and 1875 argue strongly against adopting this strategy.

A more realistic goal (and certainly a more affordable one) would be to assemble a short proof set of Three-Dollar gold pieces. I know one collector that put together a dazzling set of the Civil War issues in grades of Proof-65 and Proof-66, most with Cameo or Ultra Cameo surfaces. The fruits of his labor were sold through auction on October 29, 2004, at which time the coins realized $253,000. Assembling a 10-piece proof set focused on the 1880s is also a tempting numismatic endeavor.

Courtesy of Bowers and Merena

Given the rarity and cost of all proof Three-Dollar issues, the collector might want to consider assembling a short set instead of pursuing the entire series. The author knows one numismatist that focused on the Civil War issues of 1861-1865. The fruits of his labor were sold through auction on October 29, 2004 for a total of $253,000.

A Complete Set by Issuing Mint: The 1854-D and 1854-O are unique for Three-Dollar gold pieces struck in the Dahlonega and New Orleans Mints. Hence, I would only acquire these issues as part of either an advanced type set or a more comprehensive Southern gold collection. Indeed, these issues are usually viewed as highlights of gold sets built around the Dahlonega or New Orleans Mints.

Less prominent in numismatic circles are specialized collections of early San Francisco Mint gold coinage. Excluding the unique 1870-S, a complete set of S-mint Threes is certainly within reach of the collector with above-average means. Although short, this set is quite challenging to assemble. The rarity of the 1855-S, 1856-S, 1857-S and 1860-S in Mint State argues in favor of acquiring circulated coins in EF and AU. Focusing solely on coins that grade AU-55, plan on spending at least $45,000 for a four-coin set of S-mint Threes.

Investing Tips

Most collector interest in Three-Dollar gold pieces centers on five groups of issues: type coins such as the 1854, 1874 and 1878; Southern gold issues—the 1854-D and 1854-O; the proof-only 1873 Open 3, 1875 and 1876; low-mintage, yet relatively obtainable Mint State coins like the 1879, 1887, 1888 and 1889; and the more obtainable proof type candidates from the 1884-1889 era. I believe that each area is poised for significant price appreciation, and I suggest adding a Three-Dollar gold piece from at least one of these categories to a numismatic portfolio.

With the market's fixation on quality, an 1878, 1879, 1887, 1888 or 1889 that grades at least MS-64 has good potential for growth. The same can also be said for proofs such as the 1875, 1876 and 1884-1889. With a numeric grade of at least Proof-65 and Cameo or Deep/Ultra Cameo surfaces, these are among the most beautiful Three-Dollar gold pieces in the market. The overall scarcity of the type and, in particular, the undeniable rarity of many individual issues suggests that some Three-Dollar gold pieces might do very well in the coming decades under the right market conditions.

Courtesy of Bowers and Merena

Most collector interest in Three-Dollar gold pieces centers on five groups of issues, one of which concerns the proof-only 1873 Open 3, 1875 and 1876 deliveries. With the market's fixation on quality, an example that grades at least Proof-65 with Cameo or Deep/Ultra Cameo surfaces could perform well as part of a numismatic portfolio.

CHAPTER FIFTEEN

Four-Dollar
Gold Stellas

Courtesy of Rare Coin Wholesalers

SPECIFICATIONS

Year(s) Issued: *1879-1880*
Issuing Mint(s): *Philadelphia only*
Authorizing Act: *N/A*
Designer:
    Flowing Hair: *Charles E. Barber*
    Coiled Hair: *George T. Morgan*
Weight: *7 grams, with slight variation for those pieces struck in 1880*
Composition:
    Metric Alloy: *85.7% gold, 4.3% silver, 10% copper*
    Standard Alloy: *90% gold, 10% copper*
Diameter: *22 millimeters*
Edge: *Reeded*

History

One of the most interesting, yet confusing denominations in the United States coinage family, the federal government intended the Four-Dollar gold piece to solve two problems. First, silver and gold had to maintain a delicate balance in the international market in order for the Mint and/or mine owners to run profitable operations. When too much gold entered the market, as happened beginning with James Marshall's discovery in California during 1848, silver coins were hoarded, exported and eventually melted as their bullion value outstripped their face value. This usually happened at a net loss to the federal government. When silver flooded the market, such as occurred during the 1870s due to the richness of Nevada's Comstock Lode, prices for that precious metal fell and mine owners had a difficult time selling their product. The second problem was the perceived need for an international trade coin that, although struck in the United States Mint, would enjoy widespread acceptance among foreign governments and merchants.

In 1879, John Adam Kasson hit upon an idea that would hopefully solve both problems simultaneously. As U.S. minister to the Austro-Hungarian Empire, Kasson felt the need for his own country to have an international trade coin that could compete with the likes of Austria's 8 Florins, the Netherlands' 8 Florins, France's 20 Francs, Italy's 20 Lire and Spain's 20 Pesetas. Kasson was also a former Congressman and chairman of the Committee on Coinage, Weights and Measures, so he was keenly aware of the domestic rivalry between gold and silver. He proposed that the United States Mint strike a Four-Dollar coin in a metric alloy containing approximately 85.7% gold, 4.3% silver and 10% copper. Why a Four-Dollar coin as opposed to, say, the Three-Dollar and Five-Dollar pieces already in production? Apparently, Four-Dollars more closely approximated the value of other international trade coins and would facilitate acceptance in numerous countries. The use of the metric alloy provided Western mine owners with another outlet for their silver at a time when prices were falling and there were few other uses for the precious metal other than in coinage. Since the alloy also included gold, production of a Four-Dollar coin would not come at the expense of gold miners' interests. The Committee on Coinage, Weights and Measures selected the name "Stella" for the new denomination, "…in analogy to one [E]agle, both the star and eagle being National emblems on our coins."

Before the Stella could be produced in large quantities for circulation, the denomination required Congressional approval. In order to facilitate this, the Mint prepared patterns for presentation to Congressmen to help them evaluate the merits of a Four-Dollar gold piece. Two designs were prepared. Chief Engraver Charles E. Barber prepared the first, which depicts a left-facing portrait of Liberty with flowing hair as the central element on the obverse. Liberty is wearing a coronet inscribed LIBERTY. The second design was prepared by Assistant Engraver George T. Morgan whose portrait of Liberty is distinguishable by having the hair coiled atop the head and the word LIBERTY inscribed on a ribbon instead of a coronet. Both types are otherwise identical, the composition expressed around the obverse border as * 6 * G * .3 * S * .7 * C * G * R * A * M * S * with the date below the portrait. A five-pointed star, or Stella (the Latin word for star), serves as the focal feature on the reverse. The denomination expressed as both ONE STELLA and 400 CENTS is inscribed on the star. The mottos E PLURIBUS UNUM and DEO EST GLORIA are around the star, the legend UNITED STATES OF AMERICA is above and another expression of the denomination, FOUR DOL., is below.

Using Barber's Flowing Hair design, the Mint struck 15 Stellas in 1879 for delivery to select Congressional leaders. Demand from other Congressmen prompted Mint officials to produce additional examples in early 1880, albeit still using the dies for the 1879 Flowing Hair design. These pieces were not struck in metric alloy, but rather using the standard alloy of 90% gold, 10% copper.

Despite the influence of Kasson and his supporters, the Four-Dollar Stella did not meet with widespread approval. The Double Eagle, or Twenty-Dollar gold piece, was already being used in international commerce and was widely accepted overseas. The Stella project, therefore, was cancelled and the denomination never advanced beyond the status of a pattern. Additional examples of the 1879 Flowing Hair Stella were struck later in 1880 for sale to private collectors. The 1879 Coiled Hair, 1880 Flowing Hair and 1880 Coiled Hair specimens were also prepared for private sale, probably clandestinely and without government approval. Numismatic scholars do not know the exact mintage of any of these three issues, and even the total delivery of 1879 Flowing Hair Stellas can only be estimated.

All 1879 and 1880 Stellas were struck in proof format. Since these coins are technically patterns, they are usually referenced by Judd and/or Pollock numbers as designated by the two standard references on U.S. pattern and related issues: *United States Pattern Coins* by Dr. J. Hewitt Judd and *United States Pattern and Related Issues* by Andrew W. Pollock, III. Unlike virtually all other patterns, however, most type collectors and gold specialists consider this denomination an integral part of the United States coinage family and choose to add an example to their holdings.

Short Type Set

Due to its status as a pattern, the Four-Dollar Stella is unique from all of the other types that are traditionally collected as part of the regular-issue U.S. gold series. As such, the Stella does not readily present itself for inclusion in a short type set. Either of the following sets, however, will provide you with an opportunity to include one or two Stellas among your numismatic holdings without having to assemble a complete gold type set.

Four-Dollar Gold Stella Types, a two-piece set including:

> **Flowing Hair Four-Dollar Gold Stella**
> **Coiled Hair Four-Dollar Gold Stella**

Odd-Denomination Gold Coinage of the United States, a two-piece set including:

> *Three-Dollar Gold*
> **Four-Dollar Gold Stella**

Both of these options are very attractive when you consider the rarity and, hence, cost of the Four-Dollar Stella as a type. Either of these short sets hold particular appeal for the collector that desires to build a meaningful collection around this denomination but will require most, if not all of their numismatic budget to achieve this goal.

A two-piece set of Flowing Hair and Coiled Hair Stellas costs $460,000-$530,000 as long as you acquire the 1879 Flowing Hair and 1879 Coiled Hair in Proof-63 or Proof-64. If you opt for the second short set listed above, be prepared to spend at least $170,000 for an 1879 Flowing Hair Stella in Proof-64 and an 1878 Three-Dollar gold piece in MS-64.

Complete Type Set

With an estimated mintage of 700+ pieces, the 1879 Flowing Hair was produced in greater numbers than any other issue in the Four-Dollar gold series. Indeed, this is the most frequently encountered Stella in today's market, and it is the only realistic option for the type collector seeking a single representative of this denomination. The issue is known by the attributions Judd-1635 and Pollock-1832/1833.

Circulated Examples: As previously mentioned, all Stellas are patterns that the United States government never intended for use in commercial channels. Nevertheless, a few

1879 Flowing Hair examples have acquired light wear due to mishandling. By and large, these coins were carried as pocket pieces either by Congressmen or those that received them as gifts. These pieces can serve as a more affordable alternative to an example that grades Proof-60 or finer. In January of 2007, two 1879 Flowing Hair Stellas with light highpoint rub sold through auction. The PCGS Proof-55 realized $69,000 while the Proof-58 certified at the same service sold for $109,250. Coins at both grade levels will retain overall sharp definition to the devices.

As an aside, professional numismatists refer to proof coins with a numeric grade of less than 60 as being "impaired." This is technically correct as proof coins were not meant to acquire wear from circulation or by any other means. Stellas that are impaired due to a harsh cleaning, polishing, damage or having been mounted as jewelry will not certify at PCGS or NGC. Even if you are operating with a more limited numismatic budget, avoid purchasing a Stella with significant impairments.

Unimpaired Examples: Problem-free 1879 Flowing Hair Stellas are always regarded as highlights of the auctions in which they appear, and with good reason. These coins are very rare when viewed in the wider context of U.S. numismatics and they enjoy strong demand from type collectors and gold specialists alike. If you are looking for an example for a gold type set, I suggest acquiring a specimen that grades Proof-64. Such a piece will still be expensive at $160,000 or more, but the price for this issue jumps to more than $200,000 in Proof-65. In addition to a more affordable price, the Proof-64 grade level is characterized by a vibrant mint finish and a minimal number of wispy contact marks. For additional eye appeal, select a piece with a Cameo or Deep/Ultra Cameo designation. If you choose a Cameo or Deep/Ultra Cameo Stella, however, be prepared to pay 10-15% more than an all-brilliant specimen.

General Characteristics: Most 1879 Flowing Hair Stellas that I have seen display yellow-gold or orange-gold color. Examples that grade at least Proof-64 will possess vibrant surfaces with reflective fields and either brilliant or satiny devices. Coins in lower grades usually have numerous scattered hairlines, sometimes to such an extant that the original finish is muted and much of the mint brilliance is lost. The strike is sharp in other areas, but most, if not all survivors exhibit softness of detail over the central highpoints on one or both sides. Such pieces also reveal rollermarks, or planchet striations, at the top of Liberty's hair on the obverse and, occasionally, over the reverse star.

Words of Caution: As the foregoing price estimates confirm, even the relatively common 1879 Flowing Hair Stella is an expensive coin. Indeed, this denomination serves as a potential stopper for many gold type collectors. You might be tempted to avoid the Stella altogether by explaining it away as a pattern and thus not part of the regular-issue U.S. coinage family. I do not condone such reasoning for, as already mentioned, most numismatists consider the Stella an integral part of a complete U.S. gold type set. As a reflection of this fact, the 2008 edition of the indispensable reference *A Guide Book of United States Coins* by R. S. Yeoman ("The Official Redbook") lists the Stella in the regular-issue gold section between the Three-Dollar and Half Eagle series and not in the section for significant pattern coins.

Even if you recognize the necessity of including a Stella in your collection, you might consider mitigating the costliness of the 1879 Flowing Hair by opting for an example with one or more significant problems. Once again, I do not support this decision since the resale potential of "problem coins" is always significantly less than that of problem-free examples. You should also weigh the overall quality of your set against the possible inclusion of a significantly impaired Stella. A damaged Four-Dollar gold piece, or one that was formerly mounted in a bezel as jewelry, will not fit well into a type set of otherwise high-quality coins. If you are concerned about cost, the best strategy is to opt for a circulated Stella that has been certified by PCGS or NGC. PCGS has graded a few 1879 Flowing Hair examples as low Proof-30, including a specimen that realized $57,500 in late 2005.

One final word of caution regarding this type: traditional numismatic theory has it that the 15 Flowing Hair Stellas produced in 1879 for presentation to Congress are fully struck without rollermarks over the central highpoints. If this is true, then those pieces must have been lost sometime between 1879 and the present day. All examples that I have handled are a bit softly impressed over the central highpoints with prominent rollermarks over the top of Liberty's head. A metallurgical analysis would determine if a particular example was struck in metric or standard alloy and, thus, help to ascertain if it was struck in 1879 or 1880, respectively. In practice, however, few numismatists that submit 1879 Flowing Hair Stellas to the major certification services opt for a metallurgical analysis. This is because the issue as a whole is rare and the desirability of examples usually stems from their status as type coins. As such, you should not pay a premium for an 1879 Flowing Hair Stella with an above-average strike and few, if any, rollermarks over the central highpoints. Even if such a piece were to surface, the numismatic market has yet to define a universally accepted method of differentiating between original 1879 Flowing Hair Stellas and restrikes produced during 1880.

STRATEGIES FOR INCLUDING THE FOUR-DOLLAR GOLD STELLA IN A COMPLETE TYPE SET

Most Desirable Issue(s): *1879 Flowing Hair (Judd-1635, Pollock-1832/1833)*

Most Desirable Grade(s), Circulated Coins: *Proof-55, Proof-58*

Estimated Cost: *$70,000 and up*

Key to Collecting: *Plenty of bold-to-sharp striking detail still in evidence*

Most Desirable Grade(s), Unimpaired Coins: *Proof-64*

Estimated Cost: *$160,000 and up*

Key to Collecting: *Yellow-gold or orange-gold color; all-brilliant or cameo-finish surfaces; relatively few contact marks; sharp striking detail over all features save for the central highpoints on one or both sides*

Advanced Type Set

Rarer Issues: There is no such thing as a "rarer issue" in the Four-Dollar gold series as all four deliveries are rare and fully deserving of the high prices that they command in the market. Nevertheless, even issues in a series such as this can be ranked by increasing or decreasing rarity. After the 1879 Flowing Hair, the 1880 Flowing Hair (Judd-1657, Pollock-1857) has the largest surviving population. You must realize, however, that only 15-20 examples of the 1880 Flowing Hair Stella have survived—a fact that confirms this issue as a major numismatic rarity.

Given that there is little difference between the rarity of the 1879 Coiled Hair and 1880 Flowing Hair (approximately 10-15 pieces known vs. an estimate of 15-20 coins extant), I suggest paying an additional premium to acquire an 1879 Coiled Hair for your better-date type set. Coiled Hair Stellas dated both 1879 and 1880 are instantly recognizable as rarities, whereas the 1880 Flowing Hair is somewhat overlooked due to its association with the "common" 1879 Flowing Hair. Once again, Proof-63 and Proof-64 are optimum grades since they provide relatively strong eye appeal and technical quality for a more affordable price. An 1879 Coiled Hair Stella certified Proof-63 by PCGS traded hands for $316,250 through a January 2007 auction. The attribution for this pattern issue is Judd-1638, Pollock-1838.

Even if you are operating on a more limited budget, you can still acquire a Choice 1879 Flowing Hair Stella for inclusion in an advanced type set. In addition to 10-15 survivors struck in gold, a handful of examples are known in copper, aluminum and white metal. A few of the copper impressions (Judd-1639, Pollock-1839) have been gilt, or plated in gold, to simulate the gold impressions. This was often done by contemporary collectors that were also having difficulty locating one of the gold specimens. A gilt example will fit nicely into a type set, and it will cost significantly less than a gold striking. In a November, 2004 auction, a copper 1879 Coiled Hair Stella that had been gilt realized $57,500. The coin was certified Proof-63 by NGC.

On the other hand, gilt examples of the 1879 Coiled Hair are even rarer than their gold counterparts. Nevertheless, gilt specimens do appear from time to time.

1879 Coiled Hair Stellas struck in gold tend to come a bit softly impressed over the central highpoints. Many examples also display rollermarks over the top of Liberty's head and/or the reverse star. The copper impressions, however, are usually quite sharp. Examples of both the Judd-1638 and Judd-1639 Gilt varieties typically display yellow-gold or orange-gold color with uniform mint brilliance over the devices and in the fields. I am also aware of a few Judd-1638 specimens with a Cameo finish.

STRATEGIES FOR INCLUDING THE FOUR-DOLLAR GOLD STELLA IN A TYPE SET OF RARER ISSUES

Most Desirable Issue(s): *1879 Coiled Hair struck in gold (Judd-1638, Pollock-1838), 1879 Coiled Hair struck in copper and gilt (Judd-1639 Gilt, Pollock-1839)*

Most Desirable Grade(s): *Proof-63*

Estimated Cost:

    Judd-1638: *$320,000+*

    Judd-1639 Gilt: *$60,000+*

Key to Collecting: *Yellow-gold or orange-gold color; bold striking detail in most areas (Judd-1638) or an overall sharp strike (Judd-1639 Gilt)*

Major Subtypes: Acquiring an example of both designs in the Four-Dollar gold series will increase your expenditure significantly, but it will also increase the value of your collection when the time comes to sell. By value in this context I mean not only monetary value, but also the value of your accomplishment in the eyes of other collectors.

As the most frequently encountered representatives of their respective designs, the 1879 Flowing Hair and 1879 Coiled Hair are perfect candidates for inclusion in an advanced type set of major subtypes. Focus on coins that grade Proof-63 or Proof-64. You must plan on spending at least $445,000 to acquire one example of each issue that grades Proof-63.

Issuing Mint: All Four-Dollar gold pieces were struck in the Philadelphia Mint. If you adopt this strategy to build your gold type set, therefore, you need acquire only a single Stella.

Proof Type Set

All Four-Dollar gold pieces were struck in proof format, so the strategies for including an example in a proof gold type set are the same as those presented above for representing the Stella in a complete type set.

Assembling a Complete Set

Year Set: Produced solely in 1879 and 1880, a year set of Stellas requires the purchase of just two coins. This is a deceptively easy task, as all issues in this short-lived series are rare and costly. Nevertheless, you can complete this two-piece set if you focus on the Proof-63 grade level and have at least $300,000 to spend. The most realistic issues to acquire are the 1879 Flowing Hair and 1880 Flowing Hair.

Date and Mint Set: This strategy requires that you purchase one example of each of the four issues in the Four-Dollar gold series. This is a formidable and costly task, to be sure, but you can complete it with patience and the requisite resources. In other words, representatives of all four issues are available for private ownership, and they appear in the market with more or less frequency depending on their absolute rarity. If you desire to assemble a set of uniform quality and keep costs relatively low without sacrificing quality, then focus on the Proof-63 grade level. Still, be prepared to spend at least $1,025,000 to assemble a complete set of Four-Dollar gold pieces in Proof-63. Nearly half of the cost will be devoted to the 1880 Coiled Hair. With only 12 coins surviving, this is the rarest and most costly Stella.

Die Variety Set: There are no die varieties in the Four-Dollar series and, thus, no way to expand a complete four-piece set in this manner.

Proof Set: As previously stated, all Four-Dollar gold pieces were struck as proofs. A complete set of proofs, therefore, is the same as a complete date and mint set.

A Complete Set by Issuing Mint: With no mintmarked issues, the Four-Dollar gold series is not eligible for inclusion in a collection of branch mint gold coinage.

Investing Tips

The Four-Dollar gold series has a low, essentially fixed supply in numismatic circles. Demand from type collectors and gold specialists, however, is likely to increase as numismatics as a whole gains in popularity.

There are two ways that you can capitalize on the favorable relationship between supply and demand in the Four-Dollar gold series. First, consider acquiring a single representative of the series' primary type coin: the 1879 Judd-1635 Flowing Hair. Proof-64 is a desirable grade for this purpose as such coins are usually highly attractive, yet more affordably priced than pieces that grade Proof-65 or finer. What's more, this issue already has a strong track record for price appreciation:

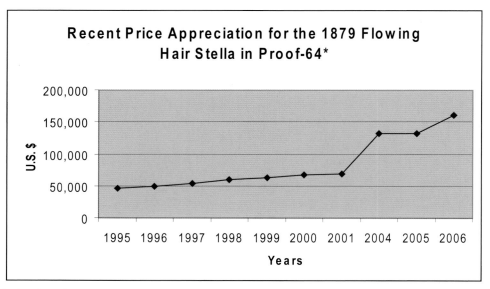

*Historic values represent prices realized for PCGS and NGC-certified examples as reported by leading numismatic auction firms.

Additionally, you could focus on the rarer issues in the Four-Dollar gold series. I particularly like the 1880 Coiled Hair, which has registered steady price appreciation over the last three decades.

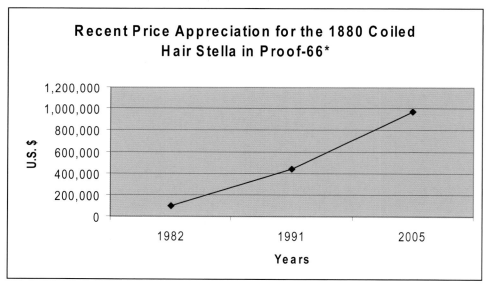

*Historic values represent prices realized for individual examples as reported by leading numismatic auction firms.

Adding an example of the 1879 Flowing Hair and/or the 1880 Coiled Hair is an excellent way to take advantage of the investment opportunities embodied in this rare gold series.

CHAPTER SIXTEEN

Capped Bust Right Half Eagles with Small Eagle Reverse

Courtesy of Bowers and Merena

SPECIFICATIONS

Year(s) Issued: *1795-1798*
Issuing Mint(s): *Philadelphia only*
Authorizing Act: *April 2, 1792*
Designer: *Robert Scot*
Weight: *8.75 grams*
Composition: *91.67% gold, 8.33% silver and copper*
Diameter: *25 millimeters (approximate)*
Edge: *Reeded*

History

During the early years of the United States, the Half Eagle was the most popular denomination among gold bullion depositors. Understandably so, the Half Eagle was the first gold coin struck in the United States Mint. The Mint delivered the initial batch of Half Eagles on July 31, 1795—a particularly proud day for Henry William DeSaussure. When President George Washington appointed him as director of the Mint earlier in the year, DeSaussure stated that one of his primary goals was to place gold into circulation.

Created by Chief Engraver Robert Scot, the first Half Eagle design displays a right-facing bust of Liberty on the obverse with 15, 16 or 13 stars divided by the portrait. Liberty is wearing a soft cap that, although once regarded as a Phyrigian-style cap, is now believed to be an article of women's clothing that was popular during the 1790s. The word LIBERTY is at the upper border, and the date is below the portrait.

On the reverse, a small spread-wing eagle is perched atop an olive branch with a circular wreath in its beak. The legend UNITED STATES OF AMERICA is around the border. As with most other early U.S. coins, the Mint did not include an expression of the denomination as part of the design for the Capped Bust Right Half Eagle. The federal government wanted the coins' bullion content and fineness to prove its worth in commerce without a new, unfamiliar denomination getting in the way. After proving its worth in export trade, the Half Eagle could include an expression of the denomination as part of the design. This happened in 1807, by which time the Capped Bust Right motif had been replaced by other designs.

The Mint struck Capped Bust Right Half Eagles with the Small Eagle reverse through early 1798. Even before that time, however, the Mint had adopted a new design with a large eagle on the reverse.

The Capped Bust Right Half Eagle with Small Eagle reverse is a rare type. All issues in this series have limited original mintages, and many examples were melted through the mid-1830s due to rising gold prices on the world market.

Short Type Set

A complete set of United States Half Eagles by type is an excellent way to highlight the Capped Bust Right Half Eagle with Small Eagle Reverse. This short set requires nine coins for completion, as follows:

Half Eagle Types, a nine-piece set including:

Capped Bust Right Half Eagle, Small Eagle Reverse
Capped Bust Right Half Eagle, Large Eagle Reverse
Capped Bust Left Half Eagle
Capped Head Left Half Eagle, Large Diameter
Capped Head Left Half Eagle, Reduced Diameter
Classic Half Eagle
Liberty Half Eagle, No Motto
Liberty Half Eagle, Motto
Indian Half Eagle

An alternative is a complete set of Capped Bust Right gold coinage. This short set is more difficult and costly to complete than the former. If you complete it, however, you will have an impressive set that can serve as either a complete holding or the basis for a larger collection.

Capped Bust Right Gold Coinage, a six-piece set including:

Capped But Right Quarter Eagle, No Stars Obverse
Capped Bust Right Quarter Eagle, Stars Obverse
Capped Bust Right Half Eagle, Small Eagle Reverse
Capped Bust Right Half Eagle, Large Eagle Reverse
Capped Bust Right Eagle, Small Eagle Reverse
Capped Bust Right Eagle, Large Eagle Reverse

Complete Type Set

I highly recommend the 1795 Small Eagle as the type candidate of choice in this early U.S. gold series. As the first gold coin struck in the Philadelphia Mint, the 1795 Small Eagle Five is a historically significant issue. In addition, the 1795 was saved in greater numbers than the other three issues in this series. It is actually the most frequently encountered Capped Bust Right Half Eagle with Small Eagle Reverse in today's market.

Circulated Examples: The two leading certification services have graded circulated 1795 Small Eagle Fives in grades as low as Very Good, but the majority of survivors grade Extremely Fine or About Uncirculated. Coins that grade at least EF-40 possess overall bold, if not sharp definition, and most retain at least some degree of original mint luster. The exact grade that you choose between EF-40 and AU-58, therefore, is a matter of cost. EF-40s sell in the neighborhood of $20,000, an AU-50 costs at least $30,000, and you will need $40,000-$55,000 to buy an AU-58.

Mint State Examples: These are definitely in the minority among surviving 1795 Small Eagle Fives. When offered at all, Uncirculated examples typically grade no finer than MS-62. This, therefore, is the grade that I recommend for Mint State type purposes, especially since MS-60s and MS-61s are usually heavily abraded and/or deficient in luster. Expect to pay at least $80,000 for a problem-free MS-62, and a PCGS-certified example in that grade did sell for as much as $149,500 in an August 2006 auction. Even the latter price is affordable relative to that realized by an NGC MS-63 example in early 2006: $218,500.

General Characteristics: Striking quality varies for this issue, but most examples that I have handled possess at least some degree of softness to the detail over the highpoints of the obverse portrait and reverse eagle. Many of the eagle's breast feathers and much of the detail on its head are sometimes completely absent. There are, however, sharply struck examples in the market, and I suggest being patient until one of those pieces is made available for purchase.

Colors include yellow-gold, orange-gold and green-gold shades. High-grade 1795 Small Eagle Fives are almost always satiny or, more commonly, semi-prooflike in finish. Semi-prooflike examples are particularly attractive in higher grades.

In circulated and lower Mint State grades, the 1795 Small Eagle Five will usually come with a generous number of small and moderate abrasions. These are well within the context of the early U.S. gold series, but avoid coins with large and/or individually distracting handling marks. Significant distractions can adversely affect a coin when you reintroduce it into the market in hopes of finding a willing buyer.

Words of Caution: In addition to individually conspicuous abrasions, avoid 1795 Small Eagle Fives that possess severe impairments. These include polishing, whizzing, damage due to scratches and other signs of mishandling. While such pieces cost appreciably less than problem-free coins in the same grade (a PCGS AU-55 realized $51,865 through a January 2007 sale while a damaged and cleaned piece with an AU-55 Details grade from ANACS commanded only $21,850 at auction five months earlier), the potential for price appreciation is much less for impaired coins. In addition, an early Half Eagle with significant problems will not do justice to a gold type set that has been assembled using otherwise problem-free coins.

As a product of the early U.S. Mint, Half Eagles of this type frequently display adjustment marks on one or both sides. These features are a normal part of the minting process, and they will not result in a lower numeric grade from PCGS or NGC in their own right. On the other hand, some collectors believe that a large number of adjustment marks limits a coin's aesthetic appeal, particularly if these marks are concentrated in a prime focal area. With this in mind, I suggest avoiding any coins with an excessive number of adjustment marks or adjustment marks that are concentrated in a prime focal area such as the obverse portrait. Go with your gut instincts and remember that other collectors will probably take focal area marks into account, thus affecting your ability to obtain a strong price when the time comes to sell.

STRATEGIES FOR INCLUDING THE CAPPED BUST RIGHT HALF EAGLE, SMALL EAGLE REVERSE IN A COMPLETE TYPE SET

Most Desirable Issue(s): *1795 Small Eagle*

Most Desirable Grade(s), Circulated Coins: *EF-40 through AU-58*

Estimated Cost: *$20,000-$55,000*

Key to Collecting: *Free of large and/or singularly distracting abrasions; few if any adjustment marks; overall bold-to-sharp definition*

Most Desirable Grade(s), Mint State Coins: *MS-62*

Estimated Cost: *$80,000 and up*

Key to Collecting: *Free of large and/or singularly distracting abrasions; few if any adjustment marks; yellow-gold, orange-gold or green-gold color; overall sharp striking detail*

Advanced Type Set

Rarer Issues: The second-year 1796/5 is the most attractive issue in this series for advanced type purposes. Not only is this issue an overdate, but it has a significantly lower surviving population than the 1795 Small Eagle. In fact, I believe that fewer than 100 examples of the 1796/5 have survived, as opposed to at least 500 pieces for the 1795 Small Eagle. On the other hand, both issues usually command similar premiums in circulated grades. For example, a 1796/5 in NGC AU-58 realized $51,750 in a December 2005 auction. This is the same price realized by a 1795 Small Eagle in PCGS AU-58 during January of 2007.

The reason for this similarity in price is that the 1795 Small Eagle enjoys greater demand due to its first-year status and historical significance. Nevertheless, you should plan to spend a bit more for a 1796/5 Half Eagle in circulated grades, particularly since the rarity is becoming more widely known in the market.

In Mint State, the 1796/5 has a combined population of only 17 examples at PCGS and NGC (April/2007). This is a much lower total than that reported for the 1795 Small Eagle, and the 1796/5 costs appreciably more in all Mint State grades. Given the rarity of this issue in Mint State, I recommend any problem-free 1796/5 Half Eagle that grades at least MS-60. This issue starts at $80,000 in Mint State.

The 1796/5 usually possesses the same striking characteristics as the 1795 Small Eagle, although it is more challenging to locate with a sharply executed strike over the reverse eagle. All other things being equal, an example with at least emerging detail over the highpoints of the eagle's head, breast and legs is preferable to a typically soft representative.

Popular as an overdate, the 1796/5 is also much rarer than the first-year 1795 Small Eagle Five. As such, it seems like an attractive issue for better-date type purposes.

STRATEGIES FOR INCLUDING THE CAPPED BUST RIGHT HALF EAGLE, SMALL EAGLE REVERSE IN A TYPE SET OF RARER ISSUES

Most Desirable Issue(s): *1796/5*

Most Desirable Grade(s), Circulated Coins: *EF-40 through AU-58*

Estimated Cost: *$25,000-$60,000*

Key to Collecting: *Free of large and/or singularly distracting abrasions; few if any adjustment marks; overall bold-to-sharp definition*

Most Desirable Grade(s), Mint State Coins: *MS-60 or finer*

Estimated Cost: *$80,000 and up*

Key to Collecting: *Free of large and/or singularly distracting abrasions; few if any adjustment marks; yellow-gold, orange-gold or green-gold color; at least emerging definition over the highpoints of the reverse eagle*

Major Subtypes: The most significant subtypes in the Capped Bust Right, Small Eagle Five-Dollar series are distinguishable by the number of stars around the obverse periphery. There are three variants, examples of which possess 15, 16 or 13 stars on the obverse. With the exception of early gold specialists, however, there is little demand for these varieties in numismatic circles. One reason for this is the rarity of all issues in this series. Most collectors, therefore, are content to own just a single example of the type. Indeed, your collecting budget might prevent you from acquiring more than one Capped Bust Right, Small Eagle Five.

Lack of sufficient financial resources could be a particularly insurmountable problem as far as the final-year 1798 Small Eagle is concerned. Only seven examples are known, and they are the only Small Eagle Fives of the 13 Stars variety. A PCGS EF-40 crossed the auction block in 2000 for $264,500. To assemble the entire three-piece set of Capped Bust Right, Small Eagle Fives by major subtype you will need at least $350,000.

> ## STRATEGIES FOR INCLUDING THE CAPPED BUST RIGHT HALF EAGLE WITH SMALL EAGLE REVERSE IN A TYPE SET OF MAJOR SUBTYPES
>
> **Required Number of Coins:** *Three*
>
> **Major Subtype #1:** *15 Stars Obverse*
>
> **Most Desirable Issue(s):** *1795*
>
> **Major Subtype #2:** *16 Stars Obverse*
>
> **Most Desirable Issue(s):** *1797 16 Stars (only option)*
>
> **Major Subtype #3:** *13 Stars Obverse*
>
> **Most Desirable Issue(s):** *1798 (only option)*

Issuing Mint: All Capped Bust Right Half Eagles with Small Eagle Reverse were struck in the Philadelphia Mint. If you are assembling a set by issuing mint, therefore, you need to acquire only a single representative of this series.

Proof Type Set

For all intents and purposes, the Capped Bust Right Half Eagle with Small Eagle Reverse is unobtainable in proof format. There is, nonetheless, a 1795 Small Eagle certified Specimen-64 at NGC (May/2007). As far as I know, that coin has never been offered for sale.

Assembling a Complete Set

Year Set: In order to build a complete year set of this type, you must acquire four coins. Enough patience and at least $215,000 are sufficient to purchase one example each of the 1795 Small Eagle, 1796/5 and 1797 (probably the 15 Stars variety) in AU-58. To this total, however, you will have to add at least $300,000 to obtain a 1798 Small Eagle. With that amount, however, you can only realistically acquire one of the two EF examples listed at PCGS and NGC (May/2007) should they become available for purchase.

Date and Mint Set: To expand a complete year set of Small Eagle Capped Bust Right Fives into a complete date and mint set requires only one additional coin. There are two major varieties of the 1797, and both the 15 Stars and 16 Stars are required for this strategy. Expect to pay at least $575,000 for a set that includes an EF 1798 Small Eagle and AU-55s or AU-58s for the other four issues.

Die Variety Set: This is one of the more popular early gold series among die variety collectors, but it is a very challenging set to complete. There are 18 different die marriages in the Capped Bust Right, Small Eagle Five-Dollar gold series. Potential stoppers include not only the 1798 Small Eagle, but also a unique variety of the 1797 16 Stars and at least one variety of the 1795 Small Eagle that has a surviving population of fewer than five coins. Given the effort and financial resources required to complete a date and mint set of this series, I advise skipping this strategy.

Proof Set: As previously mentioned, the Capped Bust Right Half Eagle with Small Eagle Reverse is a type that is essentially unobtainable in proof format.

A Complete Set by Issuing Mint: All issues in this series were delivered in the Philadelphia Mint. A complete set by issuing mint, therefore, is the same as a complete date and mint set.

Investing Tips

Due primarily to cost, there are relatively few collectors assembling complete sets of this early gold series. I would not, therefore, include an example of one of the rarer issues (read: 1797 16 Stars and 1798 Small Eagle) in your numismatic portfolio. Although these are famous rarities, finding a buyer is often as difficult as finding the coins themselves.

The first-year 1795 Small Eagle, however, is in a completely different category. This issue has been popular with type collectors for many years, and I suspect that the number of potential buyers will continue to increase as numismatics as a whole gains in popularity. Look for a problem-free Mint State example and expect to do well in the coming decades. Indeed, and as illustrated by PCGS and NGC-certified examples in MS-62, the 1795 Small Eagle has already been trending upward since the early 21st century.

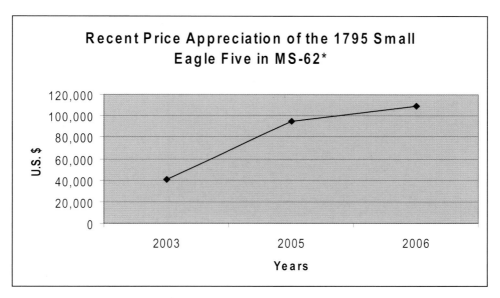

*Historic values represent prices realized for PCGS and NGC-certified examples as reported by leading numismatic auction firms.

CHAPTER SEVENTEEN

Capped Bust Right Half Eagles with Large Eagle Reverse

Courtesy of Rare Coin Wholesalers

SPECIFICATIONS

Year(s) Issued: *1797 or 1798-1807 (1795 Large Eagle coins, and possibly also the 1797 Large Eagle pieces, are backdated issues)*
Issuing Mint(s): *Philadelphia only*
Authorizing Act: *April 2, 1792*
Designer: *Robert Scot*
Weight: *8.75 grams*
Composition: *91.67% gold, 8.33% silver and copper*
Diameter: *25 millimeters (approximate)*
Edge: *Reeded*

History

The late 18th century was a dynamic time for the United States Mint. There were positive occurrences, for sure, such as the introduction of Robert Scot's new Heraldic Eagle reverse for the Capped Bust Right Half Eagle in 1797. Gone was the somewhat scrawny-looking eagle perched atop a palm branch. In its place is Scot's rendition of the Great Seal of the United States. A more powerful eagle with a shield superimposed over its breast serves as the central element of the reverse design. The eagle clutches a scroll with the motto E PLURIBUS UNUM in its beak, a bundle of arrows in its right talon and an olive branch in its left. A field of stars and an arc of clouds are above the eagle's head, and the legend UNITED STATES OF AMERICA is arranged around the border.

On the negative side, the Mint had to deal with yearly outbreaks of yellow fever during the late 1790s that forced an evacuation of Philadelphia in the fall months. These exoduses, in turn, forced a halt in coinage operations. From late August/early September through late November/early December, the Mint was unable to immediately fill orders for new coins. Thus, its employees were usually faced with a considerable backlog of warrants when they returned to their jobs at year's end. One of the denominations most frequently mentioned in these warrants was almost certainly the Half Eagle. This was the most popular gold coin among bullion depositors and those involved in export trade, and it was the denomination that they ordered in the greatest quantity.

In order to fill backdated warrants as quickly as possible and make up for time lost during the yellow fever epidemics, Mint employees grabbed whatever dies were available and struck as many Half Eagles as possible during the winter months of 1797-1798, 1798-1799 and 1799-1800. These emergency issues almost certainly explain the existence of 1795 and 1797-dated Half Eagles with the new Large Eagle reverse, as well as the 1798 Small Eagle pieces. The 1795 Large Eagle is definitely a backdated issue of 1797 and/or 1798, and the 1797 Large Eagles might also be backdated pieces from 1798.

Beginning in 1800, production of Capped Bust Right Half Eagles with Large Eagle Reverse becomes a bit less chaotic. Nevertheless, you cannot equate yearly deliveries with mintage figures for a given issue. The Mint still continued to use dies until they broke or otherwise became unusable, frequently after the calendar advanced beyond the year depicted on the obverse dies. Suitable steel was in very short supply during the late 18th and early 19th centuries, and Mint employees had to maximize usage for each die that it created.

The final Capped Bust Right Half Eagles were struck in 1807. Toward the end of that year, the Mint replaced this type with John Reich's Capped Bust Left design.

Short Type Set

Due to its close association with the Capped Bust Right Half Eagle with Small Eagle Reverse, you can highlight the Large Eagle type in one of the same short sets that I have already recommended for the preceding design.

Half Eagle Types, a nine-piece set including:
> *Capped Bust Right Half Eagle, Small Eagle Reverse*
> ***Capped Bust Right Half Eagle, Large Eagle Reverse***
> *Capped Bust Left Half Eagle*
> *Capped Head Left Half Eagle, Large Diameter*
> *Capped Head Left Half Eagle, Reduced Diameter*
> *Classic Half Eagle*
> *Liberty Half Eagle, No Motto*
> *Liberty Half Eagle, Motto*
> *Indian Half Eagle*

Capped Bust Right Gold Coinage, a six-piece set including:
> *Capped But Right Quarter Eagle, No Stars Obverse*
> *Capped Bust Right Quarter Eagle, Stars Obverse*
> *Capped Bust Right Half Eagle, Small Eagle Reverse*
> ***Capped Bust Right Half Eagle, Large Eagle Reverse***
> *Capped Bust Right Eagle, Small Eagle Reverse*
> *Capped Bust Right Eagle, Large Eagle Reverse*

Complete Type Set

For many U.S. coin series, the most readily obtainable issues are those struck during either the first year of the series or the last. This is not, however, the case with the Large Eagle Capped Bust Right Five. The "first-year" 1795 Large Eagle is a significant rarity with fewer than 50 coins surviving. The final-year 1807, while considerably more plentiful, is still not the most frequently encountered issue in this series. That honor goes to the 1806 Round Top 6, Stars 7x6. As such, this is the delivery that I recommend for gold type purposes.

Circulated Examples: By the standards of the early U.S. gold series, the 1806 Round Top 6 has a generous population of circulated survivors. Most of these coins are concentrated in the various EF and AU grades, which are attractive levels of preservation because they will usually include overall bold-to-sharp definition to the main design elements. Coins in AU often retain portions of the original mint luster, as well. An example in PCGS EF-40 sold at auction in January of 2005 for $3,450. Most AU representatives that have appeared at auction during 2006 and 2007 realized between $6,750 and $9,500.

Mint State Examples: If you specialize in higher-grade coins, I have some good news as far as this Half Eagle type is concerned. The 1806 Round Top 6 is not much more challenging to locate in Mint State than in circulated grades. In order to lessen your chances of obtaining a coin with deficient luster and/or numerous large abrasions, I advise securing an example that grades at least MS-62. A piece in that grade as certified by PCGS traded hands for $16,100 through an early 2007 auction. A PCGS MS-64 realized $46,000 in a March, 2007 sale. Gems are very rare from a condition standpoint with just two pieces graded MS-65 at PCGS and NGC combined (April/2007). The NGC-certified example appeared at auction in 2005, at which time it realized $69,000.

General Characteristics: Most high-grade 1806 Round Top 6 Half Eagles that I have handled possess thick, satiny mint luster and yellow-gold color. A few pieces have modest reflective tendencies in the fields, and color variations include green-gold and orange-gold hues. Enough well-struck coins exist that you should avoid examples with excessive lack of detail over the highpoints of the obverse portrait and the reverse eagle.

Courtesy of Bowers and Merena

A potentially desirable issue for type purposes, the 1806 Round Top 6, Stars 7x6 is the most frequently encountered Capped Bust Right Large Eagle Five in the numismatic market.

In circulated grades, be wary of coins with an inordinately large number of abrasions and/or sizeable handling marks. The latter can be particularly worrisome if they affect a key design element such as Liberty's cheek or the digits in the date on the obverse.

Words of Caution: Like its Small Eagle counterpart, the Capped Bust Right Half Eagle with Large Eagle reverse is a type that frequently displays adjustment marks on one or both sides. These as-struck features are part of the early coinage process in the U.S. Mint, and they will almost never result in a lower grade from the major third-party certification services. If you find adjustment marks particularly distracting, however, avoid coins on whose surfaces these features are present. Also be wary of early Half Eagles with adjustment marks that interfere with your ability to appreciate the major design elements.

STRATEGIES FOR INCLUDING THE CAPPED BUST RIGHT HALF EAGLE, LARGE EAGLE REVERSE IN A COMPLETE TYPE SET

Most Desirable Issue(s): *1806 Round Top 6, Stars 7x6*

Most Desirable Grade(s), Circulated Coins: *EF-40 through AU-58*

Estimated Cost: *$3,500-$10,000*

Key to Collecting: *Free of large and/or singularly distracting abrasions; few if any adjustment marks; overall bold-to-sharp definition*

Most Desirable Grade(s), Mint State Coins: *MS-62 or finer*

Estimated Cost: *$15,000 and up*

Key to Collecting: *Free of large and/or singularly distracting abrasions; few if any adjustment marks; yellow-gold, orange-gold or green-gold color; satiny mint luster; bold striking detail over the central devices*

Advanced Type Set

Rarer Issues: There are several issues in this series that I really like for better-date type purposes. These include the 1802/1, 1803/2, 1804 Normal 8 (sometimes still referred to as the Small 8), 1805 and 1807. All of these issues are rarer than the 1806 Round Top 6, but they carry similar price tags in most grades. In circulated grades, stick with coins that grade EF or AU. If you are assembling a Mint State type set, I suggest focusing on pieces certified MS-62 or finer.

STRATEGIES FOR INCLUDING THE CAPPED BUST RIGHT HALF EAGLE, LARGE EAGLE REVERSE IN A TYPE SET OF RARER ISSUES

Most Desirable Issue(s): *1802/1, 1803/2, 1804 Normal 8, 1805, 1807*

Most Desirable Grade(s), Circulated Coins: *EF-40 through AU-58*

Estimated Cost: *$4,000-$12,000*

Key to Collecting: *Free of large and/or singularly distracting abrasions; few if any adjustment marks; overall bold-to-sharp definition*

Most Desirable Grade(s), Mint State Coins: *MS-62 or finer*

Estimated Cost: *$15,000 and up*

Key to Collecting: *Free of large and/or singularly distracting abrasions; few if any adjustment marks; yellow-gold, orange-gold or green-gold color; satiny mint luster; bold striking detail over the central devices*

Major Subtypes: There are five significant design changes in this series, and each is distinguishable by the number and arrangement of stars around the obverse periphery and/ or in the reverse field above the eagle's head. Completing this set is currently impossible because one of these varieties is represented by a single coin that is impounded in the Smithsonian Institution. That coin is the 1797 Large Eagle with 16 stars on the obverse and 16 stars on the reverse.

If you are looking to obtain an example of the remaining four varieties you still have to contend with the 15 Stars obverse, 16 Stars reverse subtype. The only issues that represent this variety are the backdated 1795 Large Eagle, 1797/5 and 1797 Large Eagle, 15 Stars Obverse. All of these issues are rare and costly, a 1795 Large Eagle in PCGS AU-58 crossing the auction block at $69,000 in July of 2005. Another 1795 Large Eagle graded MS-62 at PCGS traded hands for $126,500 in early 2007.

Courtesy of Rare Coin Wholesalers

The backdated 1795 Large Eagle could serve as a representative of the 15 Stars Obverse, 16-Star Reverse subtype. Examples are costly, however, as evidenced by the sum of $126,500 realized by a PCGS MS-62 that sold through auction in early 2007.

The 13 Stars Obverse with the stars arranged 8x5 comes in two different reverse varieties. The 13-Star reverse is relatively plentiful, and you can obtain an example of the 1798 Normal 8, 1798 Large 8, 13-Star Reverse or any of the 1799-1806 issues with the exception of the 1806 Round Top 6. An 1805—one of the more frequently encountered of these issues—sold for $10,350 during a January 2007 auction. The coin was graded AU-58 by NGC at the time of sale.

The 13 Stars Obverse, Stars 8x5, 14-Star Reverse subtype is much rarer, and it is represented by only a single variety of the 1798. The Bass specimen crossed the auction block at $25,300 in 1999. The coin was certified AU-55 by NGC.

The fourth collectible subtype in this series is the 13 Stars Obverse, Stars 7x6, 13-Star Reverse. Both the 1806 Round Top 6 and the final-year 1807 represent this variety. An 1806 Round Top 6 in NGC AU-58 brought $9,775 during a January 2007 auction.

Based on the foregoing auction prices realized, you can see that it will take significant financial resources to assemble a nearly complete set of Capped Bust Right, Large Eagle Fives by major subtype. Your total expenditure for the four varieties in Choice AU is going to be at least $130,000.

STRATEGIES FOR INCLUDING THE CAPPED BUST RIGHT HALF EAGLE WITH LARGE EAGLE REVERSE IN A TYPE SET OF MAJOR SUBTYPES

Required Number of Coins: *Five*

Major Subtype #1: *15 Stars Obverse, 16 Star-Reverse*

Most Desirable Issue(s): *1795 Large Eagle*

Major Subtype #2: *16 Stars Obverse, 16 Star-Reverse*

Most Desirable Issue(s): *1797 Large Eagle, 16-Star Reverse (only option; presently unique and unobtainable for private ownership)*

Major Subtype #3: *13 Stars Obverse, Stars 8x5, 13-Star Reverse*

Most Desirable Issue(s): *1805*

Major Subtype #4: *13 Stars Obverse, Stars 8x5, 14-Star Reverse*

Most Desirable Issue(s): *1798 Large 8, 14-Star Reverse (only option)*

Major Subtype #5: *13 Stars Obverse, Stars 7x6, 13-Star Reverse*

Most Desirable Issue(s): *1806 Round Top 6, Stars 7x6*

Issuing Mint: The Philadelphia Mint struck all Half Eagles of this type.

Proof Type Set

The United States Mint did not strike any Capped Bust Right, Large Eagle Fives in proof format.

Assembling a Complete Set

Year Set: Eleven coins are required for completion of a year set of Capped Bust Right, Large Eagle Fives. This total includes the backdated issues of 1795 and 1797, and therein lies much of the potential problem should you choose to adopt this strategy. These are the two rarest dates in this series, and an example of each in AU-58 will set you back at least $150,000. Bear in mind that the 1797/5 is the only realistic option for that year since examples of both the 1797 16 Stars Obverse and 1797 15 Stars Obverse are unique and impounded in the Smithsonian Institution. As of April 2007 only two survivors of the 1797/5 have been certified AU-58 at the major grading services, both of which are listed at NGC.

Date and Mint Set: Again due to the unique 1797 16 Stars Obverse and 1797 15 Stars Obverse, it is impossible to complete this 17-piece set. It is possible, however, to assemble a nearly complete set of Capped Bust Right, Large Eagle Fives. A 15-coin partial set in AU-58 will cost a minimum of $300,000.

Die Variety Set: This is not an obtainable goal, and even the late Harry W. Bass, Jr. was unable to assemble a complete set of Capped Bust Right, Large Eagle Fives by die variety. Once again, the two unique coins that are impounded in museum collections are insurmountable roadblocks. Of the remaining 60+ die marriages, one is also unique and several are exceedingly rare with fewer than 10 coins known. Given the substantial cost of acquiring even a single Half Eagle of this type in AU-58, and the infrequency with which examples of many die varieties appear in the market, I advise concentrating your numismatic efforts in other directions.

Proof Set: As previously stated, the United States Mint did not strike any proof Half Eagles of this type.

A Complete Set by Issuing Mint: All coins of this type were struck in the Philadelphia Mint, so a complete set by issuing mint corresponds to a complete date and mint set.

Investing Tips

Obtaining a single Capped Bust Right Half Eagle with Large Eagle reverse in Mint State grade is the best way to capitalize on the most significant demand for this type in the numismatic market. Many type collectors focus on the 1806 Round Top 6, Stars 7x6 due to its relative availability. Issues that are rarer yet sell for roughly the same amount in most grades, however, are undervalued at current prices and would make a more significant addition to a portfolio. An example is the 1802/1. MS-64 is an excellent grade to obtain since it represents the highest in technical quality and eye appeal that most collectors can hope to acquire in an example of the type as a whole. As of April 2007, PCGS and NGC combined have certified 50 1806 Round Top 6 Half Eagles in MS-64, but only 33 examples of the 1802/1 in the same grade. In early 2007, an 1806 Round Top 6 in PCGS MS-64 realized $46,000 in auction, while a year earlier an 1802/1 in the same grade crossed the auction block for just $2,875 more.

CHAPTER EIGHTEEN

Capped Bust Left Half Eagles

Courtesy of Bowers and Merena

SPECIFICATIONS

Year(s) Issued: *1807-1812*
Issuing Mint(s): *Philadelphia only*
Authorizing Act: *April 2, 1792*
Designer: *John Reich*
Weight: *8.75 grams*
Composition: *91.67% gold, 8.33% silver and copper*
Diameter: *25 millimeters (approximate)*
Edge: *Reeded*

History

This is one of the shorter series in the U.S. Half Eagle family, and examples were struck for only six years from 1807-1812. Along with the Half Dollar, the Five-Dollar gold piece was the first denomination to display John Reich's Capped Bust Left design. This seems logical when one remembers that these coins were favored above all others by bullion depositors of the late 18th and early 19th centuries.

Reich's Capped Bust Left Half Eagle displays, oddly enough, a left-facing bust of Liberty on the obverse. Liberty is wearing a soft cap inscribed LIBERTY, 13 stars are arranged at the border—seven left, six right—and the date is below the bust. On the reverse, a spread-wing eagle with a shield superimposed over its breast clutches a bundle of three arrows in its left talon and an olive branch in its right. The Latin motto E PLURIBUS UNUM (Out of Many, One) is inscribed on a scroll over the eagle's head, and the legend UNITED STATES OF AMERICA is around the border. This is the first Half Eagle that includes an expression of the denomination as part of the design, with 5 D. positioned along the lower-reverse border.

John Reich engraved all of the dies that the Mint used in production of this type. His "signature," if you will, appears as a small notch on the point of star 13 that is closest to the border.

Short Type Set

Due to their rarity and corresponding cost, early U.S. gold coins are seldom featured in short type sets. These sets are traditionally reserved for types that are relatively easy to obtain in the numismatic market, such as the Liberty Half Eagle with Motto and the Saint-Gaudens Double Eagle. Nevertheless, there are significant possibilities for including a Capped Bust Left Half Eagle in a meaningful collection without assembling a complete type set of U.S. gold. I believe that two short sets are particularly suited to this purpose:

Half Eagle Types, a nine-piece set including:
> *Capped Bust Right Half Eagle, Small Eagle Reverse*
> *Capped Bust Right Half Eagle, Large Eagle Reverse*
> **Capped Bust Left Half Eagle**
> *Capped Head Left Half Eagle, Large Diameter*
> *Capped Head Left Half Eagle, Reduced Diameter*
> *Classic Half Eagle*
> *Liberty Half Eagle, No Motto*
> *Liberty Half Eagle, Motto*
> *Indian Half Eagle*

Capped Bust Left Gold Coinage, a two-piece set including:
> *Capped Bust Left Quarter Eagle*
> **Capped Bust Left Half Eagle**

The brevity of these sets camouflages the difficulty and cost that are associated with their completion. All pre-1834 Half Eagles are challenging to collect, and the Quarter Eagle counterpart to the Capped Bust Left Half Eagle is well known throughout numismatic circles as a rare, one-year type.

Complete Type Set

In my experience, the 1810 Large Date, Large 5 is the most plentiful Half Eagle of this design. The first-year 1807, 1811 Small 5 and the final-year 1812, however, are really not all that far behind in terms of availability. Any of these four issues, therefore, will serve with distinction in a type set.

Circulated Examples: As with the two preceding types in the Half Eagle series, most circulated survivors of the Capped Bust Left design grade Extremely Fine or About Uncirculated. Examples in any grade from EF-40 through AU-58 will usually have plenty of bold-to-sharp striking detail remaining, and those toward the higher end of this range possess partial mint luster. A PCGS-certified 1807 in EF-45 sold at auction for $4,600 in May of 2003. In August of 2006, an 1807 in NGC AU-58 crossed the auction block for $9,200.

Courtesy of Bowers and Merena

In the author's experience, the 1810 Large Date, Large 5 is the most frequently offered Half Eagle of this design. The first-year 1807, 1811 Small 5 and the final-year 1812, however, are really not all that far behind in terms of availability. Any of these four issues, therefore, could serve very well for type purposes. An 1812 Wide 5D in NGC MS-62 realized $12,650 at auction in April of 2006.

Mint State Examples: This is a very attractive type in Mint State grades at or the MS-63 level. With the cost of such examples in mind, however, I suggest dropping down to MS-62 to find a more affordable, yet still relatively attractive representative. An 1811 Small 5 in NGC MS-62 realized $12,650 at auction in early 2007, as did an 1812 Wide 5D in the same grade during an April 2006 sale.

In MS-63, the price for the more plentiful issues of this type moves up to the neighborhood of $20,000. There is also a realized price of $43,125 from August of 2006 for an 1810 Large Date, Large 5 in PCGS MS-64.

General Characteristics: Most examples of this type are at least boldly struck, and many are quite sharply impressed. You will not have too much difficulty locating a piece with good definition. Yellow-gold and orange-gold colors are seen most frequently, and the luster on high-grade Mint State examples is usually attractive with either a satiny or frosty texture. Occasionally, a tannish-gold or khaki-gold representative becomes available, particularly among circulated survivors. Even when worn, however, large abrasions are seldom a problem for this type, although I suggest avoiding pieces with singularly conspicuous handling marks.

Words of Caution: Adjustment marks are seen with much less frequency on survivors of the Capped Bust Left Half Eagle issues as opposed to those of the Capped Bust Right series. You should not, therefore, concern yourself with these features when searching for a suitable Capped Bust Left Half Eagle for type purposes.

STRATEGIES FOR INCLUDING THE CAPPED BUST LEFT HALF EAGLE IN A COMPLETE TYPE SET

Most Desirable Issue(s): *1807, 1810 Large Date, Large 5, 1811 Small 5, 1812*

Most Desirable Grade(s), Circulated Coins: *EF-40 through AU-58*

Estimated Cost: *$4,500-$9,500*

Key to Collecting: *Free of large and/or singularly conspicuous abrasions; bold-to-sharp definition; yellow-gold, orange-gold or tan-gold color*

Most Desirable Grade(s), Mint State Coins: *MS-62 or finer*

Estimated Cost: *$13,000 and up*

Key to Collecting: *Yellow-gold or orange-gold color; relatively vibrant satin or frosty luster for the assigned grade; bold, if not sharp striking detail*

Advanced Type Set

Rarer Issues: Although a bit rarer than issues such as the 1807 and 1810 Large Date, Large 5, the 1808/7 is still encountered fairly regularly in today's market. This issue will make a desirable addition to a better-date type set, and it is also important as one of only two overdates in this series. An example in NGC AU-55 traded hands for $8,050 in January of 2006, an NGC AU-58 sold for $10,925 in early 2007 and a coin certified MS-63 at the same service crossed the auction block for $31,625 in late 2006.

The 1808/7 typically displays deeper color than many other issues in the Capped Bust Left series. Orange-gold and khaki-gold coins are seen most often, although pieces with medium yellow-gold overtones do turn up now and then.

STRATEGIES FOR INCLUDING THE CAPPED BUST LEFT HALF EAGLE IN A TYPE SET OF RARER ISSUES

Most Desirable Issue(s): *1808/7*

Most Desirable Grade(s), Circulated Coins: *EF-40 through AU-58*

Estimated Cost: *$5,000-$13,000*

Key to Collecting: *Free of large and/or singularly conspicuous abrasions; bold-to-sharp definition; orange-gold or khaki-gold color*

Most Desirable Grade(s), Mint State Coins: *MS-62 or finer*

Estimated Cost: *$25,000 and up*

Key to Collecting: *Orange-gold or khaki-gold color; relatively vibrant satin or frosty luster for the assigned grade; bold, if not sharp striking detail*

Major Subtypes: There are no significant design changes in the Capped Bust Left Half Eagle series of 1807-1812. There are different sizes for the date and the numeral 5 in the reverse denomination, however, but this variation is due only to the use of different digit punches during the die preparation process.

Issuing Mint: Since all Half Eagles of this design were struck in the Philadelphia Mint, a single example will suffice to complete a gold type set by issuing mint.

Proof Type Set

The Capped Bust Left Half Eagle is unknown in proof format.

Assembling a Complete Set

Year Set: As a short series with no major rarities, the Capped Bust Left Half Eagle is attractive for the purpose of assembling a year set. Only six coins are required to complete this task, and you should assemble this set using examples of each of the following issues: 1807; 1808; 1809/8; 1810 Large Date, Large 5; 1811 Small 5; 1812. Selecting coins that grade AU-58 will result in a total cost of at least $52,000.

Date and Mint Set: Not all that dissimilar from a year set in scope, a date and mint set of Capped Bust Left Half Eagles requires the addition of five more coins to illustrate the 1808/7 overdate and the different-size digit punches used in 1810 and 1811. The two potential stoppers to completing this task are the 1810 Small Date, Small 5 and the 1810 Large Date, Small 5. Expect to pay more than $100,000 just to acquire examples of both of these varieties in AU-55.

Die Variety Set: There are only 15 confirmed die marriages in this six-year series. Once again, both Small 5 varieties of the 1810 delivery will cause you to pause before forging ahead with this strategy. Even excluding these two die marriages, however, I do not recommend this strategy for most collectors. The series as a whole is rare and individual examples of even the most plentiful varieties command significant premiums due to their significance as type coins.

Proof Set: This type is not eligible for inclusion in a type set of proof gold coinage because the Mint did not strike any examples with that finish.

A Complete Set by Issuing Mint: All issues in this series were delivered in the Philadelphia Mint. A complete set by issuing mint, therefore, is the same as a complete date and mint set.

Investing Tips

I find this type highly attractive in the finer Mint State grades, and such pieces are also conditionally rare and in very limited supply. Given that certified populations fall off precipitately above MS-64, you should consider adding an example in that grade to your numismatic portfolio. The more plentiful issues such as 1807 and 1810 Large Date, Large 5 appear most often in MS-64, and a lovely PCGS-certified 1807 sold at auction for $31,625 in March 2007. Examples have realized more in recent years, including an 1810 Large Date, Large 5 in PCGS MS-64 that brought $43,125 in an August 2006 sale.

CHAPTER NINETEEN

Large Diameter Capped Head Left Half Eagles

Courtesy of Rare Coin Wholesalers

SPECIFICATIONS

Year(s) Issued: *1813-1829*
Issuing Mint(s): *Philadelphia only*
Authorizing Act: *April 2, 1792*
Designer: *John Reich*
Weight: *8.75 grams*
Composition: *91.67% gold, 8.33% silver and copper*
Diameter: *25 millimeters (approximate)*
Edge: *Reeded*

History

Little has been written either by contemporary Mint employees or numismatic scholars about the exact reason for the early demise of the Capped Bust Left Half Eagle and its replacement with the Capped Head Left design in 1813. It is tempting to assume that public criticism over the former design resulted in its early retirement. If this were true, however, then why did modified versions of the Capped Bust motif remain in use on the Half Dollar through 1839?

We may never know exactly why John Reich altered the obverse design of the Half Eagle in 1813, but alter it he did. In place of a left-facing bust of Liberty there is now a left-facing head. Liberty is still wearing a soft cap with the inscription LIBERTY along its base. The date is still below, but 13 stars now encircle the periphery instead of being divided by the portrait. The reverse design of the Capped Head Left Five is essentially the same as that of its predecessor, although close examination will reveal a few light refinements to the eagle.

Reich engraved the dies for the Capped Head Left Half Eagles produced from 1813 through 1815, as evidenced by his signature notch on the point of star 13 that is closest to the border. The United States Mint did not strike any Half Eagles dated 1816 or 1817, and Reich left federal employment in the latter year. Beginning in 1818, Chief Engraver Robert Scot engraved the dies for this series, although he died in 1823 and was replaced in his post by William Kneass. While the latter gentleman probably engraved the dies for this type beginning in 1823, the possibility also exists that Christian Gobrecht executed some or all of the work. Gobrecht began working for the Mint in the 1820s in a contract capacity. He assumed most of Kneass' duties after the latter suffered a debilitating stroke in 1835 and was eventually elevated to the position of chief engraver in 1840.

All Half Eagles produced from 1813 through early 1829 were struck in an open collar. This device did not allow for uniformity of diameter and the execution of the devices in particularly high relief. In these ways the early Capped Head Left Half Eagles differ from their counterparts introduced later in 1829 and delivered through May of 1834.

The Large Diameter Capped Head Left Half Eagle is one of the most challenging types to collect in all of U.S. numismatics, and this statement is not confined merely to the gold denominations. Yearly mintage figures are actually quite generous for the era, and the type as a whole was produced in significantly greater numbers than the Capped Bust Left series. Why, then, are Large Diameter Capped Head Left Fives such elusive coins in today's market? The answer to this riddle is widespread melting.

Immense quantities of silver flooded the world market from Mexican and Latin American mines beginning in the early 19th century, gradually upsetting the delicate balance between silver and gold on the world market. By the early 1820s, the price of gold reckoned in silver had risen to the point where U.S. gold coins were no longer seen in domestic circulation. Most Large Diameter Capped Head Left Half Eagles, therefore, were shipped overseas and eventually melted. Many examples that initially remained stateside as part of bank reserves were also exported through the mid-1830s by bullion dealers and speculators, these coins again meeting with destruction overseas. Beginning in 1834, countless other pieces that were still within the United States' borders may have been returned to the Mint and melted to provide bullion for the coinage of the new, lighter-weight Classic Quarter Eagles and Half Eagles. Very few Large Diameter Capped Head Left Fives of all issues escaped one of these possible fates and survived to the present day.

Short Type Set

If you succeed in including a problem-free example of this type among your holdings, you will have accomplished a significant numismatic feat. Limitations imposed by time or financial resources should not serve as an impediment to placing a Large Diameter Capped Head Left Half Eagle in a meaningful set. There are actually two short type sets in which this series figures prominently, and they are organized either along denominational lines or based upon similarity of the coins' designs.

Half Eagle Types, a nine-piece set including:

Capped Bust Right Half Eagle, Small Eagle Reverse
Capped Bust Right Half Eagle, Large Eagle Reverse
Capped Bust Left Half Eagle

Capped Head Left Half Eagle, Large Diameter
Capped Head Left Half Eagle, Reduced Diameter
Classic Half Eagle
Liberty Half Eagle, No Motto
Liberty Half Eagle, Motto
Indian Half Eagle

Capped Head Left Gold Coinage, a four-piece set including:

Capped Head Left Quarter Eagle, Large Diameter
Capped Head Left Quarter Eagle, Reduced Diameter
Capped Head Left Half Eagle, Large Diameter
Capped Head Left Half Eagle, Reduced Diameter

Complete Type Set

By a wide margin, the first-year 1813 is the most plentiful Half Eagle of this type in numismatic circles. Apparently, the contemporary public set aside a fair number of examples as novelties, and then developed enough of an affinity for the coins to save them from being melted in later years. You should not make the mistake of classifying the 1813 as a common coin, however, for the word "common" has no place in a discussion of any pre-1834 U.S. gold issue. Nevertheless, the 1813 is the most realistic type candidate in this series.

Courtesy of Bowers and Merena

In addition to its first-year status, the 1813 is a popular issue for type purposes because it exists in greater numbers than any other Half Eagle of the Capped Head Left, Large Diameter design.

Circulated Examples: Half Eagles of this type did not circulate to an appreciable degree. Most examples that have survived did so by remaining in bank reserves or, to a lesser extent, private holdings. Indeed, the vast majority of circulated 1813 Half Eagles that have survived grade AU-50 through AU-58. Examples in those grades are costlier than coins in EF or VF, but they have significant advantages over lower-grade pieces. Coins that grade at least AU-50 possess only light wear, and their surfaces retain overall bold striking detail and partial mint luster.

You will pay at least $6,500 for an 1813 Half Eagle in AU-50. An example in that grade as certified by PCGS sold for $6,900 in a February 2007 auction. One month prior to that sale, an NGC AU-58 crossed the auction block at $8,050.

Mint State Examples: The rarity of this type as a whole suggests that any Mint State example will make an impressive addition to your numismatic holdings. Since gold coins in MS-60 and MS-61 are often noticeably abraded and/or possessed of inferior luster, I still believe that you should obtain an 1813 Half Eagle that grades at least MS-62. Even at that level of preservation, however, be wary of coins that possess individually distracting abrasions, particularly if they are located in a prime focal area such as Liberty's cheek or in the obverse field before the portrait.

Three PCGS MS-62s sold at auction in January and February of 2007 for $12,650 each. In Mint State-63, the 1813 costs approximately $20,000. The price nearly doubles in MS-64, as evidenced by a pair of near-Gems (one certified by PCGS and the other by NGC) that traded hands for $40,250 and $46,000 during an August, 2006 sale. Coins that grade MS-65 or finer are exceedingly rare, and they number just seven pieces at the major certification services (April/2007). The single highest-graded survivor of this issue is a PCGS MS-66 that realized $230,000 at auction in January of 2005 and $316,250 exactly two years later.

General Characteristics: Most high-grade 1813 Half Eagles are sharply struck, and I advise avoiding the occasional example that is noticeably soft over the eagle's talons and at the junction of the left shield border and the eagle's right shoulder. The luster is usually satiny in texture and quite thick when fully intact and vibrant. Color is predominantly yellow-gold or orange-gold, sometimes with warmer green-gold undertones evident as the surfaces turn away from a direct light source. An excessive number of distracting abrasions is seldom a problem for this issue even in the various grades, and sizeable marks are also seldom seen. Nevertheless, keep a look out for examples that do possess these detractions so that you can avoid them in favor of a more desirable coin.

Words of Caution: Many circulated 1813 Half Eagles are impaired from having been mounted as jewelry. Still others have been cleaned. The rarity and consequent cost of the issue might make discounted examples seem attractive. I believe, however, that you should focus only on problem-free survivors that possess solid technical quality for the assigned grade and pleasing eye appeal. These are the pieces that enjoy the greatest level of current demand from type collectors, and they are the coins that have the best chance of appreciating in value in the coming years.

STRATEGIES FOR INCLUDING THE LARGE DIAMETER CAPPED HEAD LEFT HALF EAGLE IN A COMPLETE TYPE SET

Most Desirable Issue(s): *1813*

Most Desirable Grade(s), Circulated Coins: *AU-50 through AU-58*

Estimated Cost: *$6,500-$8,500*

Key to Collecting: *Free of large and/or singularly conspicuous abrasions; overall bold, if not sharp striking detail; portions of the original luster still intact*

Most Desirable Grade(s), Mint State Coins: *MS-62 or finer*

Estimated Cost: *$13,000 and up*

Key to Collecting: *Yellow-gold, orange-gold or green-gold color; satiny mint luster; sharply struck devices*

Advanced Type Set

Rarer Issues: After the first-year 1813, the most frequently encountered Half Eagles of this type are those dated 1814/3, 1818 and 1820. Each of these deliveries is still significantly rarer than the 1813 and, as such, they are attractive for better-date type purposes.

Costs for these three issues vary depending on the date as well as the individual die marriage. An 1818 with STATESOF as one word on the reverse sold for $9,488 through a May 2004 auction. The coin was certified AU-58 by NGC at the time of sale. Graded MS-62 by PCGS, an 1814/3 brought $23,000 when it appeared at auction in early 2007.

STRATEGIES FOR INCLUDING THE LARGE DIAMETER CAPPED HEAD LEFT HALF EAGLE IN A TYPE SET OF RARER ISSUES

Most Desirable Issue(s): *1814/3, 1818, 1820*

Most Desirable Grade(s), Circulated Coins: *AU-50 through AU-58*

Estimated Cost: *$6,500 and up*

Key to Collecting: *Free of large and/or singularly conspicuous abrasions; overall bold, if not sharp striking detail; portions of the original luster still intact*

Most Desirable Grade(s), Mint State Coins: *MS-62 or finer*

Estimated Cost: *$23,000 and up*

Key to Collecting: *Yellow-gold, orange-gold or green-gold color; satiny mint luster; sharply struck devices*

Major Subtypes: Although Robert Scot and William Kneass (or Christian Gobrecht) prepared new device punches for Liberty's portrait in 1818 and 1823, respectively, the differences between these two variations and Reich's original design are minor and easily overlooked except perhaps by dedicated students of the series. For all intents and purposes, therefore, there are no major design changes in this series.

Issuing Mint: As with the preceding three series of United States Half Eagle, the Large Diameter Capped Head Left is a product of only the Philadelphia Mint. You need acquire just one coin to represent this series in an advanced type collection by issuing mint.

Proof Type Set

The subject of proof Large Diameter Capped Head Left Half Eagles is a tricky one, as prooflike examples are known for some issues. A few of these pieces have been classified as proofs in the past. For all intents and purposes, however, true proofs of this type are not available for private ownership as none have been certified by PCGS or NGC (May/2007).

Assembling a Complete Set

Assembling a complete set of this type using any strategy is a task that is beyond the reach of virtually all collectors. There are three exceedingly rare issues that, on their own, are sufficient for me to steer you away from specializing in this series. The 1815 has a surviving population of fewer than 12 coins, and an example in an NGC MS-62 holder for $165,000 in 1999.

Another significant stopper in this series is the 1822—one of the rarest and most famous of all United States gold coins. Only three examples are known, two of which are impounded in the Smithsonian Institution. The third was formerly part of the Eliasberg Collection and was auctioned in 1982 for $687,500. The coin now resides in an NGC EF-40 holder and would probably fetch several million dollars were it to appear in the market of the early 21st century. Finally, the 1829 Large Diameter has an extant population of fewer than 10 coins. An example graded MS-65 by PCGS crossed the auction block in 1999 for $241,500.

Additional world-famous rarities in this series include the 1825/4 (only two examples known) and 1828/7 (no more than five coins survive). There are several other individual die varieties in the Large Diameter Capped Head Left Half Eagle series that are either unique or have surviving populations of fewer than 10 coins.

Investing Tips

Some coins are so rare and so costly as to preclude a large following among collectors. This is certainly the case for the Large Diameter Capped Head Left Half Eagle series, in which many issues and/or die varieties appeal to only a select group of highly specialized and well-funded collectors. Nevertheless, all serious gold type collectors are going to have to tackle this series at some point if they are to complete their sets, and here is where you will find the best investment opportunity in this series. Mint State 1813 Half Eagles appear in the market often enough to present numerous buying opportunities each year. As a first-year issue with the largest surviving population in the series, the 1813 has long enjoyed strong demand among type collectors. Given the impressive eye appeal that high-quality examples possess, as well as the extreme rarity of coins that grade any finer, I suggest obtaining a coin that grades MS-64. This is the highest grade that most collectors will be able to acquire in a Half Eagle of this type and, if their numismatic goals dictate a high-quality representative, relative availability and cost means that they will have to target the 1813.

CHAPTER TWENTY

Reduced Diameter Capped Head Left Half Eagles

Courtesy of Bowers and Merena

SPECIFICATIONS

Year(s) Issued: *1829-1834*
Issuing Mint(s): *Philadelphia only*
Authorizing Act: *April 2, 1792*
Designer: *William Kneass, after John Reich*
Weight: *8.75 grams*
Composition: *91.67% gold, 8.33% silver and copper*
Diameter: *23.8 millimeters*
Edge: *Reeded*

History

The initial press run for this type corresponds to introduction of new technology in the United States Mint. In 1829, Mint employees started using a close collar to strike Half Eagles. This innovative piece of equipment allowed the production of coins with a uniform diameter. In addition to this feature, Half Eagles of this type differ from their Large Diameter counterparts in that they possess beaded borders, raised rims, more intricate detail to the devices and smaller letters, stars and dates. These modifications were carried out by Chief Engraver William Kneass.

Reduced Diameter Capped Head Left Half Eagles were produced from 1829 through 1834 during a time when U.S. gold coins were no longer seen in domestic circulation. High gold prices on the world market meant that the bullion value of these coins outstripped their face value from the day they were struck. Most examples of this type, therefore, were immediately exported, and few escaped being melted overseas to return to the United States. All issues exist in very limited quantities in today's market—a fact that confirms this type as one of the most difficult to collect in all of numismatics.

The second Philadelphia Mint was completed in 1833 by architect William Strickland. The first Half Eagles struck in this facility were examples of the now exceedingly rare Capped Head Left type with Reduced Diameter. (Image Courtesy of *Philly*History.org, a project of the Philadelphia Department of Records)

Short Type Set

I can think of only two short sets of U.S. gold coins that highlight this rare Half Eagle design.

Half Eagle Types, a nine-piece set including:

Capped Bust Right Half Eagle, Small Eagle Reverse
Capped Bust Right Half Eagle, Large Eagle Reverse
Capped Bust Left Half Eagle
Capped Head Left Half Eagle, Large Diameter
Capped Head Left Half Eagle, Reduced Diameter
Classic Half Eagle
Liberty Half Eagle, No Motto
Liberty Half Eagle, Motto
Indian Half Eagle

Capped Head Left Gold Coinage, a four-piece set including:

Capped Head Left Quarter Eagle, Large Diameter
Capped Head Left Quarter Eagle, Reduced Diameter
Capped Head Left Half Eagle, Large Diameter
Capped Head Left Half Eagle, Reduced Diameter

Complete Type Set

No issue in this series appears in the market on a regular basis, and none readily present themselves for type purposes. Three issues that are appreciably rarer than the others are the first-year 1829, 1832 Curl Base 2, 12 Stars and the final-year 1834 Crosslet 4. This leaves the balance of the issues in the series as the most realistic type candidates.

Circulated Examples: Since this series did not circulate domestically, and most examples were hoarded and melted, examples are rarely encountered with extensive wear. With so few worn survivors (PCGS and NGC have certified just 67 coins in all grades from VF through AU-58, April/2007), this is one type for which you should not place too much emphasis on numeric designation. Instead, acquire an example that you find attractive and that fits into your budget.

An 1834 Plain 4 in PCGS VF-30 sold at auction for $19,550 in early 2004. The same coin would have brought closer to $22,000 had it appeared at auction in early 2007. An 1830 Large 5D in NGC EF-40 that sold in July of 2005 traded hands for $29,900. Another 1830 Large 5D, this time an NGC AU-58, commanded $54,625 from the winning bidder when it was offered in a March 2007 sale.

Mint State Examples: Even taking into account the possibility of resubmissions, Mint State Reduced Diameter Capped Head Left Half Eagles are actually more plentiful than circulated pieces in today's market. These are still very rare coins in an absolute sense, however, the two major grading services having certified just 143 survivors of all issues from MS-60 through MS-67 (April/2007). Once again, rarity and the infrequency with which these coins trade means that you should not place too much emphasis on numeric designation. Of course, higher grades are always accompanied by stronger technical quality and eye appeal. If you find a lower-grade Mint State coin with which you are happy and that is a comfortable fit with your budget, however, there is no reason why you should not acquire the piece for your type set.

Even in the lowest Mint State grades, Reduced Diameter Capped Head Left Half Eagles command a significant premium. An 1831 in NGC MS-61 changed hands for $55,200 at an early 2005 auction. The price climbs rapidly as you progress up the grading scale, as evidenced by a lovely 1830 Large 5D in PCGS MS-64 that sold for $126,500 during January of 2007.

General Characteristics: Half Eagles of this type usually possess semi or fully prooflike luster. Green-gold and orange-gold colors are seen quite often, with yellow-gold and reddish-gold shades much less prevalent. Most survivors are sharply struck, although I have seen several examples with slightly uneven definition. Circulated and low-grade Mint State pieces are usually scuffy, but individually conspicuous abrasions are seldom a problem for this type.

Words of Caution: Due to the extreme rarity of this type, I recommend any problem-free example in a PCGS or NGC holder. If you are in the market for a type coin and an attractive Reduced Diameter Capped Head Left Eagle in your price range becomes available, buy the coin without hesitation. There are very few examples of this type in numismatic circles, and many are already off the market in tightly held collections or portfolios.

STRATEGIES FOR INCLUDING THE REDUCED DIAMETER CAPPED HEAD LEFT HALF EAGLE IN A COMPLETE TYPE SET

Most Desirable Issue(s): *1830 Small 5D, 1830 Large 5D, 1831 Small 5D, 1831 Large 5D, 1832 Square Base 2, 13 Stars, 1833 Large Date, 1833 Small Date, 1834 Plain 4*

Most Desirable Grade(s), Circulated Coins: *VF through AU-58*

Estimated Cost: *$19,000 and up*

Key to Collecting: *Overall bold, if not sharp striking detail; portions of the original luster still intact on coins that grade EF-45 or finer*

Most Desirable Grade(s), Mint State Coins: *MS-60 or finer*

Estimated Cost: *$50,000 and up*

Key to Collecting: *Orange-gold or green-gold color; sharp striking detail; semi or fully prooflike luster*

Advanced Type Set

Rarer Issues: Not as rare as the 1829 Reduced Diameter or 1832 12 Stars, yet a bit more elusive than the other issues in this series, the 1834 Crosslet 4 is highly recommended for advanced type purposes. Bear in mind, however, that only 17 examples have been certified in all grades by PCGS and NGC (April/2007). Only five of these coins are circulated, and they range in grade from EF-40 through AU-58; the rest are Mint State. An NGC MS-62 realized $71,875 in an auction conducted in late 2006, and a coin certified MS-64 by the same service went to the winning bidder at $109,250 during an early 2007 sale.

As a word of caution, many Crosslet 4 1834 Capped Head Left Fives are softly struck over the obverse stars with many of the radial lines indistinct. Even such pieces, however, will usually possess bold-to-sharp striking detail over the balance of the devices.

STRATEGIES FOR INCLUDING THE REDUCED DIAMETER CAPPED HEAD LEFT HALF EAGLE IN A TYPE SET OF RARER ISSUES

Most Desirable Issue(s): *1834 Crosslet 4*

Most Desirable Grade(s), Circulated Coins: *EF-40 through AU-58*

Estimated Cost: *$27,000 and up*

Key to Collecting: *Overall bold, if not sharp striking detail; portions of the original luster still intact on coins that grade EF-45 or finer*

Most Desirable Grade(s), Mint State Coins: *MS-61 or finer*

Estimated Cost: *$65,000 and up*

Key to Collecting: *Orange-gold or green-gold color; sharp striking detail in most areas; semi or fully prooflike luster*

Major Subtypes: There are no significant design changes in this series, the type remaining the same from its inception in 1829 through 1834. The 1832 12 Stars represents a blundered die error on the part of the engraver and not a distinct subtype.

Issuing Mint: All Half Eagles of this design were struck in the Philadelphia Mint, so there is no way to expand a gold type set by including mintmarked examples.

Proof Type Set

The 1831 and 1834 Capped Head Left are currently unknown in proof, and the only verified proofs of the 1829 Reduced Diameter issue are impounded in museum collections. In terms of coins available for private ownership, the 1830 and 1832 are unique. If you are a proof gold type collector, therefore, the only realistic option as far as the Reduced Diameter Capped Head Left Half Eagle is concerned is the 1833. Even that is a rare issue, however, with just five coins certified at PCGS and NGC (April/2007). The PCGS Proof-67 is a Large Date example that was formerly part of the John Jay Pittman Collection. The coin sold for $977,500 in a later auction conducted in January of 2005.

Assembling a Complete Set

Year Set: It is possible to complete a year set of Reduced Diameter Capped Head Left Half Eagles, but the task will be very difficult. In fact, I only recommend this strategy for collectors with uncommonly deep pockets. The first-year 1829 Reduced Diameter is the most difficult to obtain, as I am aware of fewer than 15 survivors in all grades. In Mint State, this issue costs at least $300,000.

For the balance of the set, you need to include one example each of the following issues: 1830 (Large 5D or Small 5D); 1831 (probably Large 5D); 1832 Curl Base 2, 13 Stars; 1833 (Large Date or Small Date); and 1834 Plain 4. In MS-64, each of these issues will set you back $110,000 or more.

Date and Mint Set: Due to the considerable cost involved in assembling a year set of this type, I do not recommend trying to acquire two examples each of the 1830, 1831, 1832, 1833 and 1834 to represent the different date logotypes and device punches. With the exception of early gold variety specialists with considerable financial resources, this is not a popular collecting strategy for this type.

Die Variety Set: The same also applies to a die variety set of this type—the cost of acquiring a single example of a "common" die marriage is the most that the majority of collectors should consider spending on the Reduced Diameter Capped Head Left Half Eagle. What's more, it is currently impossible to complete a variety set for this series because one variety of the 1834 Crosslet 4 is unique. That coin is impounded in the Harry W. Bass, Jr. Core Collection. Three other die marriages have surviving populations of fewer than 10 coins, and then there's always the key-date 1829 to consider.

Proof Set: As previously stated, not all issues in this series are known in proof format, and the only confirmed examples of the 1829 are impounded in museum collections. You could, nevertheless, acquire one example each of the 1830, 1832 and 1833, although the cost is prohibitive. Remember, the Pittman specimen of the proof 1833 Half Eagle commanded a winning bid of $977,500 when it sold at auction in early 2005. In addition, the proof 1830 and 1832 are unique in private hands.

A Complete Set by Issuing Mint: All issues in this series were delivered in the Philadelphia Mint. Since there are no major varieties, a year set also functions as a complete set by issuing mint.

Investing Tips

This is another series that is a thorn in the side of many gold type collectors. As such, the Reduced Diameter variant of the Capped Head Left Half Eagle offers considerable investment opportunities. Anyone wishing to complete a type set of U.S. gold coinage needs to acquire an example of this design, but there are precious few examples in all grades from which to choose. You would do very well by acquiring the highest-grade example that your budget will allow and "sitting on the coin" as it matures over the course of five or more years. By taking even a single coin off the market, you will contribute to the perceived rarity of this type and, therefore, help to promote significant price appreciation.

Under the right market conditions, I believe that Mint State Reduced Capped Head Left Half Eagles will outperform their circulated counterparts. Mint State coins possess stronger technical and aesthetic merits, which almost always translate into greater demand in numismatic circles.

CHAPTER TWENTY ONE

Classic Half Eagles

Courtesy of Bowers and Merena

SPECIFICATIONS

Year(s) Issued: *1834-1838*
Issuing Mint(s): *Philadelphia, Charlotte, Dahlonega*
Authorizing Act: *June 28, 1834 and January 18, 1837*
Designer: *William Kneass*
Weight: *8.36 grams*
Composition:
    1834-1836: *89.92% gold, 10.08% silver and copper*
    1837-1839: *90% gold, 10% silver and copper*
Diameter: *22.5 millimeters*
Edge: *Reeded*

History

The year 1834 was a pivotal one for the United States Half Eagle series. For more than a decade, vast quantities of silver flooded the world market from Mexican and Latin American mines. As the price of gold reckoned in silver rose, the bullion value of Half Eagles eventually outstripped the coins' face value. By the early 1830s, the situation had become so egregious that newly minted examples of the Reduced Diameter Capped Head Left design never even reached general circulation. The coins were hoarded, and many were exported and eventually melted overseas. Clearly, the federal government had to do something to correct a situation in which merchants and bullion dealers were having difficulty procuring gold coins for commercial use. In addition, there was a continual drain on the nation's gold supply as newly minted coins immediately left the country.

In 1834, Congress finally acted by reducing the weight and fineness of the Half Eagle. The vehicle of the legislature's change is the Mint Act of June 28, 1834. After its passage, Half Eagles were required to weigh 8.36 grams instead of the previously acceptable 8.75 grams. The new composition was set at 89.92% gold, 10.08% silver and copper, although this was modified again in 1837 to 90% gold, 10% copper.

Such profound changes to the composition necessitated a new design for the Half Eagle, one that would be easily distinguished from its predecessors and allow the contemporary public to readily identify pieces struck to the new specifications. Calling upon the talents of Chief Engraver William Kneass, the Mint began delivery of Classic Half Eagles on August 1, 1834—the effective date of the new Mint Act.

As with most of his "new" designs, Kneass relied on the work of his predecessors when creating the Classic Half Eagle. A portrait of Liberty once again faces left on the obverse with 13 stars arranged around the border and the date below. Gone, however, is the soft cap that, in one form or another, had been atop Liberty's head since the denomination's inception in 1795. Instead, Liberty is wearing a headband inscribed LIBERTY, the top of her head adorned with curly locks. The reverse is even more similar to that used for the Capped Head Left series, although apparently Mint personnel felt that the removal of the Latin motto E PLURIBUS UNUM from the field above the eagle's head was sufficient to distinguish the new type.

The Dahlonega Mint as pictured in an 1872 engraving. The facility produced Gold Dollars, Quarter Eagles and Half Eagles from 1838 until the start of the Civil War in 1861. The first Half Eagles struck within its walls were 20,583 examples of the Classic type. (Public Domain Image)

Using this design, the Philadelphia Mint struck greater numbers of Half Eagles from 1834-1838 then in any previous year. The destruction of old tenor gold coins that had either been returned to the Mint or were retained at the time of striking provided much of the bullion for these issues. This is particularly true of the 1834 and 1835 deliveries. The newly opened branch mints in Charlotte and Dahlonega also delivered limited quantities of Classic Half Eagles during the series' final year. The mintmark position is on the obverse in the field between the date and the truncation of Liberty's portrait. With the exception of the 1839-C and 1839-D Liberty, the 1838-C and 1838-D Classic are the only Half Eagles that carry the mintmark on the obverse.

PCGS and NGC have certified proofs for each year in this series except 1837 and 1838, although the latter service does report an 1838 graded Specimen-65 (April/2007).

The 1834, 1835 and 1836 are exceedingly rare in proof format with only a handful of examples known.

Short Type Set

I have not met many numismatists that are assembling short type sets of United States gold coins that could include a Classic Half Eagle. Nevertheless, there are two sets that require an example of this type:

Half Eagle Types, a nine-piece set including:

> *Capped Bust Right Half Eagle, Small Eagle Reverse*
> *Capped Bust Right Half Eagle, Large Eagle Reverse*
> *Capped Bust Left Half Eagle*
> *Capped Head Left Half Eagle, Large Diameter*
> *Capped Head Left Half Eagle, Reduced Diameter*
> ***Classic Half Eagle***
> *Liberty Half Eagle, No Motto*
> *Liberty Half Eagle, Motto*
> *Indian Half Eagle*

Classic Gold Coinage, a two-piece set including:

> *Classic Quarter Eagle*
> ***Classic Half Eagle***

Complete Type Set

The Classic Half Eagle is much more plentiful in today's market than any of the preceding types in the United States Half Eagle series. As such, you will have a much easier time locating a suitable example for inclusion in a type set. The best type candidates are the 1834 Plain 4, which is popular as a first-year issue, and the 1835 and 1836.

Circulated Examples: Unlike examples of the Capped Head Left design, Classic Half Eagles saw considerable circulation. Many circulated 1834 Plain 4, 1835 and 1836 Classic Half Eagles have survived, and with patience they can be found in almost any grade. In order to obtain a coin with much of the original striking detail remaining and portions of the mint luster still intact, I suggest focusing solely on the AU-55 and AU-58 grades. Based on auction prices realized from 2006-2007 for PCGS and NGC-certified examples, you will need to pay somewhere between $1,600 and $2,300 to obtain an 1834 Plain 4 in AU-55. In October of 2006, an 1834 Plain 4 in NGC AU-58 crossed the auction block for $3,220.

Mint State Examples: This is a very attractive type in Mint State, although lower-end pieces in MS-60 and MS-61 often possess inferior luster and/or an excessive number of distracting abrasions. For this reason, try to obtain a coin that grades at least MS-62.

Even through MS-63, however, this type is not always showcased in the best light. Some of the most attractive 19th century gold coins that I have ever handled are Classic Half Eagles that grade MS-64. These coins are often brightly lustrous with frosty or semi-prooflike surfaces, sharp striking detail and a minimum number of wispy handling marks. In March of 2007, an 1834 Plain 4 in NGC MS-64 crossed the auction block at $13,800.

If such a price of too rich for your blood, there are certainly many desirable Classic Half Eagles in MS-62 and MS-63. An 1836 in PCGS MS-62 sold for $6,038 during a November 2006 auction, while an 1835 certified MS-63 by NGC realized $10,925 in late 2005.

Courtesy of Bowers and Merena

The circulated type collector should be able to acquire an 1834 Plain 4, 1835 or 1836 Classic Half Eagle in almost any worn grade with more-or-less patience. In order to obtain a coin with much of the original striking detail remaining and even portions of the mint luster still intact, however, one might want to focus solely on the AU-55 and AU-58 grades.

Courtesy of Bowers and Merena

This can be a very attractive type in Mint State, although lower-end pieces in MS-60 and MS-61 often possess inferior luster and/or an excessive number of detracting abrasions. For this reason, the buyer might be well served by focusing on coins that grade at least MS-62.

General Characteristics: Half Eagles of this type are usually very well struck with bold, if not sharp definition over all elements of the design. Nevertheless, I have seen a few pieces with softer detail over the haircurls atop Liberty's brow and the eagle's left (facing) shoulder. Given the fact that examples of the 1834 Plain 4, 1835 and 1836 deliveries appear quite regularly in today's market, you should avoid pieces with a less-than-bold strike.

Examples that retain full or partial mint luster possess either a frosty or semi-prooflike texture. Color for this type ranges widely, but it is usually yellow-gold, orange-gold or green-gold in shade.

Words of Caution: This design circulated quite extensively during the 19th century, and many examples were roughly handled. Indeed, there are numerous examples in the market whose surfaces are heavily abraded. Patience will pay off, however, as there are examples in the finer AU grades whose surfaces are free of sizeable and/or individually conspicuous abrasions.

Quite a few surviving Classic Half Eagles are impaired due to scratches, cleaning or other problems. By confining your search to only those coins certified by PCGS or NGC, you can usually acquire an example that is problem free for the assigned grade. On the other hand, I distinctly remember cataloging two AU Classic Half Eagles that were certified by the leading grading services whose surfaces revealed graffiti under close inspection. This is not to disparage PCGS or NGC, for both services put out a high-quality product and employ some of the finest authenticators and graders in the numismatic market. The point is simply that graders are human like everyone else and they can make mistakes when stressed, overtired or preoccupied with life's myriad trials. I suggest closer inspection on your part when evaluating a Classic Half Eagle for potential purchase, particularly for circulated examples. Do not be afraid to use a loupe as even I have mistaken impairments such as graffiti for abrasions when looking at coins solely with the naked eye.

STRATEGIES FOR INCLUDING THE CLASSIC HALF EAGLE IN A COMPLETE TYPE SET

Most Desirable Issue(s): *1834 Plain 4, 1835 1836*

Most Desirable Grade(s), Circulated Coins: *AU-55, AU-58*

Estimated Cost: *$1,500-$3,500*

Key to Collecting: *Overall bold, if not sharp striking detail; portions of the original luster still intact; yellow-gold, orange-gold or green-gold color; no sizeable or individually distracting circulation marks*

Most Desirable Grade(s), Mint State Coins: *MS-62 or finer*

Estimated Cost: *$6,000 and up*

Key to Collecting: *Bold-to-sharp striking detail; frosty or semi-prooflike luster; yellow-gold, orange-gold or green-gold color; no sizeable or individually distracting abrasions*

Advanced Type Set

Rarer Issues: You will notice that the only Philadelphia Mint deliveries in the Classic Half Eagles series that I do not recommend for basic type purposes are the 1837 and 1838. (I consider the 1834 Crosslet 4 to be a variety of the 1834 and not a distinct issue.) Indeed, both of these issues have significantly lower mintages than the 1834, 1835 and 1836. The 1837 has an original mintage of just 207,121 pieces and the 1838 is not much higher at 286,588 pieces struck. Based on these figures, you might expect that the 1837 and 1838 are rarer than the 1834, 1835 and 1836 in all grades. This is definitely true for the 1837, and you will need to exercise considerable patience to locate a problem-free AU-55 or AU-58 for inclusion in a better-date type set. Examples in these grades start at $2,500.

Mint State 1837 Half Eagles are even rarer than circulated examples. A comparison of population data for P-mint Classic Half Eagles as reported by the two leading certification services illustrates the relative rarity of this issue in Mint State.

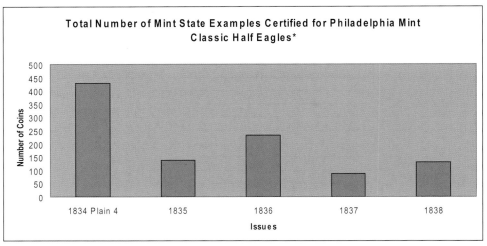

*Totals are based on combined PCGS Population and NGC Census data from www.pcgs.com and www.ngccoin.com, respectively. Websites accessed May 8, 2007.

Clearly, the 1837 has the lowest certified population in Mint State, and examples command a premium in all grades. In MS-62, a PCGS or NGC-certified coin costs at least $11,500. A beautiful PCGS MS-63 sold through an August, 2006 auction for $25,300, and the price for the issue increases sharply to $40,000+ in MS-64.

On the other hand, the above comparison suggests that the 1838 is really not all that much rarer than the 1835 in Mint State. This is a curious finding, since the 1838 usually commands a premium at or above the MS-62 grade level. (An 1835 in NGC MS-62 sold for $4,888 in November of 2005 while an 1838 in the same grade traded hands for $6,555 in a sale conducted just one year later.) The 1838 is actually a bit overrated in Mint State at current prices, and you should overlook this issue in favor of the 1837.

STRATEGIES FOR INCLUDING THE CLASSIC HALF EAGLE IN A TYPE SET OF RARER ISSUES

Most Desirable Issue(s): *1837*

Most Desirable Grade(s), Circulated Coins: *AU-55, AU-58*

Estimated Cost: *$2,500 and up*

Key to Collecting: *Overall bold, if not sharp striking detail; portions of the original luster still intact; yellow-gold, orange-gold or green-gold color; no sizeable or individually distracting circulation marks*

Most Desirable Grade(s), Mint State Coins: *MS-62 or finer*

Estimated Cost: *$11,500 and up*

Key to Collecting: *Bold-to-sharp striking detail; frosty or semi-prooflike luster; yellow-gold, orange-gold or green-gold color; no sizeable or individually distracting abrasions*

Major Subtypes: There are no major design changes in the Classic Half Eagle series, the 1834 Plain 4 and Crosslet 4 representing the use of two different date logotypes on the part of Mint employees. On the other hand, the series is similar to the Classic Quarter Eagle in that there are numerous slight modifications to Liberty's portrait throughout the series. In addition, the 1838 is known with different sizes for the reverse arrowheads. Classifying these changes as "major subtypes" or "die varieties" is a thorny problem, and researchers do not always agree. In an effort to present a balanced view, I have described the modifications to the obverse portrait in the Classic Quarter Eagle series as major design changes. For the alterations in the Classic Half Eagle series, however, I have decided to address them below under the section that deals with strategies for assembling a die variety set.

Issuing Mint: The Classic Half Eagle is the first United States gold coin of this denomination struck in more than one coinage facility. Nevertheless, the parent Mint in Philadelphia still struck most examples. The first-year 1834 Plain 4, 1835 or 1836 are all strong candidates to represent Classic Half Eagle production in the Philadelphia Mint. If your sole concern is to obtain the finest affordable example, select a coin that grades MS-62. On the other hand, and as the following discussion will make clear, the branch mint issues in this series are rare and quite costly in Mint State. If you adopt this strategy, therefore, you are probably going to have to settle for circulated examples of the 1838-C and 1838-D. If this is the case, then I also recommend acquiring a P-mint example in AU-55 or AU-58 in order to assemble a more balanced set.

The 1838-C Classic Half Eagle has an original mintage of just 17,179 pieces. Judging by the number of Mint State examples certified at the leading third-party grading services, the contemporary public did not save all that many examples at the time of issue. Indeed, most survivors found their way into circulation. Give serious consideration to any coin that grades at least AU-50. A nice About Uncirculated example will have generally bold definition over the central design elements with no large or otherwise individually conspicuous abrasions. Look for coins with yellow-gold or green-gold color, as these predominate in numismatic circles.

The popularity of the 1838-C among type collectors and Southern gold specialists alike means that you will experience considerable competition for problem-free examples. This is reflected in the cost of coins certified by PCGS and NGC. An NGC AU-50 required $9,200 from the winning bidder when it crossed the auction on July 8, 2006. By way of comparison, even lower-grade Mint State coins cost at least $35,000.

The 1838-D (20,583 pieces struck) is not quite as rare as the 1838-C, but it is still an elusive issue that becomes progressively more challenging to locate with grade. With just 24 Mint State examples reported at PCGS and NGC combined (May/2007), and such pieces starting at approximately $25,000 in MS-60, it is a more affordable strategy to look for a problem-free AU. Even in AU, however, the 1838-D is quite costly. A pair of AU-55 and AU-58 examples certified by NGC realized $9,775 and $17,250, respectively, when they sold at auction in early 2007. Colors for this issue include yellow-gold, green-gold and orange-gold shades, and most pieces are uncommonly well struck by Dahlonega Mint standards. Circulated Southern gold coins tend to come heavily abraded, but patience will be rewarded as there are some examples in the market with relatively few abrasions for the assigned grade. The same is also true for the 1838-C.

Courtesy of Bowers and Merena

The 1838-D is the first Dahlonega Mint Half Eagle, and it is an elusive delivery that becomes progressively more challenging to locate with grade. Colors for this issue include yellow-gold, green-gold and orange-gold shades, and most pieces are uncommonly well struck by the standards of the issuing Mint. Circulated Southern gold coins tend to come heavily abraded, so the quality-conscious buyer might want to hold out for a coin such as the example pictured here. This piece is relatively distraction free in the context of the Choice AU grade level.

STRATEGIES FOR INCLUDING THE CLASSIC HALF EAGLE IN A TYPE SET BY ISSUING MINT

Required Number of Coins: *Three*

Issuing Mint #1: *Philadelphia, Pennsylvania*

Most Desirable Issue(s): *1834 Plain 4, 1835, 1836*

Key to Collecting: *AU-55 or finer in grade; overall bold, if not sharp striking detail; partial or full mint luster with a frosty or semi-prooflike texture; yellow-gold, orange-gold or green-gold color; no sizeable or individually distracting abrasions*

Issuing Mint #2: *Charlotte, North Carolina*

Most Desirable Issue(s): *1838-C (only option)*

Key to Collecting: *AU-50 or finer in grade; above-average striking detail over the central design elements; yellow-gold or green-gold color; relatively abrasion free within the context of the assigned grade*

Issuing Mint #3: *Dahlonega, Georgia*

Most Desirable Issue(s): *1838-D (only option)*

Key to Collecting: *AU-50 or finer in grade; overall bold, if not sharp striking detail; yellow-gold, green-gold or orange-gold color; relatively abrasion free within the context of the assigned grade*

Proof Type Set

With solid six-to-seven figure price tags and market appearances that are usually separated by considerable periods of time, I do not recommend including the Classic Half

Eagle in a proof type set of U.S. gold. On the other hand, I am also very fond of proof Classic Half Eagles. The few specimens known are highly attractive with full striking detail and appreciable, if not bold field-to-device contrast. Buying opportunities are few and far between, however, as this is an exceedingly rare type in proof format. Indeed, there are no more than 12-15 examples of all issues in private hands. The late John Jay Pittman owned three confirmed proofs of this type: two examples dated 1835 and a single 1836. I had the extremely good fortune of cataloging the finer of Pittman's two 1835s when it appeared at a subsequent auction in August of 2006. The coin is an exquisite NGC Proof-68 Ultra Cameo and, although it did not sell in that auction, the value in the 2007 market is certainly between $750,000 and $1,000,000. (The coin did sell in its prior auction appearance in January of 2005. Housed in a PCGS Proof-67 holder at that time, it traded hands for $690,000.)

Courtesy of Bowers and Merena

The finer of two proof 1835 Classic Half Eagles once owned by renowned collector John Jay Pittman. The author had the opportunity to catalog this coin when it appeared at auction in August of 2006, at which time it was graded Proof-68 Ultra Cameo by NGC. In the 2007 market, the coin is probably worth $750,000-$1,000,000.

Assembling a Complete Set

Year Set: This is a readily obtainable goal inasmuch as the Classic Half Eagle was struck for only five years from 1834 through 1838. There is only one option for each of the first four years in this series, and you should also acquire a P-mint coin as far as 1838 is concerned. Either a high-grade circulated or Mint State coin will make an attractive addition to a collection, particularly if you are patient and focus on pieces with above-average technical quality and eye appeal. Acquiring one example each of the 1834 Plain 4, 1835, 1836, 1837 and 1838 in AU-55 will cost at least $10,000. Expect to pay more than $35,000 if you choose to assemble this set in MS-62.

Date and Mint Set: When compared to assembling a year set of the type, a date and mint set of Classic Half Eagles requires just two additional pieces. Both are the leading rarities in this series, however, and they are particularly costly in Mint State. With these facts in mind, I offer two possible strategies. First, you could acquire Mint State examples of the Philadelphia Mint deliveries and opt for AU examples of the 1838-C and 1838-D. Or, you could assemble a more uniform set by selecting AU examples of all seven issues. Either option will work, but you must consider the relative cost between the two. The first option carries a total price tag of at least $50,000, assuming a minimum grade of MS-62 for the P-mint coins and AU-50 for the two mintmarked pieces. The second option is less expensive at $30,000-$35,000 for a set with a uniform grade of AU-55.

Die Variety Set: This type is just beginning to gain a limited following among variety collectors, and there is much fertile ground in the series if you are willing to take a close look at Liberty's portrait. Employees at the Philadelphia Mint used several different portrait styles to produce Classic Half Eagles, and they differ in the curvature of the truncation, the width of the bust point and/or the design of some of the haircurls. Additionally, there are differences in the size of the reverse arrowheads between some of the P-mint coins dated 1838. At least some of these differences can be explained by the fact that Christian Gobrecht assumed William Kneass' responsibility for engraving the dies after the latter suffered a debilitating stroke in 1835.

There are fewer die varieties for the mintmarked issues in the Classic Half Eagle series. The 1838-C has just two varieties, the differences between which are minor, and only a single die marriage has been confirmed for the 1838-D.

Although I do not consider the die varieties for any issue in this series to be significant, they have been garnering increased attention among catalogers in recent years. Individual examples still rarely sell for a premium based either on the relative or absolute rarity of their die marriage, which means that there are still opportunities to cherrypick a scarcer variety. Given the cost of Mint State Classic Half Eagles, I recommend obtaining coins that grade EF or AU if you choose to collect this series by die variety. In addition to significantly lower price tags, such coins usually have a greater tendency to trade outside of auction, where the seller is less likely to have taken the time to attribute the coin. This is especially true for Philadelphia Mint examples.

Proof Set: It is not possible to assemble a complete set of proof Classic Half Eagles because the 1837 is not available for private ownership in this format. In addition, the only "proof" 1838 Half Eagle known to PCGS and NGC is a coin that has been graded Specimen-65 (as opposed to Proof-65) at the latter service (May/2007).

If you insist on collecting proof Classic Half Eagles, you are going to have to settle for a partial set. Even then, be prepared to face a formidable challenge that requires considerable time and plentiful financial resources. Assembling a partial set that includes one example each of the proof 1834 Classic, 1835 and 1836 is a multi-million dollar venture.

A Complete Set by Issuing Mint: A compete set of Classic Half Eagles struck in the Philadelphia Mint is more likely to be classified as a year set than as a complete set by issuing mint in today's market. Most collectors that specialize in gold coins struck within a specific Mint often overlook the Philadelphia Mint. Additionally, you cannot realistically speak of assembling a complete set of C or D-mint Classic Half Eagles because each coinage facility contributed just a single issue to this series. The 1838-C and 1838-D, however, are extremely important if you are assembling a complete set of Charlotte and/or Dahlonega Mint coinage.

Investing Tips

Focus on acquiring a single type coin in order to represent the Classic Half Eagle in your numismatic portfolio. The 1834 Plain 4 would work very well since its first-year status has long been popular among type collectors and other buyers. This is an attractive issue in MS-64, and coins in that grade are of further significance due to the paucity of higher-grade examples at PCGS and NGC. Since MS-64 is the finest grade that most buyers can afford, much of the demand from high-grade type collectors is concentrated at that level. The intersection of limited supply and strong demand is a highly desirable situation for numismatic investment purposes.

CHAPTER TWENTY TWO

No Motto Liberty Half Eagles

Courtesy of Rare Coin Wholesalers

SPECIFICATIONS

Year(s) Issued: *1839-1866*
Issuing Mint(s): *Philadelphia, Charlotte, Dahlonega, New Orleans, San Francisco*
Authorizing Act: *January 18, 1837*
Designer: *Christian Gobrecht*
Weight: *8.359 grams*
Composition: *90% gold, 10% copper*
Diameter:
    1839-1840: *22.5 millimeters*
    1840-1866: *21.6 millimeters*
Edge: *Reeded*

History

After only five years of production, William Kneass' Classic Half Eagle yielded to the Liberty design of Christian Gobrecht (his successor in practice if not yet in title). The reason for the quick abandonment of the Classic series is not readily apparent, as the design is not unattractive and the Mint does not appear to have had difficulty striking the coins. The Liberty design, however, would be much more difficult to eject, remaining in production for 70 years until finally stepping down in 1908. This is by far the longest run for any Half Eagle series.

The initial variant of the Liberty Half Eagle differs little from the preceding Classic design. A left-facing portrait of Liberty is again the focal feature on the obverse, 13 stars being arranged around the border and the date positioned below. This time, however, Liberty is wearing a coronet inscribed LIBERTY instead of a headband. Additionally, Liberty's hair is more tightly cropped without many of the distinct curls of the Classic design. The reverse eagle has been slightly reworked, but it is still perched atop an olive branch and bundle of arrows with its wings outstretched. The upper field on that side remained open until the addition of a scroll with the motto IN GOD WE TRUST in 1866. Mintmark location is below the eagle.

No Motto Liberty Half Eagles were struck in five mints: Philadelphia; Charlotte; Dahlonega; New Orleans; and San Francisco. The Philadelphia Mint also struck proofs during most years from 1839-1865, initially in extremely limited quantities but in slightly larger numbers beginning in 1858/1859.

Short Type Set

This is the earliest series in the U.S. Half Eagle series that is truly popular for inclusion in short type sets. The No Motto Liberty Half Eagle can be grouped with the other Liberty types from the Quarter Eagle through the Double Eagle. I also like the short set that focuses solely on the Half Eagle series.

Half Eagle Types, a nine-piece set including:
Capped Bust Right Half Eagle, Small Eagle Reverse
Capped Bust Right Half Eagle, Large Eagle Reverse
Capped Bust Left Half Eagle
Capped Head Left Half Eagle, Large Diameter
Capped Head Left Half Eagle, Reduced Diameter
Classic Half Eagle
Liberty Half Eagle, No Motto
Liberty Half Eagle, Motto
Indian Half Eagle

Liberty Gold Coinage, a four or eight-piece set depending on how many types the collector wants to represent for the larger denominations. The eight-piece set includes:
Liberty Quarter Eagle
Liberty Half Eagle, No Motto
Liberty Half Eagle, Motto
Liberty Eagle, No Motto
Liberty Eagle, Motto
Type I Liberty Double Eagle
Type II Liberty Double Eagle
Type III Liberty Double Eagle

Complete Type Set

Produced as it was during 28 years in one or more of five different Mints, there are numerous possible type candidates in the No Motto Liberty Half Eagle series. Due to the fact that they were usually produced in greater numbers and/or saved in more significant quantities, the Philadelphia Mint deliveries are preferable to the mintmarked issues for basic type purposes. I must advise, however, that while issues such as the 1843, 1845 and 1856 are fairly easy to obtain in circulated grades, Mint State survivors are very rare. This is due primarily to two factors. First, there was little, if any numismatic interest in saving business strike coins during the years in which the No Motto Liberty Half Eagle was struck. What little collector demand existed in the United States of the 1840s, 1850s and 1860s was focused almost exclusively on proof coinage. Second, the No Motto Liberty Half Eagle was a workhorse series and the individual issues saw considerable circulation.

Although all Mint State coins of this type are conditionally rare, the 1861 exists in the greatest numbers and appears in the market often enough that there are numerous buying opportunities each year. As such, this is the best type candidate in the No Motto Liberty Half Eagle series in both circulated and Mint State grades.

Circulated Examples: Over the past decade or so, I have handled circulated 1861 Half Eagles in virtually all grades from VG-8 through AU-58. The vast majority of pieces, however, grade no lower than VF, and there are also generous numbers of EF and AU survivors listed at PCGS and NGC. With the emphasis on technical quality in the numismatic market of the 21st century, I suggest obtaining an example that grades AU-58. During 2006, a leading numismatic auctioneer sold no less than 10 examples certified by PCGS or NGC in that grade. In each case, the realized price fell within the $460-$660 range.

Mint State Examples: Far fewer Mint State 1861 Half Eagles have traded hands than circulated examples, and most have been in lower grades through MS-62. As with most other gold types, MS-62 represents a potentially good cutoff point if you are seeking a suitably lustrous coin without an excessive number of large and/or singularly distracting abrasions. Select auction prices realized from the early years of the 21st century include:

> **NGC MS-62**, *realized $2,645 in July of 2004*
> **PCGS MS-63**, *sold for $6,614 during a December 2005 auction*
> **PCGS MS-64**, *traded hands at $9,488 on April 29, 2006*

General Characteristics: The 1861 Half Eagle has a relatively large mintage (688,084 pieces) for a gold coin produced in the mid 19th century, and striking quality varies widely for the issue. Nevertheless, most examples are boldly, if not sharply struck. The dominant luster types are satiny and frosty, and most of the pieces that I have seen possess either yellow-gold or orange-gold color.

Courtesy of Bowers and Merena

With such a large number of coins produced by the standards of the mid-19th century, it is no surprise to read that striking quality varies for the 1861 Half Eagle. Even so, most examples are at least as boldly impressed as the coin pictured here.

Words of Caution: With so many AU-58s in numismatic circles, I urge patience when it comes to this issue. Given enough time and energy, you can locate an example with overall sharp striking detail, attractive color, relatively few abrasions and much of the original luster still intact.

Since Mint State examples exist in far fewer numbers, do not be too patient when searching for a suitable example as you might overlook important buying opportunities. Nevertheless, pieces that grade at least MS-62 do appear frequently enough that you should not have to settle for a coin with inferior striking quality, deficient luster or individually distracting abrasions. Bear in mind, however, that most No Motto Liberty Half Eagles in MS-62 are somewhat lackluster and/or noticeably abraded. For this reason, and if your budget allows, consider purchasing an example that grades MS-63 or finer.

STRATEGIES FOR INCLUDING THE NO MOTTO LIBERTY HALF EAGLE IN A COMPLETE TYPE SET

Most Desirable Issue(s): *1861*

Most Desirable Grade(s), Circulated Coins: *AU-58*

Estimated Cost: *$460-$660*

Key to Collecting: *Overall sharp striking detail; plenty of original luster remaining; yellow-gold or orange-gold color; no sizeable or individually distracting circulation marks*

Most Desirable Grade(s), Mint State Coins: *MS-62 or finer*

Estimated Cost: *$2,500 and up*

Key to Collecting: *Sharp striking detail; satiny or frosty luster; yellow-gold or orange-gold color; relatively few abrasions for the assigned grade, and none that are individually bothersome*

Advanced Type Set

Rarer Issues: Despite its status as the most plentiful Liberty Half Eagle of the No Motto type, the 1861 does not boast the highest mintage in this series. That honor goes to the 1847 with 915,981 pieces produced. Nevertheless, the 1847 is not as plentiful in Mint State as the 1861, and it is a strong candidate for inclusion in a better-date type set. Once again, focus solely on those coins that grade at least MS-62 in order to avoid surfaces with noticeably deficient luster and/or large, individually distracting abrasions. Expect a certified MS-62 to cost at least $3,500. In MS-63, the price advances to the neighborhood of $6,000, while a realized price from a December 2005 auction provides a value of $10,000 for the 1847 in MS-64.

Since it is among the most frequently encountered No Motto Half Eagles in worn condition, the 1847 is not a good candidate for use in an advanced type set of circulated coins. Instead, consider the 1839. Popular as a first-year issue, the 1839 is also one of only three Liberty Fives struck during the 1830s. The 1839 is certainly scarce in AU-55 and AU-58, but examples in those grades usually appear at auction several times yearly. In early 2007, an NGC AU-55 realized $1,093, while during the same month a PCGS AU-58 crossed the auction block at $2,760.

STRATEGIES FOR INCLUDING THE NO MOTTO LIBERTY HALF EAGLE IN A TYPE SET OF RARER ISSUES

Most Desirable Issue(s):

  Circulated Grades: *1839*

  Mint State Grades: *1847*

Most Desirable Grade(s), Circulated Coins: *AU-55, AU-58*

Estimated Cost: *$1,100 and up*

Key to Collecting: *Overall bold definition; portions of the original luster still intact; yellow-gold or orange-gold color; no sizeable or individually distracting circulation marks*

Most Desirable Grade(s), Mint State Coins: *MS-62 or finer*

Estimated Cost: *$3,500 and up*

Key to Collecting: *Bold-to-sharp striking detail; satiny or frosty luster; yellow-gold or orange-gold color; no sizeable or individually distracting abrasions*

Major Subtypes: Prior to the addition of the motto IN GOD WE TRUST in 1866, the Mint did not alter the design of the Liberty Half Eagle. As such, you need acquire only a single No Motto example if you are assembling a type set of U.S. gold that includes major design changes.

Issuing Mint: This is one of the most enjoyable series to pursue for inclusion in a gold type set by issuing mint. Five coins are required, one example each from the Philadelphia, Charlotte, Dahlonega, New Orleans and San Francisco Mints. I have already provided enough information about several P-mint issues to equip you with the tools needed to obtain a suitable example from that coinage facility.

Courtesy of Bowers and Merena

The most plentiful Charlotte Mint Liberty Half Eagle from an absolute standpoint is almost certainly the 1847-C. There is a relatively large number of AU examples surviving, any of which would probably satisfy the type collector as long as they were problem free and certified by one of the two leading third-party grading services. The example pictured here possesses the orange-gold color for which many survivors are known.

As far as Charlotte Mint issues are concerned, the most plentiful Liberty Half Eagle from an absolute standpoint is the 1847-C. There is a relatively large number of AU examples surviving, any of which would make a lovely addition to a type set as long as they are problem free and certified by PCGS or NGC. Many examples possess yellow-gold, green-gold or orange-gold color, and most will have their fair share of distracting abrasions. If you locate a coin with relatively few distractions and none that are individually conspicuous, you will have found an above-average example. Striking quality for the 1847-C ranges from soft to overall bold, and I recommend acquiring only those coins that possess above-average definition. Expect to pay between $2,500 and at least $5,750 for the 1847-C in the AU-50 through AU-58 grade range.

Moving on to the Dahlonega Mint, we find that perhaps the most realistic type candidate is the 1853-D. Nevertheless, Mint State survivors are still rare when viewed in the wider context of U.S. numismatics. I believe that AU examples are preferable for ease of acquisition and less of a financial burden. While strike is often a problem for this issue, I have cataloged several boldly struck examples for auction. Hold out for the opportunity to acquire one of these pieces. Color is usually yellow-gold, orange-gold or green-gold in shade, and those AU survivors that still retain original mint luster will tend to be satiny or frosty in texture. Exercising a modicum of patience should be sufficient to locate an example whose surfaces are free of sizeable abrasions or noticeable distractions in the prime focal areas. AU-50s cost at least $3,750, while AU-58s require between $4,500 and $5,000.

Courtesy of Bowers and Merena

The 1853-D has the greatest certified population among Dahlonega Mint Liberty Half Eagles both in an absolute sense and in terms of examples that grade Mint State. Survivors at the latter level are still quite rare when viewed in the wider context of U.S. numismatics, however, so the type collector might want to focus on the AU grades for ease of acquisition and less of a financial burden.

In my experience, the most plentiful No Motto Half Eagle struck in the New Orleans Mint is the 1844-O. This should come as no surprise when you consider that the issue's original mintage of 364,600 pieces is the largest in this O-mint Liberty Half Eagle series. As with the 1847-C and 1853-D, the 1844-O is usually encountered in circulated condition. Indeed, AU-55 and AU-58 are the preferred grades for type purposes. In Choice AU, the '44-O usually displays overall sharp striking detail and either orange-gold or green-gold color. Some pieces, however, tend more toward a yellow-gold cast. On examples that retain most of the original luster, expect to find either a frosty or modestly semi-prooflike sheen. An AU-55 will sell for approximately $1,000, while problem-free AU-58s are worth $1,750-$2,750.

Courtesy of Bowers and Merena

In the author's experience, the most plentiful No Motto Half Eagle struck in the New Orleans Mint is the 1844-O. The vast majority of surviving examples are circulated with the result that AU-55 and AU-58 represent the finest grades that most collectors will probably be able to afford. An AU-55 should probably sell for somewhere in the neighborhood of $1,000, while in AU-58 a problem-free example will likely require $1,750-$2,750 from the buyer.

Courtesy of Bowers and Merena

With a record mintage of 105,100 pieces for an S-mint issue of this design, the reader will probably agree that the 1856-S is an attractive coin for type purposes. In an absolute sense, however, there are just not all that many '56-S Half Eagles around, and even in circulated grades the buyer is likely to experience more difficulty finding a suitable example than they will for the 1847-C, 1853-D and 1844-O.

The final coinage facility to become active in the production of No Motto Liberty Half Eagles is the San Francisco Mint. With a record mintage of 105,100 pieces for an S-mint No Motto Liberty Half Eagle, the 1856-S is an attractive coin for type purposes. In an absolute sense, there are just not all that many '56-S Half Eagles around, and even in circulated grades this issue is much rarer than the 1847-C, 1853-D and 1844-O. With just 12 Mint State coins certified at PCGS and NGC combined (May/2007), I suggest opting for a problem-free survivor in AU-55 or AU-58. The typically offered example possesses yellow-gold or orange-gold color with generally sharp definition over the devices. As a heavily circulated issue, the 1856-S is also apt to display numerous detracting abrasions. All other things being equal, therefore, a relatively smooth example in Choice AU represents an important buying opportunity. A pair of coins in AU-55 crossed the auction block in early 2007. One was certified by PCGS and the other by NGC, but both sold for $1,495. Given the rarity of Mint State examples, this issue is worth considerably more in AU-58 at approximately $4,000.

STRATEGIES FOR INCLUDING THE NO MOTTO LIBERTY HALF EAGLE IN A TYPE SET BY ISSUING MINT

Required Number of Coins: *Five*

Issuing Mint #1: *Philadelphia, Pennsylvania*

Most Desirable Issue(s): *1861*

Key to Collecting: *AU-58 or higher grade; sharp striking detail; satiny or frosty luster; yellow-gold or orange-gold color; no sizeable or individually distracting circulation marks*

Issuing Mint #2: *Charlotte, North Carolina*

Most Desirable Issue(s): *1847-C*

Key to Collecting: *AU-50 or higher grade; overall bold definition; yellow-gold, green-gold or orange-gold color; no individually bothersome abrasions*

Issuing Mint #3: *Dahlonega, Georgia*

Most Desirable Issue(s): *1853-D*

Key to Collecting: *AU-50 or higher grade; relatively sharp striking detail; yellow-gold, green-gold or orange-gold color; no individually bothersome abrasions*

Issuing Mint #4: *New Orleans, Louisiana*

Most Desirable Issue(s): *1844-O*

Key to Collecting: *AU-55 or higher grade; sharp striking detail; orange-gold or green-gold color; no individually bothersome abrasions*

Issuing Mint #5: *San Francisco, California*

Most Desirable Issue(s): *1856-S*

Key to Collecting: *AU-55 or higher grade; overall sharp definition; yellow-gold or orange-gold color; no individually bothersome abrasions; orange-gold or rose-gold color*

Proof Type Set

Even judging by proof gold standards, the No Motto Liberty Half Eagle is an extremely difficult type to acquire in this format. For each year in this series prior to 1859, the Philadelphia Mint either refrained from striking proof Half Eagles or it produced an extremely limited number of pieces for distribution as part of complete proof sets of gold, silver and minor coinage. Today, PCGS and NGC have certified examples of only nine issue in the pre-1859 proof Liberty Half Eagle series (May/2007): 1839; 1841; 1842 Small Letters; 1843; 1845; 1846; 1848; 1857; and 1858. In each case, the combined population is fewer than seven coins.

Two recent auction appearances best illustrate the extreme rarity of proof Half Eagles from the 1839-1858 era. During March of 2006, an NGC-certified 1858 in Proof-66 * Ultra Cameo realized $195,500. Nearly a year later (January of 2007, to be exact), an 1857 in NGC Proof-65 Cameo crossed the auction block for $230,000.

Beginning in 1858, the Mint made a conscious effort to market proof coinage to collectors. Two more pivotal events occurred in the following year: proof production for the Liberty Half Eagle increased significantly and federal employees began recording the total number of specimens produced each year. While the No Motto issues from 1859-1865 are more plentiful than their predecessors in today's market, they are still very rare in an absolute sense. Nevertheless, these later-date issues represent the only realistic options for the majority of proof gold type collectors.

An important type candidate is the 1864, which has the highest combined PCGS and NGC population for any issue in the proof No Motto Liberty Half Eagle series (May/2007). Even this is a rare issue, however, with fewer than 20 coins surviving. As such, do not be overly picky when it comes to numeric grade. Any problem-free example with pleasing eye appeal will make an impressive addition to a proof type set. An April 2006 auction appearance for an NGC Proof-63 Cameo resulted in a realized price of $23,000.

STRATEGIES FOR INCLUDING THE NO MOTTO LIBERTY HALF EAGLE IN A PROOF TYPE SET

Most Desirable Issue(s): *1864*

Most Desirable Grade(s): *Proof-63 Cameo or finer*

Key to Collecting: *Full striking detail; bold field-to-device contrast; orange-gold or reddish-gold color; a minimum number of wispy hairlines and/or contact marks*

Assembling a Complete Set

Year Set: This is an obtainable set, although I would like to impose two sensible parameters before getting started. First, the Philadelphia Mint issues are by far the most readily obtainable issues for virtually all years in the No Motto portion of the Liberty Half Eagle series. The only exceptions are 1865 and 1866, where the S-mint issues either exist in greater numbers than their P-mint counterpart or are the year's only option. Obtain an example of each P-mint issue from 1839-1864 and then complete your set with the 1865-S and 1866-S No Motto.

Second, even many of the more plentiful Philadelphia Mint issues are conditionally rare in Mint State, and the 1865-S and 1866-S No Motto are exceedingly so. As such, assemble this set using circulated examples. A selection of EF-AU pieces will present very well, and acquiring them is still a challenging task. A complete 28-coin year set comprised of mostly EF examples with a sprinkling of AU pieces for some of the more plentiful issues will set you back at least $23,000. The most challenging issues to obtain are the 1862, 1863 and 1864, as well as the aforementioned 1865-S and 1866-S No Motto.

Date and Mint Set: This is not realistic strategy if you are operating on a limited budget. The 1854-S is essentially uncollectible since there are only two examples in private hands from a scant original mintage of 268 pieces. Even discounting this issue, there are still numerous stoppers in the No Motto Liberty Half Eagle series. Just a few examples are the 1842-C Small Date, 1842-D Large Date, 1861-D and 1864-S. Avoid becoming frustrated with a task or placing severe strain on your numismatic budget by limiting specialization in the No Motto Liberty Half Eagle series to assembling a year set.

Die Variety Set: To date, the reception that this series has received from die variety collectors has been rather cold. There are a number of reasons for this, the most significant of which is that hardly any research has been done on varieties for the Philadelphia and San Francisco Mint issues. This is an example of the old riddle of what came first, the chicken or the egg? With the exception of some fairly dramatic misplaced dates for the 1847, varieties for the Philadelphia and San Francisco Mint issues are really not all that exciting. As such, I cannot fault researchers for seeking more dramatic series upon which to focus their time and effort. On the other hand, there might be some fascinating varieties in this series that are awaiting discovery by collectors that are willing to sift through many of the more mundane die marriages. Perhaps the riddle will be answered some day, if only for this one specific application.

The No Motto issues from the Charlotte, Dahlonega and, to a lesser extent, New Orleans Mints have been the subject of detailed and scholarly variety studies, and they have attracted limited numbers of specialized collectors. To the best of my knowledge, however, no one has ever succeeded in assembling a complete set of No Motto Liberty Half Eagles by die variety.

Proof Set: Assembling even a partial set of proof No Motto Liberty Half Eagles is not a task for you if you are limited on time and/or financial resources. Many issues are either unknown in proof format or unobtainable for private ownership, while all others are very rare and seldom represented at even the largest numismatic gatherings. Even Ed Trompeter, the California industrialist who assembled one of the finest collections of proof gold coinage ever known, seldom ventured earlier than 1858 when acquiring No Motto Half Eagles for inclusion in his set.

A Complete Set by Issuing Mint: For many years, the Charlotte and Dahlonega Mint issues in this series have served as centerpieces in specialized collections of Southern gold coinage. Indeed, these are two of the most popular and romanticized Mints in United States history, and they continue to attract new adherents year after year. Numerous collections have been assembled and sold, often as part of complete sets of all gold denominations struck in one or both of these branch mints. The Ashland City Collection is an example, and it even included representatives of many gold issues from the New Orleans, San Francisco and Carson City Mints. The portion of the collection concerned with No Motto Half Eagles from Charlotte and Dahlonega was complete for all issues and significant varieties, and it also included several duplicates. The coins graded AU and Mint State, and most sold when offered at auction in January of 2003. The total prices realized for the Charlotte and Dahlonega Mint examples that actually sold is $1,017,635.

The author knows two collectors who specialize in No Motto Half Eagles from the New Orleans Mint, one of whose accomplishment was sold through auction in 1999. The other is still active in this segment of the market, and he is being joined by a growing number of collectors that are coming to appreciate this "forgotten branch mint." Nevertheless, the value of many O-mint No Motto Half Eagles in today's market is still too low relative to many Charlotte and Dahlonega Mint issues. The New Orleans Mint definitely has a long way to go toward gathering a strong following among Southern gold collectors. On the other hand, the opportunity still exists to acquire many O-mint Half Eagles for prices that are not commensurate with their true rarity.

The Philadelphia and San Francisco Mint issues in this series are not popular among gold collectors that specialize in a single coinage facility.

Investing Tips

There are several investing strategies to consider for the No Motto Liberty Half Eagle series. First, you could acquire a single example of the design in the highest grade that you can afford and hedge your bets on an increase in type collector demand. An excellent issue for this strategy is the 1861. As illustrated by the following graph, the value of this issue in MS-64 has increased steadily from 2003-2006.

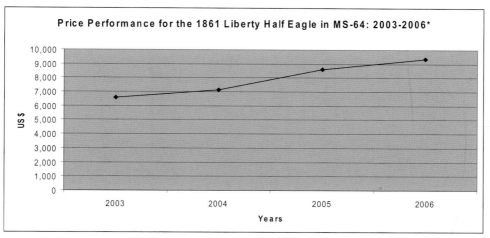

*Values represent average prices realized for PCGS and NGC-certified examples as reported by a leading rare coin auction house.

Early proof issues in this series are also excellent investment vehicles based on past price performance. Take for example the 1857, of which just two examples have been confirmed. Since the issue is so rare that specific grade looses much of its significance (the coins are similar in technical quality anyway at Proof-64 and Proof-65), I have combined their past auction appearances to illustrate a dramatic increase in value during the 25-year period from 1982-2007.

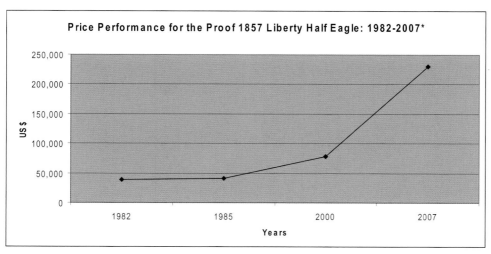

*Values represent prices realized for the two proof 1857 Liberty Half Eagles known as reported by leading rare coin auction houses.

One final segment of the No Motto Liberty Half Eagle series that has performed very well in the market is the Charlotte and Dahlonega Mint issues. Take for example the 1861-D. This is a key-date rarity with just 1,597 pieces originally struck, and survivors have long enjoyed strong demand among Southern gold specialists. Since the beginning of the 21st century, this issue has increased steadily in value in AU-55.

As numismatics in general continues to grow in popularity due to modern Mint programs such as the Presidential Dollar series and other factors, and if some of today's newer collectors eventually develop into advanced gold specialists, then certain issues in the No Motto Liberty Half Eagle series cannot help but to increase in value in the coming years.

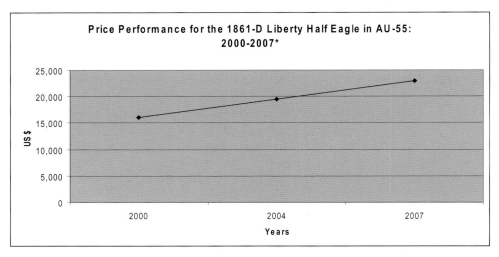

*Values represent prices realized for PCGS and NGC-certified examples as reported by a leading rare coin auction house.

Courtesy of Rare Coin Wholesalers

A key-date rarity with just 1,597 pieces struck, the 1861-D Half Eagle has long enjoyed strong demand among Southern gold specialists. Adding an example to a portfolio might be one way to capitalize on the investment potential of the No Motto Liberty Half Eagle series.

CHAPTER TWENTY THREE

Liberty Half Eagles with Motto

Courtesy of Rare Coin Wholesalers

SPECIFICATIONS

Year(s) Issued: *1866-1908*
Issuing Mint(s): *Philadelphia, Carson City, Denver, New Orleans, San Francisco*
Authorizing Act: *January 18, 1837 (supplemented by the Acts of March 3, 1865 and February 12, 1873)*
Designer: *Christian Gobrecht*
Weight: *8.359 grams*
Composition: *90% gold, 10% copper*
Diameter: *21.6 millimeters*
Edge: *Reeded*

History

The unexpected duration and bloodletting of the Civil War resulted in a religious revival in the United States that began to impact the nation's coinage in 1864. In that year, the newly introduced Two-Cent piece became the first U.S. coin to include the motto IN GOD WE TRUST as part of the design. The Act of March 3, 1865 expanded on this theme and required that the Mint include the motto on all coins of sufficient size. For the gold series, the smallest coin affected was the Half Eagle.

The Mint added the motto to the upper reverse field of the Liberty Half Eagle in 1866 without altering any other aspects of the design. James Barton Longacre, who had replaced Christian Gobrecht as chief engraver in 1844, engraved the motto upon a simple scroll. The Liberty Half Eagle with Motto remained in production through 1908, during which time the Philadelphia, Carson City, Denver, New Orleans and San Francisco Mints all struck examples. When you also consider the No Motto issues delivered in the Charlotte and Dahlonega Mints, the Liberty Half Eagle is the only United States coin to have been struck in all of the mints that operated at one time or another during our nation's history.

Short Type Set

One of the most popular and readily obtainable coins in the entire U.S. gold coin series, the Liberty Half Eagle with Motto has long been favored for inclusion in short type sets. If you are drawn to this type but do not have the desire or the means to build an entire gold type set, I suggest including an example in a meaningful collection by assembling one of the following short sets.

Half Eagle Types, a nine-piece set including:

Capped Bust Right Half Eagle, Small Eagle Reverse
Capped Bust Right Half Eagle, Large Eagle Reverse
Capped Bust Left Half Eagle
Capped Head Left Half Eagle, Large Diameter
Capped Head Left Half Eagle, Reduced Diameter
Classic Half Eagle
Liberty Half Eagle, No Motto
Liberty Half Eagle, Motto
Indian Half Eagle

Liberty Gold Coinage, a four or eight-piece set depending on how many types the collector wants to represent for the larger denominations. The eight-piece set includes:

Liberty Quarter Eagle
Liberty Half Eagle, No Motto
Liberty Half Eagle, Motto
Liberty Eagle, No Motto
Liberty Eagle, Motto
Type I Liberty Double Eagle
Type II Liberty Double Eagle
Type III Liberty Double Eagle

Popular U.S. Gold Types, an eight or ten-piece set including:

Liberty Quarter Eagle
Indian Quarter Eagle
Liberty Half Eagle, Motto
Indian Half Eagle
Liberty Eagle, Motto
Indian Eagle (No Motto and/or Motto)
Liberty Double Eagle (usually a Type III example)
Saint-Gaudens Double Eagle (No Motto and/or Motto)

Complete Type Set

Whereas the highest-mintage issue in the No Motto Liberty Half Eagle series is the 1847 at 915,981 pieces, there are no less than 14 Motto issues with original mintages of more than 1 million coins. Indeed, there are numerous possible type candidates in this series, each of which has a relatively sizeable number of examples from which to choose in many of the more popular grades. Some of the earlier-dated deliveries that are strong type candidates are the 1880, 1881, 1881-S and 1882. These issues, however, are conditionally rare above MS-64. If you assembling a Gem-quality type set, look to such later-date issues as the 1900, 1901, 1901-S and 1908.

Courtesy of Bowers and Merena

Some of the earlier-dated deliveries in the Liberty Half Eagle with Motto series that are perhaps readily recognizable as type candidates are the 1880, 1881, 1881-S and 1882. These issues, however, are conditionally rare above MS-64, so the collector who desires a Gem-quality example might want to look to such later-date issues as the 1900, 1901, 1901-S and 1908.

Circulated Examples: The frequency with which Mint State examples appear in the market argues against including a circulated Liberty Half Eagle with Motto in a gold type set. I understand, however, that you may be assembling a circulated set due to the cost of some other gold types in Mint State. If this is the case, it is perfectly acceptable to acquire a circulated example of this type. Additionally, you might be able to afford a Motto Liberty Half Eagle in MS-61 or MS-62 but may be unwilling to accept the deficient luster and/or heavily abraded surfaces that characterize gold coins in these grades. A high-grade circulated survivor with relatively smooth surfaces and much of the original luster still intact is sometimes preferable to a baggy and/or subdued BU example.

Regardless of exactly what your motivation is for acquiring a circulated Liberty Half Eagle with Motto, I would not purchase a coin that grades lower than AU-58. Bear in mind that the value of common-date Liberty Half Eagles in circulated grades fluctuates with the spot price of gold. During the spring of 2007, AU-58 examples of issues such as the 1880 and 1901-S were selling at auction for approximately $200.

Mint State Examples: Since this is the earliest Half Eagle type that is relatively obtainable through MS-65, I strongly advise adding a Gem to your type set. A 1900 in NGC MS-65 sold for $2,530 in January of 2007, while a PCGS MS-65 traded hands for $3,450 four months later.

If you want to spend a bit less without sacrificing too much on quality, look to the 1880 or 1881-S in MS-64. Two examples of the 1881-S appeared at auction in early 2007. The PCGS coin brought $1,725 while the NGC piece realized $1,610.

There are also some truly exquisite survivors of this type in numismatic circles, and Superb Gems are among the most beautiful gold coins that I have ever handled. A 1901-S in PCGS MS-67 sold for $14,950 in early 2007.

General Characteristics: With so many possible type candidates from which to choose, you should have no difficulty finding a Liberty Half Eagle with Motto that satisfies your aesthetic requirements. I have handled numerous examples with yellow-gold, orange-gold, rose-gold or reddish-gold surfaces. Most pieces are satiny or frosty in luster quality. While the occasional piece with slight striking incompleteness over the central highpoints does turn up, there are enough sharply impressed examples to satisfy much of the current market demand.

Words of Caution: This is one type that you can acquire without undue stress. That said, it is still a good idea to keep at least one point in mind: there are enough type coins from which to choose that you can afford to wait until confronted with an example that meets all of your requirements. These requirements can include not only technical aspects such as strike and surface preservation, but also aesthetics along the lines of color and specific luster type.

STRATEGIES FOR INCLUDING THE LIBERTY HALF EAGLE WITH MOTTO IN A COMPLETE TYPE SET

Most Desirable Issue(s): *Numerous, including 1880, 1881, 1881-S, 1882 (issues such as these probably only through MS-64), 1900, 1901, 1901-S and 1908*

Most Desirable Grade(s), Circulated Coins: *AU-58*

Estimated Cost: *$200-$250*

Key to Collecting: *Sharp striking detail; plenty of original luster remaining; yellow-gold, orange-gold, rose-gold or reddish-gold color; no sizeable or individually distracting circulation marks*

Most Desirable Grade(s), Mint State Coins: *MS-64 or finer*

Estimated Cost:

   Issues such as the 1880 and 1881-S in MS-64: *$1,600-$2,000*

   Issues such as the 1900 and 1901-S in MS-65: *$2,500-$3,750*

Key to Collecting: *Sharp striking detail; satiny or frosty luster; yellow-gold, orange-gold, rose-gold or reddish-gold color; a minimal number of wispy bagmarks*

Advanced Type Set

Rarer Issues: Your options here are limited only by the length of the Liberty Half Eagle with Motto series. Nevertheless, certain issues are more appealing for advanced type purposes than others. I particularly like the 1891-CC. This is the most plentiful Half Eagle struck in the Carson City Mint, and a relatively large number of examples have survived in grades through MS-63. Given the long-standing popularity of this frontier-era branch mint in numismatic circles, a high-quality '91-CC will serve as a highlight in a better-date gold type set.

Courtesy of Bowers and Merena

A Motto Liberty Half Eagle that might hold particularly strong appeal for the advanced type collector is the 1891-CC. This is the most plentiful Half Eagle struck in the Carson City Mint, and a relatively large number of examples have survived through Choice Mint State. Given the long-standing popularity of this frontier-era coinage facility in numismatic circles, a high-quality '91-CC could serve as a highlight in a better-date gold type set.

The 1891-CC Half Eagle typically displays overall bold, if not sharp striking detail and frosty mint luster. While color varies among survivors, the most dominant shades are orange-gold and rose-gold. Pieces with one of these color variations can also reveal pretty green-gold undertones as the surfaces turn away from a direct light source.

The price for the 1891-CC Half Eagle in AU-58 is modest at approximately $600, and an example in MS-63 as certified by PCGS or NGC costs only $2,750-$3,500. In fact, MS-63s do not cost much more than the common issues such as the 1900 and 1901-S in MS-65. An 1891-CC in PCGS MS-64 sold for $5,750 in early 2007.

STRATEGIES FOR INCLUDING THE LIBERTY HALF EAGLE WITH MOTTO IN A TYPE SET OF RARER ISSUES

Most Desirable Issue(s): *1891-CC*

Most Desirable Grade(s), Circulated Coins: *AU-58*

Estimated Cost: *$600-$700*

Key to Collecting: *Overall bold definition; ample remaining luster; orange-gold, rose-gold or green-gold color; no sizeable or individually distracting circulation marks*

Most Desirable Grade(s), Mint State Coins: *MS-63, MS-64*

Estimated Cost:

   MS-63: *$2,750-$3,500*

   MS-64: *$5,000 and up*

Key to Collecting: *Bold-to-sharp striking detail; frosty luster; orange-gold, rose-gold or green-gold color; no sizeable or individually distracting abrasions*

Major Subtypes: After the addition of the motto IN GOD WE TRUST in 1866, the Liberty Half Eagle design remained unchanged through its termination in 1908. A single example, therefore, will suffice to represent the Motto series in a gold type set that includes major subtypes.

Issuing Mint: As with its No Motto counterpart, the Motto Liberty Half Eagle was struck in five different Mints. Fortunately, there are relatively obtainable issues from each of these Mints. In fact, this is one series for which I recommend focusing exclusively on Mint State coins. A quintet of Motto Liberty Half Eagles that range in grade from MS-62 through MS-65 is even a meaningful set in its own right.

For approximately $2,500-$3,750, you can obtain a pleasing 1900 Half Eagle in MS-65 and satisfy the Philadelphia Mint requirement for this strategy. The Carson City Mint has also been addressed above, and the 1891-CC is an excellent choice in MS-63 or MS-64. Returning to one of the series' most plentiful issues, the 1901-S in MS-65 is an excellent representative from the San Francisco Mint.

The other two Mints that struck Motto Liberty Half Eagles contributed only a limited number of issues to this series. In the case of the New Orleans Mint, there are only three issues dated 1892-1894. The 1893-O has the highest mintage in this group, yet it is still a scarce coin in all Mint State grades that becomes conditionally rare in MS-63. Still, there are enough MS-62s listed at PCGS and NGC that you can acquire one without too much difficulty. An NGC MS-62 traded hands for $2,530 at one of the earliest auctions of 2007. Most '93-O Half Eagles that I have handled are generally bold in strike with frosty luster and orange-gold or rose-gold color. This issue almost always displays a considerable number of abrasions at the MS-62 level; a coin that is free of large and/or individually conspicuous bagmarks certainly numbers among the nicer BU survivors.

Courtesy of Bowers and Merena

There are only three New Orleans Mint issues in the Liberty Half Eagle with Motto series, and the 1893-O has the highest mintage. Most '93-O Fives that the author has handled are generally bold in strike with frosty luster and orange-gold or rose-gold color. This issue will almost always display a considerable number of abrasions—the example pictured here is among the finest that the author has ever had the privilege of cataloging for auction.

Opening its doors as a coinage facility in 1906, the Denver Mint struck Liberty Half Eagles both in that year and during 1907. The 1907-D is more plentiful in today's market, and it is even fairly obtainable through MS-65. An NGC MS-65 crossed the auction block at $3,450 on April 7, 2006. Vibrant luster, overall bold striking detail and yellow-gold or orange-gold color characterize most high-grade 1907-D Half Eagles that I have handled.

STRATEGIES FOR INCLUDING THE LIBERTY HALF EAGLE WITH MOTTO IN A TYPE SET BY ISSUING MINT

Required Number of Coins: *Five*

Issuing Mint #1: *Philadelphia, Pennsylvania*

Most Desirable Issue(s): *Numerous, including 1900*

Key to Collecting: *MS-65 grade; sharp striking detail; satiny or frosty luster; yellow-gold, orange-gold or rose-gold color; a minimal number of wispy bagmarks*

Issuing Mint #2: *Carson City, Nevada*

Most Desirable Issue(s): *1891-CC*

Key to Collecting: *MS-63 or MS-64 grade; bold-to-sharp striking detail; frosty luster; orange-gold, rose-gold or green-gold color; no sizeable or individually distracting abrasions*

Issuing Mint #3: *Denver, Colorado*

Most Desirable Issue(s): *1907-D*

Key to Collecting: *MS-65 grade; overall bold striking detail; yellow-gold or orange-gold color; satiny or frosty luster; a minimal number of wispy bagmarks*

Issuing Mint #4: *New Orleans, Louisiana*

Most Desirable Issue(s): *1893-O*

Key to Collecting: *MS-62 grade; overall sharp striking detail; orange-gold or rose-gold color; frosty mint luster; no sizeable or individually bothersome abrasions*

Issuing Mint #5: *San Francisco, California*

Most Desirable Issue(s): *1901-S*

Key to Collecting: *MS-65 grade; sharp striking detail; satiny or frosty luster; yellow-gold, orange-gold or rose-gold color; a minimal number of wispy bagmarks*

Proof Type Set

Along with the Indian type, the Liberty design with Motto is the most frequently encountered Half Eagle in proof format. If you would like to assemble a type set of proof gold coinage, therefore, you must be prepared to obtain a Motto Liberty Half Eagle. Of course, all proof gold coins are rare in an absolute sense, and you will require a considerable sum of money to acquire an attractive example of this type.

While the 20th century issues are a bit more obtainable, most proof Half Eagles from the 1902-1907 era do not possess a significant degree of field-to-device contrast. Given the desirability of Cameo and Deep/Ultra proof coinage in many numismatic circles, I prefer the 1890s issues for type purposes. Examples that grade at least Proof-64 display few, if any wispy hairlines and will allow you to readily appreciate the field-to-device contrast. Demand a full strike, and expect the color to be a rich shade of yellow-gold or orange-gold. Many proof Liberty Half Eagles from the 1890s also possess a lovely "orange peel" texture which is best described as a rippled effect over the surfaces. This feature is eagerly sought by proof gold specialists and adds considerably to the desirability of an individual example.

A beautiful 1892 in PCGS Proof-64 Cameo sold at auction for $13,800 during the summer of 2004. Two specimens graded NGC Proof-65 Cameo realized $29,900 when they appeared in distinct 2005 sales. The coins were dated 1895 and 1898. The following year, another 1895 in NGC Proof-66 Cameo commanded $34,400 from the winning bidder. One final example that I would like to share is an exquisite 1898 graded Proof-66 Ultra Cameo by NGC. The coin crossed the auction block in early 2007 at $36,225.

Courtesy of Rare Coin Wholesalers

As this 1895 illustrates, the proof Liberty Half Eagles struck during the 1890s often display bold field-to-device contrast that is usually rewarded with a Cameo or Deep/Ultra Cameo designation at the major certification services. This can be a highly desirable attribute for the proof gold type collector.

STRATEGIES FOR INCLUDING THE LIBERTY HALF EAGLE WITH MOTTO IN A PROOF TYPE SET

Most Desirable Issue(s): *1891-1899*

Most Desirable Grade(s): *Proof-64 Cameo or finer*

Key to Collecting: *Bold field-to-device contrast; yellow-gold or orange-gold color; full striking detail; a minimum number of wispy hairlines; "orange-peel" texture*

Assembling a Complete Set

Year Set: It is possible to assemble a year set of Liberty Half Eagles with Motto, although the task is made considerably more difficult by the pre-1878 issues. With the exception of the 1873 Closed 3 and 1873 Open 3, both the Philadelphia and branch mint issues from 1866-1877 are scarce-to-rare in all grades. Compromise a bit on numeric grade and opt for EF examples in order to keep such issues as the 1866, 1869-S and 1875-S relatively affordable. Beginning with the 1878, you could advance to AU or Mint State coins without putting too much of a strain on the purse strings. Then again, this is a sizeable set (43 coins are required for completion), and I believe that it is better to focus solely on circulated examples in EF and AU to keep the total cost at a more manageable level. Comprised of circulated coins, a year set of Liberty Half Eagles with Motto will require at least $20,000-$25,000 for completion.

Date and Mint Set: Due to the rarity and high cost of several issues, I do not recommend this strategy for the Motto Liberty Half Eagle. Chief among the series' stoppers are the 1870-CC, 1875 (only 200 business strikes and 20 proofs struck), 1878-CC and the proof-only 1887. Even if you were to select a slightly impaired 1887 in Proof-58 and examples of the other three issues in AU, you would be looking at a price tag of at least $115,000 for only an extremely small percentage of a complete date and mint set.

Die Variety Set: With the exception of the Carson City Mint issues, no portion of the Motto Liberty Half Eagle series has been the subject of a serious die variety study. Struck as they were during an era of fairly standardized die production, there are few significant die varieties in this series. As such, I suspect that the popularity of the Motto Liberty Half Eagle among die variety specialists will remain limited.

Proof Set: The cost and difficultly associated with assembling a complete set of proof Liberty Half Eagles excludes most collectors from adopting this strategy. Nevertheless, this is an obtainable goal, at least insofar as it has been done before. California industrialist Ed Trompeter once owned a complete set of proof Liberty Half Eagles with Motto as part of his collection of 1858-1915 U.S. gold coinage. These coins were sold in 1998 along with the No Motto Half Eagles, all of the Eagles and Double Eagles and the fabled Amazonian gold pattern set for a total of sum of $15,177,500.

A Complete Set by Issuing Mint: The most popular coinage facility that struck Liberty Half Eagles of this type is the Carson City Mint, and CC-mint Fives are widely collected either in their own right or as part of larger collections of frontier-era gold. A complete 19-coin set in AU-50 will cost at least $170,000-$175,000.

The Denver and New Orleans facilities did not contribute enough issues to the series to become the focus of attention among specialized collectors. Finally, the Philadelphia and San Francisco Mints remain unpopular with collectors that specialize in gold coinage by issuing mint.

Investing Tips

All Liberty Half Eagles with Motto that grade MS-67 or finer are rare coins, as evidenced by the combined PCGS and NGC population data for some of the more popular type issues in this series.

Acquiring, say, a 1901-S in MS-67 and keeping the coin off the market for at least five years as part of a numismatic investment portfolio is an excellent way to capitalize on a highly specialized portion of the gold market. Superb Gem Liberty Half Eagles exist in such small numbers that even the introduction of a handful of new collectors will result in dramatic price increases under the right overall market conditions.

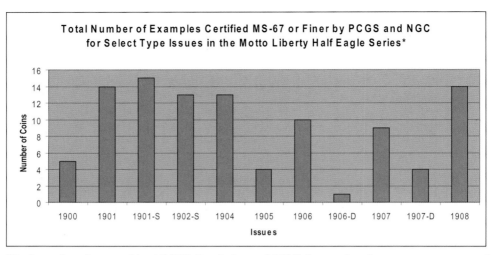

Total Number of Examples Certified MS-67 or Finer by PCGS and NGC for Select Type Issues in the Motto Liberty Half Eagle Series*

*Totals are based on combined PCGS Population and NGC Census data from www.pcgs.com and www.ngccoin.com, respectively. Websites accessed May 9, 2007.

CHAPTER TWENTY FOUR

Indian Half Eagles

Courtesy of Rare Coin Wholesalers

SPECIFICATIONS

Year(s) Issued: *1908-1929*
Issuing Mint(s): *Philadelphia, Denver, New Orleans, San Francisco*
Authorizing Act: *January 18, 1837 (supplemented by the Acts of March 3, 1865 and February 12, 1873)*
Designer: *Bela Lyon Pratt*
Weight: *8.359 grams*
Composition: *90% gold, 10% copper*
Diameter: *21.6 millimeters*
Edge: *Reeded*

History

Even before taking up residence in the White House, Theodore Roosevelt felt that the long-standing, relatively banal Liberty design was no longer representative of the United States of the late 19th and early 20th centuries. During his tenure as the 26th president, Roosevelt used his political clout to push through some of the most revolutionary changes in the history of U.S. coin design. Desiring a "look" for the nation's gold coinage that was at once more modern yet clearly influenced by the great artists of Ancient Greece, Roosevelt commissioned two prominent American sculptors to create new designs for the Quarter Eagle, Half Eagle, Eagle and Double Eagle. To execute the new Quarter Eagle and Half Eagle, Roosevelt employed the skills of Bela Lyon Pratt. Roosevelt first became acquainted with Pratt through a mutual friend, Dr. William Sturgis Bigelow of Boston, who also shared the president's desire to improve the nation's coinage.

Like his Quarter Eagle, Pratt's Indian Half Eagle features a revolutionary design that is unlike any preceding type in the U.S. coinage family. Rather than being raised above the fields, the devices are incuse (or set below) the coin's surfaces. Contemporary criticisms that focused on the penchant for this design to collect contagious germs, the susceptibility of the incuse design to counterfeiting and the questionable ability of the coins to stack were easily brushed aside once the first examples entered circulation in 1908. The design proved its worth in commercial channels, and it is now widely regarded as one of the most attractive of all U.S. coin types.

The obverse of the Indian Half Eagle features a left-facing portrait of a Native American wearing a feathered headdress. Thirteen stars are arranged at the border six left, seven right. The word LIBERTY is above the portrait, and the date is below. On the reverse, a bald eagle strides powerfully to the viewer's left. The eagle is perched atop a bundle of arrows and it is holding an olive branch in place with its right talon. The motto IN GOD WE TRUST is present in the right field, while the Latin motto E PLURIBUS UNUM is in the left. Along the top border is the legend UNITED STATES OF AMERICA, and the denomination FIVE DOLLARS is at the bottom. The mintmark, if present, will be at the lower-left reverse rim before the arrowheads.

The Indian Half Eagle was struck from 1908-1929, most examples being produced in the Philadelphia, Denver and San Francisco Mints. The New Orleans facility contributed a scant 34,200 pieces in 1909—its final year of coinage operations. No coins of this denomination were produced from 1917-1928, and no more would ever be struck for circulation after 1929.

The Philadelphia Mint also struck proof Indian Half Eagles, albeit only from 1908 through 1915.

Short Type Set

This inspired design has long been a favorite among gold type collectors, and it readily lends itself to inclusion in several short type sets.

Half Eagle Types, a nine-piece set including:

Capped Bust Right Half Eagle, Small Eagle Reverse
Capped Bust Right Half Eagle, Large Eagle Reverse
Capped Bust Left Half Eagle
Capped Head Left Half Eagle, Large Diameter
Capped Head Left Half Eagle, Reduced Diameter
Classic Half Eagle
Liberty Half Eagle, No Motto
Liberty Half Eagle, Motto
Indian Half Eagle

20th Century Gold Coinage, a four or six-piece set including:

Indian Quarter Eagle
Indian Half Eagle
Indian Eagle (No Motto and/or Motto)
Saint-Gaudens Double Eagle (No Motto and/or Motto)

Popular U.S. Gold Types, an eight or ten-piece set including:

Liberty Quarter Eagle
Indian Quarter Eagle
Liberty Half Eagle, Motto
Indian Half Eagle
Liberty Eagle, Motto
Indian Eagle (No Motto and/or Motto)
Liberty Double Eagle (usually a Type III example)
Saint-Gaudens Double Eagle (No Motto and/or Motto)

Complete Type Set

In terms of total number of coins known, the Indian Half Eagle is one of the more plentiful coins of this denomination in today's numismatic market. With the exception of the 1908-S, 1909-O, 1911-D, 1911-S, 1912-S, 1915-S, 1916-S and 1929, I recommend any issue in this series for inclusion in a circulated type set. This type can be challenging to locate in the finer Mint State grades, however, and you are likely to see one issue above all others at or above the MS-63 level. That coin is the 1909-D, and it is the most logical choice for Mint State type purposes.

Circulated Examples: There is very little difference in value for common-date Indian Half Eagles in AU-58 and examples in the lower Mint State grades. Some realized prices for the 1909-D in PCGS and NGC AU-58 from late 2006/early 2007 range from $322 to $488, while an example of the same issue in NGC MS-61 traded hands for $575 in April of 2007. With an approximate difference of just $100-$250, it might not seem logical to pursue this type in circulated grades.

Keep in mind that Indian Half Eagles in MS-60, MS-61 and MS-62 are heavily abraded, lackluster and otherwise unattractive coins. What's more, the conditionally challenging nature of the type as a whole means that even the common 1909-D advances to several thousand dollars in MS-63. If you are on a tighter budget but would still like to acquire a relatively smooth, suitably lustrous Indian Half Eagle, I suggest purchasing an AU-58. Be selective, however, and try to find an example that is above average for the grade.

Courtesy of Bowers and Merena

The Indian Half Eagle can be a challenging type to locate in the finer Mint State grades, and the buyer is likely to see one issue above all others at or above the MS-63 level. That coin is the 1909-D, and it seems to be the most logical choice for the Mint State type collector.

Mint State Examples: Focusing on the 1909-D, you can acquire a pleasing Indian Half Eagle with good luster and a minimum number of distracting abrasions at the MS-64 grade level. Coins certified by PCGS or NGC cost about $3,500-$4,000. In keeping with the series' conditionally challenging nature, expect the price of the 1909-D to increase exponentially as you progress up the grading scale. A PCGS MS-65 went to the winning bidder at $14,950 during an early 2007 sale.

General Characteristics: Striking quality varies for this type, and some issues (like the 1911) are known for poor definition over the feathers in the Native American's headdress. There are enough coins to choose from, however, that patience will be rewarded with a sharply struck example.

The 1909-D is usually well produced with satiny or softly frosted luster. Color ranges from yellow-gold on the lighter side of the spectrum to deeper orange-gold and green-gold shades.

Words of Caution: I have encountered a few Indian Half Eagles with what appears to be dirt adhering to some of the recessed areas of the devices. Most of those coins were circulated, although a few lower-grade Mint State coins were also included. Avoid these coins as the foreign matter in the recesses has an adverse effect on eye appeal. I feel the same way about examples with alloy spots. While alloy spots are becoming less common in the numismatic market, I still encounter Indian Half Eagles with those features once in a while.

Some branch mint issues in this series are notorious for possessing a poorly struck mintmark. Examples include the 1909-O, 1913-S and 1914-S, which are nearly impossible to locate with a sharp mintmark. This problem is not as pronounced for other issues, however, one of which is the 1909-D. If you are searching for an '09-D, therefore, I would absolutely hold out until you find a coin with a boldly impressed D mintmark.

STRATEGIES FOR INCLUDING THE INDIAN HALF EAGLE IN A COMPLETE TYPE SET

Most Desirable Issue(s):

　　Circulated Grades: *Most, including 1908, 1909-D and 1915*

　　Mint State Grades: *1909-D*

Most Desirable Grade(s), Circulated Coins: *AU-58*

Estimated Cost: *$325-$525*

Key to Collecting: *Sharp striking detail including, if applicable, a well-defined mintmark; portions of the original luster still intact; relatively abrasion-free surfaces*

Most Desirable Grade(s), Mint State Coins: *MS-64 or finer*

Estimated Cost: *$3,500 and up*

Key to Collecting: *Sharp striking detail including a well-defined D mintmark; satiny or frosty luster; yellow-gold, orange-gold or green-gold color; a minimal number of wispy bagmarks*

Advanced Type Set

Rarer Issues: Most of the San Francisco Mint issues in this series are lower-mintage and/or scarce coins, but they usually appear in the market often enough that you should have little difficulty locating an example for inclusion in a better-date type set of circulated coins. I particularly like problem-free AU-58s for this purpose. Recent prices realized for scarcer S-mint Indian Half Eagles in AU-58 include:

> **1908-S:** *$1,265 for an NGC-certified example in February 2007*
> **1909-S:** *$518 for an NGC-certified example in November 2006*
> **1910-S:** *$518 for an NGC-certified example in February 2007*
> **1912-S:** *$633 for an NGC-certified example in February 2007*
> **1913-S:** *$604 for an NGC-certified example in February 2007*
> **1914-S:** *$863 for an NGC-certified example in February 2007*
> **1915-S:** *$805 for a PCGS-certified example in April 2007*

Mint State type collectors should focus on the Philadelphia Mint issues from 1908-1915. All have considerably lower certified populations than the 1909-D, yet they sell for only $1,000-$1,500 more in MS-64. In MS-65, however, these P-mint issues command at least several thousand dollars more than the 1909-D.

STRATEGIES FOR INCLUDING THE INDIAN HALF EAGLE IN A TYPE SET OF RARER ISSUES

Most Desirable Issue(s):

Circulated Grades: *1908-S, 1909-S, 1910-S, 1912-S, 1913-S, 1914-S, 1915-S*

Mint State Grades: *1908, 1909, 1910, 1911, 1912, 1913, 1914, 1915*

Most Desirable Grade(s), Circulated Coins: *AU-58*

Estimated Cost: *$525-$1,500*

Key to Collecting: *Overall sharp definition, including a bold-to-sharp S mintmark, if possible; ample remaining luster; no sizeable or individually distracting circulation marks*

Most Desirable Grade(s), Mint State Coins: *MS-64 or finer*

Estimated Cost: *$4,500 and up*

Key to Collecting: *Bold-to-sharp striking detail; satin or frosty luster; yellow-gold, orange-gold, rose-gold or green-gold color; a minimum number of wispy bagmarks*

Major Subtypes: The Indian Half Eagle underwent no design changes during its operational lifetime, and there are no major subtypes in this series.

Issuing Mint: With only four coins required, assembling a complete set of Indian Half Eagles that includes a representative of each issuing mint might sound like an easy task. The conditionally challenging nature of this type and the rarity of the series' only O-mint delivery, however, pose problems for many collectors. With these thoughts in mind, and with the goal of assembling a set that is as uniform in quality as possible, I suggest pursuing this strategy with a mix of AU and lower Mint State coins.

With the exception of the key-date 1929, any Philadelphia Mint issue in this series will serve as a fitting addition to a type set. Coins such as the first-year 1908, 1910 and 1915 are fairly easy to locate in MS-62, and they cost only $1,000-$1,500.

You can also meet the Denver Mint requirement with a Mint State coin, such is the prevalence of the 1909-D in MS-62. As with the 1908, 1910 and 1915, the '09-D typically sells for $1,000-$1,500 in this grade.

The New Orleans Mint is the real stopper to assembling a complete type set of Indian Half Eagles by issuing mint. There is only a single O-mint issue in this series, and the 1909-O is a low-mintage, key-date rarity with just 34,200 pieces struck. Survivors are scarce in worn condition, nothing short of rare in Mint State and enjoy strong demand at all levels of preservation. Given the elusiveness and cost of even marginal Mint State examples, obtain a coin that grades AU-58. This is an attractive grade for the issue, particularly if you insist on a piece with pleasing color, a suitably bold O mintmark and relatively smooth surfaces. The cost will be substantial. Some early 2007 auction appearances for this issue resulted in realized prices for AU-58s in the range of $11,000-$15,550.

Courtesy of Rare Coin Wholesalers

The 1909-O is the only New Orleans Mint issue in the Indian Half Eagle series. It is also a rare, key-date delivery with just 34,200 pieces struck. Obtaining an example will likely be a considerable obstacle to completing an advanced type set by issuing mint.

Generally speaking, S-mint Indian Half Eagles are more challenging to obtain in Mint State than their Philadelphia and Denver Mint counterparts. Nevertheless, the 1911-S and 1916-S are plentiful enough through MS-62 that you should have little difficulty acquiring a Mint State example. As certified by PCGS or NGC, the 1911-S sells for $1,500-$2,000 in MS-62. The price range for the 1916-S in the same grade might be a bit wider, an example selling for $1,150 through a 2005 auction while another traded hands for $2,760 in an early 2007 sale.

Avoid any 1911-S Half Eagle with poor striking detail over the lowermost feathers in the Native American's headdress and/or the reverse mintmark. The 1916-S is almost always a bit poorly defined over the mintmark, so an example with above-average detail to the S is preferable. Luster for these two issues ranges from satiny to frosty, and the color is typically an orange-gold or green-gold shade.

STRATEGIES FOR INCLUDING THE INDIAN HALF EAGLE IN A TYPE SET BY ISSUING MINT

Required Number of Coins: *Four*

Issuing Mint #1: *Philadelphia, Pennsylvania*

Most Desirable Issue(s): *1908-1915*

Key to Collecting: *MS-62 grade; bold-to-sharp striking detail; satin or frosty luster; yellow-gold, orange-gold, rose-gold or green-gold color*

Issuing Mint #2: *Denver, Colorado*

Most Desirable Issue(s): *1909-D*

Key to Collecting: *MS-62 grade; sharp striking detail including a well-defined D mintmark; satiny or frosty luster; yellow-gold, orange-gold or green-gold color*

Issuing Mint #3: *New Orleans, Louisiana*

Most Desirable Issue(s): *1909-O (only option)*

Key to Collecting: *AU-58 grade; bold definition to the O mintmark; yellow-gold, rose-gold or, occasionally, green-gold color; relatively distraction-free surfaces*

Issuing Mint #4: *San Francisco, California*

Most Desirable Issue(s): *1911-S, 1916-S*

Key to Collecting: *MS-62 grade; sharp striking detail including sharp (1911-S) or bold (1916-S) definition to the S mintmark; orange-gold or green-gold color; satin or frosty mint luster*

Proof Type Set

The Philadelphia Mint struck proof Indian Half Eagles each year from 1908 through 1915. This was a time of experimentation in the United States Mint as far as proof gold production is concerned, and several different finishes are represented on surviving Indian Half Eagles. The 1908 and 1911-1915 deliveries typically display a form of matte or sandblast finish that varies in the number and size of the surface granules as well as the color. The 1909 and 1910, however, exhibit the unusual Roman Gold finish that is a blend of satin and semi-reflective qualities.

None of these finishes struck a particularly receptive chord among the contemporary public, and all proof Indian Half Eagles are rarer than their original mintages might suggest. Many examples failed to sell and were eventually melted in the Mint. Even today, surviving matte specimens are often overlooked by collectors and investors. For one thing, the coins' surfaces are usually quite dark, a feature that is particularly pronounced for the first-year 1908. In addition, the matte texture is delicate and easily marred, and contact marks are readily evident as shiny spots on the surfaces. For these reasons, I do not recommend the 1908, 1911, 1912, 1913, 1914 or 1915 for proof type purposes.

The Roman Gold issues of 1909 and 1910, however, are relatively bright with warm, medium intensity, yellow-gold color. A small percentage of examples possess more of a green-gold cast. Examples that grade at least Proof-64 are largely free of wispy handling marks, and all specimens that I have seen possess razor-sharp striking detail. A 1909 in PCGS Proof-64 sold for $16,100 in 2004. The price for both the 1909 and 1910 increases dramatically with grade, however, and a bidder paid the hefty sum of $48,875 for a 1910 in PCGS Proof-65 PCGS in a 2006 auction.

Courtesy of Rare Coin Wholesalers

With brighter surfaces that the 1908 and 1911-1915 deliveries, the Roman Gold issues of 1909 and 1910 might be the most desirable options to represent the Indian Half Eagle in a type set of proof coinage.

STRATEGIES FOR INCLUDING THE INDIAN HALF EAGLE IN A PROOF TYPE SET

Most Desirable Issue(s): *1909, 1910*

Most Desirable Grade(s): *Proof-64 or finer*

Key to Collecting: *Needle-sharp striking detail; bright Roman Gold surfaces; yellow-gold or green-gold color; a minimum number of wispy contact marks*

Assembling a Complete Set

Year Set: Relying almost exclusively on the Philadelphia Mint issues, you can assemble a nearly complete 10-coin year set of Indian Half Eagles without too much difficulty. Of course, the 1916-S is that year's only Half Eagle delivery, and an example is absolutely required for completion of this set. The only other year in this series with just a single delivery reported is 1929, and a survivor of the year's P-mint issue will be considerably more costly to obtain than a 1916-S. Indeed, the 1929 is the rarest Half Eagle of this type in terms of total number of coins known, and it is the obvious "stopper" to assembling a complete year set of the type.

The majority of 1929 Half Eagles that have survived are Mint State, and the issue did not see widespread circulation at the time of delivery. It is a good idea to concentrate on the rarer issues when undertaking any numismatic task, and I recommend obtaining a 1929 Half Eagle in MS-62, MS-63 or MS-64 to begin your Indian Half Eagle year set. In these grades the 1929 varies in price from $12,000 to $40,000. Your collecting budget, as well as your willingness to live with scattered bagmarks and/or somewhat deficient luster, should dictate exactly which grade in this range you choose to select. Avoid examples in MS-60 and MS-61 if at all possible as they tend to be overly abraded, sometimes also with dull, lackluster surfaces.

Courtesy of Bowers and Merena

The 1929 is the rarest Half Eagle of this type in terms of total number of coins known and, since neither the Denver nor San Francisco Mints struck coins of this denomination that year, it is perhaps the obvious "stopper" to assembling a complete year set of this type.

Depending on your collecting budget and/or the grade you select for the 1929, the balance of an Indian Half Eagle year set could be assembled with Mint State coins in the 62-64 range. A Choice-quality set using MS-64s for the 1908-1915 deliveries and MS-63s for the 1916-S and 1929 will be well matched in terms of technical quality. What's more, MS-63s and MS-64s offer considerable eye appeal if chosen carefully. Built using this strategy, an Indian Half Eagle year set will require at least $60,000-$65,000. One third of this total cost is required for the 1929.

Date and Mint Set: If you reconcile yourself to the cost associated with acquiring the 1909-O and 1929, assembling a date and mint set of Indian Half Eagles is a readily obtainable goal. Even the key-date 1909-O and 1929 trade frequently enough in today's market that you should not have too much difficulty locating an example in most grades. In the interest of keeping costs at a more manageable level, assemble the set using a mix of AU and lower Mint State coins. Expect to pay $11,000-$16,000 for the 1909-O in AU-58. Although the 1929 is actually an inverse condition rarity with fewer circulated survivors than Mint State ones, AU-58s do exist and they are offered now and then in the market. An example certified by PCGS sold through auction in early 2007 for $17,250.

Even though they are somewhat pricey, I would still purchase the semi key-date Indian Half Eagles in MS-62. Several examples of the 1908-S in MS-62 sold between $2,000 and $2,750 at auction during 2005. The 1911-D is another semi key-date issue in this series, and it is a costlier proposition than the 1908-S at $10,000-$15,000 in MS-62. The 1915-S is a $4,500-$5,500 coin in the same grade. Finally, the 1909-S, 1910-S, 1912-S, 1913-S, 1914-S and 1916-S are obtainable at $3,000-$5,000 each in MS-62.

This leaves the 1908, 1908-D, 1909, 1909-D, 1910, 1910-D, 1911, 1911-S, 1912, 1913, 1914, 1914-D and 1915. You can acquire one example of each of these issues in MS-62 for $1,000-$2,000. The total cost for this 24-piece set in AU-BU, therefore, is in the range of $75,000-$110,000.

Die Variety Set: Due to the Mint's use of standardized dies in the production of this series, there are no significant die varieties in the Indian Half Eagle series.

Proof Set: Being that there are only eight issues in the proof Indian Half Eagle series, assembling a complete set of these coins is within reach if you have considerable financial resources. Due to the delicate nature of their surfaces, the matte issues of 1908 and 1911-1915 usually show numerous distracting shiny spots in grades at or below the Proof-64 level. In order to avoid this problem, assemble your proof Indian Half Eagle set in Proof-65. Based on select auction prices realized from 2006 and 2007, this eight-piece set in PCGS and NGC Proof-65 requires at least $350,000-$400,000 to complete.

A Complete Set by Issuing Mint: While there are many ways to collect Indian Half Eagles, focusing on a specific issuing mint is not among the more popular. The brevity of this series explains why it is so conducive to year or date and mint collecting. For example, a complete set of P-mint issues would require the addition of just one coin—a 1916-S—for conversion to a year set.

Investing Tips

As previously mentioned, the Indian Half Eagle is a conditionally challenging type that is quite rare in the finer Mint State grades. This is most readily evident when you look solely at those grades at or above the MS-66 level. PCGS and NGC combined have certified only 132 Indian Half Eagles in MS-66, MS-67 and MS-68 (May/2007). In order to understand exactly how limited this number is, it helps to remember that the United States Mint struck 14,078,066 Indian Half Eagles from 1908-1929. When you also consider that the number of high-grade type collectors is always expanding and that the beauty of this type is best appreciated in the finest Mint State grades, an expertly preserved Gem or Superb Gem will make a desirable addition to an investment portfolio. That certain issues have already had an impressive track record at these levels is evident by looking at the first-year 1908 in MS-66.

A market correction for this issue is noted between late 2006 and early 2007, but the 1908 has still trended upward nicely since the early 21st century. And don't forget, market corrections are excellent buying opportunities, particularly for issues that are still demonstrating growth over an extended period of time.

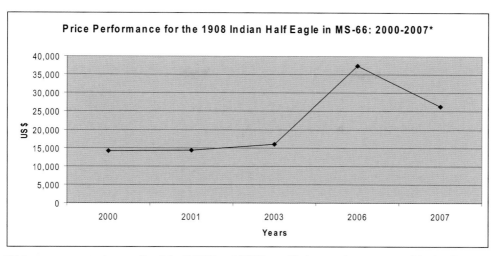

*Values represent prices realized for PCGS and NGC-certified examples as reported by leading rare coin auction houses.

CHAPTER TWENTY FIVE

Capped Bust Right Eagles with Small Eagle Reverse

Courtesy of Rare Coin Wholesalers

SPECIFICATIONS

Year(s) Issued: *1795-1797*
Issuing Mint(s): *Philadelphia only*
Authorizing Act: *April 2, 1792*
Designer: *Robert Scot*
Weight: *17.50 grams*
Composition: *91.67% gold, 8.33% silver and copper*
Diameter: *33 millimeters (approximate)*
Edge: *Reeded*

History

Although the Half Eagle was the preferred denomination among the contemporary public during the late 1700s and early 1800s, the Eagle had the greatest face value of any United States coin until the commencement of regular-issue Double Eagle production in 1850. It must have been an occasion of tremendous national pride, therefore, when the chief coiner delivered the first Ten-Dollar gold pieces on September 22, 1795. Other countries almost certainly noticed that it took the United States less than two decades since declaring its independence from Great Britain to obtain the ability to place such a large and valuable gold coin into the avenues of commerce. And perhaps no other peoples looked upon such an event with more trepidation than the British. For while the American Revolution established the United States' political independence from the Great Britain, the former 13 colonies were still very much under the economic yoke of their former masters. The issuing of the first Eagles, therefore, can be seen as one more significant step in the

American Revolution—a struggle that would not really reach a definable end until the War of 1812 settled important economic issues between the United States and Great Britain.

The task of designing the first Ten-Dollar gold piece fell to Chief Engraver Robert Scot. In keeping with a practice that was to become more-or-less standard in the United States Mint until the early 20th century, Scot chose the same design for the Eagle that he used for the Half Eagle. On the obverse, a bust of Liberty faces right with an arrangement of stars at the border, the word LIBERTY above and the date below. Liberty is wearing a soft cap that appears to have been modeled after a popular women's headdress of the late 18th century. On the reverse, a rather frail-looking eagle with spread wings is perched atop an olive branch with a wreath clutched in its beak. The legend UNITED STATES OF AMERICA is around the border.

The United States Mint at Philadelphia used this design in the production of Eagles for just shy of three years from September 22, 1795 through May 2, 1797. During that time period, only 13,344 coins were struck. This figure probably represents the total original mintage for the entire Capped Bust Right, Small Eagle Ten-Dollar series. The word "probably" is used here because the records left by early Mint personnel make it impossible to tell conclusively when the Large Eagle design completely replaced its Small Eagle predecessor.

The survival rate for pre-1834 U.S. gold coins is quite low, and no more than 5-6% of Small Eagle Tens produced have survived. Most of the examples that have been lost were claimed by bullion depositors and speculators during the run up in gold prices through the 1830s.

Short Type Set

Any set of United States Ten-Dollar gold types would, of course, have to begin with an example of the Capped Bust Right with Small Eagle design. This short set requires only six coins, as follows:

Eagle Types, a six-piece set including:

> ***Capped Bust Right Eagle, Small Eagle Reverse***
> *Capped Bust Right Eagle, Large Eagle Reverse*
> *Liberty Eagle, No Motto*
> *Liberty Eagle, Motto*
> *Indian Eagle, No Motto*
> *Indian Eagle, Motto*

Another short set in which this early Eagle figures prominently focuses on use of the Capped Bust Right design in the U.S. gold series.

Capped Bust Right Gold Coinage, a six-piece set including:

> *Capped Bust Right Quarter Eagle, No Stars Obverse*
> *Capped Bust Right Quarter Eagle, Stars Obverse*
> *Capped Bust Right Half Eagle, Small Eagle Reverse*
> *Capped Bust Right Half Eagle, Large Eagle Reverse*
> ***Capped Bust Right Eagle, Small Eagle Reverse***
> *Capped Bust Right Eagle, Large Eagle Reverse*

Complete Type Set

Judging by auction appearances, certified population data at PCGS and NGC and my experience tracking these coins, the first-year 1795 with 13 leaves in the reverse branch is the most common Capped Bust Right Eagle with Small Eagle Reverse. This makes sense since a small number of coins were probably set aside at the time of delivery for their novelty and historical significance. As the United States' first Ten-Dollar gold piece and the most plentiful issue of its design, I highly recommend the 1795 13 Leaves as a type coin.

Circulated Examples: When numismatists speak of "circulation" in connection with early United States gold coins, we are not envisioning commercial use with which someone in the 21st century would be familiar. Denizens of late 18th century America did not walk around with their pockets full of Quarter Eagles, Half Eagles and Eagles. Likewise, they did not have a "coin jar" at home into which they would deposit loose change at the end of a day's excursions. Instead, circulation for an early U.S. gold coin refers to use in international trade or sequestration as part of a bank's bullion reserves. We can accept this theory as fact for the Eagle based not only on the considerable amount of money that ten dollars represented in the 1790s, but also on the distribution of surviving examples of the Small Eagle type. Most worn survivors are concentrated at the EF and AU levels, suggesting that the coins saw very little day-to-day use.

A 1795 13 Leaves Eagle certified EF-40 by PCGS crossed the auction block in early 2006 for $54,625. This is an uncommonly large sum of money to pay for the assigned grade, and I believe that this coin is more accurately described as an AU. A range of $35,000-$40,000 is more appropriate for an EF-40. An example in NGC AU-53 sold for $44,563 in November of 2005, while a PCGS AU-58 required $86,250 from a winning bidder during one of the earliest auctions of 2007.

Courtesy of Bowers and Merena

Most worn 1795 Eagles encountered in today's market are concentrated at the EF and AU levels. A problem-free piece that falls within the 40-58 numeric grade range would probably be viewed with pleasure by its owner.

Mint State Examples: All Mint State 1795 13 Leaves Eagles are highly prized in today's market, and even MS-60s as graded by PCGS or NGC serve as centerpieces in gold type sets. A PCGS MS-60 sold at auction for $161,000 in 2004. I am aware of at least one PCGS MS-63 that realized $201,250 during an early 2007 auction, and it was followed one month later by an NGC MS-64 with a sale price of $345,000. Gems number just four coins at PCGS and NGC, and the sole PCGS MS-65 traded hands for $506,000 in 2003.

General Characteristics: As a product of the early United States Mint, you might expect the 1795 13 Leaves Eagle to have some peculiar striking characteristics. Perhaps surprisingly, many high-grade survivors that I have handled possess overall bold, if not sharp definition. While a few survivors are quite sharply impressed over the highpoint of the obverse portrait, as well as the eagle's head and breast on the reverse, it is a good idea to expect to see some softness to the detail in these areas. The color is typically a yellow-gold, orange-gold or green-gold shade. Pieces that retain partial or complete mint luster are often satiny or semi-prooflike in appearance. Circulated and low-grade Mint State examples almost always come with liberally abraded surfaces. With patience, however, you can locate a few examples through MS-62 that are free of sizeable and/or individually distracting abrasions. Coins that grade at least MS-63 display only small-size abrasions, and their number diminishes as you progress up the grading scale.

Some Capped Bust Right Eagles display adjustment marks on one or both sides. These features are as made and are a normal part of the production process in the early United States Mint. While adjustment marks will not result in a lower numeric grade from PCGS or NGC, they can be distracting if excessive or concentrated in a prime focal area.

Words of Caution: Even a quick perusal of auction catalogs provides sufficient evidence that many surviving 1795 13 Leaves Eagles are impaired for one reason or another. Some coins are scratched, plugged or otherwise damaged, while others have been the recipients of an overzealous cleaning, tooling or more-or-less inconspicuous repairs. This is a rare and historic issue, and it makes sense that earlier generations of numismatists saved pieces that may have been passed over were they examples of a less desirable issue or type. In addition, many cleaned and repaired early Eagles were not subject to such treatment with the intent to deceive. Rather, many practitioners of these numismatic "arts" probably felt as though they were improving the appearance and enhancing the desirability of coins that had significant problems.

The U.S. rare coin market of the 21st century looks upon impairments such as repairs, tooling and whizzing in a different light than, say, numismatists in the 1940s or 1950s. Today, significantly impaired early Eagles are rejected for certification at PCGS and NGC, the coins instead finding their way into ANACS, NCS or other holders that make mention of the impairment(s) on the insert. Due to the significant cost of this issue, you might be tempted to acquire a 1795 13 Leaves Eagle with AU or even Mint State details that is being offered at a lower price due to one or more problems. I do not recommend this course of action since impaired examples always appreciate less than problem-free pieces. If you simply cannot afford an AU or Mint State coin as certified by PCGS or NGC, acquire a problem-free coin in a lower grade. Your financial investment in the coin will be better protected if you follow this advice.

One final word of caution is perhaps in order before you begin searching for a 1795 13 Leaves Eagle. Many early U.S. gold coins have been lightly cleaned at one time or another and even PCGS and NGC sometimes accept such pieces for certification. These services have even been known to lower an example's numeric grade to compensate for a light cleaning. This was certainly the case with the 1795 13 Leaves example in PCGS VF-30 that appeared in a major auction during September of 2006. The coin was cataloged as showing "evidence of cleaning" with a "degree of wear [that] is less than expected for the grade." The coin realized $46,000, a price that is more in line with an EF grade than VF-30. While the market accepts such coins at competitive price levels, do not purchase any early Eagle with which you are fully satisfied. Buyer's remorse is a terrible feeling and I have seen it sap the enthusiasm of many promising collectors.

STRATEGIES FOR INCLUDING THE CAPPED BUST RIGHT EAGLE WITH SMALL EAGLE REVERSE IN A COMPLETE TYPE SET

Most Desirable Issue(s): *1795 13 Leaves*

Most Desirable Grade(s), Circulated Coins: *EF-40 through AU-58*

Estimated Cost: *$35,000 and up*

Key to Collecting: *Free of large and/or singularly distracting abrasions; few if any adjustment marks; yellow-gold, orange-gold or green-gold color; overall bold-to-sharp definition*

Most Desirable Grade(s), Mint State Coins: *MS-60 or finer*

Estimated Cost: *$100,000 and up*

Key to Collecting: *Free of large and/or singularly distracting abrasions; few if any adjustment marks; yellow-gold, orange-gold or green-gold color; overall sharp striking detail*

Advanced Type Set

Rarer Issues: After the first-year 1795 13 Leaves, the Capped Bust Right, Small Eagle Ten that you are most likely to encounter in today's market is the 1796. This second-year delivery is twice as rare as the 1795 13 Leaves, but it is still more plentiful than the 1795 9 Leaves and the 1797 Small Eagle. For such a rare and desirable issue, it hardly seems appropriate to suggest a grade range for type purposes. As long as the coin fits into your budget, is attractive and has been certified by PCGS or NGC, then you should consider including it in your set. The 1796 starts at $40,000 in EF-40 and progresses through the $75,000-$85,000 range in AU-55 before commanding $100,000+ in MS-62.

The quality of strike for this issue is similar to that of the 1795 13 Leaves. Once again, color varies from yellow-gold to orange-gold and green-gold shades. Scattered abrasions are the norm, but avoid examples with large distractions or an excessive number of adjustment marks.

STRATEGIES FOR INCLUDING THE CAPPED BUST RIGHT EAGLE WITH SMALL EAGLE REVERSE IN A TYPE SET OF RARER ISSUES

Most Desirable Issue(s): *1796*

Most Desirable Grade(s): *EF-40 or finer*

Estimated Cost: *$40,000 and up*

Key to Collecting: *Free of large and/or singularly distracting abrasions; few if any adjustment marks; yellow-gold, orange-gold or green-gold color; overall bold-to-sharp definition*

Major Subtypes: There are four major subtypes in the Capped Bust Right Small Eagle Ten-Dollar series, each of which represents a variation on the basic design. These subtypes differ either in the number of leaves in the reverse branch or the number or arrangement of the obverse stars. This is an extremely challenging series to collect using this strategy, but take note that achieving this goal would also give you a complete date and mint set of the type.

Obtaining one example each of the 1795 13 Leaves, 1795 9 Leaves, 1796 and 1797 Small Eagle in AU-55 requires that you have at least $380,000 to spend. The 1795 9 Leaves and 1797 Small Eagle will monopolize much of your effort and financial resources, as both issues are considerably rarer than the 1795 13 Leaves and 1796.

STRATEGIES FOR INCLUDING THE CAPPED BUST RIGHT EAGLE W/ SMALL EAGLE REVERSE IN A TYPE SET OF MAJOR SUBTYPES

Required Number of Coins: *Four*

Major Subtype #1: *15 Stars Obverse, 13 Leaves*

Most Desirable Issue(s): *1795 13 Leaves (only option)*

Major Subtype #2: *15 Stars Obverse, 9 Leaves*

Most Desirable Issue(s): *1795 9 Leaves (only option)*

Major Subtype #3: *16 Stars Obverse, Stars 8x8*

Most Desirable Issue(s): *1796 (only option)*

Major Subtype #4: *16 Stars Obverse, Stars 12x4*

Most Desirable Issue(s): *1797 Small Eagle (only option)*

Issuing Mint: All Eagles of this type were struck in the Philadelphia Mint.

Proof Type Set

The United States Mint did not strike Small Eagle Capped Bust Right Tens in proof format.

Assembling a Complete Set

Year Set: As far as the Small Eagle portion of the Capped Bust Right Eagle series is concerned, this strategy differs from a type set of major subtypes through the subtraction of just a single coin. You need only one example with the date 1795, and the rarity of the 9 Leaves argues in favor of including a 13 Leaves coin in your year set. To acquire one example each of the 1795 13 Leaves, 1796 and 1797 Small Eagle in AU-55, plan on spending at least $225,000-$250,000.

Date and Mint Set: As previously mentioned, a date set of Capped Bust Right Eagles with Small Eagle Reverse corresponds to a set of major subtypes.

Die Variety Set: There is enough variation between individual die marriages in this series to make the Small Eagle Capped Bust Right Ten an appealing series to collect by die variety. A major stumbling block for many collectors, however, is the cost. Acquiring even a single Capped Bust Right Eagle with Small Eagle Reverse is a costly undertaking, while the financial commitment increases markedly for a three-coin year set or a four-piece date and mint set. I am aware of only one collector who has completed a set of this early Eagle type by die variety: Harry W. Bass, Jr.

On the other hand, the Small Eagle Capped Bust Right Ten has relatively few individual die marriages as far as early U.S. gold series are concerned. Furthermore, you will already own examples of the two rarest die marriages (1795 9 Leaves and the 1797 Small Eagle) if you have completed a set by major subtype. There is only a single die variety confirmed for the 1796, and the other four varieties of the 1795 (each with 13 Leaves in the reverse branch) are more prevalent than the 9 Leaves variety. A complete die variety set of Capped Bust Right, Small Eagle Tens requires seven coins and, using examples that grade AU-55, will cost at least $550,000.

Proof Set: Once again, the United States Mint did not strike proof Eagles of this type.

A Complete Set by Issuing Mint: Since all Small Eagle Capped Bust Right Tens were struck in the Philadelphia Mint, a complete set by issuing mint is the same as a complete date and mint set.

Investing Tips

The most popular issue in this series, as well as one of the most significant coins in all of United States coinage history, is the first-year 1795. The 13 Leaves variant has long enjoyed considerable interest among type collectors and gold specialists, and the gap between supply and demand for high-quality Mint State survivors continues to widen. This relationship between critical market forces is best illustrated by looking at the price appreciation for the issue in MS-64 over a 25-year period beginning in 1982.

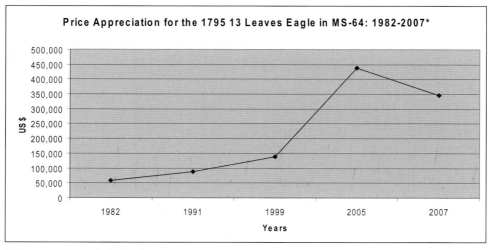

*Values represent individual or average prices realized as reported by leading rare coin auction houses.

The combined PCGS and NGC population for this issue in MS-64 is only eight coins (May/2007). This is certainly a small total even by early 21st century standards, and these coins are becoming even rarer from an availability standpoint as more type collectors become active in the market.

While limited supply and increasing demand are sufficient reasons for you to acquire a Choice 1795 13 Leaves Eagle, the slight decrease in price between 2005 and 2007 noted in the above graph provides an even greater sense of urgency. I believe that this price decrease represents a short-term market correction and not a long-term trend. Take advantage of this situation by adding a high-grade 1795 13 Leaves Eagle to your portfolio before the issue rallies.

CHAPTER TWENTY SIX

Capped Bust Right Eagles with Large Eagle Reverse

Courtesy of Rare Coin Wholesalers

SPECIFICATIONS

Year(s) Issued: *1797-1804*
Issuing Mint(s): *Philadelphia only*
Authorizing Act: *April 2, 1792*
Designer: *Robert Scot*
Weight: *17.50 grams*
Composition: *91.67% gold, 8.33% silver and copper*
Diameter: *33 millimeters (approximate)*
Edge: *Reeded*

History

In 1797, the Mint instituted the first of five major design changes in the Eagle series. Robert Scot's new reverse design for the Capped Bust Right Eagle closely followed the Great Seal of the United States, the eagle larger than that of its predecessor with a shield superimposed over its breast. Above its head is a field of 13 stars and an arc of clouds, and its beak clutches a scroll upon which the Latin motto E PLURIBUS UNUM is inscribed. A bundle of arrows is in the eagle's right (or Dexter) claw while the olive branch of peace is in the left (or less honorable) claw. While the late Walter Breen (1988) suggests that the reversal of these two design elements may have been a bit of "ill-timed saber rattling" by the federal government, it is more probable that it was merely a blunder by Scot. The chief engraver was probably not up to snuff on the study of heraldry. The legend UNITED STATES OF AMERICA continued in its original position around the periphery. Additionally, the basic Capped Bust Right design on the obverse remained unchanged.

Yearly mintages for Large Eagle Tens are sporadic, the year 1798 representing a low point with just 1,742 pieces produced. On the other hand, a record (for that era) delivery of 44,344 coins was achieved during 1801, which is a result of a sudden increase in demand for this denomination among bullion depositors. Remember, mintage figures from the early years of U.S. Mint operations represent the total number of coins struck during a specific calendar year and may not correspond to the number of examples produced bearing a specific date. Since high-grade steel was in short supply in the 1790s and early 1800s, the Mint often used dies until they were irretrievably broken even if the date on the resulting coin did not match the date on the calendar. Older dies were also sometimes pressed back into service if they were still usable, a situation that could result in, say, an 1800-dated coin being struck after an example dated 1801. As a result, we can only estimate original mintages for specific issues based on the number of coins that have survived.

The final Capped Bust Right Eagles with Large Eagle Reverse struck for circulation were delivered in 1804. They also turned out to be the final business strike Eagles produced in the United States Mint until 1838. On December 31, 1804, President Thomas Jefferson halted production of Eagles because the coins were being exported and melted by bullion dealers at a net loss to the nation's economy.

As it turned out, however, 1804 did not see the final use of the Large Eagle Capped Bust Right design on a Ten-Dollar gold piece. In 1834, President Andrew Jackson requested that the Mint strike special proof sets for presentation to foreign governments. These sets were to include one example of each denomination that was still considered current at that time. In the case of the Eagle, this presented an interesting situation because no examples of this coin had been struck for circulation in 30 years. Accordingly, Mint personnel created a new set of dies that bore the date of the most recent Eagle delivery: 1804. Unlike the business strikes that were actually produced that year, however, the proofs created in 1834/1835 display a plain 4 in the date and a beaded border. The coins were also struck in a close collar that imparted a more uniform diameter.

The proof 1804 Plain 4 Eagle is one of the classic rarities in the United States coinage series. It is a legitimate Mint issue and should be considered an important part of the Capped Bust Right series. Only four gold examples have been traced, one of which is still part of the exquisite King of Siam Proof Set for which it was originally created. Four additional examples are known, but those coins are silver impressions (Judd-34) that represent either die trial strikings from 1834/1835 or a fantasy issue made by Mint officials during or after the late 1850s for private purposes. I had the extremely good fortune of researching the history and pedigree for one of the silver impressions in late 2006 for a prominent Southern California dealer, and I also closely examined the gold example in the King of Siam Proof Set at around the same time.

Short Type Set

In addition to a set of United States Eagle types, a short type set of Capped Bust Right gold coinage will highlight the Large Eagle Ten. Both sets require six coins for completion, and both could serve as either an impressive numismatic holding in their own right or the beginning of a more comprehensive type set of U.S. gold coinage.

Eagle Types, a six-piece set including:

Capped Bust Right Eagle, Small Eagle Reverse
Capped Bust Right Eagle, Large Eagle Reverse

Liberty Eagle, No Motto
Liberty Eagle, Motto
Indian Eagle, No Motto
Indian Eagle, Motto

Capped Bust Right Gold Coinage, a six-piece set including:

Capped But Right Quarter Eagle, No Stars Obverse
Capped Bust Right Quarter Eagle, Stars Obverse
Capped Bust Right Half Eagle, Small Eagle Reverse
Capped Bust Right Half Eagle, Large Eagle Reverse
Capped Bust Right Eagle, Small Eagle Reverse
Capped Bust Right Eagle, Large Eagle Reverse

Complete Type Set

As a rule, Large Eagle Tens appear in the market more frequently than their Small Eagle predecessors. This is particularly true of the 1799 Small Stars Obverse, 1799 Large Stars Obverse and 1801, which are the most plentiful issues of the former design and the three that I recommend for type purposes.

Courtesy of Bowers and Merena

Along with the 1801, the 1799 is the most frequently encountered Capped Bust Right, Large Eagle Ten-Dollar gold piece in today's market. Both issues, therefore, seem ideal for both circulated and Mint State type purposes.

Circulated Examples: 1799 and 1801 Eagles are seldom encountered in grades lower than EF-40. As with the Small Eagle type, Ten-Dollar gold pieces of this design were used almost exclusively in export trade and as part of bank reserves. Many examples, therefore, acquired only light wear.

Examples in EF-40 cost between $12,000 and $15,000. An 1801 in PCGS EF-45 sold at auction for $17,250 during March of 2007. Interestingly, this is the same price realized by an 1801 in PCGS AU-50 in May of that year—a fact that confirms the need to always evaluate a coin on its own merits instead of taking the grade on the third-party insert at face value. A 1799 and 1801 Eagle that grades AU-58 at PCGS or NGC will require you to pay $20,000-$30,000.

Mint State Examples: Any Mint State Capped Bust Right Eagle with Large Eagle Reverse is highly desirable for high-grade type purposes. An 1801 in NGC MS-60 traded hands for $25,300 in May of 2007. A 1799 Small Stars Obverse certified MS-63 at the same service commanded $41,688 from the winning bidder at an April 2007 auction. Another 1799, this piece a Large Stars Obverse example in PCGS MS-64, realized $97,750 when it appeared at auction in early 2007. An 1801 in the same grade sold for even more—$126,500—when it crossed the auction block in 2004.

General Characteristics: Eagles of this type often display yellow-gold, green-gold or orange-gold color. The dominant luster type among 1799s and 1801s is satiny, although some pieces possess semi-reflective tendencies in the fields. Striking quality varies from sharp to a bit soft over isolated highpoints in the centers and around the peripheries. Enough well-struck examples have survived, however, that you should not have too much difficulty in this area. On the other hand, large and/or singularly distracting abrasions can be a problem, particularly in circulated and lower Mint State grades. Avoid these features by focusing on higher-grade Mint State examples or exercising a bit of patience when searching for a coin in EF, AU or BU. There are relatively smooth-looking survivors in lower grades, and these coins are preferable.

Many 1799 and 1801 Eagles display adjustment marks. These features are usually few in number, singularly inconspicuous and do not adversely affect the coin's eye appeal. On the other hand, you should avoid pieces with an excessive number of adjustment marks, particularly if they are concentrated in one or more of the prime focal areas. While these as-struck features will not result in a lower numeric grade from PCGS or NGC, they can be distracting in certain instances.

Words of Caution: As evidenced by some of the auction prices realized mentioned above, values for Large Eagle Tens can fluctuate widely even within a single grade. As with their Small Eagle predecessors, the leading third-party certification services are often more lenient with Large Eagle Capped Bust Right Tens than they are with many later-date types in the U.S. gold series. The expert graders at PCGS and NGC understand that a fair number of these rare coins have been lightly cleaned at one time, usually long ago when standards for grading and numismatic conservation were different than they are in the market of the 21st century. Pieces that have been treated in such a manner can still be highly desirable, however, and PCGS and NGC frequently encapsulate these coins, sometimes assigning a lower numeric grade to compensate for the cleaning. While the market accepts this practice, sale prices reflect a coin's technical quality and eye appeal and not just the numeric grade assigned by PCGS or NGC. Always evaluate any Large Eagle Ten in person prior to making a purchase to be sure that you are comfortable with the assigned grade and find the coin aesthetically pleasing. You should also enlist the services of a trusted dealer or other numismatic professional to gain additional insight into a coin's technical merits before deciding whether or not to add the piece to your collection.

Finally, I wish to make it clear that PCGS and NGC have a policy of not encapsulating any coin that has been harshly cleaned, polished or otherwise significantly impaired. This also applies to early Eagles, and pieces with major problems are returned to the submitter without being placed in a PCGS or NGC holder.

STRATEGIES FOR INCLUDING THE CAPPED BUST RIGHT EAGLE WITH LARGE EAGLE REVERSE IN A COMPLETE TYPE SET

Most Desirable Issue(s): *1799 Small Stars Obverse, 1799 Large Stars Obverse, 1801*

Most Desirable Grade(s), Circulated Coins: *EF-40 through AU-58*

Estimated Cost: *$12,000 and up*

Key to Collecting: *Free of large and/or singularly distracting abrasions; few if any adjustment marks; yellow-gold, orange-gold or green-gold color; overall bold-to-sharp definition*

Most Desirable Grade(s), Mint State Coins: *MS-60 or finer*

Estimated Cost: *$30,000 and up*

Key to Collecting: *Free of large and/or singularly distracting abrasions; few if any adjustment marks; yellow-gold, orange-gold or green-gold color; overall sharp striking detail*

Advanced Type Set

Rarer Issues: The 1800 and 1803 occupy the second rarity tier in the Capped Bust Right, Large Eagle Ten-Dollar series. Survivors of these issues usually appear less frequently in the market than those of the 1799 and 1801, but still often enough that you should not have much difficulty locating either a circulated or Mint State example. Extremely Fine representatives start at $13,000. An 1803 Small Stars Reverse in PCGS AU-53 brought $19,550 at auction in early 2007, while another example in PCGS AU-55 traded for $25,300 six months earlier.

Certified MS-60 by NGC, an 1800 Eagle crossed the block for $27,500 at a major auction house during the first month of 2007. And a sum of $63,250 was required from the winning bidder by an 1803 Small Stars Reverse in NGC MS-63. The date of the final-listed sale was May 12, 2007.

Striking quality and surface characteristics for the typically encountered 1800 and 1803 Eagle are similar to those of the 1799 and 1801.

Courtesy of Bowers and Merena

Within the Capped Bust Right, Large Eagle Ten-Dollar series, the second rarity tier is occupied by the 1800 and 1803. Survivors of these issues usually appear less frequently in the market than those of the 1799 and 1801, but still often enough that the better-date type collector should not have too much difficulty locating either a circulated or Mint State example.

STRATEGIES FOR INCLUDING THE CAPPED BUST RIGHT EAGLE WITH LARGE EAGLE REVERSE IN A TYPE SET OF RARER ISSUES

Most Desirable Issue(s): *1800, 1803 Small Stars Reverse, 1803 Large Stars Reverse*

Most Desirable Grade(s): *EF-40 or finer*

Estimated Cost: *$13,000 and up*

Key to Collecting: *Free of large and/or singularly distracting abrasions; few if any adjustment marks; yellow-gold, orange-gold or green-gold color; overall bold-to-sharp definition*

Major Subtypes: Since Eagles of this type were struck in relatively large numbers, and dies in the early U.S. Mint were engraved by hand, it should come as no surprise to read that there are as many as nine different subtypes in this series. In practice, few collectors other than early gold variety specialists take notice of these differences. You, too, should be content to own just a single example of the Large Eagle type. For the sake of completion, however, I have included a list of distinct subtypes in this series.

STRATEGIES FOR INCLUDING THE CAPPED BUST RIGHT EAGLE WITH LARGE EAGLE REVERSE IN A TYPE SET OF MAJOR SUBTYPES

Required Number of Coins: *Nine*

Major Subtype #1: *16 Stars Obverse, 13-Star Reverse, Long Thin Neck*

Most Desirable Issue(s): *1797 Large Eagle (only option; a single die marriage of the issue)*

Major Subtype #2: *16 Stars Obverse, 13-Star Reverse, Long Thick Neck*

Most Desirable Issue(s): *1797 Large Eagle (only option; a single die marriage of the issue)*

Major Subtype #3: *16 Stars Obverse, 13-Star Reverse, Short Thin Neck*

Most Desirable Issue(s): *1797 Large Eagle (only option, a single die marriage of the issue)*

Major Subtype #4: *13 Stars Obverse, Stars 9x4, Short Thin Neck*

Most Desirable Issue(s): *1798 Stars 9x4 (only option)*

Major Subtype #5: *13 Stars Obverse, Stars 7x6, Short Thin Neck*

Most Desirable Issue(s): *1798 Stars 7x6 (only option)*

Major Subtype #6: *13 Stars Obverse, Stars 8x5, Small Stars Obverse, Short Thick Neck, Small Stars Reverse*

Most Desirable Issue(s): *1799 Small Stars Obverse (only option)*

Major Subtype #7: *13 Stars Obverse, Stars 8x5, Large Stars Obverse, Short Thick Neck, Small Stars Reverse*

Most Desirable Issue(s): *1799 Large Stars Obverse, 1801*

Major Subtype #8: *13 Stars Obverse, Stars 8x5, Large Stars Obverse, Short Thick Neck, Large Stars Reverse*

Most Desirable Issue(s): *1803 Large Stars Reverse (only option)*

Major Subtype #9: *13 Stars Obverse, Stars 8x5, Large Stars Obverse, Short Thick Neck, Medium Stars Reverse*

Most Desirable Issue(s): *1804 Plain 4 (only option; essentially unobtainable as only four proofs are known, one of which is part o the King of Siam Proof Set and another of which is impounded in the Harry W. Bass, Jr. Core Collection)*

Issuing Mint: The Philadelphia Mint struck all Capped Bust Right, Large Eagle Reverse Ten-Dollar gold pieces.

Proof Type Set

For all intents and purposes, this type is unobtainable in proof format. The United States Mint did not strike proofs of this type as we would describe them today during the 1797-1804 era. Nevertheless, NGC does list a single 1800 in Specimen-65 in their online Census (May/2007). I have not seen that coin.

On the other hand, the 1804 Plain 4 Eagles are unequivocally proofs that were painstakingly prepared as such by Mint personnel in 1834 and/or 1835. One of the classic rarities in U.S. numismatics, this issue is out of reach for most collectors. Only four examples have been confirmed, one of which is still part of the fabled King of Siam Proof Set. A prominent Southern California dealer acquired the entire set in November of 2005 for $8,500,000, and a market analysis that I conducted suggests that it is worth at least $15,000,000 in the 2007 market.

Courtesy of Rare Coin Wholesalers

Among the classic rarities in all of U.S. numismatics, the proof 1804 Plain 4 Eagles were painstakingly prepared by Mint employees in 1834 and/or 1835 for inclusion in special presentation proof sets. Only four examples struck in gold have been traced. The specimen pictured here is still part of the fabled King of Siam Proof Set, which changed hands in November of 2005 for the amazing sum of $8,500,000.

One of the other 1804 Plain 4 Eagles that has survived is impounded in the Harry W. Bass, Jr. Core Collection. The remaining two pieces, however, are individually owned by private parties. To the best of my knowledge, neither specimen has appeared at public auction between 2000 and 2007.

Assembling a Complete Set

Few collectors have attempted to assemble a complete set of Capped Bust Right Eagles with Large Eagle Reverse, and even fewer have succeeded. Even the more plentiful issues such as 1799 and 1801 are expensive in an absolute sense, and the series is rife with rare issues (1798 Stars 9x4, 1798 Stars 7x6 and 1804 Plain 4) and die varieties. Even having the requisite financial resources might not be enough to complete a set of this early Eagle type in a timely manner. The infrequency with which some coins trade can lead to frustration that, in turn, might lead you to refocus your numismatics efforts away from this series.

Nevertheless, at least three collectors have succeeded (or nearly succeeded) in forming complete sets of Large Eagle Capped Bust Right Tens. And what one man can do, another can do.

Year Set: In July of 2004, the gold portion of the impressive Richmond Collection crossed the auction block. Included among the lots was a complete seven-coin year set of Large Eagle Tens (actually, both varieties of the 1798/7 were represented, although the Stars 9x4 is the more obvious candidate for inclusion in a year set). The coins ranged in grade from AU-53 through MS-63, and their prices realized are as follows:

> **1797 Large Eagle**: *NCG AU-55, realized $23,000*
> **1798/7 Stars 9x4**: *NGC AU-55, realized $52,900*
> **1799**: *NGC MS-61, realized $23,000*
> **1800**: *NGC AU-53, realized $15,525*
> **1801**: *NGC MS-61, realized $19,550*
> **1803**: *NGC MS-63, realized $46,000*
> **1804 Crosslet 4**: *NGC MS-62, realized $50,600*

Date and Mint Set: Defined in terms that are applicable to this series, a date and mint set of Large Eagle Capped Bust Right Tens includes one example each of those issues and varieties that are significant enough to have gained individual listings at the major certification services. A complete set must include 10 coins, one example each of the 1797 Large Eagle, 1798 Stars 9x4, 1798 Stars 7x6, 1799 Small Stars Obverse, 1799 Large Stars Obverse, 1800, 1801, 1803 Small Stars Reverse, 1803 Large Stars Reverse and 1804 Crosslet 4. Louis E. Eliasberg, Sr. nearly completed this task as he was missing only the 1803 Large Stars Reverse. (The variety was probably not considered significant enough at the time Eliasberg formed his collection.) The gold portion of his collection was auctioned in October of 1982 under the title of *The United States Gold Coin Collection*.

Die Variety Set: As far as I know, Harry W. Bass, Jr. is the only collector that nearly completed this task. He obtained at least one example of each of the 26 known die marriages save for one, including the proof-only 1804 Plain 4.

Proof Set: Defined in a strict sense, a complete set of proof Capped Bust Right, Large Eagle Tens comprises only a single coin: the 1804 Plain 4. As previously stated, only two of these coins are available for private ownership on an individual basis, and neither has appeared at auction during the eight-year period from 2000-2007. In the numismatic market of the early 21st century, each of these coins would command in excess of $1,000,000.

A Complete Set by Issuing Mint: Since all Large Eagle Tens were struck in Philadelphia, a complete set by issuing mint is the same as a complete date and mint set.

Investing Tips

Since the rarity and cost of this type narrows the playing field among specialized collectors, your investing goals would be best served by including a single type coin in the highest grade that you can afford in your portfolio. Issues such as the 1799, 1800, 1801 and 1803 have traditionally enjoyed strong demand among type collectors, and Mint State pieces are particularly rare from a market availability standpoint. Focusing solely on the scarcer 1803 in MS-63, we see the following positive trend from 1995-2007.

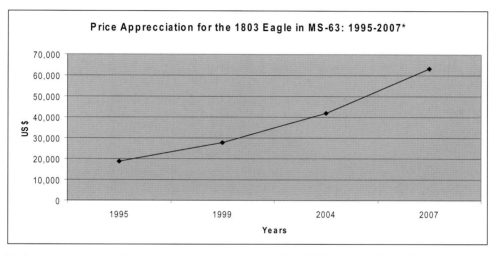

*Values represent individual or average prices realized for PCGS and NGC-certified examples as reported by leading rare coin auction houses.

As with all other U.S. gold series, demand for high-grade Large Eagle Tens such as the 1803 will continue to increase in the coming decades as more type collectors become active in this segment of the market.

Courtesy of Bowers and Merena

Early Eagles such as the 1799, 1800, 1801 and 1803 have traditionally enjoyed strong demand among collectors who require a representative of this type for their set. Mint State pieces can seem particularly rare from a market availability standpoint, and they may offer stronger growth potential than circulated examples through AU.

CHAPTER TWENTY SEVEN

No Motto
Liberty Eagles

Courtesy of Rare Coin Wholesalers

SPECIFICATIONS

Year(s) Issued: *1838-1866*
Issuing Mint(s): *Philadelphia, New Orleans, San Francisco*
Authorizing Act: *January 18, 1837*
Designer: *Christian Gobrecht*
Weight: *16.718 grams*
Composition: *90% gold, 10% copper*
Diameter: *27 millimeters*
Edge: *Reeded*

History

No Eagles were struck for circulation from 1805-1837 because the denominations' weight and fineness as originally stipulated in the Act of April 2, 1792 were high enough to make the coins attractive to bullion dealers and speculators. As s result, examples were disappearing from circulation at an alarming rate by 1804, and President Thomas Jefferson had no choice but to halt production at the end of that year. By 1838, however, the United States Congress had passed the Mint Acts of June 28, 1834 and January 18, 1837, both of which altered the weight and fineness of the nation's gold coinage. Armed with these new laws, the secretary of the Treasury believed that the time had finally come to resume production of Ten-Dollar gold pieces.

Accordingly, Mint Director Robert Maskell Patterson received orders in 1838 to begin striking Eagles. To design the new coin, the director turned to Christian Gobrecht, who had been deputizing for Chief Engraver William Kneass since 1836. For the obverse, Gobrecht chose a left-facing portrait of Liberty, her hair tied in a bun and a coronet inscribed LIBERTY above the brow. Thirteen stars are arranged around the border, and the date is below. His reverse displays a spread-wing eagle clutching a bundle of arrows in its left talon and an olive branch in its right. There is a shield superimposed over the eagle's breast. The legend UNITED STATES OF AMERICA is above and TEN D. is below—the first use of the denomination as an element of the design in the Eagle series. The mintmark, if present, can be found in the reverse field below the eagle. Gobrecht would go on to adapt this Liberty design for use on the Half Eagle (1839) and Quarter Eagle (1840).

With the exception of two isolated spikes in production at the Philadelphia Mint in 1847 and 1849, production of Liberty Eagles initially remained limited at that facility as well as in the New Orleans and San Francisco branch mints. Clearly, the Half Eagle was still the favored denomination for most transactions involving gold coins. Furthermore, the onset of the California Gold Rush in 1848-1849 prompted the federal government to create a new, larger denomination—the Double Eagle—to serve as a convenient storehouse for the vast quantities of precious metal being mined on the West Coast.

Short Type Set

A complete type set of United States Ten-Dollar gold pieces must include a No Motto Liberty Eagle. Additionally, this coin is very similar in design to the other Liberty gold series designed by Christian Gobrecht and James Barton Longacre, a fact that also serves as a unifying theme for a short type set.

Eagle Types, a six-piece set including:

Capped Bust Right Eagle, Small Eagle Reverse
Capped Bust Right Eagle, Large Eagle Reverse
Liberty Eagle, No Motto
Liberty Eagle, Motto
Indian Eagle, No Motto
Indian Eagle, Motto

Liberty Gold Coinage, a four or eight-piece set depending on how many types the collector wants to represent for the larger denominations. The eight-piece set includes:

Liberty Quarter Eagle
Liberty Half Eagle, No Motto
Liberty Half Eagle, Motto
Liberty Eagle, No Motto
Liberty Eagle, Motto
Type I Liberty Double Eagle
Type II Liberty Double Eagle
Type III Liberty Double Eagle

Complete Type Set

I believe that this is one of the most underrated types in the entire U.S. gold series of 1795-1933. All Liberty Eagles without Motto are scarce-to-rare coins, and they are offered for sale much less frequently than No Motto Half Eagles and Type I Double Eagles. The two most plentiful No Motto Eagles in today's market are the 1847 and 1847-O, although the 1849 and 1851-O are only marginally less rare and are also potential candidates for inclusion in a type set.

Courtesy of Bowers and Merena

Perhaps the two most readily obtainable No Motto Liberty Eagles in today's market are the 1847 and 1847-O, both of which could be attractive for type purposes.

Circulated Examples: Survivors of these four issues are fairly plentiful through the AU-58 grade level, and you can acquire a near-Mint example without too much difficulty. A selection of auction prices realized from 2005-2007 gives an idea what you will need to spend should you adopt this strategy.

> **1847**: *NGC AU-55, realized $633 in March of 2007*
> **1847**: *NGC AU-58, realized $1,006 in December of 2006*
> **1847-O**: *NGC AU-55, realized $840 in March of 2007*
> **1847-O**: *NGC AU-58, realized $1,438 in March of 2006*
> **1849**: *NGC AU-55, realized $633 in February of 2007*
> **1849**: *NGC AU-58, realized $1,150 in June of 2006*
> **1851-O**: *PCGS AU-55, realized $2,415 in February of 2007*
> **1851-O**: *NGC AU-58, realized $3,450 in June of 2005*

Mint State Examples: All No Motto Liberty Eagles are conditionally challenging in Mint State, and there are only 151 survivors from the entire series that grade finer than MS-62 at PCGS and NGC (May/2007). Even the recovery of the treasure of the *S.S. Republic*, which sank off the coast of Savannah, Georgia on October 25, 1865, has not materially altered the availability of No Motto Liberty Eagles in high grades. Most examples from the

S.S. Republic that NGC has conserved and certified as of May 2007 range in grade from AU-55 through MS-62.

Given the rarity of examples that grade any finer, I suggest acquiring a No Motto Liberty Eagle that grades MS-62. Even in that grade, however, the otherwise relatively obtainable 1847 and 1849 are conditionally rare. At least two 1847s in MS-62 did cross the auction block in April of 2006: the NGC example realized $5,175 and the PCGS coin traded hands for $8,050. An 1849 in PCGS MS-62 sold for 5,463 in late 2005.

The 1847-O and 1851-O are so rare in all Mint State grades (combined PCGS and NGC populations as of May 2007: 25 and 18 coins, respectively) that I do not recommend either issue for high-grade type purposes. If you are still interested in these issues, however, note than one of the finest surviving 1847-O Eagles—an NGC MS-61—sold through auction in March of 2007 for $7,475.

General Characteristics: No Motto Liberty Eagles often display blunt striking detail over the obverse stars, the tips of the eagle's wings on the reverse and/or the central highpoints on both sides. While the 1847, 1847-O, 1851 and 1851-O are among the better-produced issues from their respective Mints, softly impressed examples are encountered now and then. Avoid these pieces in favor of a sharper-looking example. Examples that retain full or partial luster are usually frosty or modestly prooflike, and color for these issues is often yellow-gold, orange-gold or green-gold in shade.

Courtesy of Bowers and Merena

While the 1847, 1847-O, 1851 and 1851-O are among the better-produced issues from their respective Mints, softly impressed examples are encountered now and then. The '51-O pictured here is noticeably deficient in detail over the obverse stars and at the tips of the eagle's wings on the reverse. The buyer might want to avoid coins such as this in favor of a sharper-looking example.

As one of the United States' larger gold coins, Eagles of all types tend to come liberally abraded in circulated and lower Mint State grades. Survivors from the No Motto Liberty series are no exception, and you are going to have to accept a coin with some degree of scuffiness in AU or lower Mint State grades. You will be much happier with your purchase, however, if you hold out for an example that is free of large or otherwise unduly distracting abrasions.

Words of Caution: There is not much more advice that I can dispense about the No Motto Liberty Eagle as a type other than to reiterate that this is a challenging and, in my opinion, underrated type. Choice AU and Mint State survivors of even relatively plentiful issues such as the 1847 and 1849 are anything but common when viewed in the wider context of U.S. numismatics. As such, be sure to evaluate every buying opportunity carefully, particularly if the coin in question is sharply struck, free of an excessive number of abrasions and aesthetically pleasing. Such examples are genuinely rare and they do not appear all that often in today's rare coin market.

STRATEGIES FOR INCLUDING THE NO MOTTO LIBERTY EAGLE IN A COMPLETE TYPE SET

Most Desirable Issue(s):

Circulated Grades: *1847, 1847-O, 1849, 1851-O*

Mint State Grades: *1847, 1849*

Most Desirable Grade(s), Circulated Coins: *AU-55, AU-58*

Estimated Cost: *$750 and up*

Key to Collecting: *Free of large and/or singularly distracting abrasions; yellow-gold, orange-gold or green-gold color; overall bold, if not sharp definition*

Most Desirable Grade(s), Mint State Coins: *MS-62*

Estimated Cost: *$5,000 and up*

Key to Collecting: *Free of large and/or singularly distracting abrasions; frosty or modestly semi-prooflike luster; yellow-gold, orange-gold or green-gold color; overall sharp striking detail*

Advanced Type Set

Rarer Issues: There are numerous issues in the No Motto Liberty Eagle series that would fit comfortably into an advanced type set of rarer issues. For a bit of a challenge, consider the 1840 or 1841. Both are early-date issues in this series, and neither is encountered with any degree of frequency in today's market. Expect the 1840 to command at least $2,250 in AU-55 and closer to the $3,500-$4,000 range in AU-58. Prices are fairly similar for the 1841 in these grades.

Both the 1840 and 1841 are major rarities in Mint State, and I cannot remember cataloging an example for auction since at least the early 21st century. If you are able to locate even an MS-60 I suggest jumping at the opportunity to add a very rare and seldom-encountered coin to your set. An 1840 in that grade passed through auction in August of 2004 for $7,475. The coin was certified by NGC. One year earlier an 1841 in PCGS MS-62 traded hands for $12,650.

The 1840 and 1841 are usually free of bothersome striking incompleteness, although isolated bluntness to the detail may be present over a few of the obverse star centrils. Color is frequently orange-gold or green-gold in shade, and the luster will invariably be semi-prooflike or satiny. Locating an example that is relatively abrasion free for the assigned grade is a nearly impossible task. Given the elusiveness of these issues in numismatic circles, it is best to ignore this criterion in this one instance and accept some scattered abrasions as "par for the course." On the other hand, purchasing a coin with a large mark in a prime focal area such as Liberty's cheek is an unacceptable risk. Do not add a coin to your collection that you might have difficulty selling down the road.

STRATEGIES FOR INCLUDING THE NO MOTTO LIBERTY EAGLE IN A TYPE SET OF RARER ISSUES

Most Desirable Issue(s): *1840, 1841*

Most Desirable Grade(s): *AU-55 or finer*

Estimated Cost: *$2,250 and up*

Key to Collecting: *Orange-gold or green-gold color; generally sharp striking detail; satiny or semi-prooflike luster*

Major Subtypes: There are two distinct types in the No Motto Liberty Eagle series, although you may be unfamiliar with the first one. Christian Gobrecht's initial obverse design for this type features a noticeably different hair style and deeper curvature to the truncation of the neck than later issues. For unknown reasons, the Mint altered this design partway through 1839, also taking the opportunity to decrease the size of the letters in the legend UNITED STATES OF AMERICA and the denomination TEN D. on the reverse. The 1838 and 1839/8 Type of 1838 (a.k.a. Large Letters) constitute a distinct subtype in this series and one that you must represent in an advanced type set.

Courtesy of Bowers and Merena

The 1838 and 1839/8 Type of 1838 (a.k.a. Large Letters) constitute a distinct subtype in the No Motto Liberty Eagle series and one that the advanced collector may want to represent in their set. Christian Gobrecht's initial obverse design for this type features a noticeably different hair style and deeper curvature to the truncation of the neck than later issues. For unknown reasons, the Mint altered this design partway through 1839, also taking the opportunity to decrease the size of the letters in the legend UNITED STATES OF AMERICA and the denomination TEN D. on the reverse.

The 1838 and 1839/8 Large Letters are both scarce-to-rare in all grades. As such, you will have difficulty locating an affordable example in the market. The 1839/8 Large Letters starts at $5,000 in AU-50, and you can expect the scarcer 1838 to bring at least $8,500 in the same grade. Strike poses a problem for this type, and the stars around the obverse border are usually quite blunt with little, if any detail to the radial lines. With this in mind, I suggest concentrating solely on examples that grade at least AU-50 to guarantee as much as possible that the coin you select will possess sufficiently sharp detail in most areas.

Other attributes of this type include semi-to-fully prooflike luster and color that ranges from yellow-gold to deeper orange-gold and green-gold shades. Be prepared to deal with a decent number of abrasions and somewhat scuffy surfaces when searching for an 1838 or 1839/8 Large Letters Eagle. Indeed, I have seen very few overall smooth examples during the decade from 1998-2007.

A pair of Choice AU Eagles of this type sold through auction in early 2007 for $12,650. Both were certified AU-55, the 1839/8 Large Letters in a PCGS holder and the 1838 graded by NGC and pedigreed to the Richmond Collection. Both issues are very rare in Mint State and they command premiums that reflect that fact. An 1839/8 in NGC MS-62 sold for $33,350 at auction in March of 2007 and an exceptional 1838 graded MS-63 at PCGS crossed the block at $115,000 a few months earlier. The finest-known example of the type is an 1839/8 Large Letters in PCGS MS-66 from the Gold Rush Collection that commanded $402,500 when it appeared in a January 2005 auction.

The better-known design of the Liberty Eagle that the Mint introduced in 1839 and continued to use through the end of the No Motto type is much more obtainable than the Type of 1838. Issues such as the 1847, 1847-O, 1849 and 1851-O are strong candidates to represent the Type of 1839.

STRATEGIES FOR INCLUDING THE NO MOTTO LIBERTY EAGLE IN A TYPE SET OF MAJOR SUBTYPES

Required Number of Coins: *Two*

Major Subtype #1: *Portrait Style of 1838, Large Letters Reverse*

Most Desirable Issue(s): *1838, 1839/8 Type of 1838 (only options)*

Major Subtype #2: *Portrait Style of 1839, Small Letters Reverse*

Most Desirable Issue(s): *1847, 1847-O, 1849, 1851-O*

Issuing Mint: Only three Mints were active in the production of No Motto Liberty Eagles, and I have already presented the best type candidates from the Philadelphia and New Orleans Mints. This leaves the San Francisco Mint. Unlike its identically dated Quarter Eagle and Half Eagle counterparts, the 1854-S Eagle is one of the more plentiful San Francisco Mint issues of its type. This establishes the '54-S as a desirable type coin, especially since it is also historically significant as the premier Eagle from this branch mint.

If you choose to acquire P and O-mint No Motto Liberty Eagles that grade at least AU-55, you should do likewise for the 1854-S for the sake of uniformity. Two NGC-certified AU-55s sold at auction in early 2007 for between $1,495 and $1,725. Just a single grade increase makes a big difference in price for this issue, and you will have to pay at least $4,500 for an 1854-S in AU-58.

Much of this price increase for the 1854-S in AU-58 is due to the rarity of Mint State survivors. While most collectors should resign themselves to acquiring an example in AU-55 or AU-58, you can own a Mint State 1854-S Eagle as long as you are willing to spend at least $10,000 for the privilege.

The '54-S is similar to many No Motto Liberty Eagles in that the strike varies from overall sharp to a bit soft in isolated peripheral areas. Yellow-gold, orange-gold and green-gold colors are all represented among the survivors that I have examined. When present, original luster is often satiny in texture. While many examples are quite extensively abraded, relatively smooth-looking survivors do turn up from time to time. The latter are free of sizeable and/or individually conspicuous abrasions, and I highly recommend them as some of the finest survivors at their respective levels of preservation.

The New Orleans Mint. Although the facility commenced operations in 1838 when the first Liberty Eagles were being struck in Philadelphia, the earliest O-mint gold coin of this denomination is dated 1841. The branch mint ceased operations in 1861 due to the start of the Civil War, reopened as a coinage facility in 1879 and struck its last coins in 1909. (Public Domain Image)

Courtesy of Bowers and Merena

Unlike its identically dated Quarter Eagle and Half Eagle counterparts, the 1854-S is one of the more plentiful San Francisco Mint issues in the No Motto Liberty Eagle series. This could make the '54-S desirable for type purposes, especially since it is also historically significant as the premier Eagle from this branch mint.

STRATEGIES FOR INCLUDING THE NO MOTTO LIBERTY EAGLE IN A TYPE SET BY ISSUING MINT

Required Number of Coins: *Three*

Issuing Mint #1: *Philadelphia, Pennsylvania*

Most Desirable Issue(s): *1847, 1849*

Key to Collecting: *AU-55 or finer grade; free of large and/or singularly distracting abrasions; yellow-gold, orange-gold or green-gold color; overall sharp striking detail; frosty or semi-prooflike luster*

Issuing Mint #2: *New Orleans, Louisiana*

Most Desirable Issue(s): *1847-O, 1851-O*

Key to Collecting: *AU-55 or AU-58 grade; free of large and/or singularly distracting abrasions; yellow-gold, orange-gold or green-gold color; overall bold, if not sharp definition*

Issuing Mint #3: *San Francisco, California*

Most Desirable Issue(s): *1854-S*

Key to Collecting: *AU-55 or AU-58 grade; relatively abrasion free for the assigned grade; overall bold-to-sharp definition; traces of original satiny luster; yellow-gold, orange-gold or green-gold color*

Proof Type Set

The rarity of survivors from all issues in this series means that I do not recommend the No Motto Liberty Eagle for inclusion in a proof type set. The Philadelphia Mint struck only limited numbers of proof No Motto Liberty Eagles, in most cases far fewer than 10 coins per year. A few issues such as the 1854, 1855 and 1856 are unknown in proof at either PCGS or NGC (May/2007), and I suspect that the Mint either did not produce proof Eagles in those years or no examples have survived. On the other hand, at least one branch mint proof is known for this type—the unique 1844-O that has been alternatively certified Proof-64 by PCGS and Proof-65 Ultra Cameo at NGC.

Courtesy of Rare Coin Wholesalers

All proof Motto Liberty Eagles are exceedingly rare coins. This piece, an 1862 certified Proof-65 Ultra Cameo by NGC, would probably fetch well in excess of $100,000 were it consigned to auction.

In reality, the only proof No Motto Liberty Eagles that I recommend for type purposes are those dated 1859-1865. These issues were produced in greater numbers than their predecessors, and more examples have survived. In all cases, however, the surviving populations are much lower than original mintages might suggest due to lagging collector sales and the unfortunate tendency of the Mint to melt unsold examples at year's end. The result is that even the more frequently encountered proofs of this type—the 1863 and 1864—are still very rare coins when viewed in the wider context of U.S. numismatics.

Nevertheless, you can purchase a proof 1863 or 1864 given enough time and financial resources. Most examples that I have seen display Cameo or Deep/Ultra Cameo surfaces, and these are particularly attractive if largely free of distracting hairlines. Look for an example with a numeric grade of at least Proof-64, orange-gold or reddish-gold color and a full strike from the dies.

Extreme rarity and awe-inspiring beauty in the numismatic market are always accompanied by a hefty price tag, and such is the case with high-grade proof 1863 and 1864 Eagles. An 1863 certified Proof-64 Cameo by NGC sold at auction for $103,500 in mid-2005, while an 1864 that appeared in a 2006 sale commanded $74,750 from the winning bidder. The 1864 was housed in an NGC Proof-64 Ultra Cameo holder at the time of sale.

STRATEGIES FOR INCLUDING THE NO MOTTO LIBERTY EAGLE IN A PROOF TYPE SET

Most Desirable Issue(s): *1863, 1864*

Most Desirable Grade(s): *Proof-64 Cameo or finer*

Key to Collecting: *Full striking detail; bold field-to-device contrast; orange-gold or reddish-gold color; a minimum number of wispy hairlines and/or contact marks*

Assembling a Complete Set

Year Set: This is the only complete set of No Motto Liberty Eagles that I recommend you trying to assemble. Even so, be prepared for a hard, uphill battle if you adopt this strategy. I suggest using coins that grade EF to complete this set, although you will still have difficulty with the 1838, the Philadelphia and/or San Francisco Mint issues from the later Civil War era and the 1866-S No Motto. In fact, acquiring examples of only the 1838, 1863-S, 1864, 1865 and 1866-S No Motto in EF-40 will set you back at least $20,000, and that's providing that you can even find pieces for sale. Again assuming that you focus on the EF-40 grade level, the remaining 24 coins in this set will range in price from a low of $350-$450 for the relatively common 1847 to at least $3,500 for the 1839 Large Letters.

Date and Mint Set: The steep obstacles standing in the way of completing a year set of No Motto Liberty Eagles are both more significant and more numerous as far as a date and mint set are concerned. To assemble a year set, you can choose between such issues as the 1839/8 Large Letters and 1839 Small Letters, 1863 and 1863-S and 1864 and 1864-S. In order to complete a date and mint set of this type you must acquire one example of each of these rare issues. And then there are additional rarities such as the 1858 (just 2,521 pieces produced) and 1859-O (original mintage: only 2,300 coins) with which to contend.

I do not even recommend this strategy if you have enough persistence to go the distance against a series with numerous issues that trade only infrequently in the numismatic market. Even if you can find examples of all issues, you will need at least $160,000-$175,000 to assemble the complete 67-coin set in Extremely Fine. This total includes overdates such as the 1846/5-O and 1853/2 as well as other varieties like the 1850 Large and Small Date and the intriguing 1865-S 865/Inverted 186.

Die Variety Set: As of the early 21st century, the New Orleans Mint issues in this series are just beginning to gather a following among a limited number of die variety specialists. The Philadelphia and San Francisco Mint issues, on the other hand, are still largely overlooked by this segment of the numismatic community. I see this as an opportunity if you are willing to take a closer look at this series, although a word of caution is in order here. As it is premature to speak of a market for die marriages in the No Motto Liberty Eagle series, you should not pay a premium for a variety that is being touted as a significant rarity. At the very least you should seek the counsel of a recognized expert in the field or a trusted dealer before paying a premium for a rare variety in this series.

Proof Set: This is another strategy that I do not recommend for the No Motto Liberty Eagle series. The pre-1859 issues are either uncollectible or unknown, and even those coins struck from 1859-1865 are rare and quite costly. On the other hand, the idea of assembling a partial set of proof No Motto Liberty Eagles from the Civil War era does appeal to me. The coins are relatively obtainable by the standards of this series, and they have an indelible link to that turbulent period in U.S. history. In Proof-65 grade, expect one example each of the 1861, 1862, 1863, 1864 and 1865 Eagle to cost at least $550,000.

A Complete Set by Issuing Mint: The only Mint in which No Motto Liberty Eagles were struck that has attracted at least some measure of interest among specialized collectors is the New Orleans Mint. Even so, I am not aware of too many collectors that are focusing solely on O-mint Eagles, although there are a few. This mintmarked series can gain in popularity only if more Southern gold specialists begin to realize that the Charlotte and Dahlonega facilities are not the only branch mints that were once located south of the Mason-Dixon line.

The S-mint No Motto Liberty Eagle series is shorter than its O-mint counterpart (14 issues/major varieties vs. 21 issues/major varieties), but the San Francisco Mint is even less popular among mintmarked collectors than the New Orleans Mint. As well, virtually all early S-mint Eagles are scarce-to-rare even in lower grades—a fact that rules out this strategy for collectors with more limited resources of time and money.

Investing Tips

With so few examples certified in higher grades at PCGS and NGC (only 151 coins, May/2007), selecting a No Motto Liberty Eagle in MS-63 or finer condition is an excellent way to invest in this 19th century gold series. The issues that you will have the most opportunities to acquire in the finer Mint State grades are the 1847, 1848, 1849, 1850 Large Date, 1853, 1855, 1856 and 1861. Bear in mind, however, that even these issues exist in extremely small quantities at or above the MS-63 grade level, as evidenced by the following chart:

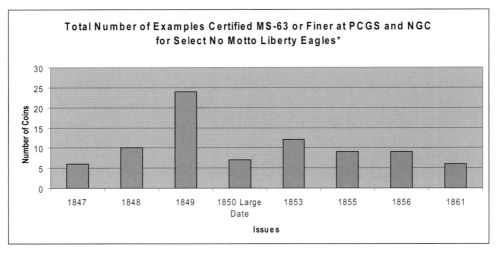

*Totals are derived from the online PCGS Population Report and NGC Census at www.pcgs.com and www.ngccoin.com, respectively. Websites accessed May 13, 2007.

Focusing on the 1849 for a moment, I am aware of three examples in MS-63 that have appeared at auction during the seven-year period from 2000 through 2006. The two final pieces in this trio each realized more than their predecessor(s), as follows:

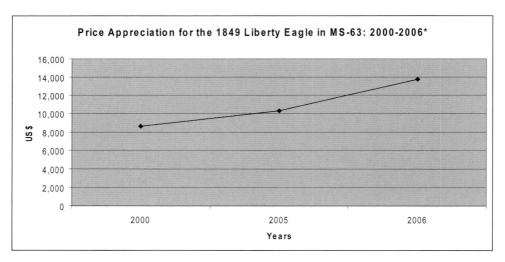

*Values represent individual prices realized for PCGS and NGC-certified examples as reported by leading rare coin auction houses.

This positive trend serves as an indicator of the growth potential for the No Motto Liberty Eagle series as a whole in the finer Mint State grades.

CHAPTER TWENTY EIGHT

Liberty Eagles with Motto

Courtesy of Rare Coin Wholesalers

SPECIFICATIONS

Year(s) Issued: *1866-1907*
Issuing Mint(s): *Philadelphia, Carson City, Denver, New Orleans, San Francisco*
Authorizing Act: *January 18, 1837 (supplemented by Acts of March 3, 1865, and February 12, 1873)*
Designer: *Christian Gobrecht*
Weight: *16.718 grams*
Composition: *90% gold, 10% copper*
Diameter: *27 millimeters*
Edge: *Reeded*

History

Like its Half Eagle counterpart, the Liberty Eagle was affected by the Mint Act of March 3, 1865 that mandated inclusion of the motto IN GOD WE TRUST on all silver and gold coins of sufficient size. In order to help the Mint conform to this law, Chief Engraver James Barton Longacre designed a simple scroll upon which the motto could be inscribed. Longacre positioned the scroll in the reverse field above the eagle, where it took its place beginning in 1866. This is the second of the two major types in the Liberty Eagle series, and it remained in use until the design as a whole was eclipsed by Augustus Saint-Gaudens' Indian Eagle in 1907.

Although initially remaining at the same low levels as its No Motto predecessor, production of Liberty Eagles with Motto increased sporadically beginning in the late

1870s/early 1880s. Even if delivered in relatively limited numbers, issues from circa 1879 through the series' end in 1907 are generally much easier to obtain than Eagles produced during the 1838-1878 era. This is because later-date Liberty Eagles were not subject to as high a rate of attrition from circulation and/or melting as their predecessors. Indeed, significant percentages of many issues probably survived as part of bank reserves either in the United States or abroad in Latin America and Europe, where the coins were shipped in exchange for foreign goods or as payment for debts owed by the federal government. There are still some rare coins in the later Liberty Eagle with Motto series, to be sure, and the Carson City Mint issues figure prominently among the types' key and semi-key dates.

In addition to the fabled Nevada branch mint, Liberty Eagles with Motto were struck in Philadelphia, Denver, New Orleans and San Francisco. The mintmark position remains the same as for the No Motto type, i.e. in the reverse field below the eagle.

Short Type Set

More frequently encountered in today's market than any of the preceding Eagle types struck by the United States Mint, the Liberty design with Motto is a favorite among type collectors due to the relative ease with which examples can be obtained in today's market. In fact, circulated and low-end Mint State survivors of the series' more common issues are often referred to as "generic Ten-Dollar Libs" (or a derivative of that descriptive phrase) in many numismatic circles.

I am aware of three short type sets in which you can highlight the Liberty Eagle with Motto.

Eagle Types, a six-piece set including:

Capped Bust Right Eagle, Small Eagle Reverse
Capped Bust Right Eagle, Large Eagle Reverse
Liberty Eagle, No Motto
Liberty Eagle, Motto
Indian Eagle, No Motto
Indian Eagle, Motto

Liberty Gold Coinage, a four or eight-piece set depending on how many types the collector wants to represent for the larger denominations. The eight-piece set includes:

Liberty Quarter Eagle
Liberty Half Eagle, No Motto
Liberty Half Eagle, Motto
Liberty Eagle, No Motto
Liberty Eagle, Motto
Type I Liberty Double Eagle
Type II Liberty Double Eagle
Type III Liberty Double Eagle

Popular U.S. Gold Types, an eight or ten-piece set including:

Liberty Quarter Eagle
Indian Quarter Eagle
Liberty Half Eagle, Motto
Indian Half Eagle

Liberty Eagle, Motto
Indian Eagle (No Motto and/or Motto)
Liberty Double Eagle (usually a Type III example)
Saint-Gaudens Double Eagle (No Motto and/or Motto)

Complete Type Set

There are numerous issues in the later portion of the Motto Liberty Eagle series that are strong candidates for inclusion in both circulated and Mint State type sets. Examples include the 1895, 1899, 1901, 1901-S and the final-year 1907. I must inform you, however, that the 1901-S is the most common Liberty Eagle with Motto in MS-65. For this reason, the '01-S is my primary choice for a type coin in this series.

Courtesy of Bowers and Merena

The 1901-S is the most readily obtainable Liberty Eagle with Motto in the finer Mint State grades. For this reason, this issue will probably be the type candidate of choice for many buyers.

Circulated Examples: Most 1901-S Eagles are Mint State or, at most, minimally circulated. Mint State examples are actually so common in the market that there is little price difference between AU and BU survivors. For example, two coins graded AU-58 by NGC both realized $299 at auction at the end of 2005. During the same month, two examples in NGC MS-62 sold for an average of $446 each. The spread between the two grades as evidenced by these four pieces is only $147—a difference that is minimal enough for me to recommend that you purchase a Mint State 1901-S Eagle for your type set.

If you must buy a circulated 1901-S Eagle, get an AU-58 and hold out for a coin that meets with your complete satisfaction. In this grade, the 1901-S is common enough that dealer asking prices and auction prices realized fluctuate with the prevailing spot price of gold.

Mint State Examples: This is one type in the Eagle series for which you can locate an attractive Mint State survivor with relative ease and at fairly minimal cost. I particularly like MS-64s as they reveal a minimum number of wispy bagmarks. In this grade, the 1901-S costs between $1,300 and $2,000. I am, however, aware of at least one PCGS MS-64 that sold for $2,530 during an early 2007 auction. MS-65s are scarcer than MS-64s and start at $4,250.

PCGS and NGC have seen some truly exceptional 1901-S Eagles. A PCGS MS-66 traded hands for $5,170 at an auction session conducted May 12, 2007. Superb Gems number just a handful of coins at PCGS and NGC, and an NGC MS-67 commanded $15,525 from the winning bidder when it appeared in an early 2005 sale.

General Characteristics: The 1901-S almost always comes sharply struck with yellow-gold, orange-gold or rose-gold color. Some pieces will tend more toward a green-gold cast. Mint luster is usually vibrant with a richly frosted texture; prooflike examples are distinctly in the minority among survivors.

Words of Caution: With the exception of the finest Mint State grades, there are many 1901-S Eagles from which to choose in today's market. You should, therefore, be as selective as possible when pursuing this issue. Do not buy any example that does not meet with your full approval. Rest assured that a more desirable coin will become available in a fairly short period of time.

STRATEGIES FOR INCLUDING THE LIBERTY EAGLE WITH MOTTO IN A COMPLETE TYPE SET

Most Desirable Issue(s): *Numerous, including 1895, 1899, 1901, 1901-S and 1907*

Most Desirable Grade(s), Circulated Coins: *AU-58*

Estimated Cost: *$300-$350*

Key to Collecting: *Free of large and/or singularly distracting abrasions; yellow-gold, orange-gold, green-gold or rose-gold color; sharp striking definition; plenty of original mint luster remaining*

Most Desirable Grade(s), Mint State Coins: *MS-64 or finer*

Estimated Cost: *$1,300 and up*

Key to Collecting: *Free of large and/or singularly distracting abrasions; full, frosty mint luster; yellow-gold, orange-gold, green-gold or rose-gold color; a sharply executed strike*

Advanced Type Set

Rarer Issues: Due to its relative availability among Liberty Eagles from the popular Carson City Mint, the 1891-CC is my favorite choice for inclusion in a better-date type set. AU-58s appear at auction several times yearly. In addition, there are enough AU-58s in the market that you should have no difficulty locating a pleasing example. This issue tends to come well struck with good luster, although locating a lightly circulated representative whose surfaces are overall smooth could represent a significant challenge. A better strategy is to look for an example that is free of large and/or individually distracting abrasions, particularly in the prime focal areas. Several PCGS and NGC AU-58s that sold in late 2006 and early 2007 realized between $715 and $1,040.

As a rule, the manner in which CC-mint gold issues were distributed, stored and transported were not conducive to the survival of relatively smooth-looking Mint State examples. This is definitely the case with the 1891-CC Eagle, and the issue is very scarce-to-rare in grades above MS-62. For this reason, I recommend MS-62s for Mint State type purposes. Expect a BU 1891-CC to possess a generous number of abrasions, but I have handled a few pieces that are at least free of individually conspicuous distractions. A group of seven examples in PCGS and NGC MS-62 that passed through auction during January-May 2007 realized between $1,955 and $3,738.

Courtesy of Bowers and Merena

The most plentiful Eagle from the extremely popular Carson City Mint, the 1891-CC might be a strong candidate for inclusion in a better-date type set. Examples that grade AU-58 usually appear at auction several times yearly, which means that the numismatist should have ample opportunity to acquire an attractive representative.

STRATEGIES FOR INCLUDING THE LIBERTY EAGLE WITH MOTTO IN A TYPE SET OF RARER ISSUES

Most Desirable Issue(s): *1891-CC*

Most Desirable Grade(s): *AU-58 through MS-62*

Estimated Cost: *$700-$3,850*

Key to Collecting: *Yellow-gold, orange-gold, rose-gold or green-gold color; overall sharp striking detail; frosty mint luster; no sizeable abrasions in prime focal areas*

Major Subtypes: The addition of the motto IN GOD WE TRUST in 1866 constitutes the final design change for the Liberty Eagle. As such, there are no major subtypes in the Motto portion of this series

Issuing Mint: In order to represent Motto Liberty Eagle production at each coinage facility that was active in the production of this type, you need to acquire five coins. The best P-mint type candidates are the 1899, 1901 and 1907, examples of which will command similar prices to the 1901-S in grades from AU-58 through MS-64.

I have already addressed the 1891-CC and 1901-S above. These issues are the most suitable type candidates in the Motto Liberty Eagles series from their respective Mint.

The 1906-D and 1907-D are the only two Eagles of this type struck in the Denver Mint. In addition to its popularity as the first D-mint Eagle in U.S. coinage history, the 1906-D is a bit easier to obtain in the finer Mint State grades than the 1907-D and is the better choice for gold type purposes. MS-62s are worth between $375 and $450, while in MS-64 the 1906-D advances to approximately $1,500-$2,500. If you are assembling a circulated type set, expect to pay no more than $350-$400 for a 1906-D Eagle in AU-58.

Opening its doors as a coinage facility in 1906, the Denver Mint contributed just two issues to the Liberty Eagle series. This postcard view depicts the branch mint as it looked in the early 20th century. (Public domain image)

Courtesy of Bowers and Merena

In addition to its popularity as the first D-mint Eagle in U.S. coinage history, the 1906-D is usually a bit easier to obtain in the finer Mint State grades than the 1907-D and may be the better choice for the gold type collector.

Courtesy of Bowers and Merena

Along with the 1901-O and 1904-O, the 1903-O is probably the most plentiful New Orleans Mint Eagle of the Liberty, Motto type. In AU-58 an example will usually cost at least $300, while the price range for an MS-62 is probably best estimated at $725-$950.

One final coinage facility helped to produce Liberty Eagles with Motto: the New Orleans Mint. In terms of total number of coins that have survived, the 1901-O, 1903-O and 1904-O are the most plentiful O-mint Eagles of this type. The distribution of these issues is similar to that of the 1891-CC and certified populations dwindle rapidly above MS-62. In AU-58 these O-mint issues cost at least $300, while the price range for MS-62s is best estimated at $725-$950. If you are willing to stretch a bit to obtain a higher-grade example, consider a coin in MS-63. A 1903-O in that grade as certified by PCGS sold for $2,760 at an auction conducted in May of 2007.

The attentive reader will notice that I have not provided price estimates for the 1899, 1901 or 1907 in MS-65. The persistence and financial resources required to obtain Carson City, Denver and New Orleans Mint Liberty Eagles in MS-65 means that you should concentrate on lower-grade examples for this strategy as a whole. A set built around coins that grade MS-62 through MS-64 will make an attractive and noteworthy addition to any collection.

STRATEGIES FOR INCLUDING THE LIBERTY EAGLE WITH MOTTO IN A TYPE SET BY ISSUING MINT

Required Number of Coins: *Five*

Issuing Mint #1: *Philadelphia, Pennsylvania*

Most Desirable Issue(s): *1899, 1901, 1907*

Key to Collecting: *AU-58 through MS-64 grade; free of large and/or singularly distracting abrasions; yellow-gold, orange-gold, rose-gold or green-gold color; sharp striking detail; relatively vibrant luster for the assigned grade*

Issuing Mint #2: *Carson City, Nevada*

Most Desirable Issue(s): *1891-CC*

Key to Collecting: *AU-58 through MS-62 grade; yellow-gold, orange-gold, rose-gold or green-gold color; overall sharp striking detail; frosty mint luster; no sizeable abrasions in prime focal areas*

Issuing Mint #3: *Denver, Colorado*

Most Desirable Issue(s): *1906-D*

Key to Collecting: *AU-58 through MS-64 grade; free of large and/or singularly distracting abrasions; yellow-gold, orange-gold or green-gold color; sharp striking detail; relatively vibrant luster for the assigned grade*

Issuing Mint #4: *New Orleans, Louisiana*

Most Desirable Issue(s): *1901-O, 1903-O, 1904-O*

Key to Collecting: *AU-58 through MS-62 grade; yellow-gold, orange-gold or green-gold color; overall sharp striking detail; frosty mint luster; no sizeable abrasions in prime focal areas*

Issuing Mint #5: *San Francisco, California*

Most Desirable Issue(s): *1901-S*

Key to Collecting: *AU-58 through MS-64 grade; free of large and/or singularly distracting abrasions; frosty mint luster; yellow-gold, orange-gold, green-gold or rose-gold color; a sharply executed strike*

Proof Type Set

It is much easier to locate a proof Motto Liberty Eagle in today's market than an example of the earlier No Motto design. Of course, all proof U.S. gold coins are rare, and this segment of the market is the province of well-funded collectors. If you are in this category, look for a proof Liberty Eagle dated 1899, 1900 or 1901. The issues are more plentiful than the earlier 1890s deliveries in today's market, and survivors often display the Cameo or Deep/Ultra Cameo finishes that are so appealing.

Courtesy of Bowers and Merena

The proof type collector might find the 1899, 1900 and 1901 deliveries preferable as far as the Liberty Eagle with Motto series is concerned. These issues are a bit more plentiful than the earlier 1890s deliveries in today's market, and survivors will often display the Cameo or Deep/Ultra Cameo finishes that many numismatists find so appealing.

Proof Eagles are fairly large coins, and their delicate fields acted like magnets for grade-limiting hairlines and other contact marks. As such, I recommend Proof-64 as a minimum cutoff point in order to minimize the number of wispy handling marks on a coin's surface. Expect to pay at least $20,000 for a near-Gem with a Cameo designation. Prices realized from 2005-2006 for examples in Proof-64 Cameo include:

1899*: PCGS-certified, sold for $25,300 in 2005*
1900*: PCGS-certified, sold for $22,800 in 2006*

Anticipate a price increase to $35,000-$40,000 if you are interested in looking at these issues in Proof-65 Cameo.

Proof Liberty Eagles with Motto are invariably full strikes, the 1899-1901 issues often displaying yellow-gold, orange-gold or even rose-gold color. Cameo or Deep/Ultra Cameo specimens exhibit bold contrast between frosty devices and mirror-finish fields, and the latter areas will sometimes exhibit a rippled "orange peel" texture. I am particularly fond of the "orange peel" finish, as are most proof gold specialists.

STRATEGIES FOR INCLUDING THE LIBERTY EAGLE WITH MOTTO IN A PROOF TYPE SET

Most Desirable Issue(s): *1899-1901*

Most Desirable Grade(s): *Proof-64 Cameo or finer*

Key to Collecting: *Bold field-to-device contrast; yellow-gold, orange-gold or rose-gold color; full striking detail; a minimum number of wispy hairlines; "orange peel" texture*

Assembling a Complete Set

Year Set: Even if you on a limited collecting budget, assembling a partial year set of Motto Liberty Eagles from 1878-1907 is still a workable strategy. This is particularly true if you focus on circulated grades, for in EF all years from that era have at least one issue that costs no more than $350 (depending, of course, on the current spot price of gold). Stretching to AU for many of these years will not cost significantly more as the asking price for common-date Motto Liberty Eagles in worn condition is closely tied to the value of the precious metal that the coins contain.

With the possible exception of the 1874-P, the Liberty Eagles with Motto struck from 1866 through 1877 are much more elusive than their later-date counterparts. Buying an EF of even the most common issues from that era will result in a total cost of at least $27,000 to complete your year set. If you are contemplating this strategy, be aware that the only two business strike deliveries for the year 1875 are both significant rarities: the 1875-P with just 100 coins struck for circulation and the 1875-CC at an original mintage of just 7,715 pieces.

Date and Mint Set: If you complete a date and mint set of Liberty Eagles with Motto you will have accomplished a significant numismatic feat. Before you rush headfirst into this strategy, however, remember the approximate cost of the series' 15 rarest issues: 1867-S; 1870-CC; 1871-CC; 1872-CC; 1873; 1873-CC; 1875; 1875-CC; 1876; 1876-CC; 1877; 1877-CC; 1878-CC; 1879-CC and 1883-O. Acquiring an example of each of these deliveries even in EF-40 will require you to spend at least $200,000.

Die Variety Set: What little research has been done on die marriages in the Liberty Eagle with Motto series has discovered mostly minor varieties. This is one form of collecting Liberty Eagles that is still in its infancy.

Proof Set: Due to the rarity of all issues in this series, and particularly those delivered during the 1860s and 1870s, I do not recommend this strategy. What I do recommend if you have sufficient finances, however, is to complete a partial proof set. The 1890s issues would make a pleasing set, as would the 20th century issues from 1900 through the series' end in 1907. If you choose to assemble a 20th century set, remember that the Mint changed its method of proof manufacture in 1902 and most Liberty Eagles struck during and after that year possess an all-brilliant finish. Even pieces that have received a Cameo designation from PCGS or NGC do not resemble Cameo examples from, say, the 1890s.

An eight-piece set of proof 1900-1907 Liberty Eagles will set you back at least $150,000. This total assumes a numeric grade of Proof-64 for each example in the set.

A Complete Set by Issuing Mint: The Carson City Mint issues in the Liberty Eagle series are extremely popular among specialized collectors. They are sometimes collected on their own, but more frequently obtained as part of a larger set of all CC-mint gold issues. A potential problem facing many collectors that aspire to one of these strategies, however, is the cost associated with several issues in the Carson City Mint Liberty Eagle series. The first-year 1870-CC is a major numismatic rarity, an example in NGC EF-45 trading for $32,200 in October of 2006. Other elusive CC-mint Eagles include the 1871-CC ($16,100 paid for a PCGS AU-50 in early 2007), 1873-CC ($16,675 paid for a PCGS EF-45 in 2006) and 1879-CC ($18,400 paid for a PCGS AU-50 during an early 2007 auction).

If CC-mint Liberty Eagles are too rich for your blood, consider completing a set of the O-mint issues. You must still contend with such key-date deliveries as the 1879-O and 1883-O, EF-40s costing at least $5,000 and $8,000, respectively. Once clear of these two issues, you will find the remaining 14 O-mint issues in this series surprisingly affordable. This is particularly true if you look for EF and AU examples, many of which are obtainable for less than $1,000 each. More plentiful issues such as the 1888-O, 1892-O and 1906-O actually sell for less than $600 in AU-58.

Investing Tips

Some of the early San Francisco Mint deliveries in the Liberty Eagle with Motto series are extremely undervalued in today's market, particularly when compared to the Carson City Mint issues from the same era. I have drawn a comparison between those years from 1870-1878 during which both the Carson City and San Francisco Mints were active in the production of Liberty Eagles. Although third-party grading data is largely skewed by resubmissions, the total number of coins listed at PCGS and NGC is helpful for assessing relative rarity between multiple issues. For the purposes of this comparison, I have focused solely on coins that grade AU-55 or finer. Early-date Motto Liberty Eagles struck in both the Carson City and San Francisco Mints circulated quite extensively, and even locating a problem-free AU-55 is a formidable task.

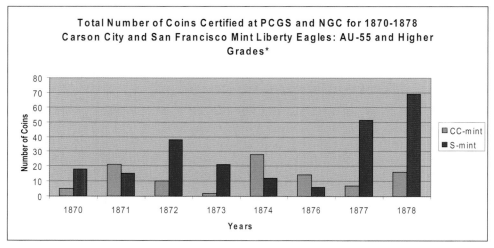

*Totals are derived from the online PCGS Population Report and NGC Census at www.pcgs.com and www.ngccoin.com, respectively. Websites accessed May 13, 2007.

The data reveals that three issues—1871-S, 1874-S and 1876-S—have lower certified populations at PCGS and NGC at or above the AU-55 grade level than their identically dated CC-mint counterparts. Auction prices realized hardly reflect this fact, however, as evidenced by a few examples:

1871-CC: *A PCGS AU-55 realized $19,550 at auction in February 2007.*
1871-S: *An NGC AU-55 realized $6,613, also during an early 2007 sale.*
1874-CC: *A PCGS AU-55 sold for $11,500 in April of 2006.*
1874-S: *An NGC AU-55 crossed the block at $6,290 during an auction conducted in May of 2006.*

1876-CC: *A PCGS AU-55 realized $23,000 at auction in 2002.*
1876-S: *An NGC AU-55 sold for $20,700 during a 2005 auction, while an identically graded example realized just $9,200 in a 2006 sale. The latter price seems closer to the 2007 market value for this issue in AU-55.*

Even taking into account the strong likelihood of resubmissions skewing the population data for these six issues, these S-mint issues are obviously undervalued in the current market.

Of course, I acknowledge that the San Francisco Mint still lags far behind the Carson City Mint in terms of popularity among gold specialists. Indeed, the unique double mintmark and storied history of the Carson City Mint explains its greater desirability vis-à-vis the San Francisco Mint. Both branch mints produced Liberty Eagles during the frontier era, however, and their coins saw equally heavy commercial use. If early S-mint gold coinage gains a significant following among specialized collectors, high-grade 1871-S, 1874-S and 1876-S Eagles will increase markedly in value in the coming decades. You should take a closer look at this portion of the Motto Liberty Eagle series and evaluate its potential for representation in your portfolio.

Courtesy of Bowers and Merena

Early San Francisco Mint deliveries in the Liberty Eagle with Motto series such as the 1871-S and 1874-S might be undervalued in today's market, particularly when compared to the Carson City Mint issues from the same era. The '71-S pictured here has a weakly impressed mintmark, a feature seen quite often on San Francisco Mint Half Eagles and Eagles from the late 1860s and early 1870s.

CHAPTER TWENTY NINE

No Motto Indian Eagles

Courtesy of Rare Coin Wholesalers

SPECIFICATIONS

Year(s) Issued: *1907-1908*
Issuing Mint(s): *Philadelphia, Denver*
Authorizing Act: *January 18, 1837 (supplemented by Acts of March 3, 1865, and February 12, 1873)*
Designer: *Augustus Saint-Gaudens*
Weight: *16.718 grams*
Composition: *90% gold, 10% copper*
Diameter: *27 millimeters*
Edge: *46 raised stars, one for each state in the Union during the years in which this type was produced*

History

Considered by many numismatists to be one of the most beautiful coins ever struck in the United States Mint, the Indian Eagle made its debut in 1907. Inspired by President Theodore Roosevelt as part of his plans to increase the beauty of United States coinage, Augustus Saint-Gaudens executed this powerful design. The artist, one of the preeminent American sculptors of the early 20th century and a friend of Roosevelt, modified one of his earlier head studies of Liberty for use on the obverse of this coin. Saint-Gaudens placed a Native American headdress atop Liberty's head, the word LIBERTY inscribed along its base. Thirteen stars are present along the upper border, and the date position is at the lower border.

Saint-Gaudens' reverse design for the Indian Eagle displays a bald eagle powerfully striding to the viewer's left atop a bundle of arrows around which an olive branch is intertwined. The legend UNITED STATES OF AMERICA is above, the Latin motto E PLURIBUS UNUM is in the field behind the eagle and the denomination TEN DOLLARS is below.

Although few can successfully debate Saint-Gaudens' skill as a sculptor (some of his most famous works include the Sherman Monument in New York City's Central Park, the Robert Gould Shaw Memorial on Boston Common and the *Diana* statue that now resides in New York's Metropolitan Museum of Art), he did not fully understand the requirements of coinage created primarily for commercial use. As a result, his original design for the Indian Eagle, although possessed of great beauty, was impractical for mass production. When utilized for trial purposes in 1907, this design produced coins with a raised outer rim that would have never worked in circulation. Such a feature prevented the coins from stacking, among other things. Chief Engraver Charles E. Barber modified this Wire Rim design (as it is now known) in an effort to improve its practicality for regular production.

The second variant of the Indian Eagle struck in the Mint during 1907 is the Rolled Edge. Although Barber removed the troublesome wire rim and the Mint struck 20,000 examples with the intent of placing them into circulation, the design was still found wanting in the eyes of at least some government officials. Going back to the drawing board, Barber then produced the No Periods variant. This type derives its name from Barber's removal of the periods, or triangular dots, at the beginning and end of the legend, Latin motto and denomination on the Wire Rim and Rolled Edge pieces. The No Periods design is the one that Mint officials finally settled upon for long-term Indian Eagle production.

The driving force behind the creation of the Indian Eagle and Saint-Gaudens Double Eagle in 1907 was our nation's 26th president, Theodore Roosevelt. One of "Teddy's" pet projects while residing at 1600 Pennsylvania Avenue concerned improving the designs of the denominations then being struck in the United States Mint. Focusing first and foremost on the gold coins, Roosevelt believed that the long-lived Liberty designs were banal and no longer indicative of the United States' growing status as a major player on the world stage. (Public Domain Image)

In addition to the basic Saint-Gaudens design, Wire Rim, Rolled Edge and No Periods Indian Eagles all have one thing in common: they do not display the motto IN GOD WE TRUST on either side. This omission was no accident, but rather the result of personal preference on the part of President Theodore Roosevelt who believed that the use of a deity's name on coinage was blasphemy. Congress mandated the inclusion of the motto in 1908, thus ending production of the short-lived No Motto type.

With the exception of 210,000 pieces struck in the Denver Mint in early 1908, all No Motto Indian Eagles were coined in Philadelphia. The mintmark for the '08-D No Motto can be found at the left-reverse rim above the final leaf on the branch. Interestingly, the mintmark position moved to the field area below the end of the olive branch with the introduction of the Motto type.

Short Type Set

There are three short type sets in which you can include an example of the No Motto Indian Eagle. Please note that you can expand or truncate the second and third collecting strategies that I have outlined below depending on whether or not you want to include both No Motto and Motto examples of the Indian Eagle and Saint-Gaudens Double Eagle.

Eagle Types, a six-piece set including:

Capped Bust Right Eagle, Small Eagle Reverse
Capped Bust Right Eagle, Large Eagle Reverse
Liberty Eagle, No Motto
Liberty Eagle, Motto
Indian Eagle, No Motto
Indian Eagle, Motto

20th Century Gold Coinage, a four or six-piece set including:

Indian Quarter Eagle
Indian Half Eagle
Indian Eagle (No Motto and/or Motto)
Saint-Gaudens Double Eagle (No Motto and/or Motto)

Popular U.S. Gold Types, an eight or ten-piece set including:

Liberty Quarter Eagle
Indian Quarter Eagle
Liberty Half Eagle, Motto
Indian Half Eagle
Liberty Eagle, Motto
Indian Eagle (No Motto and/or Motto)
Liberty Double Eagle (usually a Type III example)
Saint-Gaudens Double Eagle (No Motto and/or Motto)

Complete Type Set

In addition to having been produced in greater numbers than any other issue of this type, the 1907 No Periods was set aside in fairly significant numbers as the first Indian Eagle to actually reach general circulation. Due to the relative availability of circulated and Mint State survivors, I wholeheartedly recommend this issue as the type candidate of choice in the No Motto Indian Eagle series.

Circulated Examples: You will have little, if any difficulty locating a pleasing 1907 No Periods Indian Eagle that grades AU-58. The going rate for AU-58s certified by PCGS and NGC is between $475 and $725.

Mint State Examples: From the standpoint of market availability, the 1907 No Periods is fairly common through the MS-65 grade level. Gems, however, command significant premiums due to their significance as high-grade type coins. I am aware of at least seven examples graded MS-65 by PCGS or NGC that sold through auction in late 2006/early 2007. The realized price for each of these coins fell within the range of $8,050 and $8,625.

If you are on a tighter budget but still desire an overall smooth-looking 1907 No Periods Indian Eagle, buy a coin that grades MS-64. Based on a quick perusal of auction prices realized from early 2007, I believe that you will have to pay $4,500-$6,500 for an MS-64.

Due to the manner in which Chief Engraver Barber prepared this design, the 1907 No Periods always exhibits softness of detail over the central obverse haircurls and reverse feathers. When combined with scattered abrasions and/or somewhat muted luster as frequently seen in lower Mint State grades, this striking characteristic can inhibit a coin's eye appeal. For this reason, I suggest that you avoid examples that grade MS-60, MS-61, MS-62 or MS-63.

If your collecting budget makes it well nigh impossible to acquire a 1907 No Periods Indian Eagle in MS-64 or MS-65, you can still succeed in procuring a desirable piece in MS-62 or MS-63. Be prepared for a longer search, though, as most MS-62s and MS-63s that I have seen are not the most attractive coins. In MS-63 this issue sells between $2,750 and $4,000, while MS-62s can be had for $1,000-$1,750

General Characteristics: In addition to the aforementioned softness of detail over the central highpoints, the 1907 No Periods is usually characterized by satiny mint luster that is quite vibrant in the finer Mint State grades. Most examples exhibit yellow-gold color, although you will occasionally encounter a piece with green-gold surfaces.

Words of Caution: The 1907 No Periods Indian Eagle has a "look" all its own. Do not approach this issue with the aim of locating a coin that looks like a high-grade 1926 or 1932 Indian Eagle. For starters, the 1926 and 1932 typically come with frosty luster while the 1907 No Periods almost always exhibits a softer, satiny sheen. What's more, most other Philadelphia Mint issues in this series tend to come sharply struck. The 1907 No Periods, however, is always softly defined over the central highpoints.

It is not my intention to deter you from pursuing the 1907 No Periods for circulated or Mint State type purposes. Rather, my goal is to familiarize you with the characteristics of this issue and equip you with the tools you need to recognize an attractive example when one is offered for sale.

STRATEGIES FOR INCLUDING THE NO MOTTO INDIAN EAGLE IN A COMPLETE TYPE SET

Most Desirable Issue(s): *1907 No Periods*

Most Desirable Grade(s), Circulated Coins: *AU-58*

Estimated Cost: *$475-$725*

Key to Collecting: *Free of large and/or singularly distracting abrasions; yellow-gold, green-gold or rose-gold color; overall bold definition*

Most Desirable Grade(s), Mint State Coins: *MS-64 or finer*

Estimated Cost: *$4,500 and up*

Key to Collecting: *Free of large and/or singularly distracting abrasions; full, satiny mint luster; yellow-gold or green-gold color; bold striking detail in most areas*

Advanced Type Set

Rarer Issues: Although the 1908 No Motto was produced in far fewer numbers than the 1908-D No Motto (33,500 pieces vs. 210,000 coins), the Philadelphia Mint issue is a more realistic option for advanced type purposes. This is particularly true in Mint State grades, where the 1908 No Motto has a slightly higher certified population at PCGS and NGC (May/2007). Survivors of this P-mint issue have the added benefit of being relatively sharply struck with pleasing satin luster.

Courtesy of Bowers and Merena

Although the 1908 No Motto was produced in far fewer numbers than the 1908-D No Motto (33,500 pieces vs. 210,000 coins), the Philadelphia Mint delivery seems like the more realistic option for advanced type purposes in the Indian Eagle series. Look for coins with orange-gold or green-gold color, relatively sharp striking detail and satiny mint luster.

Two 1908 No Motto Eagles in NGC AU-58 sold at auction during March 2007, one for $633 and the other for $690. The 1908 No Motto is much rarer than the 1907 No Periods in Mint State, particularly in MS-64, MS-65 and higher grades. In MS-62, the 1908 No Motto sells for $1,600-$2,500, while the price for MS-63s increase to the range of $3,750-$4,500. An example in PCGS MS-64 realized $5,750 at auction during May of 2007.

In MS-65, the 1908 No Motto is very scarce and commands between $12,500 and $20,000. Due to this cost, I suggest that you acquire a coin that grades MS-62, MS-63 or MS-64 when pursuing the 1908 No Motto Indian Eagle.

STRATEGIES FOR INCLUDING THE NO MOTTO INDIAN EAGLE IN A TYPE SET OF RARER ISSUES

Most Desirable Issue(s): *1908 No Motto*

Most Desirable Grade(s): *AU-58 through MS-64*

Estimated Cost: *$600-$6,000*

Key to Collecting: *Orange-gold or green-gold color; relatively sharp striking detail; satiny mint luster*

Major Subtypes: To be considered complete, a set of No Motto Indian Eagles that represents every design change in the series must include three coins. Not only must you obtain an example the No Periods design, but also the Wire Rim and Rolled Edge issues of 1907. The 1907 Wire Rim and Rolled Edge are among the rarest 20th century U.S. gold coins, and they are highly prized as representatives of a design that is more akin to Augustus Saint-Gaudens' original vision for the Indian Eagle.

Most 1907 Wire Rim Eagles were saved by the dignitaries that received the coins from the Mint, and a sizeable percentage of the 500-piece mintage has survived in Mint State. Relative rarity and strong demand, however, always result in strong prices for this issue. Since even an example in MS-62 will set you back at least $30,000, I recommend that you purchase any problem-free piece that grades at least that high. In MS-64, the 1907 Wire Rim is a $40,000-$50,000 coin, while an exquisite Gem in PCGS MS-66 commanded $92,000 at auction in early 2007. Some MS-66s have sold for even more, such as the piece that brought $120,750 during a 2004 sale.

Courtesy of Bowers and Merena

Since most examples of the 1907 Wire Rim Eagle were saved by the dignitaries to whom they were presented, a sizeable percentage of the 500-piece mintage has survived in Mint State. Relative rarity and strong demand, however, will almost always result in strong prices for this issue. Even a coin that grades MS-62 is likely to set the buyer back at least $30,000.

The 1907 Rolled Edge Indian Eagle is even rarer than its Wire Rim counterpart. Although the Mint struck 20,000 Rolled Edge examples, it destroyed all but 42 pieces. Most of the coins that escaped the melting pot were set aside for Assay purposes or obtained by contemporary collectors directly from the Mint. As such, this issue is almost always encountered in Mint State. In fact, I have seen very few examples that grade lower than MS-64. A PCGS MS-64 sold at auction in late 2006 and realized $43,125. The price for this issue increases markedly with grade. For example, an NGC MS-65 realized $195,500 at auction in early 2007 and an exceptional PCGS MS-67 traded for a record price of $402,500 in the same sale.

1907 Wire Rim and Rolled Edge Indian Eagles usually possess satiny surfaces, the Wire Rim issue almost always yellow-gold or green-gold in color. The Rolled Edge, however, is sometimes a bit deeper in color with more of an orange-gold appearance. Both issues exhibit numerous swirling die polish lines in the fields. These are as-struck features and, as they are raised on the surface of the coin, you should not mistake them for hairlines imparted from cleaning or other mishandling. Striking definition in the centers ranges from soft to relatively sharp, but the peripheral definition is invariably weak. Much of this lack of detail is due not to inadequacies with the strike, but rather the manner in which Mint personnel prepared the dies.

STRATEGIES FOR INCLUDING THE NO MOTTO INDIAN EAGLE IN A TYPE SET OF MAJOR SUBTYPES

Required Number of Coins: *Three*

Major Subtype #1: *Wire Rim*

Most Desirable Issue(s): *1907 Wire Rim (only option)*

Major Subtype #2: *Rolled Edge*

Most Desirable Issue(s): *1907 Rolled Edge (only option)*

Major Subtype #3: *No Periods*

Most Desirable Issue(s): *1907 No Periods*

Issuing Mint: This is a fairly easy strategy to undertake as far as the No Motto Indian Eagle series is concerned. If you choose to build a type set of No Motto Indian Eagles by issuing mint, you must obtain one example from the Philadelphia Mint and a second from the Denver Mint. The 1907 No Periods is an excellent general type coin and it also serves as a good example of No Motto Indian Eagle production in the Philadelphia Mint.

As far as the Denver Mint requirement is concerned, the 1908-D No Motto is your only option in the No Motto Indian Eagle series. This issue is quite rare in the finer Mint State grades, so I recommend avoiding any coin that grades MS-64 or finer unless you have at least $12,000 to spend. On the other hand, this issue is usually softly struck with inferior luster, and I also urge you to stay away from circulated examples or low-end Mint State coins through MS-62.

With these considerations in mind, MS-63 is a good compromise grade for the 1908-D No Motto Eagle. MS-63s will command a price in the $5,000-$5,500 range. While scattered bagmarks are usually present on a Ten-Dollar gold piece of any type in MS-63, a little persistence will be rewarded with an example that is free of singularly distracting abrasions. Also try to find a coin with above-average luster for the 1908-D No Motto is usually somewhat deficient in this category.

STRATEGIES FOR INCLUDING THE NO MOTTO INDIAN EAGLE IN A TYPE SET BY ISSUING MINT

Required Number of Coins: *Two*

Issuing Mint #1: *Philadelphia, Pennsylvania*

Most Desirable Issue(s): *1907 No Periods*

Key to Collecting: *MS-64 or finer grade; free of large and/or singularly distracting abrasions; full, satiny mint luster; yellow-gold or green-gold color; bold striking detail in most areas*

Issuing Mint #2: *Denver, Colorado*

Most Desirable Issue(s): *1908-D No Motto (only option)*

Key to Collecting: *MS-63 grade; yellow-gold or orange-gold color; above average striking detail; satiny or softly frosted luster that is above average in vibrancy for the issue; no individually distracting bagmarks*

Proof Type Set

Although some numismatists have described the 1907 Wire Rim and Rolled Edge Indian Eagles as proofs, I believe that the Mint prepared these issues in business strike format. Indeed, PCGS and NGC certify these coins using the Mint State grading scale.

On the other hand, NGC does report a single Rolled Edge specimen in Satin Proof-67 (May/2007). To the best of my knowledge, that coin and a lone 1907 No Periods in NGC Proof-64 are the only two No Motto Indian Eagles that the Mint deliberately prepared in proof format. Since there are only two coins from which to choose, do not try to include a No Motto Indian Eagle in a proof type set.

Assembling a Complete Set

Year Set: This strategy requires just two coins for completion, and you have the added benefit of being able to target issues that are fairly plentiful in today's market. The No Periods is the most realistic choice for 1907, while the 1908 No Motto works well for that year. A two-coin year set of No Motto Indian Eagles in AU-58 will cost only $1,000-$1,500. If you desire higher-quality examples, set aside at least $10,000 before trying to obtain a 1907 No Periods and 1908 No Motto in MS-64.

Date and Mint Set: Although requiring only five coins, a complete set of all issues in the No Motto Indian Eagle series will cost a considerable amount of money due to the 1907 Wire Rim and 1907 Rolled Edge issues. Since the Rolled Edge is hardly ever encountered circulated, and the Wire Rim is also typically offered in Mint State, you should consider assembling this set in a relatively high grade. You will, however, need to have ample financial resources in order to complete this five-coin set in Choice Mint State. Using coins that grade MS-63 or MS-64, one example each of the 1907 Wire Rim, 1907 Rolled Edge, 1907 No Periods, 1908 No Motto and 1908-D No Motto will cost at least $95,000-$100,000.

Die Variety Set: I have neither seen nor heard of a comprehensive study on die marriages in the Indian Eagle series, and I do not believe that any significant varieties exist. In addition, I have never met a specialized Indian Eagle collector that has shown an interest in die varieties for the No Motto portion of this series.

Proof Set: With only two proof No Motto Indian Eagles of all dates and issues certified by PCGS and NGC (May/2007), only a single collector could own a complete set of this type in proof format at any one time. I am not aware of any public auction appearances for either of these coins that are more recent than the 1970s.

A Complete Set by Issuing Mint: With so few issues, the No Motto Indian Eagle series is not a candidate for specialization by issuing mint.

Investing Tips

The 1907 Wire Rim and Rolled Edge Indian Eagles are very popular with advanced collectors. They are the only two issues in this series that are relatively true to Augustus Saint-Gaudens' original vision for the Indian Eagle—a design that I believe actually eclipses that of the Saint-Gaudens Double Eagle as the most beautiful coin ever produced in the United States Mint. With a net mintage of just 42 coins, the 1907 Rolled Edge exists in a much smaller quantity than the 1907 Wire Rim. As such, I believe that the Rolled

Edge has a more favorable relationship between the critical market forces of supply and demand. The 1907 Rolled Edge Indian Eagle is an extremely attractive coin in the finest Mint State grades, and such examples have performed very well during the 12-year period from 1992-2004.

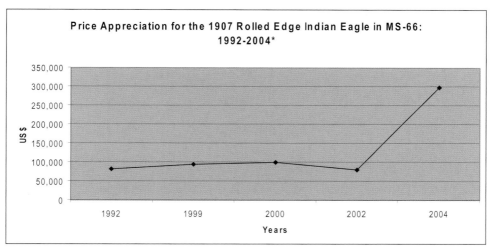

Price Appreciation for the 1907 Rolled Edge Indian Eagle in MS-66: 1992-2004*

*Values represent individual or average prices realized for PCGS and NGC-certified examples as reported by major rare coin auction houses.

After a slight market correction in 2002, the Rolled Edge Eagle rebounded strongly in 2004. If the beauty of Saint-Gaudens' Indian Eagle continues to win adherents, high-quality survivors of the Rolled Edge issue will go on to establish new price records in the coming years.

Courtesy of Bowers and Merena

The Wire Rim and Rolled Edge are the only two issues in this series that are relatively true to Augustus Saint-Gaudens' original vision for the Indian Eagle. With a net mintage of just 42 coins, the Rolled Edge exists in a much smaller quantity than the Wire Rim and, as such, may have a more favorable relationship between the critical forces of supply and demand. The Rolled Edge Indian Eagle can be an extremely attractive coin in the finest Mint State grades, and such examples appear to have performed quite well for their owners during the 12-year period from 1992-2004.

CHAPTER THIRTY

Indian Eagles with Motto

Courtesy of Bowers and Merena

SPECIFICATIONS

Year(s) Issued: *1908-1933*
Issuing Mint(s): *Philadelphia, Denver, San Francisco*
Authorizing Act: *January 18, 1837 (supplemented by Acts of March 3, 1865, and February 12, 1873)*
Designer: *Charles E. Barber, after Augustus Saint-Gaudens*
Weight: *16.718 grams*
Composition: *90% gold, 10% copper*
Diameter: *27 millimeters*
Edge:
    1908-1911: *46 raised stars*
    1912-1933: *48 raised stars, the two additional stars signifying the admission of Arizona and New Mexico as states*

History

In 1908, Congress mandated that the Mint include the motto IN GOD WE TRUST as part of the design for the Indian Eagle. This was done in deference to the Mint Act of March 3, 1865 (which stated that all U.S. coins of sufficient size display this motto) and over the objection of Theodore Roosevelt. It was at the president's request that the Mint omitted the motto from the coins struck in 1907 and early 1908. Chief Engraver Charles E. Barber modified the design of the Indian Eagle once again to include the motto in the left-reverse field. He also made a few additional, albeit minor, changes that include a slight repositioning of the Latin motto E PLURIBUS UNUM in the right-reverse field. Another modification introduced with the production of Motto Indian Eagles is the movement of the mintmark position. While the 1908-D No Motto displays the mintmark at the left-reverse border above the leaves at the tip of the olive branch, the Denver and San Francisco Mint examples struck after the addition of the Motto show the mintmark below the end of the olive branch.

Indian Eagles with Motto were struck for circulation yearly from 1908-1916, in 1920, 1926 and 1930 and finally from 1932-1933. The Philadelphia Mint prepared proofs for sale for collectors only from 1908-1915, and these coins display either a matte or Roman Gold finish depending on the specific year of issue.

In 1933, President Franklin Delano Roosevelt issued the Gold Recall Act that banned the hoarding and exportation of U.S. gold coins and ordered the return of all such pieces in private hands to the federal government "for compensation at the official price." The act was one of Roosevelt's many attempts to halt and reverse the dire economic conditions of the Great Depression. While coins with numismatic value were exempt from the Gold Recall Act, many pieces that did not command a premium as collectibles by 1933 standards were turned over to government control by compliant citizens. These coins were melted. Particularly hard hit among Indian Eagles were the 1920-S, 1930-S and 1933 issues, most examples of which were still awaiting distribution in government vaults at the time the Gold Recall Act became law. The wholesale destruction of the majority of the coins struck accounts for the extreme rarity of these three issues in all grades.

In worn condition, most other Indian Eagles of this type can be found with relative ease in today's market. Possible exceptions are the 1908-S, 1911-D, 1911-S, 1913-S and 1915-S. These issues are scarce not because of widespread melting, but rather because they were struck in limited quantities. On the other hand, many Motto Indian Eagles are extremely challenging to locate in the finer Mint State grades. Indeed, this type is much rarer at or above the MS-65 grade level than its popular contemporary in the 20th century gold series: the Saint-Gaudens Double Eagle.

Short Type Set

As one of the United States' more easily obtainable Ten-Dollar gold pieces, the Indian Eagle with Motto is popular for inclusion in short type sets. In addition to a set that focuses solely on the Ten-Dollar denomination, the Motto Indian Eagle can be grouped with the other 20th century gold series or the more plentiful Liberty designs to form a meaningful set. I have seen several sets that include just a single representative of each series, but you can expand short sets of 20th century and popular gold types to include both No Motto and Motto examples of the Indian Eagle and Saint-Gaudens Double Eagle.

Eagle Types, a six-piece set including:
Capped Bust Right Eagle, Small Eagle Reverse
Capped Bust Right Eagle, Large Eagle Reverse
Liberty Eagle, No Motto
Liberty Eagle, Motto
Indian Eagle, No Motto
Indian Eagle, Motto

20th Century Gold Coinage, a four or six-piece set including:
Indian Quarter Eagle

Indian Half Eagle
Indian Eagle (No Motto and/or Motto)
Saint-Gaudens Double Eagle (No Motto and/or Motto)

Popular U.S. Gold Types, an eight or ten-piece set including:
Liberty Quarter Eagle
Indian Quarter Eagle
Liberty Half Eagle, Motto
Indian Half Eagle
Liberty Eagle, Motto
Indian Eagle (No Motto and/or Motto)
Liberty Double Eagle (usually a Type III example)
Saint-Gaudens Double Eagle (No Motto and/or Motto)

Complete Type Set

At 4.4 million pieces struck, the 1932 boasts the highest mintage in the entire Indian Eagle series. Since most of this delivery seems to have been distributed prior to the president's issuance of the Gold Recall Act, and a substantial number of examples subsequently escaped the melting pot, the 1932 is the most plentiful issue of the Motto type in today's market. There is a close contender for this status, however, and that is the 1926. Indeed, I recommend both issues for inclusion in gold type sets.

Circulated Examples: The Indian Eagle with Motto is one coin in the U.S. gold coin family that it I would not acquire in circulated condition for type purposes. For starters, the vast majority of examples submitted to PCGS and NGC are Mint State. Additionally, and perhaps most importantly, there is only a minimal difference in price for AU-58s and examples in the lower Mint State grades. For example, whereas a 1932 in NGC AU-58 sold for $460 through auction in February of 2006, a coin in NGC MS-60 sold for less than $30 more during the same month.

If you still insist on adding a circulated 1926 or 1932 Indian Eagle to your type set, focus solely on coins that grade AU-58. At that level of preservation you should be able to find a coin that is overall sharply defined, predominantly lustrous and free of an excessive number of abrasions.

Mint State Examples: While Mint State 1926 and 1932 Indian Eagles are relatively plentiful in an absolute sense, the type as a whole can be challenging to locate in higher grades. As a result, prices for these two issues increase sharply as you progress up the Mint State grading scale. Against this you must weigh the fact that 1926 and 1932 Indian Eagles in MS-60, MS-61, MS-62 and MS-63, while often possessing vibrant mint luster, usually display a generous number of distracting bagmarks. If your budget permits, target the MS-64 grade level to obtain a lustrous example with a minimum number of scattered abrasions. In MS-64, 1926 and 1932 Indian Eagles start at $1,800-$2,600.

I realize that MS-64s may be out of your reach. Fortunately, you can still acquire a pleasing Indian Eagle in MS-62 or MS-63 while keeping costs at a more manageable level. Be prepared to exercise more patience during this search process. Most Mint State 1926 and 1932 Indian Eagles grade below MS-64 due to scattered bagmarks. These pieces typically retain fully vibrant luster. On the other hand, the occasional lackluster piece with relatively smooth surfaces does come along in an MS-62 or MS-63 holder. This is a positive as there is some opportunity to choose what in your mind is the lesser of two evils: a sizeable number of bagmarks or slightly deficient luster. Either way, 1926 and 1932 Indian Eagles in MS-63 will run $1,000-$1,500, while in MS-62 these issues drop down to the $800-$1,000 range.

If you want to go the other way and select a coin that grades MS-65 for your type set, anticipate spending at least $4,000-$5,000 for a 1926 or 1932 Indian Eagle.

General Characteristics: In Mint State, the 1926 and 1932 usually display rich, frosty mint luster. Green-gold and orange-gold colors are dominant among survivors, but a rose-gold 1932 does turn up now and then. Both issues seldom display bothersome striking incompleteness. On the other hand, scuffy surfaces are the norm in lower Mint State and circulated grades. Some examples that grade MS-60 through MS-62 possess large, individually detracting bagmarks.

Courtesy of Bowers and Merena

In Mint State, the 1932 will typically display rich, frosty mint luster. Green-gold and orange-gold colors seem to predominate among survivors, but a rose-gold example could turn up now and then. This issue is seldom plagued by bothersome striking incompleteness.

Words of Caution: Indian Eagles dated 1926 and 1932 sometimes possess scattered copper (or alloy) spots on one or both sides. These will not result in a lower numeric grade from PCGS or NGC, and I have even met one or two collectors that value these features as a sign of originality. Generally speaking, however, an excessive number of copper spots, or even a single one in a prime focal area, will diminish a coin's eye appeal. Consequently, a reduction in eye appeal could result in a reduction in price, so you should avoid examples with bothersome copper spots. Protecting your financial investment must be an important consideration every time you add a coin to your collection.

STRATEGIES FOR INCLUDING THE INDIAN EAGLE WITH MOTTO IN A COMPLETE TYPE SET

Most Desirable Issue(s): *1926, 1932*

Most Desirable Grade(s), Circulated Coins: *AU-58*

Estimated Cost: *$450-$550*

Key to Collecting: *Free of large and/or singularly distracting abrasions; orange-gold or green-gold color; overall sharp definition; plenty of original luster remaining*

Most Desirable Grade(s), Mint State Coins: *MS-64 or finer*

Estimated Cost: *$1,800 and up*

Key to Collecting: *Free of large and/or singularly distracting abrasions; full, frosty mint luster; orange-gold or green-gold color; a sharp strike*

Advanced Type Set

Rarer Issues: In circulated grades, the 1908-S, 1911-D, 1911-S, 1913-S and 1915-S are strong candidates for inclusion in an advanced type set. These issues have low mintages, which is a desirable attribute. Prices in AU-58 range from $750-$1,600 for a 1911-S to upward of $2,500 for a 1911-D or 1913-S. Some auction appearances for premium-quality examples have resulted in even higher realized prices, and this is due to the rarity of these issues in Mint State.

Most 1908-S, 1911-D, 1911-S, 1913-S and 1915-S Indian Eagles possess orange-gold or green-gold color and frosty surfaces. Abrasions for AU-58s can be substantial, but enough searching will procure a relatively smooth-looking example. Many 1911-S and 1913-S Indian Eagles exhibit a curious patch of roughness along the lower-left obverse border that sometimes affects the first two digits in the date. This feature is as struck. Speaking of the strike, most examples of these issues are quite sharp. Luster, on the other hand, varies from vibrant for the 1908-S to somewhat inferior for the 1913-S.

Courtesy of Bowers and Merena

In circulated grades, the advanced type collector might want to select a 1908-S, 1911-D, 1911-S, 1913-S or 1915-S Indian Eagle for inclusion in their set. These issues possess low mintages, a feature that is often desirable to collectors. The 1913-S will probably cost upward of $2,500 in AU-58.

If you are assembling a better-date type set using Mint State coins, the early Philadelphia issues, as well as the 1910-D, are rarer than the 1926 and 1932 in MS-64. Cost varies depending on the specific issue, but it will be in the range of $2,750-$5,000. Look for a coin with sharp striking detail and vibrant, frosty or satiny luster.

STRATEGIES FOR INCLUDING THE INDIAN EAGLE WITH MOTTO IN A TYPE SET OF RARER ISSUES

Most Desirable Issue(s):

    Circulated Grades: *1908-S, 1911-D, 1911-S, 1913-S, 1915-S*

    Mint State Grades: *1908 Motto, 1909, 1910, 1910-D, 1911*

Most Desirable Grade(s):

    Circulated Examples: *AU-58*

    Mint State Examples: *MS-64*

Estimated Cost:

    Circulated Examples: *$750-$2,500*

    Mint State Examples: *$2,750-$5,000*

Key to Collecting:

    Circulated Examples: *Overall sharp definition; relatively smooth-looking surfaces for the AU-58 grade level; portions of the original luster still intact*

    Mint State Examples*: Sharp striking detail; full, frosty or satiny luster; no sizeable and/or individually distracting bagmarks*

Major Subtypes: There are no major subtypes in the Indian Eagle with Motto series, the design remaining unchanged through the series' end in 1933.

Issuing Mint: Three Mints were active in the production of this type, and you can easily fulfill the Philadelphia Mint requirement with a 1926 or 1932. And as the most plentiful mintmarked issue in the series, the 1910-D is the best choice for a Motto Indian Eagle struck in the Denver Mint.

Courtesy of Bowers and Merena

The 1909-S probably exists in greater numbers at the MS-64 level than any other San Francisco Mint Indian Eagle. Look for coins with a sharp strike, good luster and pretty color.

Things are a little more complex as far as the S-mint Indian Eagle series is concerned, particularly if you desire a Mint State example. The 1909-S exists in greater numbers at the MS-64 level than any other S-mint delivery of this type, but it is still conditionally challenging and quite rare in that grade. On the positive side, the 1909-S tends to be sharply struck with good luster and pretty color. Indeed, a minimally abraded MS-64 is a very attractive coin. A quartet of '09-S Eagles graded MS-64 by PCGS and NGC that sold through various auctions during 2006 and early 2007 realized $5,750-$6,900. The relative ease with which you can acquire a 1910-D, 1926 and/or 1932 in MS-64 means that you should stretch for the 1909-S in this grade in order to assemble a set of uniform technical quality.

STRATEGIES FOR INCLUDING THE INDIAN EAGLE WITH MOTTO IN A TYPE SET BY ISSUING MINT

Required Number of Coins: *Three*

Issuing Mint #1: *Philadelphia, Pennsylvania*

Most Desirable Issue(s): *1926, 1932*

Key to Collecting: *MS-64 grade; free of large and/or singularly distracting abrasions; full, frosty mint luster; orange-gold or green-gold color; sharp striking detail*

Issuing Mint #2: *Denver, Colorado*

Most Desirable Issue(s): *1910-D*

Key to Collecting: *MS-64 grade; free of large and/or singularly distracting abrasions; full, frosty mint luster; orange-gold or green-gold color; sharp striking detail*

Issuing Mint #3: *San Francisco, California*

Most Desirable Issue(s): *1909-S*

Key to Collecting: *MS-64 grade; free of large and/or singularly distracting abrasions; frosty or satiny mint luster; rose-gold or green-gold color; sharp striking detail*

Proof Type Set

Unlike its No Motto predecessor, the Indian Eagle with Motto is a type that you can realistically include in a proof type set of U.S. gold. As with the proof Indian Quarter Eagle and Indian Half Eagle, the Mint used several different experimental finishes in the production of this series. The first-year 1908 Motto is not a good choice for type purposes because most examples that I have seen display a fairly dark matte texture to their surfaces. Although the Mint also imparted a matte, or sandblast finish to the proof Eagles struck in 1911, 1912, 1913, 1914 and 1915, these issues are lighter in color with more of a fine-grain, sparkling texture.

In the U.S. rare coin market of the 21st century, however, the most appealing coins are those with the brightest, flashiest surfaces. In the case of the proof Indian Eagle with Motto series, the only two issues that really meet this criterion are the 1909 and 1910.

Struck with a Roman Gold finish that blends satin and semi-reflective characteristics, the typically encountered 1909 and 1910 looks markedly different from most other proof Indian Eagles. In addition to bright, yellow-gold or orange-gold color, these issues possess a surface texture that is better at hiding wispy contact marks than those of their matte counterparts. As a result, you can keep costs down somewhat by acquiring a Proof-64 while still acquiring a relatively smooth-looking example. The 1909 and 1910 are pricy in Proof-64, however, and you will have to part with at least $30,000-$40,000 to make the purchase.

In higher grades, the asking price for the proof 1909 and 1910 increases accordingly. A 1910 in PCGS Proof-65 sold for $66,125 during an early 2007 auction, while a 1909 in NGC Proof-66 traded for $51,750 at around the same time. Proof-67s start at $80,000.

Courtesy of Rare Coin Wholesalers

Struck with a Roman Gold finish, the 1909 and 1910 are typically brighter than the proof Indian Eagles delivered in 1908 and from 1911-1915. A 1909 certified Proof-66 by NGC sold for $51,750 during an early 2007 auction.

STRATEGIES FOR INCLUDING THE INDIAN EAGLE WITH MOTTO IN A PROOF TYPE SET

Most Desirable Issue(s): *1909, 1910*

Most Desirable Grade(s): *Proof-64 or finer*

Key to Collecting: *Full striking detail; bright Roman Gold surfaces; yellow-gold or orange-gold color, sometimes with rich green-gold undertones; few, if any wispy contact marks*

Assembling a Complete Set

Year Set: This is the least expensive way to assemble a complete set of Motto Indian Eagles, although the necessity of including all three of the series' key-date issues will still result in substantial cost. The final-year 1933 is available only in Mint State as far as PCGS and NGC-certified coins are concerned (May/2007). An NGC MS-64 commanded $276,000 at auction in 2004. I also know of two PCGS MS-65s that appeared at auction during the first decade of the 21st century. The first realized $517,500 in 2005 while the second brought $546,250 in early 2007.

While the 1920-S and 1930-S are available in circulated condition, in practice the 1930-S is seldom encountered in grades below MS-60. (As of May 2007, in fact, the lowest-graded 1930-S Eagles at PCGS and NGC are AU-58s.) In MS-64, the 1930-S is at least a $40,000-$50,000 coin, while in PCGS MS-65 an example traded hands for $63,250 at auction in January of 2007. Even in MS-62 the '30-S commands in excess of $30,000, as evidenced by a PCGS coin in that grade that realized $33,350 in 2006.

The Old Mint, also known as the Granite Lady, is actually the second building to house the San Francisco Mint. From 1874-1930, it helped strike gold coins for use in circulation. The final two regular-issue gold coins struck within this building—the 1930-S Indian Eagle and 1930-S Saint-Gaudens Double Eagle—are both major numismatic rarities since most examples were destroyed on government authority. (Image Courtesy of the San Francisco History Center, San Francisco Public Library)

Courtesy of Bowers and Merena

Although obtaining one coin from each year in the series is probably the least expensive way to assemble a complete set of Motto Indian Eagles, the necessity of including all three of the series' key-date issues is still likely to result in substantial cost. The 1930-S is seldom encountered in worn condition, which means that the buyer will almost certainly have to acquire a Mint State representative. Even in MS-62 this issue will often command in excess of $30,000, as evidenced by a PCGS-certified coin in that grade that realized $33,350 in 2006.

The 1920-S, on the other hand, occasionally appears in circulated grades. Bear in mind that this is a rare issue at all levels of preservation. A PCGS AU-58 brought $29,900 when it sold during an early 2005 auction.

In order to offset the significant financial requirement for the 1920-S, 1930-S and 1933, I suggest acquiring circulated examples for the other 11 years represented by the Motto Indian Eagle series. One representative each of the 1908 Motto, 1909, 1910-D, 1911, 1912, 1913, 1914, 1915, 1916-S, 1926 and 1932 in AU-58 will require you to spend at least $5,000.

Date and Mint Set: Several complete sets of Indian Eagles with Motto have been assembled and sold over the years, almost always as part of collections that also included examples of the No Motto issues. Among others, the Dr. Thaine B. Price Collection crossed the auction block in 1998 and the Indian Eagles in the Richmond Collection sold in 2004. The Richmond Collection coins ranged in grade from MS-61 through MS-64, and the total realized price for all 27 pieces was $420,720.

Die Variety Set: Indian Eagles with Motto are rarely collected by die variety. The dies that the Mint used to produce this series are virtually indistinguishable from one another.

Proof Set: Excluding the rare Roman Gold variant of the 1908 Motto, a complete set of proof Indian Eagles with Motto requires eight coins. The extensive Richmond Collection also included a complete set of this series. The individual coins in that collection graded Proof-63, Proof-64, Proof-65 and (in the case of the 1913 and 1914) Proof-66 at NGC. Total prices realized amounted to $228,275.

A Complete Set by Issuing Mint: I do not know any collectors that are assembling sets of Indian Eagles with Motto by focusing solely on the Philadelphia, Denver or San Francisco Mint issues. Indeed, I recommend assembling a complete date and mint set of all issues from 1907-1933 if you would like to specialize in the Indian Eagle series.

Investing Tips

I am particularly fond of the 1908-S Indian Eagle as a numismatic investment vehicle. It is the first San Francisco Mint issue in the entire Indian Eagle series (No Motto and Motto), and it is a low-mintage coin with just 59,850 pieces produced. Mint State examples are definitely in the minority among survivors, but they are also some of the more attractive Indian Eagles that I have ever handled. The strike is almost always sharp, and luster tends to be frosty and quite vibrant. I recommend adding one of the few Gems or Superb Gems to your portfolio. The combined PCGS and NGC population for coins graded MS-65 or finer is only 55 pieces (May/2007)—a total that almost certainly includes more than a few resubmissions.

Perhaps surprisingly, the 1908-S is not the most conditionally challenging issue in the Motto Indian Eagle series. The 1913-S, for example, has a combined PCGS and NGC certified population of a mere six coins at or above the MS-65 level (May/2007). Past performance is not a guarantee of future appreciation in the rare coin market, but it could be an indicator under the right circumstances. I am aware of two 1913-S Eagles in PCGS MS-66 that sold through auction from 2000-2007, the more recent appearance representing a four-fold price increase over its predecessor.

Other Motto Indian Eagles that are in very limited supply above MS-64 include the 1909-D, 1910-S, 1911-D, 1912-S, 1915-S and the key-date 1920-S. Along with the 1908-S and 1913-S, high-grade examples of any one of these issues are highly recommended for numismatic investment purposes.

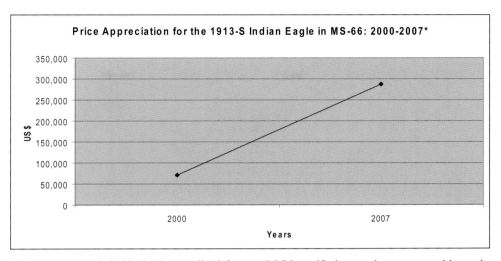

*Values represent individual prices realized for two PCGS-certified examples as reported by major rare coin auction houses.

CHAPTER THIRTY ONE

Type I Liberty Double Eagles

Courtesy of Bowers and Merena

SPECIFICATIONS

Year(s) Issued: *1850-1866*
Issuing Mint(s): *Philadelphia, New Orleans, San Francisco*
Authorizing Act: *March 3, 1849*
Designer: *James Barton Longacre*
Weight: *33.436 grams*
Composition: *90% gold, 10% copper*
Diameter: *34 millimeters*
Edge: *Reeded*

History

The largest-denomination coin ever struck for circulation in the United States Mint is the Double Eagle, or Twenty-Dollar gold piece. This impressive coin came into existence as a direct result of James Marshall's 1848 discovery of gold in California's American River. Beginning the following year, this precious metal became available in large quantities for the first time in the nation's history. (The Lower Appalachian Gold Rush of the 1820s and 1830s was handily outstripped by that in California in terms of quantity of gold mined.) In order to convert newly mined gold into coin form as rapidly and expeditiously as possible, Congress felt that a denomination larger than the Eagle would be useful. As such, it authorized production of the Double Eagle with the Act of March 3, 1849.

Designed by Chief Engraver of the United States Mint James Barton Longacre, the nation's first Double Eagle displays a left-facing portrait of Liberty as the central design element on the obverse. Liberty is wearing a coronet inscribed LIBERTY, 13 stars are around the border and the date is below. On the reverse, a spread-wing eagle with a shield superimposed over its breast clutches an ornate scroll in its beak. The Latin motto E PLURIBUS UNUM is inscribed upon the scroll. An olive branch is in the eagle's left (facing) talon and a bundle of arrows is in the right (facing) talon. A circle of 13 stars and a glory of rays are above the eagle's head. The legend UNITED STATES OF AMERICA is along the upper border, while the denomination is expressed as TWENTY D. at the lower border. The mintmark, if present, is positioned in the lower-reverse field between the eagle's tailfeathers and the denomination.

A single pattern dated 1849 is known; the coin is part of the National Numismatic Collection in the Smithsonian Institution. Regular-issue production began in 1850 at the Philadelphia and New Orleans Mints, the San Francisco facility joining in 1854. Mintages were fairly heavy at first, although they became more irregular beginning in the late 1850s, particularly in New Orleans where much of the gold came from local sources. The Philadelphia Mint struck proofs in limited numbers beginning in 1858.

The Type I Liberty Double Eagle, as the original design for this denomination is now known, yielded to the Type II series in 1866 with the introduction of the motto IN GOD WE TRUST.

Short Type Set

A six-piece set of Double Eagle types will make an attractive addition to your collection and, of course, highlight the Type I Liberty design. I have also seen several short sets comprised solely of Liberty Double Eagle types or Liberty gold coinage. In addition, the Type I Double Eagle is one of seven U.S. gold coins designed by James Longacre.

Double Eagle Types, a six-piece set including:
> ***Liberty Double Eagle, Type I***
> *Liberty Double Eagle, Type II*
> *Liberty Double Eagle, Type III*
> *Saint-Gaudens Double Eagle, High Relief*
> *Saint-Gaudens Double Eagle, No Motto*
> *Saint-Gaudens Double Eagle, Motto*

Liberty Double Eagle Types, a three-piece set that includes:
> ***Type I Liberty Double Eagle***
> *Type II Liberty Double Eagle*
> *Type III Liberty Double Eagle*

Liberty Gold Coinage, a four or eight-piece set depending on how many types the collector wants to represent for the larger denominations. The eight-piece set includes:
> *Liberty Quarter Eagle*
> *Liberty Half Eagle, No Motto*
> *Liberty Half Eagle, Motto*
> *Liberty Eagle, No Motto*
> *Liberty Eagle, Motto*
> ***Type I Liberty Double Eagle***
> *Type II Liberty Double Eagle*
> *Type III Liberty Double Eagle*

Gold Coin Types Designed by James Barton Longacre, a seven-piece set including:

Type I Gold Dollar
Type II Gold Dollar
Type III Gold Dollar
Three-Dollar Gold
Type I Double Eagle
Type II Double Eagle
Type III Double Eagle

Complete Type Set

The location and salvage of several important shipwreck treasures during the late 20th and early 21st centuries has dramatically altered the absolute, high-grade and/or relative rarity of numerous issues in the Type I Double Eagle series. Of particular importance were the treasures yielded by the *S.S. Central America* (sunk September 12, 1857 with more than 5,000 1857-S Double Eagles on board, many of them Mint State), *S.S. Brother Jonathan* (sunk January 30, 1865 carrying at least 1,000 Double Eagles, including many 1865-S in Mint State) and *S.S. Republic* (sunk October 25, 1865; the resulting excavation has yielded several thousand Double Eagles, many dated 1861, 1865 and 1865-S). Based on the sheer number of examples that have entered the numismatic market since 2000, the 1857-S has become the most readily obtainable Type I Double Eagle in the finer circulated and Mint State grades, although the 1861 is a close second in worn condition. I recommend both the 1857-S and 1861 for circulated type purposes. My choice for a Mint State type coin is definitely the 1857-S.

Circulated Examples: To obtain a coin with sufficient detail remaining, look for an 1857-S or 1861 Double Eagle that grades at least EF-40. Both issues start at about $700 in that grade.

Courtesy of Bowers and Merena

After the 1857-S, the 1861 is the most plentiful Type I Double Eagle in worn condition. The circulated type collector can find an example with considerable detail remaining beginning in EF-40, at which grade level the 1861 will probably start at about $700.

In AU-50 the 1857-S and 1861 sell for $1,000-$1,100, while AU-55s will cost $1,200 or so. In AU-58 the price for these two issues diverge quite markedly. An 1861 in PCGS AU-58 brought $2,185 at auction in March of 2007. During the same month, however, an identically graded 1857-S from the *S.S. Central America* commanded $3,738.

Mint State Examples: To minimize the number of small, moderate and large-size abrasions as much as possible, do not purchase an 1857-S Double Eagle that grades less than MS-62. Several MS-62s from the *S.S. Central America* sold between $4,600 and $5,700 at auction in early 2007. MS-63s start at $5,750 and can reach as high as $7,250, while the price for this issue in MS-64 is in the range of $7,250-$8,500.

Even despite the fact that a fair number of Gem 1857-S Double Eagles were included in the treasure of the *S.S. Central America*, pressure from high-grade gold type collectors usually results in relatively strong prices for such pieces. A random sampling of coins graded MS-65 by PCGS that sold through auction in early 2007 reveals prices in the $10,350-$13,800 range.

Courtesy of Bowers and Merena

Based on the sheer number of examples that have entered the numismatic market due to the excavation of shipwrecks such as that of the *S.S. Central America*, the 1857-S has become the most readily obtainable Type I Double Eagle in Mint State grades.

General Characteristics: Most Extremely Fine and About Uncirculated 1861 Double Eagles that I have handled possess warm green-gold or orange-gold color. Overall definition is usually bold, if not sharp, and traces of mint luster are often present in grades as low as EF-40.

1857-S Double Eagles from the *S.S. Central America* shipwreck are generally characterized by yellow-gold, orange-gold or rose-gold color and sharp striking detail. Lustrous pieces are typically frosty in texture.

Words of Caution: Deep, detracting abrasions are sometimes a problem for Type I Double Eagles regardless of issue, as these were large coins that were often roughly handled in commercial channels. Be particularly selective when evaluating circulated and low-end Mint State examples for purchase. A bit of patience will be rewarded with a relatively abrasion-free representative.

The 1857-S Double Eagles from the *S.S. Central America* were expertly preserved after decades of immersion in saltwater to reveal, at least in most cases, beautiful surfaces. Some pieces, even those that are certified by PCGS and NGC, still reveal areas of haziness on one of both sides where the surface build up must have been particularly thick. I have even seen a few examples on which one side is bright and lustrous and the other is hazy and quite subdued. While these coins are technically problem free, I believe that you should buy a different example. Areas of haziness can detract significantly from a coin's eye appeal.

STRATEGIES FOR INCLUDING THE TYPE I LIBERTY DOUBLE EAGLE IN A COMPLETE TYPE SET

Most Desirable Issue(s):

  Circulated Grades: *1857-S, 1861*

  Mint State Grades: *1857-S*

Most Desirable Grade(s), Circulated Coins: *EF-40 through AU-58*

Estimated Cost: *$700 and up*

Key to Collecting: *Free of large and/or singularly distracting abrasions; orange-gold, green-gold or, in the case of the 1857-S, rose-gold color; overall bold-to-sharp definition; portions of the original luster still intact*

Most Desirable Grade(s), Mint State Coins: *MS-62 or finer*

Estimated Cost: *$4,600 and up*

Key to Collecting: *Free of large and/or singularly distracting abrasions; frosty mint luster; yellow-gold, orange-gold or rose-gold color; sharply struck devices*

Advanced Type Set

Rarer Issues: Several issues in the Type I Double Eagle series are scarcer than the 1861 in circulated grades but do not command much a premium in EF and AU. Included in this group are the 1851, 1852, 1853, 1854 Small Date, 1857 and 1860. At the lower end of the spectrum, you can acquire an 1852 or 1854 Small Date in EF-40 for not much more than what it would cost for an 1861 in the same grade. In AU-58, a more conditionally challenging delivery such as the 1857 is worth $2,200-$2,500.

Although the number of Mint State 1865-S Double Eagles discovered with the shipwreck of the *S.S. Brother Jonathan* was not as great as the cache of 1857-S examples on board the *S.S. Central America*, the 1865-S has still become one of the more frequently encountered Type I issues in high grades. I like this issue for Mint State type purposes, and MS-62s will cost at least $7,000. In MS-63, expect to pay at least $8,000 for an 1865-S Double Eagle. MS-64s sell for $9,000-$10,000, and MS-65s are $15,000-$20,000 coins.

The strike for the 1865-S varies from overall sharp to noticeably soft in isolated areas. Luster also varies, and I have seen pieces with both frosty and satiny textures. The color is usually an orange-gold or rose-gold shade.

STRATEGIES FOR INCLUDING THE TYPE I LIBERTY DOUBLE EAGLE IN A TYPE SET OF RARER ISSUES

Most Desirable Issue(s):

  Circulated Grades: *1851, 1852, 1853, 1854 Small Date, 1857, 1860*

  Mint State Grades: *1865-S*

Most Desirable Grade(s):

  Circulated Examples: *EF-40 through AU-58*

Mint State Examples: *MS-62 or finer*

Estimated Cost:

Circulated Examples: *$750 and up*

Mint State Examples: *$7,000 and up*

Key to Collecting:

Circulated Examples: *Overall bold-to-sharp definition; no sizeable or individually distracting abrasions; portions of the original luster still intact*

Mint State Examples: *Relatively sharp striking detail; full, frosty or satiny luster; no sizeable and/or individually distracting bagmarks; orange-gold or rose-gold color*

Major Subtypes: The Liberty Double Eagle series of 1850-1866 includes a major variation on the standard Type I design. That is the Paquet Reverse found on two 1861s and a larger, albeit still relatively small number of 1861-S examples. This variety represents an attempted redesign of the Type I Double Eagle on the part of Assistant Engraver Anthony C. Paquet. Unlike the standard Type I motif, the Paquet Reverse features tall lettering in the legend and denomination as well as a narrow rim.

If you desire a Paquet Reverse Double Eagle for inclusion in an advanced type set, I strongly advise that you focus on the 1861-S. Although a number of 1861 Paquet Reverse Double Eagles were struck in the Philadelphia Mint, all but two were recalled and destroyed. Mint officials feared that the narrow rim would not adequately protect the coins in circulation. By the time the recall order reached the West Coast, however, the San Francisco Mint had released 19,250 examples into circulation.

Although not in the same rarity class as its P-mint counterpart, the 1861-S Paquet Reverse Double Eagle is still an elusive coin. In fact, this is the rarest S-mint issue in the Type I Double Eagle series, and examples command a significant premium irrespective of

Courtesy of Rare Coin Wholesalers

In 1861, Assistant Engraver Anthony C. Paquet created a new reverse design for the Type I Liberty Double Eagle characterized by tall letters in the legend and denomination and a narrow rim. The design was deemed inadequate for commercial use, but not before 19,250 examples were distributed from the San Francisco Mint. Today, the 1861-S Paquet Reverse is a rare coin, an NGC AU-55 trading for $109,250 during a mid-2006 auction.

grade. With this in mind, as well as the fact that no Mint State examples are reported at PCGS or NGC (May/2007), I recommend any problem-free example in VF, EF or AU. A PCGS VF-30 commanded $48,875 at an auction conducted in early 2007, while an NGC EF-45 traded hands for $57,500 two years earlier. Another significant price for this issue is $109,250 that the winning bidder paid for an NGC AU-55 in a mid-2006 sale.

Expect any 1861-S Paquet Double Eagle that you encounter to be liberally abraded. Given the rarity and significance of this issue, however, do not be obsessed with finding a smooth-looking example. (Actually, few survivors are accurately described as such anyway.) Definition is usually only average for the assigned grade, and the typical color for this issue is a warm shade of green-gold.

STRATEGIES FOR INCLUDING THE TYPE I LIBERTY DOUBLE EAGLE IN A TYPE SET OF MAJOR SUBTYPES

Required Number of Coins: *Two*

Major Subtype #1: *Standard Type I Design*

Most Desirable Issue(s): *1857-S, 1861*

Major Subtype #2: *Paquet Reverse*

Most Desirable Issue(s): *1861-S Paquet Reverse (only realistic option given the rarity of the 1861 Paquet Reverse)*

Issuing Mint: Due to the conditionally challenging nature of all New Orleans Mint issues in the Type I Double Eagle series, I advise using Choice AU coins to fulfill this strategy. For the Philadelphia and San Francisco Mints, focus on the 1861 and 1857-S, respectively.

Courtesy of Bowers and Merena

The most likely candidates for representing Type I Double Eagle production in the New Orleans Mint are probably the 1851-O and 1852-O. Examples in AU-55 and AU-58, however, will still almost certainly command a significant premium due to the rarity of Mint State survivors. An 1851-O in PCGS AU-55 sold for $8,050 at auction in 2006.

Lest you tread into the area of rare, key-date issues, use the 1851-O or 1852-O to represent Type I Double Eagle production in the New Orleans Mint. Examples in AU-55 and AU-58, however, still command a significant premium due to the rarity of Mint State survivors. An 1851-O in PCGS AU-55 sold for $8,050 at auction in 2006, while an 1852-O in NGC AU-58 commanded $11,500 in an early 2007 sale. Overall detail for these issues is usually a bit soft due to deficiencies with the strike, but rich green-gold or orange-gold color enhances the eye appeal. If you are fortunate enough to locate a relatively distraction-free example, you will have found one of the nicer circulated survivors. Most 1851-O and 1852-O Double Eagles that I have seen are liberally abraded.

STRATEGIES FOR INCLUDING THE TYPE I LIBERTY DOUBLE EAGLE IN A TYPE SET BY ISSUING MINT

Required Number of Coins: *Three*

Issuing Mint #1: *Philadelphia, Pennsylvania*

Most Desirable Issue(s): *1861*

Key to Collecting: *AU-55 or AU-58 grade; free of large and/or singularly distracting abrasions; orange-gold or green-gold color; overall bold-to-sharp definition; portions of the original luster still intact*

Issuing Mint #2: *New Orleans, Louisiana*

Most Desirable Issue(s): *1851-O, 1852-O*

Key to Collecting: *AU-55 or AU-58 grade; free of large and/or singularly distracting abrasions, if possible; orange-gold or green-gold color; relatively bold definition*

Issuing Mint #3: *San Francisco, California*

Most Desirable Issue(s): *1857-S*

Key to Collecting: *AU-55 or AU-58 grade; free of large and/or singularly distracting abrasions; orange-gold, green-gold or rose-gold color; overall bold-to-sharp definition; much of the original luster still intact*

Proof Type Set

With the exception of a unique specimen striking of the rare 1856-O that I examined in 2002 while working for a major Texas auction house, the only proof Type I Liberty Double Eagles available for private ownership are P-mint examples struck during the 1858-1865 era. All of these issues are rare, however, and in most cases much more so than even a limited original mintage might suggest. The Mint destroyed many unsold examples at the end of each year, and contemporary collectors may have accidentally or intentionally placed additional pieces into circulation at a later date.

If you have considerable financial resources, there are enough 1864s extant that you should be able to include an example in your proof type set. An NGC Proof-64 Cameo sold during an early 2007 auction for $184,000. I particularly like Proof-64s because they are free of all but a few wispy hairlines and/or contact marks. Gems, while even more carefully preserved, are so rare that PCGS and NGC combined have seen just two specimens that grade Proof-65 or finer (May/2007). Most proof 1864 Double Eagles that I have seen display bold Cameo contrast between the fields and devices.

Courtesy of Bowers and Merena

Although all proof Type I Double Eagles are exceedingly rare coins, the 1864 does appear in the market on occasion and might be within reach of the proof type collector with considerable financial resources. An NGC Proof-64 Cameo sold during an early 2007 auction for $184,000.

STRATEGIES FOR INCLUDING THE TYPE I LIBERTY DOUBLE EAGLE IN A PROOF TYPE SET

Most Desirable Issue(s): *1864*

Most Desirable Grade(s): *Proof-64 Cameo*

Key to Collecting: *Full striking detail; bold field-to-device contrast; orange-gold or reddish-gold color; a minimum number of wispy hairlines and/or contact marks*

Assembling a Complete Set

Year Set: The Type I Double Eagle was struck for a period of 17 years, and assembling a complete year set is an obtainable goal. In order to increase your chances of meeting with success, concentrate on the P-mint issues in EF-40 or EF-45 condition. The one exception, of course, will be the 1866-S No Motto, which is the only Type I Double Eagle produced that year. Rare in all grades, the 1866-S No Motto costs $15,000 in Extremely Fine. Expect to add $18,000 more to the cost of a '66-S No Motto to acquire an EF example of each P-mint issue in the Type I Double Eagle series. To save a few thousand dollars, use the 1859-S, 1862-S, 1863-S, 1864-S and 1865-S instead of their identically dated Philadelphia Mint counterparts.

Date and Mint Set: Due to the extreme rarity and consequent cost of key-date issues such as the 1854-O, 1856-O, 1861 Paquet Reverse and 1861-S Paquet Reverse, I do not recommend trying to complete a date and mint set of Type I Liberty Double Eagles. Consider these significant auction appearances for some of the rarest Type I Double Eagles in today's market:

1854-O: *$431,250 for an NGC AU-58 in 2005.*
1856-O: *$345,000 for a PCGS AU-50 during the summer of 2006.*
1861 Paquet Reverse: *$1,610,000 for the PCGS MS-61 that sold in 2006. This is the second finer of the two examples known.*
1861-S Paquet Reverse: *$74,750 for a PCGS AU-50 in early 2007.*

Courtesy of Bowers and Merena

Due to the extreme rarity and consequent cost of key-date issues such as the 1854-O, 1856-O, 1861 Paquet Reverse and 1861-S Paquet Reverse, a complete date and mint set of Type I Liberty Double Eagles is probably beyond reach for most numismatists. Just to provide the reader with a frame of reference, an 1856-O certified AU-50 by PCGS crossed the auction block at $345,000 during the summer of 2006.

Die Variety Set: To date, there is little collector demand for die varieties in the Type I Liberty Double Eagle series. The rarity of many issues and the consequent difficulty of assembling even a date and mint set does not bode well for this strategy gaining a substantial following in the foreseeable future.

Proof Set: The rarity and cost of the proof Liberty Double Eagles struck from 1858-1865 means that you should be content to own just one example. A single proof 1864 as part of a type set is the sign of an important collection.

A Complete Set by Issuing Mint: Of the three Mints that struck Type I Liberty Double Eagles, the New Orleans facility is the most popular among specialized collectors. Unfortunately, the Type I Double Eagle series includes two of the rarest O-mint gold coins of any denomination—1854-O and 1856-O—and other issues such as the 1855-O, 1857-O, 1858-O, 1859-O, 1860-O and 1861-O are quite costly in their own right.

I have never met a collector that specializes in Type I Double Eagles struck in the Philadelphia Mint. And the San Francisco Mint Type I Double Eagle series, while marginally more popular, includes notable rarities in the form of the 1861-S Paquet Reverse and 1866-S No Motto. In sum, I do not recommend assembling a set of Type I Double Eagles by issuing mint due to the unpopularity of the Mints or the extreme rarity of many of the coins that they produced.

Investing Tips

As the preceding sections should have made clear, the Type I Liberty Double Eagle series includes many exceedingly rare issues among both the business strikes and proofs. Key-date coins are strong performers and I believe that you should represent some of these issues in your portfolio. As far as the Type I Liberty Double Eagle series is concerned, I particularly like the proof 1860. There are fewer than 10 survivors from an original mintage of 59 pieces, and most are concentrated at the Proof-64 grade level.

Courtesy of Bowers and Merena

Key-date coins such as the proof 1860 Liberty Double Eagle can be strong performers as part of a numismatic investment portfolio. There are probably fewer than 10 survivors from an original mintage of 59 coins, and examples that grade Proof-64 and Proof-64 Cameo have performed quite well during the seven-year period from 2000-2006.

An example of a business strike Type I Twenty that has performed well through the early years of the 21st century is the key-date 1854-O in AU-50.

Courtesy of Bowers and Merena

An example of a business strike Type I Twenty that has performed well through the early years of the 21st century is the 1854-O in AU-50. As such, the numismatic investor might want to consider adding an example of this rare, key-date issue to their portfolio.

As past performance for these two issues suggests, you can do very well adding a rare Type I Double Eagle to a balanced portfolio.

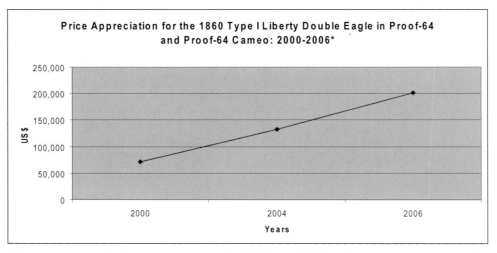

*Values represent individual prices realized for PCGS and NGC-certified examples as reported by major rare coin auction houses.

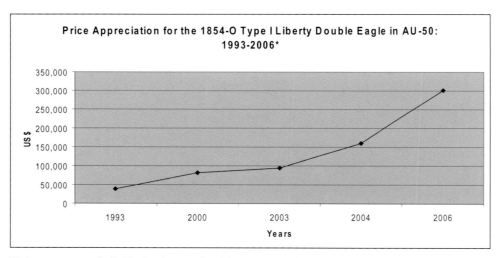

*Values represent individual prices realized for PCGS and NGC-certified examples as reported by major rare coin auction houses.

CHAPTER THIRTY TWO

Type II Liberty Double Eagles

Courtesy of Rare Coin Wholesalers

SPECIFICATIONS

Year(s) Issued: *1866-1876*
Issuing Mint(s): *Philadelphia, Carson City, San Francisco*
Authorizing Act: *March 3, 1849*
Designer: *James Barton Longacre*
Weight: *33.436 grams*
Composition: *90% gold, 10% copper*
Diameter: *34 millimeters*
Edge: *Reeded*

History

The addition of the motto IN GOD WE TRUST to the reverse of the Liberty Double Eagle in 1866 marked the birth of the Type II series. Chief Engraver Longacre placed the motto within the circle of 13 stars above the eagle's head.

The Type II Double Eagle series spans just 11 years from 1866-1876. The Philadelphia and San Francisco Mints struck examples of this type every year during that time period, with the Carson City Mint joining in from 1870-1876. In an absolute sense, the only truly rare Type II Double Eagles are the 1870-CC, 1871-CC, 1872-CC and 1873-CC. On the other hand, the type as a whole is very difficult to locate in the finer Mint State grades. The result is that even common-date examples in MS-60, MS-61 and MS-62 carry premiums that reflect strong demand from high-grade type collectors.

Short Type Set

Due to its close association with the Type I Double Eagle, you can highlight the Type II design in the same short type sets.

Double Eagle Types, a six-piece set including:

Liberty Double Eagle, Type I
Liberty Double Eagle, Type II
Liberty Double Eagle, Type III
Saint-Gaudens Double Eagle, High Relief
Saint-Gaudens Double Eagle, No Motto
Saint-Gaudens Double Eagle, Motto

Liberty Double Eagle Types, a three-piece set that includes:

Type I Liberty Double Eagle
Type II Liberty Double Eagle
Type III Liberty Double Eagle

Liberty Gold Coinage, a four or eight-piece set depending on how many types the collector wants to represent for the larger denominations. The eight-piece set includes:

Liberty Quarter Eagle
Liberty Half Eagle, No Motto
Liberty Half Eagle, Motto
Liberty Eagle, No Motto
Liberty Eagle, Motto
Type I Liberty Double Eagle
Type II Liberty Double Eagle
Type III Liberty Double Eagle

Gold Coin Types Designed by James Barton Longacre, a seven-piece set including:

Type I Gold Dollar
Type II Gold Dollar
Type III Gold Dollar
Three-Dollar Gold
Type I Double Eagle
Type II Double Eagle
Type III Double Eagle

Complete Type Set

The 1873 Open 3 is far and away the most plentiful Type II Double Eagle in today's market, and it is the most readily obtainable in the finer Mint State grades. For these reasons, the 1873 Open 3 is the leading type candidate in this series.

Circulated Examples: Circulated 1873 Open 3 Double Eagles are offered on a regular basis through AU-58. Coins in that grade display only light highpoint rub and/or friction in the fields, and the surfaces usually retain much of the striking detail and original mint luster. Some lightly worn survivors are quite heavily abraded, but enough AU-58s are available that you should be able to locate a coin that does not have too many large or distracting marks. The 1873 Open 3 is worth $650-$850 in AU-58.

Mint State Examples: The 1873 Open 3 is virtually unobtainable above MS-63, and that grade represents the finest in technical quality that you can realistically hope to procure in a Type II Double Eagle irrespective of issue. Due to the rarity of higher-grade examples, there are sometimes substantial differences in price between 1873 Open 3 Double Eagles certified MS-63 at PCGS and NGC. Average and below-average pieces sell for much less than high-end, premium-quality examples. Most MS-63s, however, are worth between $9,000 and $13,000. Be sure to carefully evaluate the strengths and weaknesses of all 1873 Open 3 Double Eagles in MS-63 rather than simply relying on the numeric designation on the insert.

If you are on a tighter budget, look for an 1873 Open 3 that grades MS-62. These coins are valued at $2,000-$2,750. Mint State examples in lower grades are apt to be very heavily abraded and/or deficient in luster. Since this type already has one strike against it due to soft definition over Liberty's portrait (more on this below), I do not recommend acquiring a baggy, lackluster example in MS-60 or MS-61. The majority of low-end Mint State coins that I have seen are not that attractive.

General Characteristics: Generally speaking, Type II Double Eagles will not show the same degree of definition to the hair over Liberty's brow as you will see on a Type I or Type III example. The 1873 Open 3 actually possesses one of the bolder strikes in the Type II series. I have seen examples with several different colors, including orange-gold, rose-gold and green-gold shades. In high grades, the 1873 Open 3 almost always displays rich, frosty luster.

Words of Caution: Be on the lookout for 1873 Open 3 Double Eagles that possess scattered alloy (or copper) spots on one or both sides. I have seen a few examples with these features. While alloy spots will not lower a coin's grade in their own right, they do inhibit the eye appeal and, consequently, the price that a coin will bring in the market.

STRATEGIES FOR INCLUDING THE TYPE II LIBERTY DOUBLE EAGLE IN A COMPLETE TYPE SET

Most Desirable Issue(s): *1873 Open 3*

Most Desirable Grade(s), Circulated Coins: *AU-58*

Estimated Cost: *$650-$850*

Key to Collecting: *Relatively free of large and/or singularly distracting abrasions; orange-gold, rose-gold or green-gold color; overall bold definition; much of the original luster still intact*

Most Desirable Grade(s), Mint State Coins: *MS-62, MS-63*

Estimated Cost:

    MS-62: *$2,000-$2,750*

    MS-63: *$9,000 and up*

Key to Collecting: *Free of large and/or singularly distracting abrasions; frosty mint luster; yellow-gold, rose-gold or green-gold color; above-average striking detail on the obverse*

Advanced Type Set

Rarer Issues: In circulated grades, I strongly recommend the 1875-CC or 1876-CC for advanced type purposes. These are the two most frequently encountered Type II Double Eagles from the Carson City Mint, which is arguably the most popular coinage facility in United States history. Examples that fall within the EF-45 through AU-58 grade range retain at least some portion of the original mint luster, and the overall definition is usually quite bold. An 1875-CC in PCGS EF-45 brought $1,380 at auction in early 2007, while an AU-58 at that service commanded $2,645 during the same month. The 1876-CC is worth more in AU-58 at $3,000-$3,500 because Mint State survivors are rarer than those of the 1875-CC.

Courtesy of Bowers and Merena

In circulated grades, the better-date gold type collector might want to consider the 1875-CC or 1876-CC. These seem to be the two most frequently encountered Type II Double Eagles from the Carson City Mint, which is one of the most popular coinage facilities in United States history.

After the 1873 Open 3, the 1875-S is one of the most frequently encountered Type II Double Eagles in Mint State grades through MS-62. It is still appreciably rarer than the 1873 Open 3, however, and the 1875-S is worth $3,000-$4,250 in MS-62. The 1875-S is very rare at or above the MS-63 grade level, and it is virtually unobtainable any finer than MS-64.

STRATEGIES FOR INCLUDING THE TYPE II LIBERTY DOUBLE EAGLE IN A TYPE SET OF RARER ISSUES

Most Desirable Issue(s):

  Circulated Grades: *1875-CC, 1876-CC*

  Mint State Grades: *1875-S*

Most Desirable Grade(s):

  Circulated Examples: *EF-45 through AU-58*

  Mint State Examples: *MS-62*

Estimated Cost:

  Circulated Examples: *$1,350-$3,500*

  Mint State Examples: *$3,000-$4,250*

Key to Collecting:

Circulated Examples: *Above-average definition to Liberty's hair and the obverse stars; no sizeable or individually distracting abrasions; portions of the original luster still intact*

Mint State Examples: *Above-average striking detail; full, frosty mint luster; no sizeable and/or individually distracting bagmarks; orange-gold or rose-gold color*

Major Subtypes: The Type II Liberty Double Eagle remained unchanged from its introduction in 1866 to its eclipse by the Type III design after 1876.

Issuing Mint: This strategy requires that you obtain three Type II Double Eagles. To represent the Philadelphia Mint, use the 1873 Open 3 and look for an example that grades MS-62 or MS-63. You should be able to assemble a uniformly high-grade set using this strategy, so consider only Mint State coins from each of the three Mints.

As far as the San Francisco Mint requirement is concerned, I recommend both the 1875-S and the 1876-S. An example in MS-62 will set you back $2,750-$4,250. Look for a coin with satiny or frosty luster and orange-gold or rose-gold color. Although it will not be easy, try to hold out for an example that is not overly abraded. You should definitely avoid any coin that possesses large, overly conspicuous abrasions.

The Carson City Mint is a much more costly endeavor, but I still believe that you should select a Mint State example in following this strategy. The 1875-CC appears fairly often in MS-62, and a trio of examples certified by PCGS and NGC passed through auction between $7,763 and $9,200 in early 2007. Hold out for one of the better-struck examples, as many 1875-CC Double Eagles are excessively soft over the obverse portrait and/or stars. Most Mint State examples are frosty in texture, sometimes with modest hints of reflectivity in the fields. Green-gold, yellow-gold and orange-gold coins are all known for this issue. Pieces with numerous abrasions are the norm, but you should avoid coins with excessive copper spots.

STRATEGIES FOR INCLUDING THE TYPE II LIBERTY DOUBLE EAGLE IN A TYPE SET BY ISSUING MINT

Required Number of Coins: *Three*

Issuing Mint #1: *Philadelphia, Pennsylvania*

Most Desirable Issue(s): *1873 Open 3*

Key to Collecting: *MS-62 grade; free of large and/or singularly distracting abrasions; frosty mint luster; yellow-gold, rose-gold or green-gold color; above-average striking detail on the obverse*

Issuing Mint #2: *Carson City, Nevada*

Most Desirable Issue(s): *1875-CC*

Key to Collecting: *MS-62 grade; free of large and/or singularly distracting abrasions, if possible; yellow-gold, orange-gold or green-gold color; frosty mint luster; above-average striking detail; no distracting copper spots*

Issuing Mint #3: *San Francisco, California*

Most Desirable Issue(s): *1875-S, 1876-S*

Key to Collecting: *MS-62 grade; above-average striking detail; full, frosty or satiny luster; no particularly large abrasions; orange-gold or rose-gold color*

Proof Type Set

As a whole, proof Type II Double Eagles are more readily obtainable than their Type I predecessors. I must stress, however, that all proof Liberty Double Eagles from the 1860s and 1870s are extremely rare coins. In fact, the highest-mintage issue in the proof Type II series is the 1867 with a mere 50 coins struck. Even so, the final-year 1876 has survived in greater numbers than any other proof Type II Double Eagle. As such, this is the issue that I recommend you pursue when assembling your type set of proof gold.

Anticipate strong competition for a proof 1876 Double Eagle, as less than one-third of the 45 pieces originally struck have survived in all grades. I realize that such pieces are very costly, but you will be most pleased by selecting an example that grades Proof-64. Lower-grade specimens are marred with numerous distracting hairlines and contact marks, while Gems are even more expensive than Proof-64s. The proof 1876 typically displays bold field-to-device contrast and rich yellow-gold or orange-gold color. A PCGS Proof-64 Deep Cameo realized $115,000 at auction in 2004.

Courtesy of Bowers and Merena

The type collector should probably anticipate strong competition for a proof 1876 Double Eagle, as it is likely that less than one-third of the 45 pieces originally struck have survived in all grades. This issue will typically display bold field-to-device contrast and rich yellow-gold or orange-gold color.

STRATEGIES FOR INCLUDING THE TYPE II LIBERTY DOUBLE EAGLE IN A PROOF TYPE SET

Most Desirable Issue(s): *1876*

Most Desirable Grade(s): *Proof-64 Cameo, Proof-64 Deep/Ultra Cameo*

Key to Collecting: *Full striking detail; bold field-to-device contrast; yellow-gold or orange-gold color; a minimum number of wispy hairlines and/or contact marks*

Assembling a Complete Set

Year Set: This is a relatively easy set to assemble, as the Type II Double Eagle series was struck for only 11 years. The pre-1873 issues are all scarce-to-rare in Mint State, however, so I urge you to pursue this strategy using only circulated coins. For most years, the San Francisco Mint issue is preferable to the Philadelphia Mint issue due to greater availability. The Carson City Mint issues all carry higher premiums than their identically dated P and S-mint counterparts.

In Extremely Fine, examples of the S-mint issues in this series are obtainable for less than $1,000 each. In AU-50 or AU-53, you will need to spend as much as $1,500 on the San Francisco Mint issues in the Type II Double Eagle series.

Date and Mint Set: Although the 1871-CC, 1872-CC and 1873-CC are rare in the finer circulated and all Mint State grades, the only real impediment to completing a date and mint set of Type II Double Eagles is the 1870-CC. A legendary rarity in the U.S. gold series and unknown in Mint State, the 1870-CC is beyond the reach of all but the wealthiest collectors. An NGC AU-50 realized $359,375 when it crossed the auction block during the summer of 2006.

Discounting the 1870-CC, you can assemble a virtually complete set of Type II Double Eagles in EF or AU. The Philadelphia and San Francisco Mint issues will cost between $650 and $3,250 in AU-50. Remember that you must purchase two examples each of the 1873 and 1873-S in order to represent both the Closed 3 and Open 3 date logotypes.

The remaining CC-mint issues carry higher price tags and vary more widely in cost than their P and S-mint counterparts. The relatively plentiful 1875-CC and 1876-CC are valued at $1,200-$1,500 in AU-50, while the 1871-CC will set you back at least $25,000-$30,000 in the same grade.

Courtesy of Bowers and Merena

Perhaps the only real impediment to completing a date and mint set of Type II Double Eagles is the 1870-CC. The 1871-CC, 1872-CC and 1873-CC, however, can also be challenging to acquire in problem-free AU and Mint State grades.

Die Variety Set: Collecting, and even studying, Type II Liberty Double Eagle by die variety is an area of numismatics that is still in its infancy. There is a chance, therefore, that you can discover a previously unreported variety. On the other hand, this area of the market is undeveloped and I would not pay a premium for a Type II Double Eagle advertised as a rare variety.

Proof Set: Although only requiring 11 coins for completion, assembling a complete set of proof Type II Double Eagles is a challenging and costly undertaking. The goal is attainable, however, as PCGS and NGC have certified examples of all proof issues in this series. Most examples grade Proof-62 through Proof-64, often with a Cameo or Deep/Ultra Cameo designation.

A Complete Set by Issuing Mint: The Carson City Mint is easily the most popular of the three coinage facilities that struck Type II Double Eagles, and it has a considerable following among specialized collectors. Most collectors that follow this strategy are assembling either a set of Type II and Type III Double Eagles from the Carson City Mint or a complete set of all gold coins struck in this Mint. As previously stated, the first-year 1870-CC is a major rarity that is a significant impediment to the completion of any set of Carson City Mint gold coinage.

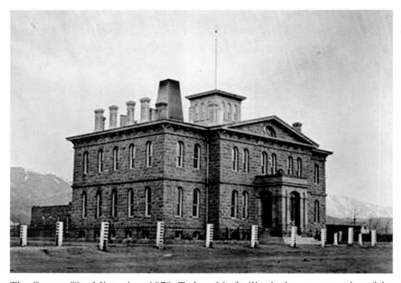

The Carson City Mint, circa 1879. Today, this facility is the most popular of the three Mints that struck Type II Liberty Double Eagles among specialized gold collectors. (Nevada State Museum, Carson City)

Although often overlooked by specialized collectors, the Philadelphia and San Francisco Mints offer excellent collecting opportunities as far as the Type II Double Eagle is concerned. You can assemble a complete 12-piece set of P or S-mint Type II Double Eagles in AU-50 for only $650-$2,000 or $650-$1,500 per coin, respectively.

Investing Tips

While you could make a strong argument for investing in the rare business strike and proof Double Eagles of this type, I believe that a better strategy is to take advantage of the conditionally challenging nature of the type as a whole. Type collectors are more numerous than specialized collectors, and the ratio between the two will probably remain fairly constant in the foreseeable future. I believe that there will be a far greater number of potential buyers for, say, an 1873 Open 3 or 1876-S in MS-63 than there will be for an 1870-CC in the coming decades.

In my opinion, the best way to capitalize on the challenging nature of the Type II Double Eagle series is to add a single high-grade example to your portfolio. At or above the MS-64 grade level, PCGS and NGC combined list just 102 Type II Double Eagles of all issues (May/2007). This is a limited total by the standards of the U.S. rare coin market in the early 21st century. What's more, these coins will become even rarer from the standpoint of market availability as the number of high-grade gold type collectors continues to increase.

CHAPTER THIRTY THREE

Type III Liberty Double Eagles

Courtesy of Rare Coin Wholesalers

SPECIFICATIONS

Year(s) Issued: *1877-1907*
Issuing Mint(s): *Philadelphia, Carson City, Denver, New Orleans, San Francisco*
Authorizing Act: *March 3, 1849*
Designer: *James Barton Longacre*
Weight: *33.436 grams*
Composition: *90% gold, 10% copper*
Diameter: *34 millimeters*
Edge: *Reeded*

History

The Mint modified the Liberty Double Eagle once more in 1877, this time spelling out the denomination in full as TWENTY DOLLARS along the lower-reverse border. The Type III Liberty Double Eagle, by which name the new design is now known, was produced into 1907 before being replaced by the Saint-Gaudens series.

The Philadelphia, Carson City, Denver, New Orleans and San Francisco Mints all struck Type III Double Eagles. They are the most numerous examples of the basic Liberty design in today's market, and many issues in the Type III series have generous mintages. The Philadelphia Mint also struck proofs every year from 1877 through 1907, and during 1883, 1884 and 1887 these were the only Double Eagles struck in that coinage facility.

Short Type Set

This is the most popular U.S. gold coin for short set type purposes. I am aware of five different parameters around which you can build a short set that includes an example of the Type III Double Eagle.

Double Eagle Types, a six-piece set including:

> *Liberty Double Eagle, Type I*
> *Liberty Double Eagle, Type II*
> **Liberty Double Eagle, Type III**
> *Saint-Gaudens Double Eagle, High Relief*
> *Saint-Gaudens Double Eagle, No Motto*
> *Saint-Gaudens Double Eagle, Motto*

Liberty Double Eagle Types, a three-piece set that includes:

> *Type I Liberty Double Eagle*
> *Type II Liberty Double Eagle*
> **Type III Liberty Double Eagle**

Liberty Gold Coinage, a four or eight-piece set depending on how many types the collector wants to represent for the larger denominations. The eight-piece set includes:

> *Liberty Quarter Eagle*
> *Liberty Half Eagle, No Motto*
> *Liberty Half Eagle, Motto*
> *Liberty Eagle, No Motto*
> *Liberty Eagle, Motto*
> *Type I Liberty Double Eagle*
> *Type II Liberty Double Eagle*
> **Type III Liberty Double Eagle**

Popular U.S. Gold Types, an eight or ten-piece set including:

> *Liberty Quarter Eagle*
> *Indian Quarter Eagle*
> *Liberty Half Eagle, Motto*
> *Indian Half Eagle*
> *Liberty Eagle, Motto*
> *Indian Eagle (No Motto and/or Motto)*
> **Liberty Double Eagle (usually a Type III example)**
> *Saint-Gaudens Double Eagle (No Motto and/or Motto)*

Gold Coin Types Designed by James Barton Longacre, a seven-piece set including:

> *Type I Gold Dollar*
> *Type II Gold Dollar*
> *Type III Gold Dollar*
> *Three-Dollar Gold*
> *Type I Double Eagle*
> *Type II Double Eagle*
> **Type III Double Eagle**

Complete Type Set

There are numerous issues in the Type III Double Eagle series that could serve well for both circulated and Mint State type purposes. A few that come readily to mind are the 1899, 1900, 1904, 1904-S and 1907, although even some of these issues are conditionally challenging above the MS-64 grade level. The 1904 is the one Type III Twenty that remains relatively available even through MS-65, however, and I suggest focusing on this issue when assembling your gold type set.

Circulated Examples: Due to the prevalence of Mint State survivors, I suggest that you remain at the AU-58 grade level for the 1904 Double Eagle. There are numerous AU-58s in the market from which to choose, and you should be able to locate a relatively smooth-looking example without too much difficulty. Insist on a coin with sharp striking detail and nearly full mint luster on both sides. Armed with $600-$750, you can acquire an example certified by PCGS or NGC. Bear in mind, however, that the value attached to circulated 1904 Double Eagles fluctuates with the spot price of gold.

Mint State Examples: I recommend selecting a 1904 Double Eagle that grades MS-64 or MS-65 for your Mint State type set. Examples in those grades are minimally abraded with full, vibrant luster. In MS-64 the 1904 costs $1,250-$1,750, while an MS-65 will set you back between $3,250 and $4,250.

Although conditionally scarce, 1904 Double Eagles in MS-66 do trade fairly often in the market. An NGC MS-66 crossed the auction block at $10,063 in late 2006.

General Characteristics: 1904 Double Eagles vary in color, and I have handled examples with yellow-gold, orange-gold and green-gold surfaces. The dominant luster type is frosty, and the strike is typically sharp.

Words of Caution: Unless you are in the market for one of the very few Superb Gems certified at PCGS and NGC or a relatively scarce Prooflike example, do not rush into a 1904 Double Eagle unless you are completely satisfied with the coin being offered. This is a plentiful issue in most grades, and you should not feel an undue sense of urgency about making a purchase.

Courtesy of Bowers and Merena

The 1904 Double Eagle is a plentiful issue in most grades, and the collector should probably not feel an undue sense of urgency about making a purchase. In fact, it might be a good idea to forestall making a purchase until one is confronted with an example that meets with 100% approval.

STRATEGIES FOR INCLUDING THE TYPE III LIBERTY DOUBLE EAGLE IN A COMPLETE TYPE SET

Most Desirable Issue(s): *1904*

Most Desirable Grade(s), Circulated Coins: *AU-58*

Estimated Cost: *$600-$750*

Key to Collecting: *No large and/or singularly distracting abrasions; yellow-gold, orange-gold or green-gold color; sharp definition; most of the original luster still intact*

Most Desirable Grade(s), Mint State Coins: *MS-64 or finer*

Estimated Cost: *$1,250 and up*

Key to Collecting: *No large and/or singularly distracting abrasions; full, frosty mint luster; yellow-gold, orange-gold or green-gold color; sharp striking detail*

Advanced Type Set

Rarer Issues: The popularity of the Carson City Mint argues strongly in favor of your including an 1890-CC Double Eagle in an advanced type set. I only recommend this issue in AU-58, however, as the 1890-CC is rare and quite costly in Mint State. (A PCGS MS-62 sold for $10,925 at auction in early 2007.) Other better-date type candidates in AU-58 are the low-mintage 1902, 1905 and 1906.

In AU-58, the 1890-CC commands a price in the $2,000-$3,000 range. For the 1902, 1905 and 1906 in AU-58, you need spend only $700-$1,250. Although this will prove particularly challenging for the 1890-CC, insist on locating an example that is relatively free of distracting abrasions.

Courtesy of Bowers and Merena

The popularity of the Carson City Mint seems to argue strongly in favor of the advanced type collector including an issue like the 1890-CC in their set. Although this may prove to be a challenging task, the buyer might want to try to locate an example that is relatively free of distracting abrasions.

The 1906-D is a highly desirable issue for inclusion in a better-date type set of Mint State coins. Historically significant as the first Double Eagle struck in the Denver Mint, the 1906-D is scarce in MS-63 and quite rare any finer. A PCGS MS-63 sold for $2,530 during an auction conducted in early 2007, while MS-64s cost at least $5,000-$6,000. Gems are seldom encountered and number just 15 coins at the two major certification services (May/2007).

Courtesy of Bowers and Merena

Another seemingly desirable issue for inclusion in a type set of rarer issues is the 1906-D. Historically significant as the first Double Eagle struck in the Denver Mint, the '06-D is also scarce in MS-63 and quite rare any finer.

The 1906-D is sometimes softly impressed in one or more areas, but you should be able to locate an overall bold-looking example without too much difficulty. The typical luster type is satiny, and the color can be yellow-gold, orange-gold or green-gold in shade.

STRATEGIES FOR INCLUDING THE TYPE III LIBERTY DOUBLE EAGLE IN A TYPE SET OF RARER ISSUES

Most Desirable Issue(s):

   Circulated Grades: *1890-CC, 1902, 1905, 1906*

   Mint State Grades: *1906-D*

Most Desirable Grade(s):

   Circulated Examples: *AU-58*

   Mint State Examples: *MS-63, MS-64*

Estimated Cost:

   Circulated Examples:

       1890-CC: *$2,000-$3,000*

       1902, 1905, 1906: *$750-$1,250*

   Mint State Examples: *$2,500-$6,000*

Key to Collecting:

   Circulated Examples: *Overall sharp definition; relatively few sizeable abrasions; portions of the original luster still intact*

   Mint State Examples: *Sharp striking detail; full mint luster, usually of a satiny texture; no sizeable and/or individually distracting bagmarks; yellow-gold, orange-gold or green-gold color*

Major Subtypes: There are no design changes in the Type III Liberty Double Eagle series.

Issuing Mint: You will need to acquire five Type III Liberty Double Eagles if you adopt this strategy. The Philadelphia Mint requirement is the easiest to fulfill as you can use the common-date 1904. I have also addressed the 1890-CC above, and it is the most plentiful Carson City Mint Double Eagle in today's market irrespective of type.

There are only two Denver Mint issues in this series: the 1906-D or 1907-D. Based on my experience, the final-year 1907-D is a bit easier to obtain in grades through MS-64.

As far as the San Francisco Mint is concerned, the high-mintage 1904-S is preferable to the other S-mint issues in the Type III Double Eagle series. This issue is conditionally scarce as a Gem, but you can obtain an MS-64 for only $1,250-$1,800.

Courtesy of Bowers and Merena

As far as type purposes are concerned, the high-mintage 1904-S might be preferable to the other S-mint deliveries of the Type III Double Eagle design. This issue is conditionally scarce as a Gem, but the buyer should be able to obtain an MS-64 at $1,250-$1,800.

We now come to the New Orleans Mint, which for the Type III Double Eagle will act as a major stumbling block to the assembly of your set. There is just one O-mint delivery in this series, and the 1879-O is a rare coin with just 2,325 pieces originally produced. Even in VF-30 an example certified by PCGS commanded $23,115 from the winning bidder when it sold in January of 2007. An NGC AU-50 realized $34,500 in 2006, while an NGC AU-58 traded hands for $40,250 one year earlier. PCGS and NGC combined report only eight Mint State examples (May/2007), a few entries of which are actually resubmissions rather than distinct examples.

STRATEGIES FOR INCLUDING THE TYPE III LIBERTY DOUBLE EAGLE IN A TYPE SET BY ISSUING MINT

Required Number of Coins: *Five*

Issuing Mint #1: *Philadelphia, Pennsylvania*

Most Desirable Issue(s): *1904*

Key to Collecting: *MS-64 grade; no large and/or singularly distracting abrasions; full, frosty mint luster; yellow-gold, orange-gold or green-gold color; sharp striking detail*

Issuing Mint #2: *Carson City, Nevada*

Most Desirable Issue(s): *1890-CC*

Key to Collecting: *AU-58 grade; overall sharp definition; relatively few sizeable abrasions, if possible; portions of the original luster still intact*

Issuing Mint #3: *Denver, Colorado*

Most Desirable Issue(s): *1906-D, 1907-D (only options)*

Key to Collecting: *MS-63 or MS-64 grade; bold-to-sharp striking detail; full, satiny or frosty luster; no sizeable and/or individually distracting bagmarks; yellow-gold, orange-gold or green-gold color*

Issuing Mint #4: *New Orleans, Louisiana*

Most Desirable Issue(s): *1879-O (only option)*

Key to Collecting: *VF or finer in grade; suitably bold detail for the assigned grade; no sizeable abrasions, if possible*

Issuing Mint #5: *San Francisco, California*

Most Desirable Issue(s): *1904-S*

Key to Collecting: *MS-64 grade; sharp striking detail; full, frosty mint luster; no individually distracting bagmarks; orange-gold or green-gold color*

Proof Type Set

As a turn-of-the-century issue with one of the more generous surviving populations in this series, the 1900 is a strong candidate to represent the Type III Double Eagle in a type set of proof gold. The issue is almost always fully struck with rich yellow-gold or orange-gold color, and many examples possess Cameo or Deep/Ultra Cameo surfaces. A Proof-64 Cameo will set you back about $40,000-$50,000, while an NGC Proof-65 Ultra Cameo sold for considerably more in 2006 at $77,625. Given this disparity in price, I recommend buying a Proof-64 Cameo or Deep/Ultra Cameo. The examples in that grade that I have seen are very attractive coins.

STRATEGIES FOR INCLUDING THE TYPE III LIBERTY DOUBLE EAGLE IN A PROOF TYPE SET

Most Desirable Issue(s): *1900*

Most Desirable Grade(s): *Proof-64 Cameo or Proof-64 Deep/Ultra Cameo*

Key to Collecting: *Full striking detail; bold field-to-device contrast; yellow-gold or orange-gold color; a minimum number of wispy hairlines and/or contact marks*

Assembling a Complete Set

Year Set: Provided that you avoid low-mintage and/or scarcer issues, the assembly of a virtually complete year set of Type III Double Eagles will not pose too much of a problem. You can obtain AU-55s for 30 of the years in this series by spending only $750-$800 per coin. Look to the Philadelphia or San Francisco Mint issues to fulfill most requirements for this strategy.

The 31st and final coin required for completion of your year set of Type III Double Eagles is another matter entirely. The Philadelphia Mint is responsible for the only Double Eagles produced in 1886, and it struck a mere 1,000 business strikes and 106 proofs. An NGC EF-45 brought $48,875 at auction in 2006. Half a year later, a PCGS AU-55 traded for $69,575.

Date and Mint Set: I only recommend this collecting strategy for the Type III Double Eagle series if you have considerable patience and substantial financial resources. The series includes many key-date rarities among the business strikes, such as the 1878-CC, 1879-CC, 1879-O, 1881, 1882, 1885, 1891 and 1891-CC.

On the other hand, I like the idea of forming a partial date and mint set of this type. The 20th century issues are attractive for this purpose, and you can assemble a complete set of the 18 issues dated 1900-1907 for less than $800 per coin. This price is for coins in AU.

Die Variety Set: There are few significant die marriages among Type III Double Eagles, and even fewer collectors that specialize in this series by variety. This is a facet of the Type III Double Eagle series that has yet to generate significant interest in the market.

Proof Set: I am sure there are many collectors that would enjoy assembling a complete set of proof Type III Liberty Double Eagles. While the task is possible, the rarity of these coins and their consequent price means that you should not adopt this strategy unless you have considerable financial resources.

A Complete Set by Issuing Mint: The most easily completed subset of Type III Double Eagles are those issues struck in the San Francisco Mint. Examples of most S-mint issues in this series cost no more than $750-$800 in AU-55. Nevertheless, the Carson City Mint enjoys a much stronger following in the market. Collectors usually acquire Type III Double Eagles from the Carson City Mint for inclusion in more comprehensive sets of CC-mint gold coinage.

The Philadelphia Mint is akin to the San Francisco Mint in terms of its popularity with specialized collectors. Even if the Philadelphia Mint were more popular among collectors assembling gold sets by issuing mint, I would not recommend this strategy. There are simply too many rare business strikes in the Type III Double Eagle series (for example, the 1881, 1882, 1885 and 1886) to make this an obtainable goal for most collectors.

Investing Tips

The Type III Liberty Double Eagle is one of the most popular series in all of U.S. numismatics, and there are several strategies that you could follow in adding an example to your portfolio. A 1904 in MS-66 is an extraordinary representative of the Type III design, and such coins are always in demand among high-grade type collectors. No other Type III Double Eagle has a significant representation at or above the MS-66 grade level, and even the 1904 is seldom encountered finer than MS-65.

Key-date issues such as the 1886 are also strong candidates for significant price appreciation. I admit that the number of collectors assembling complete sets of Type III Double Eagles is likely to remain small due to the cost associated with such a strategy. On the other hand, there are very few examples of an issue like the 1886 available to meet even limited demand. And looking solely at a selection of examples certified in AU-55 by PCGS or NGC, the 1886 has already performed quite well during the eight-year period from 1999-2007.

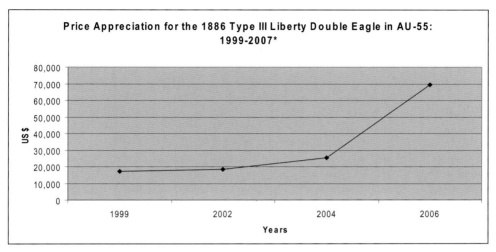

*Values represent individual or average prices realized for PCGS and NGC-certified examples as reported by major rare coin auction houses.

Finally, you could select a proof Type III Double Eagle for your portfolio. This type is more obtainable in proof than its Type I or Type II predecessors, and it has a stronger following among type collectors. In an absolute sense, however, proof Type III Double Eagles are still extremely rare coins. Even a modest increase in demand will result in significant price appreciation.

CHAPTER THIRTY FOUR

High Relief Saint-Gaudens Double Eagle

Courtesy of Rare Coin Wholesalers

SPECIFICATIONS

Year(s) Issued: *1907 only*
Issuing Mint(s): *Philadelphia only*
Authorizing Act: *March 3, 1849*
Designer: *Augustus Saint-Gaudens*
Weight: *33.436 grams*
Composition: *90% gold, 10% copper*
Diameter: *34 millimeters*
Edge: *E PLURIBUS UNUM with stars dividing the words*

History

This type is widely regarded as the most beautiful regular-issue gold coin ever struck in the United States Mint. The driving force behind the redesign of the Double Eagle in 1907 was our nation's 26th president, Theodore Roosevelt. One of "Teddy's" pet projects while residing at 1600 Pennsylvania Avenue concerned improving the designs for United States coinage. Focusing first and foremost on the gold coins, Roosevelt believed that the long-lived Liberty designs were banal and no longer indicative of the United States' growing status as a major player on the world stage. (Roosevelt himself had earned a Nobel Peace Prize for his offer of mediation that eventually led to the end of the Russo-Japanese War of 1904-1905. In a further display of the nation's power, he would send the Great White Fleet on a circumnavigation of the globe at the end of 1907.) To redesign the Double Eagle, the president commissioned Augustus Saint-Gaudens, his personal friend and one of the preeminent American sculptors of his day.

The design for this coin as finalized by Saint-Gaudens and Roosevelt depicts a full-length representation of Liberty striding toward the viewer on the obverse. Liberty is clothed in flowing robes and she holds a torch in her right hand and an olive branch in her left. A glory of rays is present behind Liberty's portrait, and the dome of the U.S. Capitol building is in the background at the lower left of Liberty's portrait. The word LIBERTY is along the upper border and the date is positioned in the lower-right field. Forty-six small stars encircle much of the periphery. The first coins struck in 1907 display the date in Roman numerals: MCMVII.

On the reverse of the Saint-Gaudens Double Eagle, a majestic bald eagle flies to the left in front of the rays of a rising sun. The legend UNITED STATES OF AMERICA and denomination TWENTY DOLLARS are above the eagle.

The first Double Eagles struck using this design are the Ultra High Relief patterns—rare and eagerly sought today as the original representatives of Saint-Gaudens' inspired design. Unfortunately, the relief was so high that the coins were impractical for regular-issue coinage. Even if the Mint could have produced them in a timely and efficient manner, they would have never functioned well in circulation. In an attempt to remedy this problem, the relief was lowered to create the coin

The Double Eagle that debuted in 1907—considered by many numismatists to be the most beautiful coin ever struck in the United States Mint—was designed by Augustus Saint-Gaudens. One of the preeminent American sculptors of his day, Saint-Gaudens was also a personal friend of President Theodore Roosevelt. (Public Domain Image)

that we now know as the High Relief Double Eagle. Even these coins required special care to impart sharp detail to the devices—each piece had to be struck three or four times on a hydraulic medal press—and the Mint could not deliver enough examples to meet the needs of commerce within the constraints of this laborious production process. Nevertheless, the Philadelphia Mint struck 12,867 High Relief Double Eagles from August-September 1907 and from November 23, 1907 through January 6, 1908. By May 7, 1908 all but 51 of these coins had left the Mint.

Complaints that the new coins were not suitable for commercial use because they would not stack mattered little at the time because the High Relief Double Eagles did not circulate anyway. President Roosevelt distributed a fair number of the coins himself, the recipients most likely friends, important government officials and possibly even the naval officers involved in the historic sailing of the Great White Fleet. Many other examples found their way into the hands of admirers who squirreled them away as keepsakes. As a result, most 1907 High Relief Double Eagles that have survived are Mint State or About Uncirculated. The occasional well-worn example that turns up in the market probably served as a pocket piece for a number of years.

Despite the issue's popularity for presentation purposes, the days were numbered for the High Relief Double Eagle. The time-consuming production process and the impracticality of the high relief design for use in circulation were significant enough drawbacks for government officials to call for another version of the design. As such, the Mint struck only a limited number of High Relief Double Eagles in late 1907 and early 1908. The survivors, however, are some of the most eagerly sought coins in all of U.S. numismatics, and they are representatives of an important one-year type in the Double Eagle series.

Short Type Set

The significant premium that even well-worn examples command in today's market explains why so few collectors seek to include a High Relief Double Eagle in short type sets. (The purpose of this strategy, after all, is to build a meaningful set at a more affordable cost.) Regardless, you must acquire a High Relief Double if you are assembling a complete set of all Double Eagle types.

Double Eagle Types, a six-piece set including:

Liberty Double Eagle, Type I
Liberty Double Eagle, Type II
Liberty Double Eagle, Type III
Saint-Gaudens Double Eagle, High Relief
Saint-Gaudens Double Eagle, No Motto
Saint-Gaudens Double Eagle, Motto

Complete Type Set

Circulated Examples: This type is much more common in Mint State than it is in worn condition. Due to the substantial cost associated with Mint State examples, however, it is perfectly understandable if you want to include a circulated coin in your type set. Fortunately, such pieces do trade from time-to-time and they are desirable alternatives to a more costly Mint State example.

A PCGS VF-30 (a former pocket piece, no doubt) sold for $8,625 in early 2007. The realized price for a PCGS AU-50 that crossed the auction block a few months earlier was $9,775, while a PCGS AU-55 traded hands for $11,500 in 2005. Finally, I am aware of a High Relief Double Eagle in a PCGS AU-58 holder that brought $12,650 from the winning bidder during a February 2007 sale.

You might have noticed that there is only a 50% difference in value between a High Relief Double Eagle in VF-30 and an example in AU-58. This is a narrow spread, and it is due to the fact that Mint State examples exist in far greater numbers in the numismatic market. In fact, there is such a preponderance of Mint State survivors that there is also a narrow spread for High Relief Double Eagles in MS-62, MS-63 and MS-64.

Mint State Examples: In my experience, and based on PCGS and NGC population figures, most Mint State High Relief Double Eagles that have survived grade MS-62, MS-63 or MS-64. Examples in all three of these grades are highly recommended for Mint State type purposes. If you want to buy an MS-62, expect to pay between $16,000 and $20,000. Seven examples certified MS-63 by PCGS appeared at auction in early 2007, at which time they realized between $18,975 and $23,000. MS-64s command $25,000-$35,000.

High Relief Double Eagles that grade MS-62 almost always possess below-average eye appeal. Most examples that I have encountered have subdued surfaces. On the other hand, those coins seldom reveal large abrasions. PCGS and NGC have graded enough High

Relief Double Eagles in MS-62 to afford you the luxury of deciding what is the lesser of two evils: liberally abraded surfaces or muted luster.

General Characteristics: Well-worn High Relief Double Eagles in VF usually possess khaki-gold, tan-gold or olive-gold color and are seldom heavily abraded. Instead, the surfaces tend to be quite smooth with a slightly glossy texture due to the coins having been used as pocket pieces. Otherwise, this issue is generally characterized by yellow-gold, orange-gold or green-gold color. Examples with strong luster are quite vibrant with a satiny texture to the surfaces. Due to the manner in which the issue was produced, the High Relief Double Eagle is always sharply detailed. EF and AU coins will possess some small and moderate-size abrasions, and examples in MS-63 and MS-64 are also apt to display scattered handling marks that help to define the grade.

Words of Caution: The substantial premium that this issue commands in all grades is due not so much to the rarity of survivors but rather to the beauty and popularity of the High Relief design. In fact, High Relief Double Eagles are really quite common from a market availability standpoint, and the typical sale conducted by one of the leading auction houses usually includes multiple Mint State examples. The same is generally true for large, national conventions, on whose bourse floors you are likely to find several dealers selling Mint State High Relief Double Eagles. Circulated survivors are much more challenging to locate, but they still trade several times yearly. In sum, do not pressure yourself into buying a High Relief Double Eagle unless you are completely satisfied with the coin. There are numerous examples from which to choose, and the issue trades on a regular basis.

STRATEGIES FOR INCLUDING THE HIGH RELIEF SAINT-GAUDENS DOUBLE EAGLE IN A COMPLETE TYPE SET

Most Desirable Issue(s): *MCMVII (1907) High Relief (only option)*

Most Desirable Grade(s), Circulated Coins: *VF-20 through AU-58*

Estimated Cost: *$8,000-$15,000*

Key to Collecting: *Relatively smooth surfaces; khaki-gold, tan-gold or olive-gold color; sharp definition; for AU examples, portions of the original luster still intact*

Most Desirable Grade(s), Mint State Coins: *MS-62 through MS-64*

Estimated Cost: *$16,000-$35,000*

Key to Collecting: *No large and/or singularly distracting abrasions, if applicable for the grade; satiny mint luster; yellow-gold, orange-gold or green-gold color; sharp striking detail*

Advanced Type Set

There is only a single issue of this type, but it does come in Wire Rim and Flat Rim varieties. The differences between the two do not represent a design change, but are rather the result of the manner in which individual High Relief Double Eagles were struck.

As previously stated, High Relief Double Eagles required multiple blows from the dies in order to impart sufficiently sharp definition to the devices. The considerable pressure that resulted from these impressions often forced some of the metal from the planchet into the space between the dies and the collar. On the finished coins, this metal usually appears as a partial wire rim on one or both sides.

The wire rim, or fin as it is also known, proved irksome to then-Mint Director Frank A. Leach. On December 14, 1907, he instructed Mint personnel to take the necessary steps to omit this feature from all subsequent examples struck. This was largely accomplished, and the coins produced on or about December 20, 1907 through January 6, 1908 are now known as the Flat Rim variety.

The majority of High Relief Double Eagles that have survived are Wire Rim examples. The scarcer Flat Rim variety, therefore, would fit well in an advanced type set. In this case, choosing a rarer coin will not result in an additional financial commitment. Flat Rim pieces seldom command a premium over their Wire Rim counterparts.

Proof Type Set

Numismatic experts disagree as to whether or not any High Relief Saint-Gaudens Double Eagles qualify as proofs. Part of the confusion stems from the criteria used to classify a coin as a proof. One of the requirements for a coin to be declared a proof is conclusive evidence of multiple impressions from the dies. All High Relief Double Eagles were struck at least three times and, as such, meet this requirement. On the other hand, there is no evidence that Mint personnel used different production processes in the delivery of some High Relief Double Eagles that would qualify those coins as proofs. Even the omission of the wire rim beginning in late December 1907 does not in its own right qualify the coins struck before or after that date as proofs.

Nevertheless, NGC lists more than 200 proof High Relief Double Eagles in their online Census (May/2007). PCGS, on the other hand, will not certify any High Relief Double Eagle as a proof. In NGC Proof-64, an example will cost you $40,000-$50,000, while an NGC Proof-65 crossed the auction block in 2006 for $69,000.

Assembling a Complete Set

A complete set of this type requires only a single coin or, at most, two examples if you choose to represent both the Wire Rim and Flat Rim varieties. This is true for both business strikes and proofs.

Investing Tips

During any given year, you will be confronted with numerous opportunities to acquire a High Relief Double Eagle through auction or for outright purchase. This issue is really not rare in an absolute sense, as most examples were set aside shortly after striking. On the other hand, coins that grade MS-65 or finer are quite rare from a market availability standpoint. In fact, for every Gem High Relief Double Eagle that I have cataloged for auction I have described at least 12-15 examples that grade MS-62, MS-63 and/or MS-64.

There are several reasons why I recommend MS-65 High Relief Double Eagles for inclusion in your numismatic portfolio. First, and as previously stated, the type is conditionally rare beginning in MS-65. Second, coins with Gem-quality surfaces are smoother and more vibrant than lower-grade examples. As such, an MS-65 will allow greater appreciation of this beautiful design. Finally, the High Relief Double Eagle is an extremely popular coin that enjoys strong demand in all grades. This demand is more acute at or above the MS-65 level where there are fewer pieces available.

Expect to pay at least $40,000 for a High Relief Double Eagle in MS-65. At the MS-66 level, the price advances to the range of $70,000-$75,000. Superb Gems are very rare, although a Flat Rim example in PCGS MS-68 did cross the auction block in early 2007. The coin realized $316,250. As impressive as this sum of money is, it nearly pales into insignificance when you compare it to the realized price reported for an MS-69 that sold through auction on two occasions in late 2005 and early 2007. The coin is a Wire Rim example certified by PCGS, and it traded first for $575,000 and then for $546,250.

CHAPTER THIRTY FIVE

No Motto Saint-Gaudens Double Eagles

Courtesy of Bowers and Merena

SPECIFICATIONS

Year(s) Issued: *1907-1908*
Issuing Mint(s): *Philadelphia, Denver*
Authorizing Act: *March 3, 1849*
Designer: *Augustus Saint-Gaudens*
Weight: *33.436 grams*
Composition: *90% gold, 10% copper*
Diameter: *34 millimeters*
Edge: *E PLURIBUS UNUM with stars dividing the words*

History

The impracticality of the High Relief type for large-scale production meant that the Mint needed a new design for the Double Eagle. The task of lowering the relief again fell to Chief Engraver Charles E. Barber, who was largely responsible for creation of the High Relief design since Saint-Gaudens had died on August 3, 1907. (Barber did, however, receive substantial help from Saint-Gaudens' assistant Henry Hering.) The new type differed dramatically from its High Relief predecessor, although the basic design remained unchanged. The relief is much lower, however, and the devices are nowhere near as visually dramatic. Additionally, the date is now expressed in Arabic numerals as opposed to the Roman numerals used on High Relief examples.

Barber's new low relief design is not the final step in the evolution of the Saint-Gaudens Double Eagle, as the type still lacked the motto IN GOD WE TRUST. Congress mandated its inclusion in 1908, thereby limiting the No Motto portion of this series to a mere three issues. Significant, however, is the first branch mint Double Eagle of the Saint-Gaudens type. The 1908-D No Motto introduced the mintmark position in the obverse field immediately above the date.

Short Type Set

As a more affordable coin than its High Relief predecessor, the No Motto Saint-Gaudens Double Eagle lends itself more readily to inclusion in short type sets of U.S. gold coinage. Sets of 20th century gold and popular U.S. gold types can be structured to include one or two Saint-Gaudens Double Eagles depending on whether or not you want to represent both the No Motto and Motto designs.

Double Eagle Types, a six-piece set including:
> *Liberty Double Eagle, Type I*
> *Liberty Double Eagle, Type II*
> *Liberty Double Eagle, Type III*
> *Saint-Gaudens Double Eagle, High Relief*
> ***Saint-Gaudens Double Eagle, No Motto***
> *Saint-Gaudens Double Eagle, Motto*

20th Century Gold Coinage, a four or six-piece set including:
> *Indian Quarter Eagle*
> *Indian Half Eagle*
> *Indian Eagle (No Motto and/or Motto)*
> ***Saint-Gaudens Double Eagle (No Motto and/or Motto)***

Popular U.S. Gold Types, an eight or ten-piece set including:
> *Liberty Quarter Eagle*
> *Indian Quarter Eagle*
> *Liberty Half Eagle, Motto*
> *Indian Half Eagle*
> *Liberty Eagle, Motto*
> *Indian Eagle (No Motto and/or Motto)*
> *Liberty Double Eagle (usually a Type III example)*
> ***Saint-Gaudens Double Eagle (No Motto and/or Motto)***

Complete Type Set

Easily the most plentiful issue of this design in today's market, the 1908 No Motto is the quintessential type candidate in this short-lived series. While examples were plentiful even before that time, the disbursement of what has come to be known as the Wells Fargo Hoard dramatically altered the high-grade rarity of this issue. Acquired in the 1990s, this hoard included more than 15,000 examples of the 1908 No Motto Double Eagle that had been stored in a Wells Fargo bank vault since 1917. The coins have since been certified and encapsulated by PCGS and NGC, and they carry the pedigree Wells Fargo Nevada Gold on the insert. The hoard was of nearly uniform high quality, most examples grading MS-65 through MS-68.

Circulated Examples: With so many high-grade Mint State examples in the market, I do not recommend acquiring a circulated 1908 No Motto Double Eagle for your type set.

If you still wish to pursue this strategy, buy an AU-58. Examples in that grade will cost no more than $725, although the price will fluctuate somewhat with the spot price of gold.

Mint State Examples: Again due to the prevalence of high-grade examples in the market, I recommend buying a 1908 No Motto Double Eagle that grades at least MS-65. Expect to pay somewhere between $1,250 and $1,850 for an MS-65. In MS-66 the price increases to $2,200-$2,750. Superb Gems are worth considerably more, as evidenced by the realized price of $6,900 that the winning bidder paid for a PCGS MS-67 during an early 2007 auction. MS-68s from the Wells Fargo Hoard have brought as much as $20,000-$25,000 through 2006, and a truly exquisite PCGS MS-69 from the same hoard sold for $80,500 during a mid-2006 sale. I am even aware of another PCGS MS-69 that realized $94,875 in late 2005.

General Characteristics: With so many high-quality survivors from which to choose, insist on acquiring a 1908 No Motto Double Eagle with a sharp strike and full, softly frosted luster. Gems are overall smooth in appearance, while a Superb Gem will possess virtually pristine surfaces. Most 1908 No Motto Double Eagles exhibit orange-gold, rose-gold or green-gold color, and some pieces even display a blend of two or more of these shades.

Words of Caution: Due to the manner in which the dies were prepared, sharply struck 1908 No Motto Double Eagles do not possess the same exactness of detail as later-date issues such as the 1927 and 1928. The highpoints of Liberty's figure are usually a tad soft, and the eagle's leg feathers are sometimes indistinct. Nevertheless, the sizeable number of coins in numismatic circles means that a little bit of patience will procure a pleasingly sharp 1908 No Motto.

STRATEGIES FOR INCLUDING THE NO MOTTO SAINT-GAUDENS DOUBLE EAGLE IN A COMPLETE TYPE SET

Most Desirable Issue(s): *1908 No Motto*

Most Desirable Grade(s), Circulated Coins: *AU-58*

Estimated Cost: *$700-$750*

Key to Collecting: *Relatively smooth surfaces; orange-gold, rose-gold and/or green-gold color; overall sharp definition; much of the original luster remaining*

Most Desirable Grade(s), Mint State Coins: *MS-65 or finer*

Estimated Cost: *$1,250 and up*

Key to Collecting: *Overall smooth, if not virtually pristine surfaces; orange-gold, rose-gold and/or green-gold color; sharp striking definition; full, softly frosted luster*

Advanced Type Set

Rarer Issues: The 1907 Arabic Numerals is scarcer than the 1908 No Motto in an absolute sense, and it is more conditionally challenging. I also like the 1907 Arabic Numerals for advanced type purposes due to its status as the premier issue in the low relief Saint-Gaudens Double Eagle series.

In AU-58, the 1907 Arabic Numerals sells for only a little more than the 1908 No Motto. Enough Choice examples have survived that you should consider obtaining an MS-64 for inclusion in a Mint State type set. In that grade, $1,250-$1,750 will suffice to acquire a PCGS or NGC-certified coin. This issue is somewhat scarce in MS-65, and you should anticipate paying $2,500-$3,250 to secure an example in that grade. The highest grade that you can realistically hope to acquire in a 1907 Arabic Numerals Double Eagle is MS-66, at which level this issue is worth $6,000-$7,000.

Courtesy of Bowers and Merena

The 1907 Arabic Numerals is scarcer than the 1908 No Motto in an absolute sense, and it is more conditionally challenging. Additionally, the former issue might be desirable for better-date type purposes due to its status as the premier issue in the low relief Saint-Gaudens Double Eagle series.

The 1907 Arabic Numerals usually displays similar striking characteristics and luster quality to the 1908 No Motto. The color is usually lighter, however, and I have handled several examples with yellow-gold surfaces.

STRATEGIES FOR INCLUDING THE NO MOTTO SAINT-GAUDENS DOUBLE EAGLE IN A TYPE SET OF RARER ISSUES

Most Desirable Issue(s): *1907 Arabic Numerals*

Most Desirable Grade(s):

    Circulated Examples: *AU-58*

    Mint State Examples: *MS-64 through MS-66*

Estimated Cost:

    Circulated Examples: *$700-$775*

    Mint State Examples: *$1,250-$7,000*

Key to Collecting: *Minimally abraded, if not overall smooth surfaces; yellow-gold, orange-gold, rose-gold or green-gold color; sharp striking definition; softly frosted luster*

Major Subtypes: There are no major design changes in the No Motto Saint-Gaudens Double Eagle series, so a single example will suffice if you choose this strategy. On the other hand, the 1908 No Motto and 1908-D No Motto were prepared using two different obverse hubs that are distinguishable by the length of the rays behind Liberty's portrait. There is, however, little collector interest in these hub varieties as of the early years of the 21st century. On the other hand, I have met one collector that was dead-set on acquiring a 1908 No Motto Double Eagle of the Short Rays variety and would not consider a Long Rays example.

Issuing Mint: You need two coins to satisfy this requirement as far as the No Motto Saint-Gaudens Double Eagle series is concerned. The 1908 No Motto is the better choice for a Philadelphia Mint coin as it is easier to obtain than the 1907 Arabic Numerals. In order to acquire a well-matched pair while compensating for the conditionally challenging nature of the 1908-D No Motto, I suggest obtaining the 1908 No Motto in MS-64. Such a coin will set you back $850-$1,000.

As the only mintmarked issue of this short-lived type, the 1908-D No Motto is a must-have coin if you choose to pursue this strategy. Once again, this is a conditionally challenging issue and MS-65s command at least $6,250. Purchasing an MS-64 is a more affordable alternative, and these coins sell for much less than MS-65s at $1,250-$1,750.

STRATEGIES FOR INCLUDING THE NO MOTTO SAINT-GAUDENS DOUBLE EAGLE IN A TYPE SET BY ISSUING MINT

Required Number of Coins: *Two*

Issuing Mint #1: *Philadelphia, Pennsylvania*

Most Desirable Issue(s): *1908 No Motto*

Key to Collecting: *MS-64 grade; overall smooth surfaces; orange-gold, rose-gold and/or green-gold color; sharp striking definition; full, softly frosted luster*

Issuing Mint #2: *Denver, Colorado*

Most Desirable Issue(s): *1908-D No Motto (only option)*

Key to Collecting: *MS-64 grade; overall smooth surfaces; orange-gold or green-gold color; relatively sharp striking detail; full, satin or softly frosted luster*

Proof Type Set

This is an exceedingly rare type in proof format, and there are only five examples of the 1907 Arabic Numerals listed at PCGS and NGC (May/2007). These coins are technically patterns or experimental pieces and, as such, are not part of a regular Mint issue.

Assembling a Complete Set

Year Set: A readily obtainable goal, you need acquire only a 1907 Arabic Numerals and a 1908-dated No Motto to complete a year set of this Double Eagle type. In MS-65 a two-piece set will require you to pay $3,750-$5,000.

Date and Mint Set: Requiring only one additional coin, you could complete a date and mint set after assembling your year set. The rarity of the 1908-D No Motto in MS-65, however, means that you should pursue this strategy independently by using coins that grade MS-64. A three-piece date and mint set of No Motto Saint-Gaudens Double Eagles in MS-64 will cost $3,350-$4,500.

Die Variety Set: With the exception of the aforementioned Short Rays and Long Rays examples of the 1908 No Motto and 1908-D No Motto, there are no significant varieties in this series.

Proof Set: The extreme rarity of this type in proof, the fact that the 1907 Arabic Numerals is the only issue known to have been struck in this format and the status of those coins as experimental pieces are all points that rule out the applicability of this strategy for the No Motto Saint-Gaudens Double Eagle.

A Complete Set by Issuing Mint: With only two Philadelphia Mint issues and a single Denver Mint issue, I do not recommend assembling a set of No Motto Saint-Gaudens Double Eagles by issuing mint. As an interesting aside, however, a year set comprised of the 1907 Arabic Numerals and 1908 No Motto doubles as a complete set of No Motto Saint-Gaudens Double Eagles from the Philadelphia Mint.

Investing Tips

Due to the emphasis on technical quality in the U.S. rare coin market of the 21st century and the popularity of the Saint-Gaudens series as a whole, I suggest that you include a high-grade 1908 No Motto in your portfolio. An example pedigreed to the Wells Fargo Hoard that grades MS-67 or MS-68, to say nothing about one of the rare MS-69s, is a beautiful, virtually pristine representative of a truly timeless design in the U.S. coinage family.

CHAPTER THIRTY SIX

Saint-Gaudens
Double Eagle with Motto

Courtesy of Rare Coin Wholesalers

SPECIFICATIONS

Year(s) Issued: *1908-1933*
Issuing Mint(s): *Philadelphia, Denver, San Francisco*
Authorizing Act: *March 3, 1849*
Designer: *Augustus Saint-Gaudens*
Weight: *33.436 grams*
Composition: *90% gold, 10% copper*
Diameter: *34 millimeters*
Edge: *E PLURIBUS UNUM with stars dividing the words*

History

Returning to the Double Eagle in 1908 on strict orders from Congress, the motto IN GOD WE TRUST was incorporated into the Saint-Gaudens design along the surface of the sun at the lower-reverse border. The remaining elements of the No Motto type were carried over unchanged. Pieces struck beginning in 1912, however, display 48 obverse stars instead of 46 in recognition of New Mexico's and Arizona's admission into the Union.

The Saint-Gaudens with Motto is the final Double Eagle type struck in the United States Mint, and the series is extremely popular with both collectors and investors. While many issues are relatively obtainable through MS-64, several are significant condition rarities that are very challenging to locate in the finer Mint State grades.

Numerous Saint-Gaudens Double Eagles struck in the 1920s and 1930s were melted in the Mint after President Franklin Delano Roosevelt issued the Gold Recall Act in 1933.

The wholesale destruction that followed this presidential order obliterated much of the original mintage for issues such as the 1920-S, 1921, 1924-D, 1924-S, 1927-D and 1932. Apparently, few examples of these and other issues were released from federal holding before issuance of the Gold Recall Act. While the 1924-D and 1924-S, for example, are now considered only scarce thanks to the repatriation of coins from European and/or Latin American banks, other issues like the 1920-S, 1921 and, especially, the 1927-D remain extremely rare at all levels of preservation.

The third Philadelphia Mint opened in 1901 and was situated on Spring Garden Avenue between 16th and 17th streets. In 1933, the final regular-issue United States gold coins—Indian Eagles and Saint-Gaudens Double Eagles—were struck in this facility. It was replaced by the fourth and current Philadelphia Mint building in 1969, although the building still stands and today is the home of Philadelphia Community College. (Historical Society of Philadelphia)

This series ends with one of the most famous rarities in the entire U.S. gold series. Although federal records indicate that the Philadelphia Mint struck 445,500 Double Eagles during 1933, the Treasury Department did not officially release any of these coins into circulation before President Roosevelt's Gold Recall Act went into effect. While almost the entire mintage was certainly destroyed in the Mint, a few examples managed to escape the melting pot and find their way into the hands of private individuals. As of early 2007, the federal government has legalized ownership of only one example. The coin in question was once owned by King Farouk of Egypt and it sold at auction for $7,590,020 in 2002.

Short Type Set

Like its No Motto predecessor, the Saint-Gaudens Double Eagle with Motto is a popular coin for inclusion in short type sets. I know of three sets in which you can include a representative of this series.

Double Eagle Types, a six-piece set including:

Liberty Double Eagle, Type I

Liberty Double Eagle, Type II
Liberty Double Eagle, Type III
Saint-Gaudens Double Eagle, High Relief
Saint-Gaudens Double Eagle, No Motto
Saint-Gaudens Double Eagle, Motto

20th Century Gold Coinage, a four or six-piece set including:
Indian Quarter Eagle
Indian Half Eagle
Indian Eagle (No Motto and/or Motto)
Saint-Gaudens Double Eagle (No Motto and/or Motto)

Popular U.S. Gold Types, an eight or ten-piece set including:
Liberty Quarter Eagle
Indian Quarter Eagle
Liberty Half Eagle, Motto
Indian Half Eagle
Liberty Eagle, Motto
Indian Eagle (No Motto and/or Motto)
Liberty Double Eagle (usually a Type III example)
Saint-Gaudens Double Eagle (No Motto and/or Motto)

Complete Type Set

While there are other issues that sell for the same amount in circulated grades, the 1924, 1927 and 1928 are the most affordable Double Eagles of this type in Mint State. I wholeheartedly recommend all three issues for both circulated and Mint State type purposes.

Circulated Examples: Due to the relative ease with you can locate a Mint State 1924, 1927 or 1928 Double Eagle, I would not acquire a coin that grades lower than AU-58 if you are assembling a circulated type set. The price for AU-58s fluctuates with the gold market, but you can expect to pay approximately $700-$750.

Mint State Examples: The 1924, 1927 and 1928 all have sizeable certified populations in MS-65. This grade is characterized by full mint luster and a minimum number of wispy abrasions. Examples are highly recommended for Mint State type purposes. A sum of $1,250-$2,000 is sufficient to acquire an MS-65.

PCGS and NGC also report generous totals of 1924, 1927 and 1928 Double Eagles in MS-66. In that grade you should anticipate paying between $2,500 and $3,500. Finally, and although conditionally scarce in Superb Gem, MS-67s also trade fairly regularly in the market. Many prices realized reported by leading rare coin auction houses for 2006 and early 2007 show examples selling between $8,500 and $12,000.

General Characteristics: In addition to relative availability in most grades, the 1924, 1927 and 1928 are popular issues for type purposes because most survivors show ample evidence of having been carefully produced in the Mint. Expect the typically encountered Gem to be sharply struck with full mint frost. Color is usually a shade of yellow-gold, orange-gold or rose-gold.

Courtesy of Bowers and Merena

In addition to relative availability in most grades, the 1924, 1927 and 1928 Double Eagles are potentially popular issues for type purposes because most survivors show ample evidence of having been carefully produced in the Mint. Expect the typically encountered Gem-quality example to be sharply struck with fully frosted luster, often with yellow-gold, orange-gold or rose-gold color.

Words of Caution: Yearly buying opportunities for 1924, 1927 and 1928 Double Eagles are numerous, and this applies equally to MS-66s as well as lower-grade pieces. With this in mind, you can afford to be patient when pursuing these issues. Do not commit to a purchase unless you are completely satisfied with the coin that you are being offered. Be sure to avoid coins with alloy spots on one or both sides. Although most 1924, 1927 and 1928 Double Eagles that I have handled are free of these features, a few coins do show scattered spotting that inhibits the eye appeal.

STRATEGIES FOR INCLUDING THE SAINT-GAUDENS DOUBLE EAGLE WITH MOTTO IN A COMPLETE TYPE SET

Most Desirable Issue(s): *1924, 1927, 1928*

Most Desirable Grade(s), Circulated Coins: *AU-58*

Estimated Cost: *$700-$750*

Key to Collecting: *Relatively smooth surfaces; yellow-gold, orange-gold or rose-gold color; overall sharp definition; much of the original luster remaining*

Most Desirable Grade(s), Mint State Coins: *MS-65 through MS-67*

Estimated Cost: *$1,250-$12,000*

Key to Collecting: *Overall smooth, if not virtually pristine surfaces; yellow-gold, orange-gold or rose-gold color; sharp striking definition; full, frosty luster*

Advanced Type Set

Rarer Issues: There are several ways that you can approach this series for better-date type purposes, as rarer issues abound. Particularly desirable issues are the low-mintage Philadelphia Mint coins struck in 1908 and 1909 and again from 1911-1915. While MS-65s are conditionally rare and carry high price tags, an MS-63 or MS-64 should fit into your budget quite nicely. In MS-63, the 1912 (just 149,750 business strikes produced) sells for between $1,250 and $2,000. For a rarer coin, consider the 1914 in MS-64. The Philadelphia Mint struck just 95,250 Double Eagles for circulation in 1914, and MS-64s command $6,000-$8,000.

If you cannot afford a Mint State example of one of the early P-mint issues in the Motto Saint-Gaudens Double Eagle series, buy a coin that grades AU-58. As an example, a 1912 in that grade is a $750-$825 coin. This price range is not appreciably higher than that for a 1924, 1927 or 1928 in AU-58.

STRATEGIES FOR INCLUDING THE SAINT-GAUDENS DOUBLE EAGLE WITH MOTTO IN A TYPE SET OF RARER ISSUES

Most Desirable Issue(s): *1908 Motto, 1909, 1911, 1912, 1913, 1914, 1915*

Most Desirable Grade(s):

Circulated Examples: *AU-58*

Mint State Examples: *MS-63 or MS-64*

Estimated Cost:

Circulated Examples: *$750-$825*

Mint State Examples: *$1,250-$8,000*

Key to Collecting: *Free of sizeable and/or individually distracting abrasions; yellow-gold, orange-gold, rose-gold or green-gold color; bold or sharp striking definition; satin or frosty mint luster*

Major Subtypes: An often overlooked design change in the Motto Saint-Gaudens Double Eagle series is the Mint's introduction of the 48 Stars Obverse in 1912 to mark the entry of New Mexico and Arizona into the Union. Consider acquiring one example each from the 1908-1911 and 1912-1933 striking periods. For a coin with 46 stars around the obverse periphery, I recommend purchasing a 1909-S. An example in MS-64 will cost $1,000-$1,500, while a Gem MS-65 is a $3,500-$4,500 coin. Strong candidates to represent the 48 Stars Obverse design are once again the 1924, 1927 and 1928.

STRATEGIES FOR INCLUDING THE SAINT-GAUDENS DOUBLE EAGLE WITH MOTTO IN A TYPE SET OF MAJOR SUBTYPES

Required Number of Coins: *Two*

Major Subtype #1: *46 Stars Obverse*

Most Desirable Issue(s): *1909-S*

Major Subtype #2: *48 Stars Obverse*

Most Desirable Issue(s): *1924, 1927, 1928*

Issuing Mint: The Philadelphia, Denver and San Francisco Mints all struck Saint-Gaudens Double Eagles of this type, so you will need to acquire three coins if you adopt this strategy. I have already sufficiently addressed the Philadelphia Mint, but to reiterate I believe that the 1924, 1927 and 1928 are the best type candidates from that Mint. For the

San Francisco Mint, take advantage of the relative availability of the 1909-S, even though you might have to stretch a bit to acquire a coin that grades MS-65. (The 1909-S is worth $3,500-$4,500 in MS-65 as opposed to a value of only $1,250-$2,000 for a 1928 in the same grade.) Finally, I recommend the 1923-D as the type candidate of choice for a Motto Saint-Gaudens Double Eagle from the Denver Mint. MS-65s command a price somewhere in the $1,250-$2,000 range.

Courtesy of Bowers and Merena

The collector will probably want to look to the 1923-D to obtain an example of Motto Saint-Gaudens Double Eagle production in the Denver Mint. Survivors that have been certified MS-65 by PCGS or NGC are likely to command a price somewhere in the $1,250-$2,000 range.

STRATEGIES FOR INCLUDING THE SAINT-GAUDENS DOUBLE EAGLE WITH MOTTO IN A TYPE SET BY ISSUING MINT

Required Number of Coins: *Three*

Issuing Mint #1: *Philadelphia, Pennsylvania*

Most Desirable Issue(s): *1924, 1927, 1928*

Key to Collecting: *MS-65 grade; overall smooth surfaces; yellow-gold, orange-gold or rose-gold color; sharp striking definition; full, frosty luster*

Issuing Mint #2: *Denver, Colorado*

Most Desirable Issue(s): *1923-D*

Key to Collecting: *MS-65 grade; overall smooth surfaces; orange-gold, rose-gold or green-gold color; sharp striking detail; full, frosty luster*

Issuing Mint #3: *San Francisco, California*

Most Desirable Issue(s): *1909-S*

Key to Collecting: *MS-65 grade; overall smooth surfaces; orange-gold, rose-gold or green-gold color; sharp striking detail; full, satin or softly frosted luster*

Proof Type Set

The regular-issue proof Saint-Gaudens Double Eagle series commenced in 1908 with the delivery of 101 examples of the Motto type. From that year through 1915, the Philadelphia Mint produced specimens for sale to collectors using either a matte or Roman Gold finish. In all cases, original mintage figures are a poor indicator of the rarity of this type in proof format. Many examples failed to sell and were later melted in the Mint. Neither the matte nor Roman Gold finishes proved popular with the contemporary public, and this issue was a poor seller in the early years of the 20th century.

Due to their brighter surfaces, I believe that the Roman Gold issues of 1909 and 1910 are the best type coins in today's market. Examples of these issues seldom reveal contact marks in the form of distracting shiny spots—a problem for matte proof gold coins that grade lower than Proof-65. You can acquire a 1909 or 1910 in Proof-64 and still own a coin that is free of overly conspicuous handling marks. Following this strategy will also lessen your financial burden, although Proof-64s are still pricey in an absolute sense at $35,000-$45,000. By way of comparison, however, a 1910 in NGC Proof-65 crossed the auction block at $60,375 in 2006.

Courtesy of Bowers and Merena

Due to their brighter surfaces, the Roman Gold Double Eagles of 1909 and 1910 are probably preferable for proof type purposes. As well, examples of these issues will seldom reveal contact marks as the potentially bothersome shiny spots that often mar the surfaces of lower-grade matte proof coins.

STRATEGIES FOR INCLUDING THE SAINT-GAUDENS DOUBLE EAGLE WITH MOTTO IN A PROOF TYPE SET

Most Desirable Issue(s): *1909, 1910*

Most Desirable Grade(s): *Proof-64*

Key to Collecting: *Full striking detail; bright Roman Gold surfaces; yellow-gold, honey-gold or green-gold color; a minimal number of wispy contact marks*

Assembling a Complete Set

Year Set: Assembling a complete year set of Saint-Gaudens Double Eagles with Motto is not a realistically obtainable goal, and not only because the final-year 1933 is virtually uncollectible. Many other years in this series are represented by issues that are very rare in all grades. Included among these are 1921 (an example of the year's only issue is a $100,000+ coin even in MS-60) and 1930 (a 1930-S Double Eagle in PCGS MS-63 sold for $74,750 during an early 2007 auction). In order to improve your chances of completing this task, I suggest that you assemble a partial year set. A run of Motto Saint-Gaudens Double Eagles dated 1908-1916 in AU-55 will cost only $700-$750 per coin.

Date and Mint Set: Given the difficulty and cost associated with completing a year set of this type, I do not recommend trying to assemble a complete date and mint set of Motto Saint-Gaudens Double Eagles. Nevertheless, some collectors have succeeded with this strategy (disregarding, of course, the 1933). The Philip H. Morse Collection of Saint-Gaudens Coinage that sold through auction in late 2005 included a complete set of Motto Double Eagles. The collection included some of the finest-known survivors of the type, and numerous duplicates were present. To give you an idea of the cost required to assemble a complete date and mint set of this type, just the rare 1929-1932 examples in the Morse Collection realized in excess of $1 million.

Die Variety Set: To the best of my knowledge, there are only a handful of significant die varieties in this series. Perhaps not surprisingly, this is not one of the more popular ways to collect Double Eagles of this type.

Proof Set: Excluding the rare 1908 Motto with Roman Gold Finish and the unique specimen striking of the 1921 that realized $203,500 when it sold at auction in 2000, a complete set of proof Motto Saint-Gaudens Double Eagles must include eight coins. Purchasing one example each of the 1908 Motto, 1909, 1910, 1911, 1912, 1913, 1914 and 1915 in Proof-64 will set you back at least $300,000.

A Complete Set by Issuing Mint: I have never cataloged a collection of Saint-Gaudens Double Eagles with Motto that was built around the Philadelphia, Denver or San Francisco Mint issues. This might seem odd, especially since this strategy is a more affordable alternative to assembling a date and mint set. All three Mints that struck this series still include key-date issues, however, so you must still have considerable financial resources to complete this task. For example, a complete 15-piece set of S-mint Saint-Gaudens Double Eagles in AU-55 will require you to part with at least $80,000. Much of this cost will be devoted to the 1920-S, 1927-S and 1930-S. In fact, you are probably going to have to pay even more for the 1930-S because virtually all survivors are Mint State.

Investing Tips

The Saint-Gaudens Double Eagles struck from 1929-1932 are all rare coins, the vast majority of examples produced having been destroyed in the Mint during the mid-to-late 1930s. On the other hand, these issues are more obtainable than the 1920-S, 1921 and 1927-D, and examples are offered at least once or twice in any given year. When sold either through auction or outright, the 1929, 1930-S, 1931, 1931-D and 1932 always receive considerable fanfare from catalogers, dealers and numismatic marketers. In sum, these are high-profile rarities in the rare coin market of the 21st century. This publicity, in turn, has resulted in impressive price appreciation for certain examples, as evidenced by the 1930-S in MS-64.

The Saint-Gaudens Double Eagle is a beautiful coin, and many gold type collectors eventually choose to specialize in this series. As this happens, demand for rare, key-date issues such as the 1930-S will continue to increase in the coming years.

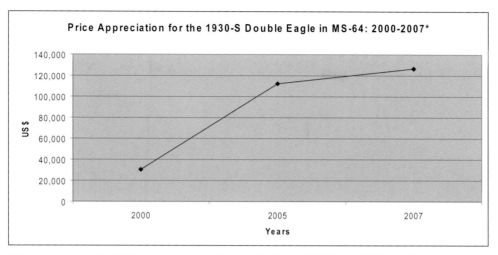

*Values represent individual or average prices realized for PCGS and NGC-certified examples as reported by major rare coin auction houses.

Glossary

About Uncirculated: The descriptive term associated with the numeric designations of 50, 53, 55 and 58 on the 70-point grading scale for United States coins. The abbreviation for About Uncirculated is AU.

Adjustment Marks: Narrow depressions in a coin's surface imparted before striking when Mint employees filed an overweight planchet in order to make it conform to the specified weight standard for the respective denomination. Adjustment marks are a normal part of the minting process for many silver and gold coins struck in the early U.S. Mint and, as such, will seldom result in a lower grade from PCGS or NGC.

Alloy Spots: Discoloration on the surface of a gold coin that are result from toning in small areas of high copper concentration. For this reason, alloy spots are sometimes also referred to as copper spots.

American Numismatic Association: Chartered by Congress in 1891, the American Numismatic Association is the leading hobby organization in U.S. numismatics. The American Numismatic Association is often referred to by the abbreviation ANA. It is a non-profit organization.

Brilliant Uncirculated: The descriptive term that corresponds to the MS-60, MS-61 and MS-62 grade levels. Brilliant Uncirculated is abbreviated as BU.

Cameo: Coins that display noticeable contrast between frosty devices/lettering and mirror-finish fields. Both PCGS and NGC use this term as a component of the grade assigned to a proof coin.

Certified: A coin that has been submitted to a third-party grading service and returned to the submitter in a sonically sealed, tamper-evident holder. Coins certified by PCGS and NGC enjoy nearly universal acceptance in the U.S. rare coin market of the early 21st century.

Choice AU: The descriptive term that corresponds to the AU-55 grade level.

Choice Uncirculated / Choice Mint State / Choice BU: Descriptive term that corresponds to the MS-63 and MS-64 grade levels.

Clashmarks: Impressions from the devices, legends or other features from one die into the surface of the opposing die in the press. Clashmarks are imparted when a pair of dies comes together in the absence of an intervening planchet. Once they become part of a die, clashmarks are transferred to the surface of a coin during the striking process.

Cleaning: The use of an abrasive substance or device to alter the surfaces of a coin. Cleaned coins often display numerous scattered hairlines on one or both sides and, as impaired examples, are usually not eligible for certification at the major third-party grading services.

Close Collar: A heavy steel plate perforated to the exact size of the coin and installed into the coinage press around the lower die to define the space in which the planchet will be struck. Introduced in many U.S. series sometime between 1829 and 1836, the close collar allowed production of coins with a uniform diameter, more pronounced rim and more intricate detail to the devices.

Copper Spots: *See Alloy Spots.*

Deep Cameo: A proof coin certified by PCGS that has especially bold field-to-device contrast. The corresponding designation at NGC is Ultra Cameo.

Die Polish Lines: *See Striations.*

Double Eagle: A United States gold coin with a face value of $20.00. Regular-issue Double Eagles were struck in the U.S. Mint from 1850 through 1933.

Eagle: A United States gold coin with a face value of $10.00. Regular-issue Eagles were struck in the U.S. Mint from 1795 through 1933.

Extremely Fine: The descriptive term associated with the numeric designations of 40 and 45 on the 70-point grading scale for United States coins. Abbreviations for Extremely Fine include EF and XF.

Fine: The descriptive term associated with the numeric designations of 12 and 15 on the 70-point grading scale for United States coins. Fine is sometimes abbreviated as F.

Gem Uncirculated / Gem Mint State / Gem BU: The descriptive term that corresponds to the MS-65, MS-66, Proof-65 and Proof-66 grade levels. Often times only the word Gem is needed to convey the same meaning.

Gilt: To cover with gold.

Hairlines: Thin lines on a coin's surfaces that, when use in reference to a business strike example, are indicative of cleaning or another form of mishandling. Hairlines are also used to describe light handling marks on proof coins and, in this case, are not always the result of cleaning. Unlike die polish lines, hairlines are set below the surface of a coin.

Half Eagle: A United States gold coin with a face value of $5.00. Regular-issue Half Eagles were struck in the U.S. Mint from 1795 through 1929.

Hub: A master die from which working dies are created.

Impaired: A descriptive term for coins that have been cleaned, damaged, whizzed, repaired or otherwise mishandled to the point where they will trade at a discounted price. It is the stated policy of major third-party grading services such as PCGS and NGC that impaired coins are not eligible for certification and will be returned to the submitter without being mounted in a plastic holder.

Insert: The small piece of paper included in the holder with coins certified by PCGS, NGC and other third-party grading services. Upon the insert are found such important information as the coin's date, denomination, grade and, if applicable, variety.

Luster: The original finish imparted to a coin at the time of striking. Or, the amount and intensity of light reflected from a coin's surface.

Matte Finish: The finish employed by the U.S. Mint to strike proof gold coins in 1908 and from 1911-1915. The surfaces of matte proof gold coins are characterized by a uniformly subdued texture that, under magnification, reveals myriad sparkling facets of large or small size.

Mint State: A coin struck for circulation but that does not display any evidence of wear. Mint State coins are graded on a numeric scale from 60-70. The term Uncirculated also describes a Mint State coin.

Near-Gem: The descriptive term that corresponds to the MS-64 and Proof-64 grade levels.

Near-Mint: The descriptive term that corresponds to the AU-58 grade level.

NGC Census: A listing of all coins certified by NGC. Up-to-date versions of the *NGC Census* are available for free viewing through the firm's website, www.ngccoin.com.

Numismatic Guaranty Corporation: Founded in 1987, NGC authenticates, grades and encapsulates coins for a fee. Along with PCGS, it is the leading third-party certification service in the U.S. rare coin market of the early 21st century.

Numismatics: The study or collection of rare coins. A person who studies, collects or invests in rare coins is known as a numismatist.

Pattern: A coin stuck for experimental purposes to test a new design or alloy. In most cases, patterns represent designs and/or coinage metals that the federal government did not adopt for regular-issue production.

PCGS Population Report: A listing of all coins certified by PCGS. Up-to-date versions of the *PCGS Population Report* are accessible for a fee through the firm's website, www.pcgs.com.

Planchet: The disk of metal upon which a coin, medal or token is struck.

Polishing: An especially severe form of cleaning. Coins that have been polished display unnaturally bright and/or glossy-textured surfaces. Technically impaired, polished coins are not eligible for certification at the major third-party grading services.

Prime Focal Areas: The most important surface areas of a coin when evaluating eye appeal and/or technical grade. Examples of prime focal areas are Liberty's cheek, the date and the mintmark. Abrasions or other distractions in prime focal areas will have a more profound effect on a coin's eye appeal than if they were located in a less-critical area.

Professional Coin Grading Service: Founded in 1986, PCGS authenticates, grades and encapsulates coins for a fee. Along with NGC, it is the leading third-party certification service in the U.S. rare coin market of the early 21st century.

Professional Numismatists Guild: An organization of rare coin and paper money experts whose members are held to high standards of integrity and professionalism. The abbreviation for the Professional Numismatists Guild is PNG. It is a non-profit organization.

Quarter Eagle: A United States gold coin with a face value of $2.50. Regular-issue Quarter Eagles were struck in the U.S. Mint from 1796 through 1929.

Resubmissions: A term that professional numismatists use to describe coins that are removed from PCGS and NGC holders and submitted to these services at least one more time in the hopes of securing a higher grade. Resubmissions skew the number of coins listed in the *PCGS Population Report* and *NGC Census* when the submitter has not returned the old insert(s) to the grading services.

Rollermarks: Marks imparted to a planchet by giant steel rollers that are used to reduce sheets of coinage metal to the proper thickness. Improperly spaced dies or inadequate striking pressure during production can leave traces of rollermarks on the surface of a finished coin, such as often seen on gold impressions of the 1879 Flowing Hair Stella.

Roman Gold Finish: The finish employed by the U.S. Mint to strike proof gold coins in 1909 and 1910. A few rare Roman Gold pieces are also known dated 1907 and 1908. This finish is a blend of satiny and semi-reflective characteristics.

Stella: In general terms, the Latin word for star. When used as a numismatic term, Stella almost always refers to the pattern Four-Dollar gold pieces struck in the Mint with the dates 1879 and 1880. These coins are called Stellas because of the five-pointed star that serves as the central design element on the reverse.

Striations: Incuse lines on the surface of a die that result from polishing during the preparation process. When transferred to a coin during striking, striations will appear as raised lines. Since these features are as struck, striations will not result in a lower numeric grade from PCGS or NGC.

Superb Gem: The descriptive term that corresponds to the MS-67, MS-68, MS-69, Proof-67, Proof-68 and Proof-69 grade levels.

Very Fine: The descriptive term associated with the numeric designations of 20, 25, 30 and 35 on the 70-point grading scale for United States coins. The abbreviation for Very Fine is VF.

Very Good: The descriptive term associated with the numeric designations of 8 and 10 on the 70-point grading scale for United States coins. The abbreviation for Very Good is VG.

Whizzing: An attempt to simulate original luster on a coin's surface through the use of a wire brush or similar device. Whizzed coins are considered to be impaired and are not eligible for certification at the major third-party grading services.

Wire Rim: A thin, raised lip of metal at the outmost edge of a coin formed when metal was forced between the dies and collar during striking. Also known as a knife rim or, less frequently, a fin.

Bibliography

Akers, David W. *A Handbook of 20th-Century United States Gold Coins: 1907-1933*. Wolfeboro, New Hampshire: Bowers and Merena Galleries, Inc., 1988.

Bowers and Merena Auctions. http://www.bowersandmerena.com/. Prices realized archives, various sales, accessed January-May, 2007.

Bowers, Q. David and Winter, Douglas. *The United States $3 Gold Pieces: 1854-1889*. Wolfeboro, New Hampshire: American Numismatic Rarities, LLC, 2005.

Breen, Walter. *Walter Breen's Complete Encyclopedia of U.S. and Colonial Coins*. New York, New York: Doubleday, 1988.

Burdette, Roger W. *Renaissance of American Coinage: 1905-1908*. Great Falls, Virginia: Seneca Mills Press, LLC, 2006.

Dannreuther, John W. and Bass, Jr., Harry W. *Early U.S. Gold Coin Varieties: A Study of Die States, 1795-1834*. Atlanta, Georgia: Whitman Publishing, LLC, 2006.

David Lawrence Rare Coins. http://www.davidlawrence.com/. Prices realized archives, Richmond Collection Part I, accessed January-May, 2007.

Garrett, Jeff and Guth, Ron. *100 Greatest U.S. Coins*, 2nd Edition. Atlanta, Georgia: Whitman Publishing, LLC, 2005.

Garrett, Jeff and Guth, Ron. *Encyclopedia of U.S. Gold Coins*: 1795-1933. Atlanta, Georgia: Whitman Publishing, LLC, 2006.

Heritage Auction Galleries. http://coins.ha.com/default.php. Prices realized archives, various sales, accessed January-May, 2007.

Ira & Larry Goldberg Auctioneers. http://www.goldbergcoins.com/index.shtml. Prices realized archives, various sales, accessed January-May, 2007.

Judd, Dr. J. Hewitt. *United States Pattern Coins*, Ninth Edition. Atlanta, Georgia: Whitman Publishing, LLC, 2005.

Numismatic Guaranty Corporation. Online Population Report. http://www.ngccoin.com/. Accessed January-May, 2007.

Pollock, Andrew, W. III. *United States Patterns and Related Issues*. Wolfeboro, New Hampshire: Bowers and Merena Galleries, Inc., 1994.

Professional Coin Grading Service. PCGS Population Report. http://www.pcgs.com/. Accessed January-May, 2007.

Stack's. http://www.stacks.com/. Prices realized archives, various sales, accessed January-May, 2007.

Stanford Coins & Bullion, Inc. Auction Values. http://www.ecoinage.com/. Prices realized archives, various U.S. gold coin issues, accessed January-May, 2007.

Superior Galleries. http://www.sgbh.com/Shop/home/index.html. Prices realized archives, various U.S. gold coin issues, accessed January-May, 2007.

Winter, Douglas and Crum, Adam. *An Insider's Guide to Collecting Type I Double Eagles*. Newport Beach, California: Newport Communications, 2002.

Winter, Douglas and Halperin, James L. *Gold Coins of the Carson City Mint*. Dallas, Texas: DWN Publishing/Ivy Press, 2001.

Winter, Douglas. *Gold Coins of the Charlotte Mint: 1838-1861*. Dallas, Texas: DWN Publishing, undated.

Winter, Douglas. *Gold Coins of the Dahlonega Mint: 1838-1861*, 2nd Edition. Irvine, California: Zyrus Press, 2003.

Winter, Douglas. *Gold Coins of the New Orleans Mint: 1839-1909*, 2nd Edition. Irvine, California: Zyrus Press, 2006

Yeoman, R. S. *A Guide Book of United States Coins*, 61st Edition. Atlanta, Georgia: Whitman Publishing, LLC, 2007.

Image Index